Leginska – Forgotten Genius of Music

Leginska

Forgotten Genius of Music

by

Marguerite and Terry Broadbent

The North West Player Piano Association
Wilmslow, Cheshire

By the same authors:

GREAT PIANISTS OF THE GOLDEN AGE

THE MELODY LINGERS ON

AN EDWARDIAN QUINTET

Published by The North West Player Piano Association
Research Section: 49 Grange Park Avenue
Wilmslow
Cheshire SK9 4AL

Copyright © 2002 by Terry Broadbent

No part of this book may be reproduced, stored in a retrieval system, or transmitted in any form, or by any means electronic, mechanical, photocopying, recording or otherwise, without the prior permission of the copyright holder.

ISBN 0 9525101 4 6

Printed and bound by Heaton Press Limited
Unit 6b, Battersea Road
Heaton Mersey Industrial Estate
Stockport
Cheshire SK4 3EA

Contents

Co-author's note	vi
List of illustrations	vii
Authors' preface	x
Acknowledgments	xii
Picture credits	xiv

Chapter:

1.	Birth of a genius	1
2.	Miss Ethel Liggins	10
3.	Apprenticeship	28
4.	Metamorphosis: the emergence of Ethel Leginska	46
5.	Marriage and a prospering career	61
6.	Hail – America!	77
7.	The great pianist	87
8.	Fame, fortune – and divorce	102
9.	Widening horizons	117
10.	Recording artist	136
11.	Pianist, composer, conductor, teacher	156
12.	The disappearing pianist: an enigma	166
13.	Leginska's orchestras	180
14.	The complete musician	207
15.	Madame Leginska – teacher	228
16.	Years of fulfilment	242
17.	Leginska – remembered by her students	262
18.	Indian summer	282
19.	Journey's end	298

Bibliography 313

Appendices:

1: (a) Liggins family tree; (b) Occupations of the Liggins' paternal forbears
   (c) Dates of birth and death of family members   316
2. Leginska the pianist: typical concert programmes   320
3: Music played in the first season of concerts of the Boston
   Philharmonic Orchestra, founded and conducted by Leginska, 1926 - 27   326
4: Leginska's musical compositions   328
5: Leginska's recordings: (a) gramophone discs (b) piano rolls (c) re-issues   330
6: Musical compositions of Ethel Leginska's husband, Emerson Whithorne   335
7: Article by Bruno David Ussher, mid-1920s, followed by the front cover of
   Leginska's 'Six Nursery Rhymes' referred to in the article   336
8: Programme of a concert, May 1960: Leginska conducting her own compositions   340

Index   344

Co-author's Note

Marguerite and I began researching Leginska's life in 1981. In 1985 we wrote the first draft of this book, using the material available up to that point. We sent a copy of the typed book to Shura Cherkassky who liked it and kindly wrote a brief Foreword for us. (I have decided not to use it as it was written so long ago and it seemed inappropriate to do so, bearing in mind that he died in 1995.) However, we knew there was little hope of attracting the interest of an established publisher of music books owing to the fact that Leginska is unknown to the present generation and would therefore not excite much interest amongst music lovers. So the possibility of publication was put on one side, temporarily, but we continued our researches and amassed more information, year by year.

After Marguerite's death in April 1994 I decided that this book, along with the companion volumes based on our 'Famous Musicians' articles written for the North West Player Piano Association, really ought to be published in a limited edition as soon as possible, not only as a long overdue celebration of Leginska's life (she has been consistently ignored by musical biographers in the past), but also as a tribute to Marguerite. Consequently, the book has now, at last, been completed. I hope that anyone who wishes to discover Leginska, a remarkable, charismatic pioneer of her time, will enjoy reading it.

Terry Broadbent

June 2002

List of Illustrations

Certified copy of the marriage certificate of Thomas Edward Liggins and Anne Peck	4
Map of Hull showing where members of the Liggins and Peck families lived and where Ethel was born	6
Liggins family tree	7
Ethel Liggins' birth certificate	8
Top: Wright Street, Hull; Lower: 22 Pemberton Street where Ethel was born	11
Tranby Croft, Hull, the home of the Wilson family	15
Mrs Russell Starr (Ethel's teacher); Ethel at the age of seven	17
Ethel's grandfather, Thomas Liggins	23
Front cover of the programme of Ethel's recital in Hull in 1897	24
Back cover of the same programme	25
James Kwast and Iwan Knorr, Ethel's teachers in Frankfurt	31
The Hoch Conservatory at Frankfurt-am-Main	33
Theodor Leschetizky, Ethel's teacher in Vienna	38
Map showing the location of 11, Wilton Terrace, Hornsea	51
11, Wilton Terrace, Hornsea at the time Ethel used to visit	52
Programme of Leginska's Promenade Concert debut under Henry Wood	56 - 58
Karl Germain on the stage of St. George's Hall, London, with Ethel Leginska assisting	62
Publicity picture hand-dated 13th August 1907	65
Picture postcards: Left: c. 1907; Right: Ethel with her husband and baby son, 1908	66
Two more publicity photographs (postcards)	67
Reverse of the above two postcards	68
Emerson Whithorne – Ethel's husband; Sketch map of Maida Vale	72
Biddulph Mansions, Maida Vale, where Ethel lived from 1906 to 1912	73
Two photographs of Leginska, 1913	82
"The phenomenal young English Pianist" ('Cleveland Leader')	85
Two more photographs of Leginska from 1913	88
Front cover of the programme of a recital in Boston, 1914	90
Back cover of the same programme	91
Leginska with a group of admiring followers	93

Two publicity pictures, 1916	99
X-ray photograph of Leginska's injured right hand, 1916	100
Leginska in 1917	105
Cedric Whittern, Ethel Leginska's son, in 1917	108
Letters from Cedric to his mother, 1917 and 1918	112 - 113
A publicity photograph from around 1918	115
"Leginska summering"	118
Leginska relaxing at Ernest Bloch's summer home, 1918	120
"Leginska, the pianistic marvel"; Leginska in her Boston garden, 1920	126
Poster of a recital in London, June 1921	128
Sheet music of 'Cradle Song'	130 - 131
A publicity portrait of Leginska, early 1920s	134
Labels of one of Leginska's Schubert recordings, 1928	138
Photographs of Leginska in music roll catalogues of the 1920s	142
Extract from 'Duo-Art Monthly', January 1926	144
Page from an Aeolian Company publicity leaflet, 1924	147
Leginska's certification on the 'leader' of an Artrio-Angelus music roll	149
Photograph of Leginska in the Wilcox & White (Artrio rolls) catalogue, 1922	150
Postcard to Ethel from her father, 1927	153
Leginska the conductor: Two publicity photographs from 1925	160
Leginska on board ship, 30th June 1925	163
Sketch of part of Manhattan Island relating to Leginska's disappearance in 1925	167
Leginska's disappearance in 1925: A few contemporary headlines	177
Leginska helping prepare for the first concert of the Boston Philharmonic Orchestra; Leginska in 1927	183
Programme cover of the first concert of the Boston Philharmonic Orchestra	184
Poster used by Leginska to promote the concerts of her new orchestra	185
Letter published in 'Duo-Art Monthly', Spring 1927	189
Two programmes of the Boston Women's Symphony Orchestra, 1928 and 1929	196
Ethel Leginska – conductor; one of her favourite pictures from the late 1920s	197
Front cover and an inside page from a concert of Leginska's Women's Symphony Orchestra, 1930	200
Leginska as seen by her audiences – as pianist and conductor, late 1920s	202
45, Richmond Street, Bridlington – Leginska's English 'home' after 1912	205

List of Illustrations

Leginska, late 1920s	211
Announcement of a Carnegie Hall concert, 1932;	
Cover of the concert programme	214
A publicity photograph used by Leginska in the early 1930s	218
Two more studies of Leginska the conductor	221
Street plan showing the location of Leginska's first and second studios	
in Los Angeles	229
Sketch plan of Leginska's studio at South Hobart Boulevard, Los Angeles	230
A publicity picture used by Leginska in the early 1940s	233
Advertisement in the 'Musical Courier' for Leginska's teaching studio, 1941	235
Publicity postcard to promote Leginska's young pupil Esther Lee Kaplan, 1943	238
Part of the 1954 brochure for the 'New Venture in Music' series	243
Poster for a concert by some of Leginska's young students, 1943	245-246
Pages from the programme of a recital by Leginska's student	
Marguerite Baum	247-249
Leginska, mid 1940s, with her student Marguerite Baum	
and concert manager Mary-V Holloway	250
Leginska: another photograph from the 1940s when Leginska was about 60	251
Programme of recitals given by 19 of Leginska's students,	
June to October 1957	257-258
Leginska's students perform in the 'Musicale' series, 1957	259
Sketch map of southern California showing Los Angeles and Laguna Beach	260
Beverly Carmen in the authors' garden in Wilmslow, 1985	267
Advertising flyer for Leginska's studio, late 1950s	272-273
Five of Leginska's students in later years	276-277
The Wilshire Ebell Theatre, Los Angeles	284
Poster advertising Leginska's opera 'Joan of Arc', 1969	289
Photograph used by Leginska in the printed programme of 'Joan of Arc'	290
Photograph dedicated to Anne Marie Biggs (Joan in 'Joan of Arc'), 1969	291
Pages from the programme of 'Joan of Arc'	293-295
Leginska's death certificate	300
Leginska's days of glory recalled	304-305
Leginska's family tree	316-317
Front cover of 'Six Nursery Rhymes'	339
Concert programme from 1960	340-343

Authors' Preface

The name 'Ethel Leginska' perhaps conjures up an image of a rather formidable lady from Eastern Europe, with a similar background to the famous Polish pianists of the nineteenth and early twentieth centuries. Nothing could be further from the truth. She was English in ancestry, birth and upbringing; a Yorkshire girl in fact, and her Polish-sounding name was adopted solely for the purpose of promoting her career.

As a child Leginska was a brilliant pianist − a prodigy. She possessed personality in abundance to complement her talent, and before she had reached her teens she was studying in Europe under the very best teachers. Such progress was very rare for a girl of humble origins in those days − it was then the end of the nineteenth century − and came about largely through her own enthusiasm and insistence. She was totally dedicated to music, an attribute which remained with her to the end of her days. Achieving success in Britain, Europe and then in the United States as an adult pianist, she became one of the leading concert pianists of her era and was ranked by the music critics of the day alongside such giants as Paderewski, Godowsky and Hofmann. Turning her attention to wider musical fields, she composed with moderate success and then became the foremost woman orchestral conductor of her time. She created, managed and conducted her own women's orchestras, thereby helping women to establish themselves as instrumentalists, and she was the first woman to conduct her own opera in a major opera house. Finally, as a teacher, she produced a constant stream of talented pianists who remember her with awe, respect and affection.

In stature Ethel Leginska was small and of slight build, but her dynamic, forceful, charismatic personality more than made up for her diminutive physique. She was, in her time, one of the world's leading musicians, and a pioneer of the role of women in music. In her long life she contributed much. But now, sadly, she is almost totally forgotten in the country of her birth. That is why we set out, in 1981, to research the life of this unique, dynamic figure and to make her story known to those who appreciate musical talent. We soon realised, as we delved into the events of her life, what a fascinating and extraordinary woman she was.

However, it did not take long to discover that attempting to bring the details of Leginska's life and achievements to the attention of the British musical establishment was going to be an uphill struggle. Until the *New Grove Dictionary of Women Composers* was published in 1994 Leginska had been ignored by each successive edition of *Grove* and it became clear that as a far as many people were concerned if she wasn't in *Grove* she was not worth knowing about. The following example illustrates this. In May 1985 we wrote to the

Authors' Preface

producer of the BBC Sunday morning radio programme *Music Weekly*, suggesting that it might be appropriate to include a small item on Leginska, perhaps with a Leginska recording, in the programme to be broadcast on Sunday morning, 13th April 1986, as a fitting celebration of the centenary of her birth on 13th April 1886. We sent them a copy of an article about Leginska, one of our *Famous Musicians* series written for the North West Player Piano Association, which outlined her life and achievements, so that no research on the BBC's part was necessary. However, a reply came back rejecting the suggestion, on the grounds that she was too marginal a figure to be of any interest to listeners. A catch-22 situation indeed! How can people ever be expected to find out about her, thus discovering that she was by no means a marginal figure, if no one is given the opportunity to bring her story to the attention of the musical public?

In the United States, Leginska's adopted country, she has received rather more attention. She lives vividly in the memories of those she taught and her name and brief details of her career appear in several American-based musical encyclopaedias. But she is now largely forgotten by the musical public in general.

In this book Leginska's story has been told in a generally chronological manner but not strictly so. For example, in probably the busiest and most productive period of her life (1918 to 1936) she was active as pianist, composer, conductor and recording artist. For this period of her life we decided that instead of saying in such-and-such a year she played at certain concerts, conducted others, composed particular pieces and recorded certain music, then in the following year she played at other concerts, composed other music, made other recordings, and so on, year by year, it was more appropriate to group her work into headings. Thus there are chapters devoted to her compositions, her recordings, her conducting, and so on. This inevitably necessitates a certain amount of jumping around chronologically but it is made very clear in the text what year(s) we are talking about at any given time and we feel it gives a more cogent picture of what Leginska was doing.

Much care has been taken in discovering and checking the details of Leginska's life from original sources for the purposes of this book. But the task has been far from onerous; indeed, the researching of Leginska's life and work has been most enjoyable and through it we have gained many friends in both Britain and the USA. We have attempted to incorporate our research into what we hope is an interesting, factually-accurate narrative. We have done the best we can with the information we have been able to discover and we hope we have succeeded in portraying in a readable form an outline of the life of this colourful, talented musician. She deserves to be remembered with honour.

Marguerite and Terry Broadbent

Acknowledgments

During our search for information on Ethel Leginska we wrote to hundreds of individuals and organisations, a large percentage of whom were kind enough to respond. Much of the research material which enabled this biography to be written arose from personal correspondence and telephone calls which followed our appeals for information. To all those who assisted we offer our heartfelt thanks. It is their generous help which has made the book possible. The lists below record, in alphabetical order, those to whom we are most indebted. To anyone inadvertently omitted we offer our apologies.

Great Britain

Gertrude M. Attwood; Mr Barry of Boosey and Hawkes; staff of the British Broadcasting Corporation Library, London; staff of the British Library Music Department; Michael Broadway; B. Cattley; Brian Chesters; staff of the Citizens' Advice Bureau, Hull; Dr and Mrs Coltman; the late David Cox, author of *The Henry Wood Proms*; Noel Cox, Warden, Royal Academy of Music; Professor E.A. Dawes; Ruth Edge, former Manager of EMI Music Archives; Barbara M. Harrison; Eric Hughes of the National Sound Archive, British Library; staff of Hornsea Public Library; staff of Hull Central Library; staff of *The Hull Daily Mail*, especially the columnist "John Humber" who publicised our quest for information on Leginska through his column of local news; Raymond Ince; the late Mrs Marjorie Langdale; Tom P. Langdale; A.H. Liggins; the Editor, *Musical Opinion*; staff of The Piano Museum, London; P. Rhodes; Glyn Roberts, Director of Leisure Services, Humberside County Council; Keith Shipley; Nicholas Simons; Norman Staveley; Margaret Stockbridge; Gerald C. Stonehill; Superintendent Registrars of Births, Deaths and Marriages, Beverley, Bridlington, Hull and London; A.T. Taylor; the secretaries of various music clubs and societies in Hull and district; Arthur Walker, former Music Librarian in the John Rylands University of Manchester Library; Martin Thacker, Librarian of the Henry Watson Music Library, Manchester; the late Walter Williams; the late John Woodhouse.

U.S.A.

Anne Marie Biggs; the late Radie Britain; staff of the Boston Public Library; Beverly Carmen; staff of John Church Co, music publishers; Dorothy Compinski; The County Recorder, Los Angeles; Thomas Curtis; Lynnore Dagg; Lucienne Bloch Dimitroff (Ernest Bloch's daughter); Herbert

Acknowledgments

Donaldson; Professor Robert Dumm; Joseph Enos; Gino Francesconi, Carnegie Hall Museum Director and Archivist; Roberta Hamilton; Marguerite Baum-Heller; Esther Lee Kaplan; Local 47 of the Los Angeles Musicians' Union; Magda Loeb; the late Robert Logan; Armando Loredo; staff of the Los Angeles Public Library; Donald Manildi, Curator, International Piano Archives at Maryland; Joan Meggett; Dr Carol Merrill-Mirsky, Director/Curator, Hollywood Bowl Museum; Professor Marilyn Neeley; staff of the New York Public Library; Daniel Pollack; staff of Schirmer, music publishers, New York; staff of Steinway & Sons, New York; Professor J. Thomson of the University of Southern California; Robert L. Watt.

Germany

Professor Dr Peter Cahn, historian of and former staff member of the Hoch Conservatory of Music, Frankfurt-am-Main; Rosemary Lawson.

Finally, thanks are due to Judith Broadbent, Susan Clews and Raymond Ince for patiently checking the typescript and for other assistance. Their unstinting help is much appreciated.

Note: In the many critical reviews from newspapers and magazines quoted in this book we have kept to the spellings used in the original reviews since it would seem wrong to do otherwise, even though this sometimes leads to differences in spellings between the various quotations when describing the same event.

Extensive use has been made of footnotes in order to add information peripheral to the main story. For instance, it seems pointless to record that Leginska studied with X, or that she worked in collaboration with Y, if the general reader has no idea who X and Y were. Some of the footnotes tell an interesting story in themselves, we believe. They can of course can be ignored if the reader wishes.

Picture Credits

Pages 4, 8: purchased from Registrars of Births, Deaths & Marriages; p. 6: authors' collection; p. 7: family tree established from information kindly supplied by Mr T.P. Langdale and Mrs M. Stockbridge; p. 11: top, courtesy of Mrs M. Stockbridge, bottom, courtesy of Messrs J. Beaty and D. Oades; p. 15: courtesy of Mrs G.A. Attwood; p. 17: left, courtesy of Mr N. Staveley, right, courtesy of Mrs G.A. Attwood (from *Hull News*, 1893); p. 23: courtesy of Mrs M. Stockbridge (from *Hull & Lincolnshire Times*, 1910); pp. 24-25: courtesy of Miss J. Levison; p. 31 (both pictures); p. 33: courtesy of Prof. Peter Cahn; p. 38: photo by H.S. Mendelssohn; pp. 51, 52: courtesy of Mr T. P. Langdale; pp. 56-58: from BBC archives, courtesy of the late Mr David Cox; p. 62: courtesy of Prof. E.A. Dawes, from *Germain and his Legerdemain* by Stuart Cramer; p. 64: courtesy of Mr T. P. Langdale (photo by Russell & Sons, London); pp. 66-68: postcards courtesy of Miss J. Levison; p. 66 (left) was published by Messrs Beitkopf & Härtel; p. 72: top, from *Composers of Today* by David Ewen, 1933, bottom, map drawn by co-author (Terry); p. 73: photograph by co-author; p. 82: left, *Musical America*, 1913, right, from an unknown newspaper (cutting in authors' collection), picture by Aperta (?), New York; p. 85: *Cleveland Leader*, 1915; p. 88: left, *Musical America*, 1913, right, *Musical Courier*, 1915; pp. 90-91: courtesy of New York Public Library; p. 93: *Musical America*, 1919; p. 99: from cuttings (unknown newspapers) in the authors' collection; p. 100: *Musical America*, 1916; p. 105: *Musical Courier*, 1917; p. 108: *Cleveland Press*, 1917; pp. 112, 113: courtesy of Mr Donald Manildi, Curator, IPAM; p. 115: photo by Underwood & Underwood, New York; p. 118: *Musical Courier*, 1918; p. 120: courtesy of Mrs Lucienne Bloch Dimitroff and the Ernest Bloch Society, via Center for Creative Photography, University of Arizona; p. 126: top, *Musical Courier*, 1918, bottom, *Christian Science Monitor*, 1920; p. 128: from authors' collection; pp. 130-131: reproduced by permission of John Church Co.; p. 134: from a Leginska advertising tract; p. 138: from the authors' collection of Leginska's '78' discs; p. 142: top, Ampico Corporation catalogue, bottom, Aeolian Company catalogue; p. 144: from *Duo-Art Monthly* (an Aeolian Co. publication), January 1926; p. 147: Aeolian Company advertising material, 1924; p. 149: from an Artrio (Wilcox & White Co.) piano roll; p. 150, from a Wilcox & White piano roll catalogue, 1922, courtesy of Dr Keith Shipley; p. 153: courtesy of Donald Manildi, Curator, IPAM; p. 160: top, cover of Aeolian Co.'s *Duo-Art Monthly*, 1927, bottom, authors' collection; p. 163: purchased from the Hulton Deutsch Collection; p. 167: authors' sketch; p. 177: from various newspapers, 1925; p. 183: top, *Boston Herald*, 1927, bottom, from an Ampico advertising brochure, 1927; pp. 184, 185, 196 (both pictures), 200: from microfilm copies purchased from Boston Public Library; p. 189: from *Duo-Art Monthly*, 1927; p. 197: one of Leginska's favourite pictures, published in the *Boston Herald*, October 1926 and elsewhere; pp. 197, 202, and front and back covers: silhouettes by Eveline Maydelle (?), 1925, courtesy Mrs M. Heller and the Hollywood Bowl Museum; p. 205: photo taken by and courtesy of Mrs M. Stockbridge; p. 211: photo from *Musical Opinion*, September 1930 and also widely used elsewhere by Leginska at that time; p. 214 (both pictures), purchased from New York Public Library; p. 218: courtesy of Mr T. P. Langdale; p. 221: top, drawing by Lydia Hess appearing in *Boston Transcript*, 1929, bottom, *Brooklyn Daily Eagle*, 1936; p. 229: standard map with authors' additions; p. 230: courtesy of Mr J. Enos; p. 233: photo by W. Jay Fredricks, New York; pp. 235, 243, 245, 246, 257, 258, 259, 272,

Picture Credits

273: courtesy of Leginska's former students; p. 238: courtesy of Miss Esther Lee Kaplan; pp. 247-249: courtesy of Mrs Marguerite Heller (née Baum); pp. 250, 251: courtesy of Mrs Marguerite Heller, photos taken by her husband Alex Heller; p. 260: authors' sketch; p. 267: authors' photo; p. 276: top, courtesy of Prof. Daniel Pollack, middle, courtesy of Prof. Marilyn Neeley, bottom, from Mr Robertson's internet site; p. 277: top, from Mr MacFarland's internet site, bottom, from sleeve booklet of Miss Kaplan's CD (Cambria 1098); pp. 284, 289, 290, 291, 293-295, courtesy of Anne Marie Biggs; p. 300: purchased from the County Registrar-Recorder, Los Angeles; pp. 304, 305: from the authors' collection of cuttings; pp. 316, 317: family tree established from information kindly supplied by Mr T.P. Langdale and Mrs M. Stockbridge; pp. 340-343: courtesy of Mrs M. Heller.

Note that in the above list the words 'courtesy of' means the person named either kindly donated or loaned the material with permission to use it in the book.

Every effort has been made to credit the sources of text and pictures and to obtain copyright clearance where possible. However, much of the material is very old and it has not always proved possible to establish who, if anyone, holds copyright at the present time. Also, some of the newspaper cuttings that came into the authors' possession, although dated, bore no identification as to which paper they came from; in those cases it was impossible to obtain copyright clearance. We apologise for any unwitting infringements.

Chapter 1

Birth of a Genius

In the mid-nineteenth century the Yorkshire town of Kingston upon Hull was a scene of bustling activity. Not yet a city, Hull (as it is usually known) was nevertheless the third most important seaport in Britain and a major seafishing centre. Industry and commerce were thriving as the town's merchants traded with Europe and outposts of Empire, and iron steamers with their tall, narrow funnels and auxiliary sails competed for berths with sea-going sailing ships and barges. The result was a thicket of masts, funnels, smoke and activity; all the ingredients of a prosperous centre of trade. As in all English towns, the whole spectrum of social status was represented in the neighbourhood, from very rich to very poor.

A small family firm which made a modest contribution to the economic life of Hull in those days was the partnership of Hockney and Liggins, builders and contractors. By the nature of their work they were not directly associated with the town's seafaring trade, but they benefited from it indirectly through the general prosperity of the district. Not only were the Hockney and Liggins families associated by business, they were also related by marriage. It is relevant to our story to consider briefly the background to these two families. [1]

In the middle and latter part of the nineteenth century the Liggins family resided less than a mile from the town's busy and flourishing dockland area. Thomas Liggins was born in 1835 and on Thursday 26th April 1860 he married Hannah Dawson Wright, a widow. [2] He was then 25 and she was 27. She and her brother Matthew were the children of Mr and Mrs John Hockney. It was thus in 1860 that the Hockney and Liggins families became related by marriage. A business partnership also emerged, and Thomas Liggins, who was a Freemason in the Humber Lodge from 1867, became a partner in the firm of Hockney and Liggins. It was a solid and dependable firm which could always be relied upon to do good sound work in the building trade. It continued in business until the end of the nineteenth century.

Thomas and Hannah Liggins lived at 10, East Parade, Holderness Road, Hull, and for many years the family firm operated from premises in Great Union Street which was nearby. In those days the boundaries between the definition of 'builder' and 'architect' were less well defined than they are today and there is evidence that Thomas Liggins performed many of the functions of an architect. It is known, for example, that he designed and built the Congregational Church in Hornsea, which is now the United Reformed

Church. [3] Though he described himself as a builder, not as an architect, he was clearly not lacking in the artistic flair needed to design buildings. His wife, Hannah, evidently also possessed artistic skills. The returns of the 1881 census list the occupation of Thomas Liggins (then aged 46) as 'Builder' and that of his wife, Hannah (48), as 'Art Student', implying that she was sufficiently interested or talented in the subject to attend some form of art classes. [4]

Six children were born to the marriage of Thomas and Hannah, of whom two died in infancy. Of those who survived to adulthood the eldest was Thomas Edward Liggins (born 2nd April 1861), who was to be the only surviving son, and, not surprisingly, he was destined to join the family business of Hockney and Liggins when he reached the necessary age. Then came three daughters, Frances Gertrude (born 1864), Katherine Anne (born 1865) and Lucy Edith (born 1868). The two children who died in infancy were William and Caroline Ellen. In the 1881 census Thomas Edward Liggins (then aged 20) was listed as 'Architect's Pupil', and the three girls, Frances, Katherine and Lucy, then 17, 16 and 12 respectively, were designated as 'Scholars'. All the family (parents and children) were born in Hull, and all lived at 10, East Parade. As an established middle-class family the Liggins clan commanded respect and was well known and highly regarded in the Hull district. Their house was substantial and 'quite stylish' for the period. [5] It was demolished only in the early 1980s.

In 1885 Thomas Edward Liggins married Anne Peck of Hull. Nothing is known of the circumstances in which Tom (as we will call him) and Anne met, but we do know something of Anne's ancestry. She was born Anne (with no other Christian names) on 1st August 1857 at the family home, 30 Queen Street, Hull. The occupation of her father, George Peck, was described on her birth certificate as 'Tailor and Outfitter's Manager' and her mother was named as Maria Peck, late Orton, formerly Spink, so she seems to have been a widow when she married George Peck. At the time of the 1881 census the family was living at 44 Wright Street, Hull; the family members were listed in the census as follows:

	Rel	Marr.	Age	Sex	Birthplace	Occupation
George Peck	Head	M	59	M	Long Riston, York	Taylor, Outfitter's Manager
Maria Peck	Wife	M	62	F	Hull	Wife
Maria Peck	Daugh	U	26	F	Hull	Dressmaker
Anne Peck	Daugh	U	23	F	Hull	Governess
Emma Peck	Daugh	U	21	F	Hull	Dressmaker
Frederick Peck	Son	U	15	M	Sheffield	Chemist's Apprentice

The marriage of Thomas Edward Liggins and Anne Peck took place at Hedon Parish Church on 27th May 1885. Hedon, a village eight miles east of the centre of Hull, was where Anne was then living, according to the marriage certificate. Banns of marriage had previously been read on three Sundays according to law and custom, on 3rd, 10th and 17th May, the couple being named therein as : "Thomas Edward Liggins Bachelor of the Parish of Drypool and Annie Peck Spinster of this Parish". The fact that Anne's name was given as "Annie" on each of these three occasions surely indicates that she was known by that name amongst her family and friends, and wished to be known as such.

Rev John H. Richardson, Vicar of Hedon, officiated. A certified copy of the marriage certificate is shown on page 4, on which the occupations of the fathers of the bride and groom are given as 'outfitter' and 'builder' respectively. As the certificate shows, there were four witnesses. Matthew Pape Hockney was the bridegroom's uncle (see page 1 and the family tree on page 7) and research has succeeded in identifying two of the three others. Rev William Henry Jones was curate of Brocklesby, a village in north Lincolnshire a few miles South of Hull. It was on the other (south) side of the River Humber but there was a regular ferry service. But significantly, he resided, according to the 1881 census, at 6 Pryme Street, Hull, where he was a tutor at the adjacent Thornton School on the same street. At the time of the 1881 census he was 28 and lived there with his wife Mary (29) and sons aged two and one. Pryme Street ran parallel with Wright Street and into Prospect Street and Wright Street where the Pecks lived in 1881. It seems likely that Mr Jones, since he lived near the Pecks, was known to the family and might have been a family friend.

Another witness, George Spink, 30, was a solicitor with the firm of Walker and Spink, solicitors and commisioners for oaths, residing at 1, Gladstone Street, Hull. Since Anne's mother's maiden name was Spink he was almost certainly one of her relatives. It has not proved possible to find who Sophie D. Green was. One may speculate that she might have been one of Anne's friends. [6]

Anne's father, as a tailor and outfitter, had a perfectly respectable job, but according to an interview Ethel Leginska gave to a musical magazine in 1919 her family was not well off financially. [7] There is evidence that the Liggins family were not too pleased about the match, whether for reasons of what they saw as differing social status or for some other cause is not known, but it was later said that Anne had "never been accepted" by Tom's family. [8] It is difficult to see why 'builder' should have been regarded as higher up the social scale than 'tailor and outfitter' even by Victorians values. Moreover, Anne must have been very intelligent to have become a governess, and if that were not enough, at least one solicitor was numbered

CERTIFIED COPY of an ENTRY OF MARRIAGE
Pursuant to the Marriage Act 1949

Registration District: SCOLCOATES

1885. Marriage solemnized at the Parish Church in the Parish of Hedon in the District of Scolcoates in the County of York

No.	When married	Name and surname	Age	Condition	Rank or profession	Residence at the time of marriage	Father's name and surname	Rank or profession of father
209	Twenty seventh May 1885	Thomas Edward Liggins	24	Bachelor	Builder	Hull	Thomas Liggins	Builder
		Anne Peck	27	Spinster	—	Hedon	George Peck	Outfitter

Married in the Parish Church aforesaid according to the Rites and Ceremonies of the Established Church after Banns by me, John H. Richardson MA Vicar

This marriage was solemnized between us, Thomas Edward Liggins / Anne Peck in the presence of us, Matthew Pape Hockney / George Spink / William H. Jones / Sophie D. Green

Deputy Superintendent Registrar } S.E. Thompson
Date 3.10. 2000.

TG 069918

Certified copy of the marriage certificate of Thomas Edward Liggins and Anne Peck

amongst Anne's relatives. It is nowadays easy to deride such attitudes but by the mores of the nineteenth century social status was very important and to marry someone seen as from a 'lower class' was not at all the done thing. There is every reason to believe that Anne was an excellent wife and that the marriage was happy. Anne seems to have been talented in both art and music and it is known that she loved nature.[9] Tom's artistic abilities were similar to those of his father in that he was able to design buildings which were not only structurally sound but were also aesthetically pleasing.

Following the marriage Tom and Anne bought a terraced house situated not very far from Tom's parents' house, at 22, Pemberton Street, just off Holderness Road (in the eastern part of Hull) and a few minutes' walk from the docks. The house was a well-built one of good class in what was then a residential area popular amongst successful businessmen.

In the Hull trade directories of the 1880s and 1890s Tom was listed as a 'surveyor', but his main work was always as a builder, in which capacity he was a major contributor to the success of the family business. All was not unbounded and continuous prosperity in Hull at that time and 'mini-recessions' occurred from time to time. But Tom Liggins possessed acute business acumen and, following his marriage, he appears to have enjoyed a modest but sound financial standing throughout the prevailing economic fluctuations. Indeed, Tom and his wife were secure enough financially to employ a maid – a not uncommon situation amongst small businessmen in those days. The maid was not always the same girl, but a succession, one at any given time.[10] Maids at that time rarely stayed in one post for long.

On Tuesday, 13th April 1886, nearly a year after Tom and Anne's marriage, a baby girl was born to the couple at their home in Pemberton Street. Tom and Anne were naturally very proud of their daughter who, as events turned out, was to be their only child. The birth was registered by Tom Liggins on Friday, 7th May, in the Registration District of Sculcoates (a part of Hull) in the sub-district of Sutton. The birth certificate is shown on page 8.[11] The little girl was named on the certificate as Ethel Annie Liggins. At her baptism soon afterwards her godfather was William H. Crofts of Caroline Place, Hull, who was a year younger than Tom Liggins and was one of his workmates at the firm of Hockney and Liggins.[12]

The arrival of an offspring to a solid, respectable couple, typical Victorian citizens immersed in the commerce of their native town, occasioned no attention other than the obvious pleasure within the family. No one had the slightest reason to imagine that a genius had entered the world or that little Ethel Liggins would become Ethel Leginska, one of the world's foremost musicians.

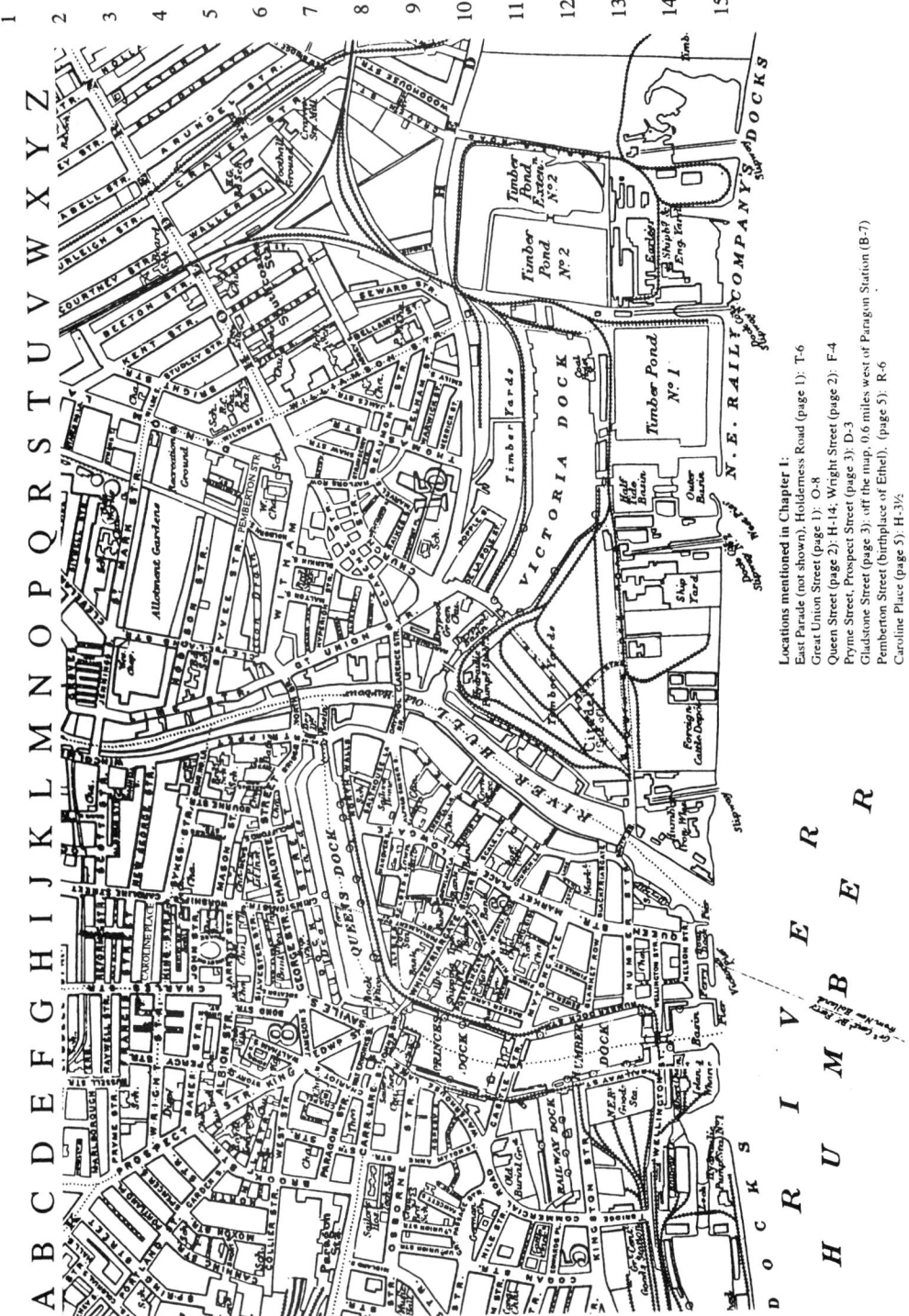

Map of Hull showing Pemberton Street, birthplace of Ethel Liggins, and other relevant streets

Birth of a Genius

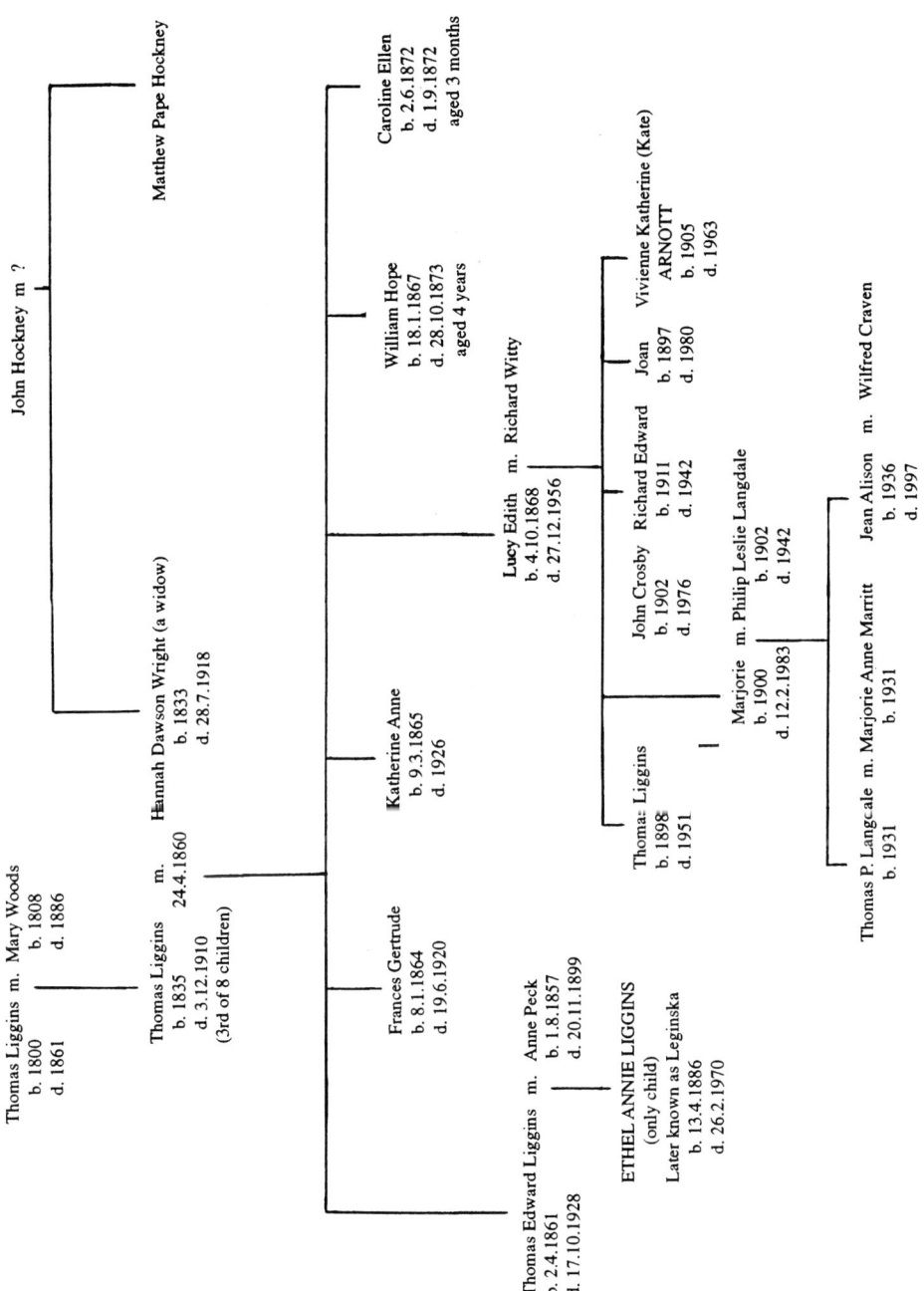

Liggins family tree
A more detailed version, drawn to a smaller scale but with more names, is shown in Appendix 1(a)

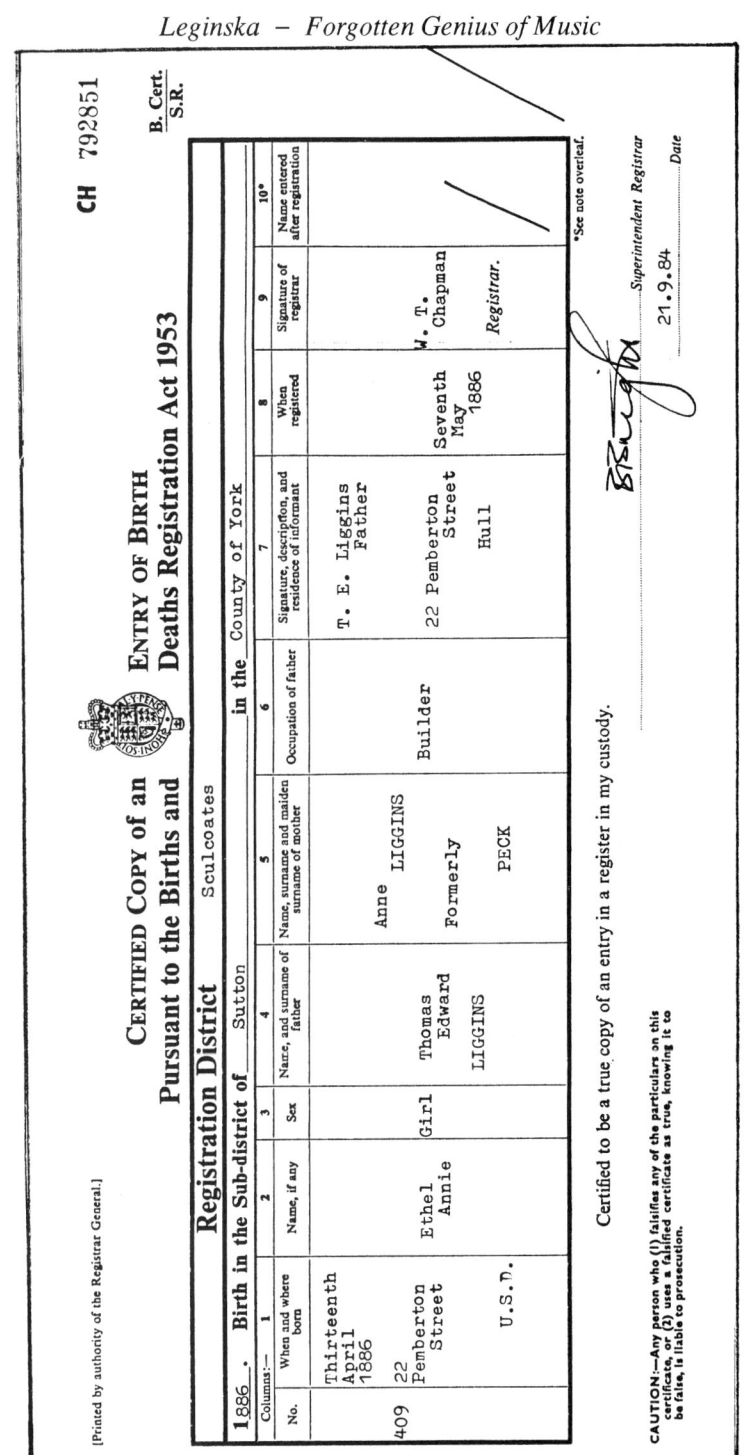

Ethel Liggins' Birth Certificate

'U.S.D.' meant Urban Sanitary District, an early form of local government designation

References: Chapter 1

1. Information about the Hockney & Liggins partnership has been built up from correspondence with numerous residents of Hull and district, in particular Mrs G.M. Attwood and Mrs Margaret Stockbridge (née Liggins), whose help is duly acknowledged, and from various Hull directories of the late nineteenth century, with assistance from the Librarians of Hull Central Library, Hornsea Library, and Mr P. Rhodes, Honorary Secretary of Hornsea Music Club.
2. Initial information concerning the Liggins family history was compiled from private correspondence in the autumn of 1982 with Mrs Marjorie Langdale of Hornsea who was Ethel Liggins' cousin (see family tree on page 7). Ethel was godmother to Mrs Langdale's youngest sister. After Mrs Langdale's death in February 1983, further factual material, including the information recorded on the family tree, was kindly provided by Mrs Langdale's son, Mr T.P. Langdale, of Beverley.
3. From private correspondence with Mr P. Rhodes of Hornsea.
4. The 1881 census was made public in 1981. The information was obtained initially with the help of staff at Hull Central Library and later by Mrs Margaret Stockbridge. This census is now available on a CD-ROM.
5. The description of the houses is by Mr B. Cattley of Beverley, Secretary of Beverley Music Lovers' Club.
6. Mrs Margaret Stockbridge spent a lot of time researching in various libraries on our behalf. It is to her that we are indebted for much of the 'fine detail' in establishing various facts concerning the marriage of Thomas Edward Peck and Anne Liggins, and related matters.
7. *The Etude*, May 1919, p. 271. This issue of the American musical magazine records an interview with Ethel Leginska in which she recalled details of her early life and paid tribute to her mother.
8. Information (in private correspondence) from Beverly Carmen, Los Angeles, recalling conversations with her former teacher Ethel Leginska (née Ethel Liggins) in which Mme Leginska, as she was then known, talked about her early years and family circumstances.
9. As reference 7.
10. Mr A.T. Taylor, Beverley. Information contained in private correspondence. Mr Taylor's mother was a maid in the Liggins household in the late 1880s.
11. Copies of Ethel Liggins' Birth Certificate and other certificates referred to in this chapter were purchased from the appropriate Superintendent Registrars.
12. The identity of Ethel's godfather is revealed in a letter to Ethel from a friend, Miss Margaret Browne of Boston Spa, dated 30th January, 1933 and his address (in 1881) was found from the 1881 census. The identity of her godmother is not known with certainty.

See also the note at the end of the list of references to Chapter 2.

Chapter 2

Miss Ethel Liggins

It was Ethel's mother who guided the upbringing of her gifted child. Anne was born of relatively poor parents but she was very bright and by her early 20s she had become a governess. Her insight and intelligence enabled her to spot her daughter's innate musical ability at an early stage. According to an interview many years later, Ethel recalled that her musical talent first showed at the age of two, "in the bathtub". [1]

"When I was about two, my mother was bathing me upstairs. All of a sudden I started to climb out of the tub. My mother grabbed me and I struggled with her. I howled, but still tried to get out. Then my mother noticed that it was when my aunt downstairs was strumming on the piano that I made my attempts to get out of the tub, and that I yelled when she stopped. My mother wondered whether there was any connection, tossed a towel around me, and rushed me, dripping, down to my aunt.

"She explained to my aunt, and had her play, both watching me. I seemed very much pleased at the sounds she made. Then my mother held me by the piano. Instead of hammering with my fist, as babies generally do, I carefully tried to imitate the action of my aunt's fingers, and listened very closely to the sound that came each time I pressed a key. My musical education began at that point."

Ethel's fascination with music became even more apparent at two years of age by:

" . . . 'haunting' the hurdy-gurdy in the street, looking big-eyed at the artist who, by the mere turning of a handle, could produce such "beautiful" music". [2]

When she was not much older her father took her to a Carl Rosa performance of *Carmen*, getting one of the cheap seats in the 'pit'.

"They thought I'd simply go to sleep, but I slept only in the intermissions. I followed everything closely, and suddenly, in the last act, I cried out, 'Run, Carmen, he'll get you; he'll get you.' " [3]

Anne Liggins, wise mother that she was, bought a music book so that Ethel could have lessons from the aunt who had first stimulated her musical awareness. She taught Ethel for a little while but she was only a moderate pianist, so the services of a professional teacher were arranged when Ethel was three or four years old, in fact as soon as she could sit comfortably on a stool in front of the keyboard. The Liggins' maid at the time later recalled that Ethel could play at sight any of the music that was purchased for her, and immediately afterwards could play it again from memory. She also had an acutely accurate sense of pitch. [4] There was no denying that Ethel's musical ability was outstanding, especially her piano playing, and by the age of five years she was the musical wonder of the neighbourhood.

Miss Ethel Liggins

A drawing of Queen Street, Hull, where Ethel's mother, Anne (Annie) Liggins, née Peck, was born in 1857 and where she spent her early years. It clearly shows the type of architecture and general scene common in Hull in the latter part of the 19th century.

The terraced house with the privet hedge, opposite the car, is 22 Pemberton Street, Hull where Ethel Annie Liggins was born and brought up. This photograph was taken in 1976. All the houses on the street were demolished in May 1979, number 22 being the last house on the street to be occupied. This house was Ethel's home in Hull from her birth in 1886 until 1913 when her father moved to Bridlington. [5]

As we have already seen, Tom Liggins' background was middle-class, in a Britain which was a very class-conscious country in those days. But Anne had come from a Yorkshire family which was not well off financially. Her parents brought her up according to sternly puritan Victorian ideals of religion and duty, which left little time for enjoying the beautiful things which made life worthwhile. Anne had rebelled at these ideals before Ethel was born. In fact, according to Ethel, Anne was a revolutionist at heart, and Ethel was to be the medium through which she chose to develop some of her principles. Ethel was to live a freer life than Anne had been able to do herself. Accordingly, when Ethel's early musical prowess became obvious, Anne decided that the child should be trained in music, which was what she liked and was gifted at above all else, and would not go to school. As Ethel's mother she would provide the child's general education herself and, in addition, Ethel would have a music lesson every day from a professional piano teacher. [6]

Ethel was allowed to go at her own pace in all things, which meant that her musical achievements were soon far in advance of what might have been expected for her age. But her music did not ruin her childhood; on the contrary, she was a happy child.

"I was naturally a very solemn child but I played a certain amount with the other children – enough. When I was six I was taught to do everything, cook – run the house. I played with my dolls and that was responsible for my starting to teach when I was scarcely more than a baby. One day my mother heard me talking in another room, although she was sure I was alone. She came in and found me explaining to my dolls what I had learned about playing the piano. I was having such a jolly time, too. Well, why not teach 'live' dolls? It would be fun for me, and it would bring me a little money. My mother took me round to the homes of people who were better off than we were – and at about six I was teaching girls in their twenties." [7]

Later, as an adult, Ethel was always grateful for the way her mother had brought her up.

"If a child has an extraordinary talent, why not allow the gift to be developed? That is the thing to do, if the child's nature is exceptional – like its talent. That is to say, if it is happy in its studies, and if its head does not become turned. It is terrible to treat every child like every other. Then if a child really is a prodigy, it will be happy if its exceptional talent is allowed to assert itself and undergo a natural rate of development. Most important, the child of great musical talent, trained the right way, acquires a routine invaluable in later life." [8]

Ethel's lack of formal schooling proved to be far from a handicap, for her mother's individual attention and tuition provided all the education she needed, and she never lagged behind her contemporaries in any way. It was Ethel's mother who encouraged her daughter's lifelong interest in nature, and she would often walk with Ethel, book in hand, through the countryside, teaching on the way. As Ethel said in adult life,

"It was all fun with such a mother, and I am sure I learned more in this individual, intimate way, than I could possibly have acquired, with my restless disposition, straight-jacketed in the ordinary school room. It was fortunate for me that my mother had experienced the severe repression of Yorkshire – repression so wonderfully described in Mrs Gaskell's classic story of the Brontës – fortunate that my mother rebelled at everything that would hinder my wholly individualistic training.

"A very great deal of time is wasted, however, in giving more than ordinary musical advantages to children who have no gift for music – children absolutely and entirely without talent. This is a ridiculous waste. No amount of cultivation will ever make a turnip bear roses – and it is cruelty to the turnip soul and ambitions to make it think it might achieve what is so out of its nature. While it was easy for me to learn to play the Mozart Fantasie, the Beethoven C minor Concerto, and the Italian Concerto of Bach, before I was nine, this was because I had a real and deep love for music, and had a music lesson every day for a long time, and no regular schooling to interrupt or divert my training. [9]

From the age of about five years news of Ethel's musical prowess was beginning to spread far and wide, and at the tender age of six years she was 'taken up' by Mrs Mary Emma Wilson (née Smith) whose interest had been attracted by reports of the young prodigy. Mrs Wilson (b. 9th August 1843, d. 22nd November 1927) was the wife of Arthur Wilson, D.L., J.P. (b. 14th December 1836, d. 21st October 1909), steamship owner, a member and at that time joint head, with his brother Charles Henry, of the Hull shipping firm of Thomas Wilson, Sons & Co with whom he had been in business since his boyhood. Arthur was the youngest son of the firm's founder, Thomas Wilson, the son of a lighterman. The company is famous in the history of Hull shipping. In 1916 it was taken over by Sir John Ellerman to become Ellerman's Wilson Line Ltd and was later part of Associated Humber Lines. [10]

For a period of several years Mary Wilson paid for Ethel's musical education. For part of the year Ethel lived at the Wilsons' large house at Tranby Croft (now a girls' school) located about four miles west of the centre of Hull. She was not by any means the only person whose career was furthered by Mary Wilson. Many other artistically gifted girls and young women were similarly helped. For instance, she did a great deal for Alice Sharrah, A.T.C.L, [11] who played the mandolin and became Principal of the Sharrah School of Music in Hull, and she was also responsible for starting off the career of Gwendolen Brogden, [12] organising her London debut, booking and paying for the hall, circularising all her influential friends and almost forcing them to come along to the performance.

There can hardly have been a better location for Ethel's talents to be shown off than at Tranby Croft, for there were many distinguished guests, and Ethel used to be brought down to play for them in the music salon.[13] She did not live with the family but resided in the nursery wing when staying at Tranby Croft where she was looked after by the Wilsons' resident staff. The Prince of Wales (later King Edward VII) had made short visits to Tranby Croft when he was in Yorkshire for the races, but had stayed there only once. It was on that visit in 1891, shortly before Ethel Liggins' association with the Wilson family began, that there occurred the incident always known afterwards as 'The Tranby Croft Affair' or 'The Baccarat Case'.[14] It concerned an allegation of cheating at cards, which led to a famous court case, and received much public attention because of the involvement of the Prince of Wales. * The trial took place from 1st to 9th June 1891 and was fully documented in the contemporary press, not only in Hull but internationally. Although the case lasted a week, the jury retired for only 13 minutes before finding the allegations proved.

---

* The basis of the case was a slander action brought by Sir William Gordon-Cumming, a well-known society figure, and a lifelong friend of the Prince of Wales, against certain fellow guests at a house-party at Tranby Croft during Doncaster race week. The alleged slander concerned a charge of cheating during two games of baccarat at Tranby Croft. It was alleged that stakes were altered after the result of hands was known. The enormous publicity engendered by the case arose purely from the social position of the parties and witnesses and in particular because the Prince of Wales gave evidence in court for Gordon-Cumming. The prince was banker at the game in question and stated that he had not noticed any cheating. The game was being played with the prince's private set of cards with his feathers on the back and this stimulated public interest even further.

The allegations originated from an accusation by the son of the house, Jack Wilson, who had been playing. Gordon-Cumming was charged with cheating, an allegation he denied, but he signed an undertaking never to play cards again, those present promising to keep silent. Nevertheless, the secret leaked out next day, allegedly through the indiscreet utterances of Lady Daisy Brooke (unkindly dubbed "the Babbling Brooke" by the popular press). She should have been a guest at the house-party but had excused herself because of a bereavement. However, she turned up at Doncaster the day after the second game, and news of the charge rapidly spread through the country. It appears that the secret agreement was entered into in the hope of avoiding publicity for the fact that the Prince of Wales was a gambler. It was also said during the trial that the prince, as Gordon-Cumming's superior officer, should have reported the charge to the proper military authority if he had thought him guilty.

During the trial, held in a packed court, the Prince of Wales sat on a bench beside the judge. There was a brilliant closing speech by the great advocate Sir Edward Clarke, who defended Gordon-Cumming, which earned a burst of applause such as is rarely heard in a law court, but it was to no avail and, as stated in the main text, the jury retired for only 13 minutes before finding the allegations proved. Seldom has there been such a swift verdict in such a hotly-disputed case. Sir Edward Clarke always maintained that his client was innocent and that there had been a miscarriage of justice.

Miss Ethel Liggins

Because of the court case and its attendant publicity, Tranby Croft was a household name throughout Britain when Ethel Liggins took up partial residence there in 1892 at the age of six years. The Prince of Wales continued to visit and many other well-known guests came and went. Ethel used to be brought down to play for them so she was known even at that early age to the Prince and the other visitors. These occasions guaranteed that her name soon became known to a wide, influential circle. Ethel was not in any way exploited by the Wilsons. They treated her well and Mary Wilson's only wish was to provide her with the funds and resources that would enable her to realise her talents and which her family, though financially comfortable, were not rich enough to provide. In later life Ethel often recalled her early years and in 1949 she composed a suite of pieces dedicated to the Wilson family. They were impressionist compositions, one of which represented the funeral procession in 1938 of Arthur Stanley ("Jack") Wilson, son of Mary Wilson. On that sad occasion the coffin was carried on a horse-drawn hearse, and the music suggested the rumbling of the cart as it was driven over muddy, rutted ground. [15]

Tranby Croft, Hull, the home of the Wilson family. It was here that Ethel Liggins, as a child, played for distinguished visitors including the Prince of Wales (later King Edward VII)

Ethel was thus established in society circles at the age of six as a child prodigy, and had there been no wise musical counsel she might well have burst across the scene like a shooting star only to disappear into obscurity. Fortunately this was not to be, for Ethel acquired an excellent new teacher shortly before her seventh birthday and this lady, Mrs Russell Starr, was to be the making of Ethel as a really skilled musician. Mrs Russell Starr * was, prior to her marriage, Miss Annie Jane Martin and was born in 1852 or 1853. From 1872 she studied at the Royal Academy of Music in London under Walter Macfarren and William Sterndale Bennett until the latter's death in 1875. She was elected an Associate of the Royal Academy of Music on 29th September of that year, and became a F.R.A.M. on 22nd March 1899. On completion of her studies in 1875 she was invited by Mr James Gough, a well-known Hull celebrity and partner in the Hull music company of Gough and Davy, to come to Hull, and accepted. She had been introduced to Mr Gough by her teacher, Walter Macfarren. She became the principal pianoforte teacher in Hull and remained so until her death. Many musicians who later made their mark studied under her. Not only did she teach piano, but she also had a wide knowledge of musical matters in general. In 1876 she criticised the performance in Hull of Sterndale Bennett's *Woman of Samaria* and, perhaps because of this and other later sub-standard orchestral performances in the town, she set up a class for orchestral sight-reading in 1886. She was on the Council and the Management Committee of the Hull and East Riding College of Music (formed in 1903) and made "a handsome gift of orchestral scores and parts". Other musical interests included membership of the Incorporated Society of Musicians, she was local representative of the Associated Boards, and was a member of the committee of the Hull Musical Festival. She died aged 80 on 15th April 1933 and was giving lessons until less than a fortnight before her death. [16]

A former pupil's tribute to Mrs Russell Starr in the *Hull Daily Mail* following her death observed:

"Thoroughness was her *mot d'ordre*, in every minutest point of technique and artistic rendering of all compositions. She was one of the first in Hull to cultivate in her pupils the gift of memorising all they studied, so they could perform their chosen composer's works from any given point selected by her. For 58 years she had indefatigably and lovingly pursued her art, with unvarying success."

Mrs Russell Starr's husband, who died in 1913, appears to have been a professional organ builder. In 1882 he was Honorary Secretary of the Hull Vocal Society and had been a singing member from around 1874. He may

---

* She was always known professionally as Mrs Russell Starr, not Mrs Annie Starr or Mrs Starr, after her marriage to Russell Starr.

well have been linked with the organ builders Bishop & Starr of London, who provided a new organ for Christ Church, Hull in the 1860s. Bishop and Starr arranged many celebrity concerts in Hull, and the *Hull Mail* reported the organisers as "very efficient". Another of Russell Starr's connections with London is that he and Dr John Hare Gibson appear to have arranged the musical part of the Shakespeare Festival Evening, probably in Hull on 24th April 1882.

Mrs Russell Starr was no ordinary piano teacher but a musician of zest and talent; she and her husband were, as we have seen, significant members of the Hull musical world. When the six-year-old Ethel Liggins was brought to Mrs Russell Starr in February 1893 she at once recognised the talents of the small, dark-haired child by the spirited, intelligent way she played a simple melody. And so the partnership of teacher and pupil began.

Mrs Russell Starr   *Ethel Liggins at the age of seven*

Mrs Russell Starr shared Anne Liggins' philosophy of life, and she taught Ethel according to her needs and not according to the requirements of the average pupil as educational systems often were, and are, organised to do. Ethel was given abundant study in ear training and elementary harmony and learned that there is a certain order in music, as in nature. Added to this was her ability to memorise music very quickly. Under Mrs Russell Starr's wise tutelage Ethel's talents were skilfully guided and she was soon allowed to make limited public appearances, the first not long after she began her studies under Mrs Russell Starr, when she was still only six years old. In April 1893, aged just seven, she played a sonata in three movements from memory and at eight she was able to play Hummel's Rondo in B flat, also from memory. The press began to take notice. The *Hull News* of 23rd June 1894 reported briefly on one of her recitals:

"On Wednesday [which would have been the 20th] the numerous pupils of Mrs Russell Starr (Miss Martin) and Mr Lancelot gave a concert. A very small performer was Miss Ethel Liggins, only eight years of age, but considerably to the front in ability, who played Hummel's Rondo in B flat, for which she received an encore."

A report of another of Ethel's recitals appeared in the *Hull Times* of Saturday 13th April 1895 – Ethel's ninth birthday: [17]

DEBUT OF MISS ETHEL LIGGINS *

"A large audience assembled by invitation at the St. George's Hall, Hull, on Tuesday [9th April] to witness the début of Miss Ethel Liggins, who is only eight years of age. She is the pupil of Miss Martin (Mrs Russell Starr), who may be justly proud of having under her tutorship a young pianist giving such high promise of some day making a name for herself and her native town. Her skill and perfect confidence for one so very young was really a surprising and pleasing revelation. Her recital embraced 23 items from the classic music of Bach, Mozart, Beethoven, and the modern composers, such as Paderewski, to the lighter music of Reinecke and Bohm. The expression contained in the rendering of Beethoven's "Nel cor picè non mi sento" and variations was a marked instance of the young pianist's ability. She was twice re-called for her playing of Reinecke's melodies, and justice was done to a minuet by Paderewski, for her playing of which she was loudly applauded."

Oh to have been there and heard the tiny talented child playing this music with, one imagines, the delicacy of her years!

Ethel's association with Mrs Russell Starr continued to prosper, and she gradually made the transition from the gifted but undisciplined musical prodigy to an accomplished child pianist. Whilst her tuition continued she divided her time between her family home and the Wilson family at Tranby Croft. She enjoyed life, and whether she was at home or at Tranby Croft music was always her prime interest.

Ethel's skills steadily matured and when she was nine years old Mrs Russell Starr deemed that the time had come for her to make her London debut. Arrangements were made for the child to play there, but

---

* Clearly it was not a true 'debut' because she had played in earlier public recitals. But perhaps this one was a rather more formal occasion than her previous appearances.

unfortunately she contracted measles and the recital had to be postponed for several weeks. Once she had recovered, a new date was arranged for the recital, and Mrs Russell Starr wisely made sure that it was well advertised. The new date was Friday, 19th June 1896 at the Queen's Hall, when Ethel was 10 years and two months old. In those days (and in fact up to and including 3rd May 1966) the front page of *The Times* consisted entirely of advertisements and notices, and a perusal of the front page of the paper dated Saturday 13th June 1896 reveals the following block notice in the centre of the page:

Miss ETHEL LIGGINS
(aged 10 years)
The Yorkshire Child Genius

MISS ETHEL LIGGINS, pupil of Miss Martin, A.R.A.M. (Mrs Russell Starr) will give a PIANOFORTE RECITAL (under the direction of Mr Daniel Mayer) in Queen's (Small) Hall on Friday afternoon next, June 19, at 3.

Grand Pianoforte with Resonator (Daniel Mayer's Patent). Tickets 5s, 2s 6d, and 1s at the usual Agents; Newman's Box Office, Queen's Hall or Concert Director Daniel Mayer, 224, Regent St. W.

The talented child's recital duly took place on the appointed day. The programme was an ambitious one of 17 pieces and was rapturously received by the public and critics. The *Hull News* reported the recital in detail: [18]

HULL PIANIST IN LONDON

Miss Liggins' debut

"Miss Ethel Liggins, the talented pupil of Mrs Russell Starr, made her debut in London last night when she appeared before a large audience comprising many distinguished musicians, at the Queen's Hall, Langham Place. Miss Liggins, who is only ten years of age, possesses exceptional ability, and her first appearance in London has been awaited with feelings of interest by a great many people in Hull who have had an opportunity of hearing her perform. The programme she rendered last night was as follows:

Prelude and fugue in B flat	Bach
Gigue in A minor	Bach
Gigue in G	Bach
Italian Concerto (finale)	Bach
Fantasia in C minor	Mozart
Sonata Op. 14, No. 2 - allegro moderato, scherzo	Beethoven
Barcarolle, Op. 28	Mendelssohn
Allegro vivace (from Lied ohne worte, No. 47)	Mendelssohn
The Rivulet	Mendelssohn

continued on next page . . .

Christmas Pieces, Nos. 3 and 5	Mendelssohn
Suite de Pieces, No. 2 in E	Sterndale Bennett
Moments Musicaux No. 3	Schubert
Mazurka, Op. 5, No. 9	Chopin
Trois Ecossaises. Op. 72, No. 3	Chopin
Valse in G flat	Chopin
Valse in D flat	Chopin
Valse Brillante	Moszkowski

"Every item was played with thought and the phrasing of a mature musician. Several recalls had to be responded to and the youthful artiste received quite an ovation at the close of the recital. The young lady's success was instantaneous and there is hardly room to doubt that in the course of a few years she will take her place among the ranks of great pianists. Both her and her teacher are to be congratulated on the splendid results achieved."

The national press attended and was lavish in its praise. *The Times* wrote: [19]

"The little girl who gave a splendid pianoforte recital yesterday afternoon in the small room of the Queen's Hall, has very decided talent and instinct for music ... Her fingers are excellently trained, and her phrasing is always correct and musicianly. That she has the makings of an artist is not to be denied, but all the greater responsibility remains with those who have the charge and training of such remarkable talent, and they must see to it that she becomes a real musician, not a mere musical acrobat."

The Daily Telegraph was equally complimentary: [20]

"Yesterday afternoon the platform of the smaller Queen's Hall was occupied by an exceedingly youthful pianist, Ethel Liggins by name, who hails from Hull, and has been taught by Mrs Russell Starr. Her programme included no less than seventeen pieces, all being played from memory with remarkable accuracy. The child has a nice touch, and her technical facility is surprising considering her tender years, though – as might be expected, there is as yet but little power. The last piece on her list was Moszkowski's Valse Brillante, which the plucky young artist dashed off in such a lively fashion as to earn a recall and plenty of applause."

Similarly enthusiastic reports appeared in the *Daily News, Morning, Manchester Courier, Morning Post, The Star, Glasgow Evening News, Irish News, Musical Courier, Lady's Pictorial, The Queen, Musical Standard, Court Journal, Liverpool Courier, Hull Mail, Eastern Morning News* and many other papers. *The Sunday Times* was not to be out-done by any of the daily newspapers and reported on Ethel's London debut as follows: [21]

"The little Yorkshire musical wonder, Miss Ethel Liggins, is undoubtedly entitled to a place in the ever-growing list of piano prodigies. She is only a child of ten, and already possesses a remarkable execution, in addition to a memory that was good enough to enable her to play some 18 pieces without music at Queen's Hall on Friday.

She has been carefully taught, and in due course should develop her excellent talents to good purpose."

Prophetic words indeed! Her later life was to fully justify all the favourable remarks of the critics.

During Ethel's childhood years of study with Mrs Russell Starr she continued to entertain the Wilsons' guests at Tranby Croft, occasions that were often reported in the society press. In 1896, for instance, this account appeared in *World*: [22]

"At Mrs Arthur Wilson's last dinner party the guests were Lord and Lady Brougham, Lord and Lady Tweedmouth, Lord and Lady Wolseley, Lord and Lady Burton, Lord and Lady Mar and Kellie, Mr and Mrs W. James, Madame von André, Mrs Ronalds and the Brazilian Minister, who were all delighted after dinner by the playing of an infant prodigy from Hull, Miss Ethel Liggins, who is only ten years old, but has a wonderful natural talent."

In the same month, "Frau Musica" wrote in *Vanity Fair*: [23]

"I am not very fond of infant prodigies; but I prophesy a great future for Miss Ethel Liggins, who was heard at Mrs Arthur Wilson's, and gave a concert at Queen's Hall – at which she played no fewer than eighteen pieces! She has evidently not been crammed, but she is a musician to her finger-tips. She touches the piano with true feeling."

On 14th January 1897, a few months after her London debut, Ethel repeated her successful Queen's Hall programme, with minor modifications, at a recital given at the Assembly Rooms, Jarratt Street, Hull. Again the recital was reported fully in the *Hull News*: [24]

Ethel Liggins

"There was a large audience at the Lecture Hall Assembly Rooms last [Thursday] evening to hear Hull's musical prodigy, Miss Ethel Liggins, aged ten years. On this occasion the clever little pianiste gave the entire recital alone and unaided. This, of course, made the performance more wonderful, but we think that a vocalist would somewhat have relieved the monotony, and would have been useful in case of accidents. Two unfortunate mishaps did indeed occur just before the concert commenced, which might have prevented its taking place, and which had the effect of upsetting the youthful musician's nerves, and spoiling the first part of the programme. She came on looking extremely pale and agitated, and played the first three pieces by Bach in a hurried, nervous manner, quite different from her usual cool and collected style. We were especially sorry that Bach's music should be so spoiled, knowing how wonderfully accurately and intelligently she can play it. The little sonata by Scarlatti and one of Mozart's were better, but Miss Liggins was clearly not herself 'till she appeared [in order] to play Beethoven's *Adagio Graziozo*, Op. 31, No. 1. Probably the lovely music itself had much to do with pulling her together, the slow, even beat having a soothing effect on her nerves. However this may be it was a delicious performance. She has improved wonderfully in execution since last year when she would probably not have been able to play such a really difficult movement, at any rate, not so perfectly. Three of

Mendelssohn's *Songs Without Words* were next played gracefully, though signs of nervousness were still apparent. After a short interval, however, she played two pieces by Schubert, with the rendering of which no fault could be found, and the clever little musician was called back again and again to make her curtsey. A set of four pieces by Chopin, three of them valses, came next. These pieces are thoroughly suited to Miss Liggins as they do not require much force, and are eminently fitted to display the beautiful lightness and quickness of her runs. One listens with delight to the fairylike quality of these, which produces an effect never obtained by more muscular players, and one wonders if, with the acquisition of more power, Miss Liggins will lose this enviable characteristic. The responsibility rests with those who have her training in hand. A nocturne by Field, which was followed by Paderewski's *Menuet* and another waltz of Chopin's, and then the little artiste gave a marvellous rendering of Raff's *La Fileuse* and of a polka by the same composer. The latter piece, which brought the recital to a conclusion, is a little too elaborate to receive full justice from the youthful musician as yet, but that she did play it at all is, indeed, a marvel. With this exception there were no signs on the programme of her being unduly pushed and much credit is due to her preceptress Miss Martin A.R.A.M. for the careful and judicious way in which she is being trained. We shall all look with interest on the future career of this, our juvenile musical genius."

The authors have been unable to ascertain the nature of the "two unfortunate mishaps" referred to in the press report. The front and back covers of the programme of the recital are shown on pages 24 and 25, the back cover bearing a charming picture of the ten-year-old girl with dark, wavy hair, dressed in an "Alice in Wonderland"- type frock.

In 1921 Mrs Russell Starr wrote a series of articles for the *Hull News* in which she recalled some of her musical memories. She mentioned a number of pupils, and then continued:

"Then there was Ethel Liggins. She was brought to me before she was seven years old – a dear little girl. This young prodigy gave two or three pianoforte recitals in Hull before she was eleven, and one in London (at the small Queen's Hall) when she was just eleven. * On this occasion before the recital the little thing clung to my hand and begged me to take her on to the platform, which of course I did. But after her first group of pieces, at the first rest when she heard the applause, she said she thought she "could go on by myself now", so I let her. All went well and the London papers from "The Times" downwards spoke enthusiastically in her praise. I believe I have the reports now somewhere. I should add that the programme consisted of items suitable to a child of genius."

---

* In fact she was only ten years and two months old. Mrs Russell Starr stated at the beginning of her newspaper articles that she was writing without references to notes. When she said that Ethel gave 'two or three piano recitals in Hull before she was eleven', she probably meant they were given before the London recital, i.e. before she was ten.

Miss Ethel Liggins

In 1918 one of Ethel's friends from her Hull days, then living in Canada, recalled her childhood performances. [25] It is interesting to note, from her account, that even at a very young age Ethel captivated her audiences and held them spellbound not only by her musicianship but also by the force of her personality — an attribute that remained with her throughout her life.

"Even at the very early age of ten she charmed the hearts of all those who listened to her. A little thing with dark curls and wonderful blue grey eyes, which seemed to hold some mystery in their depths, she would come tripping onto the platform and with a quaint little curtsey take her seat at the piano. A chord or two, a brilliant scale passage, clear and even as whistling, a crash of octaves, or a trill like a bird's note, and she would launch into Chopin — while to the audience the present became as nothing — was blotted out. Chopin's beautiful music — exquisite, haunting. It is translatable only by the few who feel and understand it. She understood it — this wonderful child with her fateful face."

Ethel's grandfather, Thomas Liggins

He lived until 1910 and his wife, Hannah, until 1918. They would have followed Ethel's early successes with great interest.

Front cover of the programme of Ethel Liggins' recital in Hull, January 1897

Back cover of the programme of Ethel Liggins' recital in Hull, January 1897

References: Chapter 2

1. Interview with Laning Humphrey (1896-1988), *Boston Sunday Post*, Boston, Mass., 22nd September 1929.
2. *The Etude*, May 1919, p. 271.
3. As ref. 1.
4. Mr A.T. Taylor, Beverley (private correspondence).
5. The photograph was kindly sent by Messrs Jim Beaty and David Oades of Hull who are cousins. Mr Oades was born at 22 Pemberton Street in the 1960s, the last person to be born there.
6. As ref. 2.
7. As ref. 1.
8. As ref. 2.
9. Ibid.
10. Information on Mrs Mary Wilson and the history of Tranby Croft was kindly supplied by Mrs G.M. Attwood of Hull, with further facts from the late Mrs M. Langdale of Hornsea and the recollections of the late Miss Rose Farbstein of Hull. For a full history of the Wilson family see *The Wilsons of Tranby Croft*, by Gertrude M. Attwood, Hutton Press, Cherry Burton, Yorks., 1988.
11. Madame Alice Sharrah, A.T.C.L. (b. January 1863, d. May 1940) founded the Hull School of Music in Storey Street, Hull, in 1887 with an initial complement of six pupils. Immediately successful, she was able to hold her first concert in the Royal Institution two years later. The next year, taking her courage in both hands and probably encouraged by Mary Wilson, she booked the Assembly Rooms and took £70 at the door, a success unheard of at that time for an amateur concert. She married William Henry Simpson in 1894, all her bridesmaids being pupils. She formed a band of mandolin players which was invited to give one of its first performances at Tranby Croft. By 1914, 1,060 pupils had passed through her hands. She had by then opened new and commodious premises in Spring Bank, Hull, which included a concert room big enough for an audience of 200. She retired from the School in 1938. (Information from Mrs G.M. Attwood.)
12. Gwendoline Brogden (b. 1889 or 1891, d. 1973) was a pupil of Mme Alice Sharrah. Many of her early performances (piano and acting) were organised from and given at Tranby Croft. Mary Wilson organised her London debut and made sure that a distinguished audience was there to listen. She played at the Gaiety Theatre just before the retirement of George Edwardes, and remained in London throughout the 1914-18 war, playing in *The Kiss Call* (1918) with Evelyn Laye, Stanley Lupino and Binnie Hale. In 1910 she married Basil Samuel Foster, also an actor and singer. There was one daughter. They were divorced in 1926. In 1936 she married Percy Waterman Pitt of Hampstead. She was a regular visitor to Muriel Wilson (youngest daughter of Arthur and Mary Wilson) who also lived in Hampstead and Muriel bequeathed a picture and items of jewellery to her. (Information from Mrs G.M. Attwood who has found there is no birth certificate for Gwendoline Brogden who claimed her birth date as 1891, but the death certificate implies it was 1889.) The authors have some of Miss Brogden's gramophone recordings which were made

during the First World War.
13. Mr A.T. Taylor, Beverley (private correspondence).
14. The Tranby Croft Affair is fully described in Mrs Attwood's book (ref. 10).
15. Recollections of the late Miss Rose Farbstein, who was well known in musical and literary circles in Hull. (Information sent by Miss Barbara M. Harrison of Filey.)
16. The authors are indebted to Mrs G.M. Attwood and Mr Norman Staveley of Hull for much of the material on Mrs Russell Starr and her husband.
17. *Hull Times*, 13th April 1895. Cutting sent by Mrs Margaret Stockbridge.
18. *Hull News,* 20th June 1896.
19. *The Times*, 20th June 1896.
20. *The Daily Telegraph*, 20th June 1896.
21. *The Sunday Times*, 21st June 1896.
22. *World,* 22nd July 1896
23. *Vanity Fair*, July 1896.
24. *Hull News*, 15th January 1897.
25. *Musical Courier*, 1st August 1918. Includes the recollections of Mrs F.R. Mackay of Alberta, Canada.

Note: When annotating sources of information by the reference numbers in this list (and also in the list of references in Chapters 1, 3 and 4 which deal with Ethel Liggins's early years), only the main source is usually quoted in order to avoid an excessively unwieldy list of sources. However, many of the facts have been checked and confirmed from a number of sources other than those quoted in the numbered references. The whole picture, as any researcher will know, is derived from many items of information fitting together like pieces in a jigsaw. Apart from the sources listed above, other people who have kindly provided facts in personal correspondence, thereby adding to or confirming the information contained in the sources quoted above, include:

Mr R. Bright, Superintendent Registrar of Births, Deaths and Marriages, Hull.
Mr B. Cattley, Hon. Secretary, Beverley Music Lovers' Circle.
Drs J.B. and K.D.M. Coltman, West Burton, Leyburn, Yorks.
Mr Noel Cox, Warden, Royal Academy of Music.
"John Humber", *Hull Daily Mail*.
Miss J. Levison, Hull.
Mr A.H. Liggins, Hull.
Mr P. Rhodes, Hon. Secretary, Hornsea Music Club.
Mr Glyn Roberts, Director of Leisure Services, Humberside County Council (on the 1881 census).
Staff of Hornsea and Hull public libraries.

The recital programme whose front and back covers are shown on pages 24 and 25 was kindly donated by Miss J. Levison. Mr T.P. Langdale provided a lot of information about the Liggins family, which enabled the family tree in Chapter 1 to be drawn. Mrs G.M. Attwood donated the photograph of Tranby Croft and Mrs M. Stockbridge found the photograph of Thomas Liggins in the *Hull and Lincolnshire Times*'s report (10th December 1910) of his funeral, and also supplied a lot of additional family history. The help of everyone who helped in these ways is duly acknowledged.

Chapter 3

Apprenticeship

After her successful London recital as a ten-year-old in 1896 and the follow-up performance in Hull in 1897, Ethel continued her studies with Mrs Russell Starr in Hull. But it was clear that she was a child of such prodigious genius that a period of full-time musical study had to be arranged at the earliest opportunity. The possibilities were investigated, and Mrs Russell Starr, Ethel and her parents and the Wilson family all agreed that Ethel must be entered for nothing less than a top-class musical school, preferably in Germany, which was then generally considered to be the centre of Europe's musical culture. And so it came about that in mid-1897 she was entered for a scholarship to study at the Hoch Conservatory of Music at Frankfurt-am-Main, Germany; her audition was successful and the scholarship was duly awarded. [1]

Ethel Liggins sailed for Germany from Hull in the autumn of 1897 when she was 11½ years old and enrolled at the Hoch Conservatory for the start of the 1897-1898 session. [2] This was a big step for a young girl to take, especially in those days, when few of her friends would have even ventured far from Hull, let alone to Europe. Indeed, some of Ethel's aunts thought it was cruel to let such a young girl go abroad for intensive study. [3] But all contemporary accounts indicate that she was a very determined young lady even at that tender age, and had set her mind on going to Europe. She was resolved even then to reach the top of the musical profession.

The Hoch Conservatory in Frankfurt-am-Main where Ethel Liggins enrolled as a student was one of the most prestigious in Germany and was generally reckoned to be amongst the top four or five in Europe. * Clara Schumann (née Wieck), widow of the composer Robert Schumann, and a famous concert pianist in her own right, had been in charge of the piano department at the Conservatory from its foundation in 1878 until she had to

---

* The Hoch Conservatory, Frankfurt-am-Main, was founded in 1878. It was endowed by the Frankfurt merchant, Joseph P. Hoch, who bequeathed his entire estate of 900,000 gold marks to establish it. Directors of the Conservatory in its earlier years included J.J. Raff (1878-82), Bernhard Scholz (1883-1908), Iwan Knorr (1909-16), W.E. Bauszern (1916-23) and Bernhard Sekles (1923-33). Standards were very high. Apart from Clara Schumann (mentioned in the text), distinguished staff included Julius Stockhausen and Engelbert Humperdinck. Pupils included (in addition to those quoted later in the text) Carl Friedberg, Hans Pfitzer, Paul Hindemith and Otto Klemperer. In 1937 the Conservatory was divided into a State High School of Music and a Conservatory which trained amateur musicians. [4] At the time Ethel Liggins was there nearly 20% of the students came from English-speaking countries. [5]

Apprenticeship

resign the post in 1892 because of worsening deafness. She had died in 1896 (the year before Ethel arrived), aged 77, but her influence still pervaded the atmosphere of the Conservatory. The Head of the piano department at the time of Ethel's arrival was James Kwast, then 45 years old.*

Kwast was greatly respected as a teacher by most of his students. He was also something of a composer, having written a piano concerto and other piano music, and had edited the works of Handel and Clementi. As the head of the piano department at the Conservatory, he was the member of staff who was to have the most influence on Ethel's future career.

Although Ethel Liggins had gained admission to the Conservatory as a result of her brilliance as a pianist, she clearly had to receive an all-round musical education whilst enrolled as a student at Frankfurt, and this entailed learning musical theory and composition. In charge of this department at the Conservatory was Iwan Knorr,† who was about the same age as Kwast.

---

* James Kwast was born in Nijerk, Holland, on 23rd November 1852. He had studied first with his father and then under Ferdinand Böhme. At the age of 22 he was appointed Instructor at the Conservatory in Cologne and from 1893 to 1903 he was at the Hoch Conservatory in Frankfurt as a piano instructor. From 1903 to 1906 he taught at the Klindworth-Scharwenka Conservatory in Berlin and then at Stern's Conservatory there. He married twice; his first wife, Antonia, who died in Stuttgart in 1931, was a daughter of Ferdinand Hiller, a well-known conductor, composer, writer and critic, who established the Cologne Conservatory, and it was in Cologne that Kwast met Antonia. But the marriage ended in divorce and he then married Frieda Hodapp (b. 13th August 1880, d. 14th September 1949), who was one of his students. She was a brilliant young musician who became a very successful concert pianist. Both James and Frieda later recorded piano rolls for J.D. Philipps & Söhne of Frankfurt (Duca rolls), including some in which they played 4-handed arrangements together. Frieda also recorded rolls for Welte & Söhne of Freiburg. James Kwast died in Berlin on 31st October 1927. [6]

† Iwan Knorr was born in Mewe, West Prussia, on 3rd January 1853. He was taken to Russia at the age of four, and later he studied with Moscheles, Richter and Reinecke at the Leipzig Conservatory. He then returned to Russia to teach at the Imperial College of Noble Ladies. In 1877, at the age of 24, whilst still unknown as a composer, he submitted one of his compositions to Brahms for an opinion. This piece was his *Variations on a Ukranian Folksong*, Op. 7, and his enterprise in approaching the famous composer was to pay dividends, for Brahms liked the piece, and as a result made a mental note of the aspiring young musician's name. In 1883 a vacancy arose on the teaching staff of the Hoch Conservatory in Frankfurt, and on the personal recommendation of Brahms, Knorr got the job. The work suited the 30-year-old musician down to the ground, and he was to stay there for most of his career. Initially he taught piano, theory and musical history, and from about 1886 he also taught composition, but two years later he gave up teaching the piano and thereafter concentrated solely on teaching theory and composition. In 1895 (two years before Ethel Liggins' arrival at the Conservatory) he was named 'Royal Professor' and in 1908, several years after her departure, he succeeded Bernhard Scholz as Director of the Conservatory. Several of his compositions were written under a pseudonym, I.O. Armand. He died in Frankfurt on 22nd January 1916. [7]

These two men were the major influences in Ethel's formal instruction, but there was also another, much younger, teacher. He was Bernhard Sekles, still in his mid-20s when Ethel arrived. * It is he who was probably responsible for much of Ethel's day-to-day instruction in musical theory, which was his special subject.

Faced by this formidable array of academic talent, the youthful Ethel Liggins (she was still only 11) entered enthusiastically into her studies and her musical education made rapid strides. It was the custom for the more talented students of the Conservatory to be allowed to make public appearances once they had satisfied their academic tutors that they had reached an appropriate standard of ability and confidence. Ethel must have impressed her new teachers very quickly as she was allowed to appear in conservatory concerts within weeks of her arrival. In her first year there she took part, with other students, in four concerts. Two of these were in December 1897, one in March 1898 (she was still only 11 for all of these) and one in May 1898, four weeks after her 12th birthday. [9] Word of this last appearance reached Hull, and the event was reported in the *Hull News*. [10]

A brilliant young Hull pianist

"A few evenings ago Miss Liggins performed at a concert by students at the Conservatoire, and the *Frankfurt Intelligenzblatt* of 9th May spoke of her playing: 'The surprise of the evening was undoubtedly the brilliant execution of Haydn's Concerto in D flat by Miss Ethel Liggins of Hull, the twelve-year-old pupil of Herr Kwast. Playing from memory and accompanied by the orchestra, the little lady interpreted this difficult work with remarkable intelligence and expression. Her technical execution was correct, tasteful and of such a childlike, heart-winning freshness, and so full of fire, that the idea of its having been acquired by heavy labour was at once dispelled. Although we are not fond of praising children's performances, still, in this case, we may reasonably expect great things from such remarkable talent, provided that it is continually guided in a quiet way to its perfect fruition.' "

Not only was Ethel's musical education benefiting from her skilled and accomplished teachers, she was also exposed to the influence of her fellow students, and probably learned as much from her contact with them as she did from the staff of the Conservatory. At the time of Ethel's arrival a dazzling array of musical talent was represented amongst her fellow students,

---

* Bernhard Sekles was born in Frankfurt-am-Main on 20th June 1872. He studied at the Hoch Conservatory in Frankfurt from 1893 to 1894 and this was followed by two years' experience as a theatre conductor at Mayence. He was appointed to the teaching staff at the Hoch Conservatory in Frankfurt in 1896 when he was still only 24 years old. He remained at the Conservatory for many years and eventually, in 1923, became its Director, a post he retained until 1933. He died in 1934, having spent almost the whole of his life in his home-town of Frankfurt. [8]

Apprenticeship

James Kwast, who taught piano

Iwan Knorr, who taught composition

Ethel Liggins' teachers in Frankfurt

including Percy Grainger from Australia * and a brilliant group of English students, namely Henry Balfour Gardiner, ** Norman O'Neill, † Roger Quilter †† and Cyril Scott. ‡ They were all several years older than Ethel Liggins and became known, variously, as the 'Frankfurt Group', the 'Frankfurt Five', or, more colloquially, the 'Frankfurt Gang'. Percy Grainger, perhaps the best known of them, had been at the Conservatory for three years when Ethel Liggins arrived. Enrolled at 13, he was still only 15 when joined at the Conservatory by Ethel. Later he recalled Ethel's arrival and remarked: "She eclipsed us all with her girlishly winsome Mozart playing." [16] Grainger was the nearest in age to Ethel though four years older. The others were three to seven years older than Grainger. Apart from Norman O'Neill who died in 1934, all the 'Frankfurt Five' lived to a good age, surviving into the second half of the 20th century.

The talents of this gifted quintet must have rubbed off in various ways on Ethel, for not only would she have been present during their studies and their performances for their teachers, but also she would have been a contributor to the musical discussions that went on. She would have absorbed the musical atmosphere engendered by these fine musicians and would no

---

* Percy Aldridge Grainger (real name George Percy Grainger; b. Adelaide, Australia, 8th July 1882) who was the youngest of the 'Frankfurt Five', was a highly eccentric individual who became famous as a concert pianist (particularly noted for his interpretation of the works of Grieg) and composer. His settings of folk songs brought him fame whilst still a young man. From the outbreak of the First World War he lived in the USA, but made concert tours all over the world up to the late 1950s. He died in White Plains, New York, on 20th February 1961. [11]

** Henry Balfour Gardiner, who achieved distinction as a composer, was born in London on 7th November 1877, six days after Roger Quilter. He had been a student at the Hoch Conservatory in Frankfurt from 1894 to 1896 but had then left to become a student at New College, Oxford. However, he used to return to Frankfurt during university vacations and Ethel would have got to know him during those visits. He died in Salisbury on 28th June 1950. [12]

† The oldest of the group, Norman O'Neill, was born in Kensington, London, on 14th March 1875 and studied at Frankfurt from 1893 to 1897, leaving about the time Ethel started, or just after. He later became a conductor and composer, and is remembered particularly for his connection with music in the theatre. He died in London on 3rd March 1934. [13]

†† Roger Quilter was born in Brighton on 1st November 1877. He was a gifted composer and made his mark at an early age as a composer of songs before turning to the composition of orchestral works. He is perhaps best remembered for his *Children's Overture*, consisting of an arrangement of nursery tunes. He was a student in Frankfurt when Ethel arrived and was there until 1898. He died in London on 21st September 1953. [14]

‡ Cyril Scott was born in Oxton, Cheshire on 27th September 1879. He became well known as a composer, writer and pianist, and perhaps best of all as a discoverer, preserver and arranger of old folk songs. He is associated with some of Percy Grainger's well-known folk song settings, having supplied Grainger with original material he had come across. He died in Eastbourne on 31st December 1970. [15]

Apprenticeship

doubt have been part of the fun and games that went on outside normal teaching hours at the Conservatory.

One of the benefits of being a student at the Hoch Conservatory was that famous musicians were regular visitors to the city, and to the Conservatory, where they played to the students. Amongst them whilst Ethel was there were Eugen d'Albert and Frederic Lamond, both Glaswegians and former pupils of Liszt. Close exposure to talent such as theirs must have given the students an insight into the particular skills of a top-class concert pianist. Lamond was regarded as a Beethoven specialist, and his physical resemblance to the great composer, which he cultivated by adopting an appropriate hairstyle, heightened the association, to the extent that Beethoven's music was demanded of him by the public at virtually every recital. Another visitor whilst Ethel was a student was Ossip Gabrilowitsch, the brilliant young Russian pianist on the threshold of a great career.

Under James Kwast, Ethel learned the Mozart A major Concerto and many other works. Photographs show Kwast as a short, bearded man who, according to Grainger, usually wore a light-coloured suit of which the trousers had shrunk to such an extent that they had to be let down to their fullest capacity. This gave the effect of fullness in the seat and a shortness in the leg which, according to Grainger, "suggested an elephant's posterior." [17]

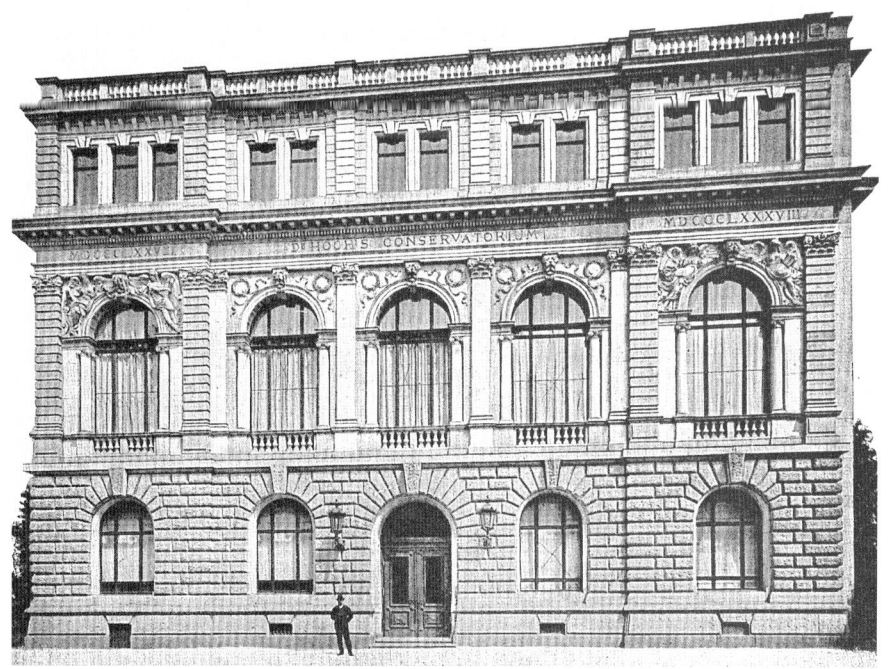

The Hoch Conservatory in Frankfurt-am-Main

Shortly after Ethel arrived in Frankfurt the 16-year-old Grainger had a brief romantic attachment with 19-year-old Mimi, daughter of his piano teacher, Kwast, by his first marriage, an affair initiated and engineered by Grainger's mother, Rose, who was with her son in Frankfurt and who organised his life for him, as she was to continue to do for many years to come. This came to nothing but the event must have been of mild passing interest to Ethel, then nearing her teens. [18]

Ethel continued to play regularly in the conservatory's concerts. When she was 14, three years after her arrival in Frankfurt, another of her appearances (on 9th November 1900) was reported in the *Hull News*: [19]

"Miss Ethel Liggins, whose wonderful skill as a musician is such a source of pride to her friends in Hull, has been playing at a concert given at Frankfort-on-the-Maine [*sic*] in connection with the Conservatorium where she is being musically educated. She chose three selections from Chopin, and achieved a great success. Three Frankfort papers commented upon this performance as follows:–

'The youthful pianist Miss Ethel Liggins played several studies from Chopin with taste and technical skill.'

'The three studies from Chopin played by the child prodigy Ethel Liggins were executed most satisfactorily and crisply.'

'The same evening we heard another child prodigy, Ethel Liggins of Hull, who, under the tuition of her teacher, Professor Kwast, has developed greatly, and who played three studies of Chopin with thorough understanding and technical skill.' "

A complete record of Ethel's appearances at the conservatory's concerts during her years of study there is shown opposite. [20]

In spite of the undoubted teaching abilities of her various tutors and the fact that she enjoyed very cordial relationships with her teachers and the other students, as shown by letters and greetings cards they sent her [21], Ethel eventually became dissatisfied with the Conservatory at Frankfurt, feeling that she was not progressing as rapidly as she would have liked. She was not alone in that respect for Percy Grainger was not happy with either Kwast or Knorr, though, mercurial character that he was, it is difficult to know to what extent the problems were associated with his teachers and to what extent they could be attributed to himself.

Early in 1902, when Ethel had been at the Conservatory for four and a half years, the impatient young 15-year-old felt she had exhausted what Frankfurt had to offer and that it was time to move on. Her thoughts had increasingly turned to Vienna, where resided Theodor Leschetizky, the most famous piano teacher in Europe. She resolved that by one means or another she would become one of his pupils, as it seemed that everybody who was anybody in the pianistic world had studied under the great teacher.

Apprenticeship

1897-98
Evening recital	6. 12. 97	Mozart: Sonata in F, K. 332, 1st movement
"	16. 12. 97	Beethoven: Variations on *Tändeln und Scherzen*
"	30. 3. 98	Haydn: Piano Concerto
Examination concert	8. 5. 98	Ditto – with orchestra

1898-99
Evening recital	21. 9. 98	Clementi: Sonata in B, 1st movement
"	12. 10. 98	Bach: Three pieces from the Partita in B
"	20. 10. 98	Mozart: Piano Concerto in A, 1st movement
Public concert	30. 11. 98 }	Bach: Three pieces from the Partita in B
Public 'people's concert'	11. 12. 98 }	
Evening recital	19. 12. 98	Mozart, Piano Concerto in A, 2nd & 3rd movts.
"	21. 12. 98	Mozart: Sonata for Keyboard and Violin in B 1st movement (with Hans Franzos, violin)
"	24. 3. 99	Beethoven: Piano Concerto No. 2 in B minor, 1st movement
"	3. 5. 99	Ditto, 2nd and 3rd movements
"	1. 6. 99	Beethoven: Rondo, Op. 129 (*Rage over a Lost Penny*)

1899-1900
Evening recital	27. 9. 99	Beethoven: Sonata No. 25 in G, Op. 79
"	2. 11. 99	Chopin: *Bolero*
"	8. 11. 99	Hummel: Piano Concerto in A minor, Op. 85, 1st movement
Public concert	12. 11. 99	Beethoven: Piano Concerto No. 2 in B minor, 2nd and 3rd movements

1900-1901
Evening recital	9. 11. 00	Chopin: Three Études; in F minor, D, A.
Public concert	22. 11. 00	Chopin: Three Études (Nos. 25 to 27)
Evening recital	20. 12. 00	Chopin: Piano Concerto No. 1 in E minor, 1st movement
"	25. 1. 01	Rameau: *Le Rappel des Oiseaux*, and Raff: *La Fileuse*
Musical performance in honour of Joseph Joachim	23. 2. 01	Beethoven: Rondo in G, Op. 129
Public concert	10. 3. 01	Mendelssohn: Piano Concerto in G minor (with orchestra)
Evening recital	13. 5. 01	Beethoven: Sonata in A, Op. 2, No. 2

1901-1902
Evening recital	3. 10. 01	Chopin: Piano Concerto in E minor, 2nd and 3rd movements
"	1. 11. 01	Beethoven: *German Dance*, and Scarlatti: Pastorale and Capriccio
"	12. 12. 01	Liszt: Hungarian Rhapsody, Number 13
"	7. 2. 02	Chopin: Préludes

Concert appearances of Ethel Liggins whilst she was a student in Frankfurt
(Details kindly provided by Professor Dr Peter Cahn)

Well known though Leschetizky * was as a teacher from the middle of the nineteenth century, it was after he taught Paderewski in the mid-1880s that he achieved worldwide fame, for Paderewski's impact on the concert platform following his first successful appearance was immediate and sensational; everyone wanted to know who had taught this brilliant young superstar, and the answer, of course, was Leschetizky. Over the years many pupils who subsequently achieved eminence flocked to him including, apart from Paderewski, Ignaz Friedman, Ossip Gabrilowitsch, Katharine Goodson, Mark Hambourg, Benno Moiseiwitsch, Elly Ney and Artur Schnabel.

The manner in which Ethel Liggins came to arrive in Vienna to be auditioned by Leschetizky early in 1902 is known from interviews she gave later in life. She was determined to study under the great teacher, and at 15 Ethel was as resolute in her intentions as she had been at 11 when she first set out for Europe. According to her own account she "ran away" from the Hoch Conservatory and went to Vienna where she "landed on Leschetizky's doorstep" and appealed to him to take her as a student. Let Ethel herself take up the story: [23]

"I was in the fourth year of my study at the Frankfurt Conservatory [†] and had become dissatisfied. I decided to run away to Vienna, but being such a child, of course, I was watched over very strictly by the directress of the 'pension' or student quarters where I lived. I took one of the other girls into my confidence. During several weeks I transferred my belongings to her house. At the same time I had her make me a dress longer than I usually wore.

"One day I got permission to go to tea at the house of a certain girl, and went to my fellow-conspirator's house instead. There I slipped the long dress on over the one I was wearing, and put on a heavy veil. I thought that disguising myself in the veil was the most wonderful idea! Then I snatched up my luggage – it didn't amount to very much – and was off. I was to find a woman who my friend knew in Vienna.

"The money for my journey was what I had saved from a little I had made now and again from concerts the Conservatory had allowed me to give. I had to put up at

---

* Theodor Leschetizky (b. Lancut, Poland, 22nd June 1830, d. Dresden, 14th November 1915) was taught to play the piano initially by his father, and at ten made his first public appearance as a pianist. In the same year the family moved to Vienna where Theodor studied with Carl Czerny (piano) and Simon Sechter (composition). From the early age of 14 years he was in demand as a piano teacher, but he also found time to study Philosophy at the University of Vienna. After he moved to St. Petersburg in 1852 he established a large circle of pupils and also played as a solo pianist, appearing before the Tsar in that role. He was a close friend of the pianist Anton Rubinstein and at Rubinstein's request became Director of Piano Studies at the St. Petersburg Conservatory in 1862. In 1878 he returned to Vienna where he taught privately almost until the end of his life and became one of the leading figures in the musical life of the city. [22]

† From the record of concerts on the previous page, she was clearly in her fifth year, not fourth. The Conservatory's yearbook verifies that Ethel was still a student there at the start of the 1901-02 session.

Apprenticeship

Nuremberg for the night, and realising that my finances would not last very long under the most favourable conditions I asked my way to the cheapest hotel in the city.

"In due time I was back on the train, and found the woman who was to take charge of me and help me get in touch with Leschetizky."

It must be remembered that Leschetizky was 71 years old when Ethel, then 15¾, arrived early in 1902. He already had a full class of students and on account of his advancing years he had let it be known that he had no wish to take any more pupils. Ethel knew this beforehand and therefore did not expect to receive a warm reception on arrival at Leschetizky's house. She described what happened:

"Send word to the master that I shall wait at his door until he comes to see me for five minutes", [24] she told the servant, who conveyed the message as to Ethel's identity to Leschetizky, but told Ethel she was unlikely to achieve the privilege she sought. All day she waited, without success. But she was not to be denied.

"Again and again I went back to Leschetizky's house – or 'villa' as they called it – and still he refused to see me. [25] I returned so many times that I was told Leschetizky was angry at the mention of my name. But I persisted. Finally he gave up the struggle. When I went before him he had nothing but dark looks for me. 'Play something!' was his greeting. I played something from Chopin, I think, and Leschetizky's only comment was, 'Play something different' – and again several times after that, he only asked me to play something else.

"Then he burst out laughing, and laughed, and laughed. 'He's an old man, and gone crazy', I thought. He picked up a letter, and put his hand over the heading, and said, 'Do you know that writing?' When I told him I did not, he took his hand away, and I saw that it was from the Hoch Conservatory in Frankfurt-am-Main. The letter said I had run away, and asked him not to see me. So that was why he had treated me that way. But after hearing me, he taught me for three years." *

In an interview with a reporter from the *Cleveland Hippodrome News* Ethel said that at her audition with Leschetizky she played for him not for the five minutes she had pleaded for but for two hours, after which he said, according to Ethel, "I will take you for my pupil free of charge and if you are unable to pay your living expenses in Vienna I will also pay those." [26]

The somewhat hostile reception, amounting initially to a rebuttal, when Ethel turned up on Leschetizky's doorstep was probably due not only to the letter he had received from the Hoch Conservatory and the known fact that he did not wish, at his age, to take any more students; the initial "rejection" amounted in effect to a test of the potential student's dedication. If a student went away meekly when rebuffed by Leschetizky he (or she) clearly lacked the motivation necessary to become a Leschetizky pupil. Benno

---

* In spite of the manner of her departure, the Frankfurt Conservatory clearly bore her no ill will. She appeared in the list of distinguished former students in their yearbooks for many years.

Moiseiwitsch, who sought to become one of the great teacher's pupils three years after Ethel, and arrived armed with a letter of recommendation, was received in an equally discouraging manner but had the determination necessary to persist, and was accepted into the select band of pupils. Leschetizky was a wise man and, at his advanced age, was prepared to accept only the most determined and dedicated of potential students.

So Ethel became one of Leschetizky's talented circle of students in 1902 and was to study with him for about two years. His influence on her progress was profound; it was he who transformed her from a highly talented prodigy into a complete pianist, equipped with a brilliant technique as well as sensitive interpretive skills. She knew the debt she owed to Leschetizky and in later years she followed his precepts when teaching her own pupils.

Leschetizky's studio was such a 'Mecca' for students that he had far more pupils than he could cope with unaided. He therefore employed a number of "preparatory teachers", whose main function was to instil into the pupils certain technical principles in which he believed, so that by the time of the first lesson with Leschetizky the worst faults should have been eradicated. A

Theodor Leschetizky, Ethel's teacher in Vienna

further purpose was to help the advanced pupils in preparing special assignments. Some pupils never progressed further than their preparatory teacher; the more talented the pupils, the more time they spent with Leschetizky. Ethel's preparatory teacher when she went to Leschetizky was Ethel Newcomb, an American, [27] but Ethel spent only a month with her and from then onwards she was taught only by Leschetizky himself.

According to Ethel, several of the two hundred or more Leschetizky pupils received a lesson only at rare intervals – only once or twice a year – others one lesson a month, others at more frequent intervals. There was no fixed 'course' – students were taught as often as Leschetizky thought appropriate. They were required to work "like a beaver" to prepare particular work assigned to them, and the ensuing lessons were very long. [28]

Leschetizky's teaching methods continued the school of Czerny but he modified it according to his own inclinations, and each student's talents were shaped individually according to his or her own particular strengths and weaknesses. Much has been written about Leschetizky's teaching system and it is unnecessary to describe it in detail here. [29] However, it should be mentioned that his method was practical rather than theoretical; he taught largely by demonstration, tailoring his instruction to the particular requirements of his pupils. According to Ethel, "He gave a great sense of economy of means. His phrasing was glorious – it was to piano playing what Caruso's was to singing." [30] Great attention was paid to detail; he studied his pupils' hands before deciding exactly what they could or could not do and he demanded that his pianists should thoroughly master every detail of the music they were set to study. Possessing a formidable memory and an infallible ear, no sloppy work was ever allowed to pass him by. He was a hard taskmaster, feared but worshipped by his pupils.

He taught only the very best pupils; those with outstanding talent. If, after an audition, there was the slightest suspicion that an aspiring student was unlikely ever to reach a high standard as a pianist however hard he or she worked, he would not enroll them, for he felt it would be unfair for them to embark on a challenge they could not meet. Once enrolled the future was in their hands – he believed in "the survival of the fittest".

Leschetizky's pupils were taught individually but an additional feature of his teaching was a group evening class every two weeks or so in which an interchange of ideas and criticism took place. Only the most gifted of his talented band of students were allowed to play at these assemblies. So far as the individual lessons were concerned the student would apply for a lesson when the work that had been set was prepared to the extent that the student dared play it to the master; for this purpose Leschetizky used a card index system in which the dates and details of the lessons were recorded. His basic idea was to bring his pupils to a certain level of excellence and at the same time let them develop their own special individuality.

Although Leschetizky was autocratic and strong-willed he soon built up a friendly rapport with most of his students. To the younger ones he was a father-figure. After they had studied with him for a while he knew each of their individual styles and foibles so well that he could recognise their playing with his eyes closed. One of his students, Benno Moiseiwitsch, has described a game Leschetizky sometimes used to play with his pupils at the group class. He would turn his back on them and ask someone (un-named) to play a certain composition; he could unfailingly pick out who it was. [31] Another student, Mark Hambourg, said that "the Professor" used to play off his students one against the other after they had played to him by telling each one, in the other's absence, that the other had done best. [32] Though he could be irritable he had a sense of humour too. Once, when an American girl was playing, Leschetizky got up, fetched a candle, lit it, and placed it under her music stool. She stopped playing and asked what he was doing. "Do not stop", he said, "I'm only trying to warm up your performance a little." He had a lively wit but could be sarcastic, and lessons sometimes ended with students in tears. On one such occasion Clara Clemens, daughter of the novelist Samuel Clemens (Mark Twain) had been so disappointed in her performance that she burst into tears afterwards. Ossip Gabrilowitsch, a fellow pupil, comforted her and from that beginning a friendship and romance developed. Eventually they were married.

Leschetizky never required excessively lengthy periods of technical practice from his students, but he demanded complete concentration on the music and insisted on the students having a thorough knowledge of every detail in it. So far as technical matters were concerned, he believed that the hand should be arched (not flat-backed) and the wrist loose. Great attention was paid to the individual needs of every pupil, so each one developed his or her individual capabilities to the fullest degree, without any fettering of originality or freedom of individual expression. If one of his pupils had a thin, bony hand, he would encourage him or her to increase the pressure of the fingers on the keys, to make the notes "sing" by bringing weight to the touch. If the hand was fat and heavy he would train the pupil to exert as little pressure as possible to counteract the natural weight.

The entire purpose of Leschetizky's teaching was to encourage dexterity of fingerwork and the production of "tone". To him, tone was paramount – tone big enough for the largest concert hall yet "so under control that it could be administered with a reserve that made its whispers potent". [33] He believed

Apprenticeship

that everything a pianist played must be beautiful in tone; alive, expressive. Never must the playing be dull, monotonous, harsh or, as he put it, "without charm". The interpretation was everything. Leschetizky knew that the ability to produce tone is the hallmark of the great pianist. He knew how to achieve it himself and he knew how to impart the secret to his pupils, which is why so many of them went on to become masters of their craft.

Not only was Leschetizky a fine teacher, he was also a composer of some renown, though underrated, with about 49 compositions to his credit, chiefly nocturnes, romances and salon pieces. During her adult career Ethel used to play some of them in her public performances, and she also played transcriptions for the piano which Leschetizky had made of non-piano works by other composers. Some of his own compositions were written essentially as studies, for example his *Intermezzo in Octaves*, Op. 14, No. 4 but, as in the case of Chopin's studies, the music rose above the level of mere mechanical exercise.

Under Leschetizky, Ethel increased her repertoire enormously and mastered the piano works of a large number of composers. Leschetizky always regarded himself as an authority on the piano works of Beethoven, on the grounds that his teacher, Czerny, had been a student of the great master; indeed, he had been one of his favourites, so it is reasonable to suppose that some of Beethoven's wishes regarding the interpretation of his music had been passed down to Leschetizky via the intermediary, Czerny.

One of Leschetizky's weaknesses was that he had "a great eye for womankind".[31] He married four times, each time to one of his pupils. As a young man Leschetizky had lived for a time in St. Petersburg and whilst there one of his duties had been to give singing lessons to the daughter of the Grand Duchess and to one of her maids of honour, Anna de Friedebourg. In 1856 Leschetizky and Mlle de Friedebourg were married. The marriage ended in divorce in 1872. In 1880 at the age of 50 he married Annette Essipoff (sometimes spelt Essipova or Esipova) who was a former pupil and also, at that time, an assistant teacher at his studio. She was a brilliant, well-known concert pianist, and together she and Leschetizky gave a celebrated series of duets until this marriage also ended in divorce, in 1892. However, she continued to work at her former husband's studio when not away on concert tours. In 1894 Leschetizky married a widow, Mme Dawimirska, a piano pupil, who was the Mrs Leschetizky in residence at the time Ethel Liggins was a pupil in Vienna, and after yet another divorce he married a fourth pupil in 1908 when he was 78. She was Marie Gabriela Rozborska, a pianist who made a number of public appearances as 'Mme Leschetizky' in London in the same year and subsequently. Ethel Liggins was only 15 when she arrived in Vienna in 1902 and not yet 18 when she left in 1904, probably too young to risk the fate of becoming yet another Mrs Leschetizky, though his pupils agreed that 'The Old Man' as he was colloquially known always had an eye for the pretty girls in his class, and the prettier they were the more attention they received. This characteristic remained with Leschetizky for the whole of his life until his death in 1915 at the age of 85.

Leschetizky had not forgotten his offer to teach Ethel Liggins free of charge. She said later: [35]

"He was wonderfully appreciative of honest effort and hard work. He knew, for example, that I was dreadfully poor, and he taught me for nothing, giving me his precious time and skill with greater liberality than to many other pupils who paid him high fees. In those days I had to keep myself on five dollars a week. And Vienna, even then, was not a cheap city. Leschetizky knew this, and once when I had played the Henselt Concerto for him at one of the classes, he told me to come to his room the next day. He disappeared into an inner room and remained for some time fussing with papers. I was fearful that I had played so badly that he was going to dismiss me. On the contrary, he reappeared at the doorway, with this little envelope in his hand – an envelope which contained one hundred kroner, in ten-kroner notes. This, he told me, was a gift to me, because I had played the concerto so much to his liking. I wanted terribly to keep the kroner, but alas, they had to go to appease the appetite of a growing girl. Fortunately I still have the envelope with his handwriting as a beloved souvenir of Leschetizky's appreciation and generosity."

During Ethel's period of study with Leschetizky she was able to hear many visiting artists in Vienna and she made occasional visits to Berlin, where she heard pianists such as Busoni and Carreño, all of which enhanced her musical education. She also returned to England from time to time for holidays and to give occasional concerts in small halls and at society functions. In the planning of these she was helped by Lady de Grey* and

---

* Lady de Grey of London (1859 - 1917) was born the Hon. Constance Gladys, sister of George Robert Charles and Sidney, 13th and 14th Earls of Pembroke. As the widow of St. George Henry (Lowther), 4th Earl of Lonsdale, she married in 1885 Frederick Oliver Robinson, (1852 - 1923), who was Earl de Grey from 1871 to 1909 and heir to the First Marquess of Ripon (a Marquessate created in 1871). He held a number of public offices and was Member of Parliament (Liberal) for Ripon, 1874-1880. He became the Second Marquess of Ripon, and Constance Gladys the Marchioness, on the death of his father in 1909.

Lady de Grey, as she was from her marriage until 1909 when she became the Marchioness of Ripon, was an active and discriminating patroness of Covent Garden opera and of the arts in general. She was remembered not only for her beauty and wit, but also for her charity work in the First World War until her death in October 1917. [36] She was described as "The most wonderful and beautiful woman, with rare distinction, unconquerable high spirits, and in her youth a *joie de vivre* and vivacity unimaginable". [37] Like Mary Wilson, Lady de Grey gave financial assistance to many talented young musicians in their quest to establish themselves. She was a frequent visitor to Tranby Croft, and Mary Wilson to Lady de Grey's residence in London. Lady de Grey would therefore have been well acquainted with Ethel Liggins.

Apprenticeship

by Mary Wilson, with whom she had kept in close touch throughout her sojourn in Frankfurt and Vienna. They both gave financial help to Ethel in such matters as the hire of halls and the printing of publicity notices. Without their generosity, Ethel's further advancement would have been virtually impossible.

It was Leschetizky's custom to tell his students when he felt that he could teach them no more and they were ready for a career on the concert platform. There is no documentary evidence to show exactly when this day came for Ethel Liggins but the facts suggest it was probably in the spring of 1904 when she was 17, or the early summer of the same year when she was just 18. * She was by then fluent in the German language and was an accomplished pianist, ready and able to embark on a concert career and to devote her energies on a full-time basis to achieving this end, given the necessary determination, which she possessed in abundance. It was with mixed feelings of sadness at leaving Leschetizky but in joyful anticipation of what lay ahead, that she returned to Britain.

---

* Ethel, in her later interviews in the USA, was a little hazy about dates and her own evidence in this regard is unreliable. In various interviews given in the USA many years later she stated the following:

1) "After getting my scholarship to the [Frankfurt] Conservatory when I was just 10 . . . " [38]
2) "I was in the fourth year of my study there [at Frankfurt], and had become dissatisfied. I decided to run away to Vienna . . ." [39]
3) "My association with him [Leschetizky] for three years was a rare privilege" [40]; and " . . . after hearing me play he [Leschetizky] taught me for three years." [41]
4) "Afterwards [after Frankfurt] I went to Leschetizky, and was with him several years, until I was 16." [42]

With regard to (1), it is known that she enrolled at Frankfurt in the autumn of 1897 when she was 11½, though she might have gained her scholarship when she was still only 10.

With regard to (2), the Frankfurt Conservatory yearbook showed that she was still there in the 1901-02 session and played in a concert on 7th February 1902 when she was 15¾; she was then in her fifth year of study. She probably left to go to Leschetizky in Vienna very soon afterwards. As the facts clearly show she was 15 when she left Frankfurt to join Leschetizky in Vienna, she could not have studied with him "for three years" as stated in (3) and also been with him "until I was 16" as stated in (4).

If she had studied with Leschetizky for three years continuously following her arrival in Vienna she would have been 18 when she left and returned to her home country. But the dates of her concert engagements on her return to Britain indicate that she began her full-time concert career there when she was still only 17, so she cannot have spent a continuous period of three years under Leschetizky's care. However, she might have studied with him full-time for two years and then gone back to him for lessons or advice on later occasions, after her departure on a full-time basis. She could then have been taught by him over a total period of three years.

Taking all the facts into account, it seems likely that she left Vienna in the spring or early summer of 1904, as stated in the main text.

References: Chapter 3

1. In an interview with Laning Humphrey in 1929 (Boston Sunday Post, Boston, Mass., 22nd September 1929), Leginska said she was "just 10" when she won her scholarship, but the Conservatory records and all other evidence point to the fact that she was 11½ when she began her studies there. She may have won her scholarship several months before the autumn start of the academic year.
2. Information communicated by Prof Dr Peter Cahn, Frankfurt.
3. The late Mrs Marjorie Langdale, Hornsea (personal correspondence, 1982).
4. *The New Grove Dictionary of Music and Musicians*, Ed. Stanley Sadie. Macmillan, London, 1980. Vol. 6, p. 801.
5. As ref. 2.
6. *The International Cyclopedia of Music and Musicians*, 4th edition, Ed. Oscar Thompson. J.M. Dent, London, 1946. p. 966. Also later editions of the same book. See also John Bird's book on Percy Grainger (ref. 16). The player piano rolls of James Kwast and Frieda Kwast-Hodapp are listed in Welte and Duca roll catalogues and in *The Classical Reproducing Piano Roll* by Larry Sitsky. Greenwood Press, Westport, Connecticut, 1990.
7. *New Grove* (ref. 4), Vol. 10, p. 125. See also John Bird's book on Percy Grainger (ref. 16).
8. *New Grove* (ref. 4), Vol. 17, p. 117.
9. As ref. 2.
10. *Hull News*, 21st May 1898.
11. *New Grove* (ref. 4), Vol. 7, p. 614. See also John Bird's book on Percy Grainger (ref. 16) and *Great Pianists of the Golden Age* by Marguerite and Terry Broadbent, North West Player Piano Association, Wilmslow, 1996, Chapter 17.
12. *New Grove* (ref. 4), Vol. 7, p. 163.
13. *New Grove* (ref. 4), Vol. 13, p. 543.
14. *New Grove* (ref. 4), Vol. 15, p. 406.
15. *New Grove* (ref. 4), Vol. 17, p. 81.
16. *Percy Grainger* by John Bird. Faber & Faber, London, 1982. (First published by Elek Books, 1976.) See p. 29. The book describes Grainger's period of study at Frankfurt (which overlapped that of Ethel Liggins) including an account of some of the students' antics.
17. *The Percy Grainger Companion* by L. Foreman. Thames Publishing Co., London, 1981.
18. As ref. 16, but pp. 37 - 39.
19. *Hull News*, 15th December 1900.
20. The list of Ethel Liggins' concert appearances in Frankfurt, and other information about the Conservatory, was kindly provided by Prof Dr Peter

Apprenticeship

Cahn, historian and former staff member of the Conservatory. He also supplied the photographs of the Conservatory, James Kwast and Iwan Knorr.
21. Copies of various letters and greeting notes from James Kwast, Frieda Hodapp and students of the Hoch Conservatory were kindly supplied by Mr Donald Manildi, Curator of the International Piano Archives at Maryland.
22. *New Grove* (ref. 4), Vol. 10, p. 689. All reputable musical encyclopaedias contain details of Leschetizky's life and work. See also *An Edwardian Quintet* by Marguerite and Terry Broadbent, North West Player Piano Association, Wilmslow, 1995. Chapter 1 tells the story of Leschetizky's life and career.
23. Interview with Laning Humphrey (see ref. 1).
24. Cleveland Hippodrome News, Cleveland, Ohio, 13th January 1908.
25. See ref. 1.
26. As ref. 24.
27. Ethel Newcomb (1875-1959) was one of several of Leschetizky's assistants who later published their recollections of him and his teaching methods. See *Leschetizky As I Knew Him* by Ethel Newcomb, D. Appleton & Co., New York and London, 1921; *Theodor Leschetizky* by Annette Hullah, John Lane, The Bodley Head, London, 1906; *Theodor Leschetizky* by Constance Jenkins (article in *The Musical Times*, 1st June 1930, written to celebrate the centenary of Leschetizky's birth).
28. *The Etude*, May 1919, pp. 271-272.
29. For an account of Leschetizky's teaching methods see references 22, 27 and 28, and also *The Groundwork of the Leschetizky Method* by Malwine Brée, G. Schirmer, New York 1902; and *The Leschetizky Method* by Marie Prentner, J. Curwen & Sons, London, 1903.
30. As reference 28.
31. *Benno Moiseiwitsch* by Maurice Moiseiwitsch, Frederick Muller Ltd, London, 1965.
32. *From Piano to Forte* by Mark Hambourg, Cassell & Co. Ltd, London, 1931.
33. As ref. 28. Page 272 (Leginska on Leschetizky's teaching).
34. This is Mark Hambourg's phrase – see ref. 32, p. 53.
35. As ref. 28. 100 kroner in 1902 was the equivalent of £4 - 3s - 0d at the time (about £250 or $375 at year 2002 values) – a generous and substantial gift.
36. *The Times*, 24th September 1923. (Obituary of the Marquess of Ripon.)
37. *The First World War* by Lt-Col Charles A'Court Repington, Vol. ii, p. 126, Constable, London, 1920. (In view of the title, one wonders how he realised the war was likely to be the prelude to another.)
38. Interview with Laning Humphrey (see ref. 1).
39. Ibid.
40. Interview in *The Etude*, see ref. 28.
41. As ref. 38.
42. *Musical America*, 24th May 1913. (Leginska interviewed by Harriette Brower.)

Chapter 4

Metamorphosis: The Emergence of Ethel Leginska

The close of Ethel Liggins' period of study with Leschetizky clearly marked the end of an important phase in her life. Little Ethel Annie Liggins, the brilliant child pianist, had long gone and had been replaced by a young woman of nearly eighteen years who was an accomplished, assured, gifted pianist, though as yet relatively inexperienced. Leschetizky was satisfied that she was able and ready to earn her living on the concert platform. She had 'grown up' as a musician during her four and a half years of study in Frankfurt and her further two years with Leschetizky.

As we have seen from the photographs in Chapter 2, Ethel as a child was small and dark-haired. Now, as a young adult, it was obvious she was destined always to be of small stature and petite build. Only 5ft 0" or 5ft 1" in height, she was to weigh no more than about 8 stones (112lb) for the whole of her life. [1, 2] But what she lacked in physical height and physique she more than made up for in vigour, energy and personal dynamism. Still dark-haired, as she would remain, and with penetrating grey-blue eyes, her hands were powerful – the result of years of training and keyboard exercise. [3] She was already a pianist to be reckoned with.

Apart from the gradual maturing and blossoming of her musical skills, two significant events had occurred during Ethel's period of study. The first one was sad; her mother died of smallpox on 20th November 1899 during an outbreak of the disease in Hull. [4] Her death took place at the newly-opened Evan Fraser Isolation Hospital in Hull. [5] She was 42. [6] This must have come as a bombshell to the 13-year-old girl and it cast a long shadow over what was otherwise a triumphant and fulfilling period of learning and achievement. Ethel had been very close to her mother, who had brought her up, educated her, and instilled into her a love of nature and literature which remained with her for the rest of her life. They were kindred spirits. In later life, Ethel sometimes spoke about her mother in conversations with her students, and said, bitterly, that her mother had never been accepted by her father's family. [7] According to Ethel's account, her mother had been taken to an isolation hospital after contracting the deadly disease and had been found dead there in a room used for storing linen. [8] Ethel was eternally indebted to her mother; it was she who had encouraged her musical talents as a child and helped her in every way possible. It was sad that she never saw Ethel's outstanding talents come to fruition, but her influence lived on throughout her daughter's life.

Metamorphosis: The Emergence of Ethel Leginska

Ethel was not present at the funeral; indeed, it is doubtful whether a normal public funeral was allowed because of the deadly, infectious nature of the disease; it is far more likely that a small private service at the hospital would have had to suffice. There is no record of an announcement of the death in the local newspapers nor of any report of a funeral. Moreover, because of the rapid way the disease develops and the slowness of communications in 1899, it is more than likely that Ethel, studying in Frankfurt, did not even learn of her mother's illness until after she had died. A glance at page 35 shows that on 12th November, only eight days before her mother's death, Ethel played the second and third movements of Beethoven's Piano Concerto No. 2 at a public concert in Frankfurt. It may have been just as well that she was unaware of the impending tragedy.

The other significant event in Ethel's life was that at the age of about 18 she changed her surname from Liggins to Leginska. From that time onwards 'Liggins' fell into disuse and 'Leginska' was used for almost all purposes. The name change came about as a result of a suggestion by Lady Maud Warrender whilst Ethel was still studying with Leschetizky but enjoying one of her periodic holidays in Britain.* At the turn of the century Lady Maud was well acquainted with the up-and-coming young pianist, Ethel Liggins, having met her on a number of earlier occasions at Tranby Croft

---

* Lady Maud Warrender was a leading figure in society and in the world of music for over 50 years. Born Lady Maud Ashley Cooper on 16th December 1870 (she died in London on 3rd September 1945) she was the fifth and youngest daughter of the 8th Earl of Shaftesbury. Most of her childhood was spent in the rigid religious atmosphere of the family seat, St. Giles' House, Dorset, but she had a good education, became fluent in French, German and Italian, and showed early promise as a singer. As she grew up she developed a fine contralto voice. She studied under a number of distinguished Italian singers and also under Henry Wood, and became an accomplished concert singer. She never sang professionally, her financial means being such that there was no need, but she was always ready to offer her considerable talents to the service of charity and in this capacity she gave about 900 concerts in all, to the benefit of numerous organisations. Noted for her good looks and commanding presence (she stood over 6ft tall), she sang throughout the British Isles and gave many concerts abroad. She was always ready to sing in hospitals and even prisons. She arranged concerts in the Royal Albert Hall, the Queen's Hall, the London Coliseum and many other places on behalf of such causes as the Union Jack Fund, the Lifeboat Fund and the League of Arts.

In February 1894 she married Sir George Warrender, 7th Baronet. He was born in 1860, the second son of Sir George Warrender, 6th Baronet, and succeeded to the title in 1901. He made the Royal Navy his career, serving in the Zulu War of 1879 whilst still a midshipman. Specialising in gunnery, he became a Commander in 1893, Captain in 1899, Rear-Admiral in 1908 and Vice-Admiral in 1913. Lady Maud was with her husband on the China Station in 1894 and was present during the visit of the Second Cruiser Squadron, commanded by her husband, to Kiel for the memorable "week" in June 1914 when Archduke Franz Ferdinand and his wife were murdered and everyone hurried home. As Admiral in charge of the Second

Footnote continued at the bottom of page 48 . . .

when Ethel played to the guests. She was always anxious to help young musicians and it was she who suggested that Ethel should change her surname. In those days, most of the top pianists were either Polish (the best-known example being Paderewski, at that time the 'Lion of the concert platform') or at least had a Polish- or Russian-sounding name, and Lady Maud suggested that Ethel should change her name in order to further her artistic career, a move which was quite common in those days. It was clear to Lady Maud's astute mind that the name 'Ethel Liggins' did nothing to help the young girl's career; she suggested that 'Ethel Leginska' would have a more charismatic ring. Ethel, ever on the lookout for ideas to help herself artistically, accepted the suggestion. Initially she used the new name only for professional purposes but from the age of about 18 or 19 onwards 'Ethel Liggins' was almost forgotten. Not only did she use the name 'Leginska' professionally, she also used it when writing to her friends in Yorkshire.[10]

The influence of Lady Maud Warrender was probably important in shaping the career of the young pianist. It is impossible to know how her career would have progressed had she remained 'Liggins'. 'Ethel Leginska' she remained to the end of her life, though the authors have found no trace of an official name change; the change was purely one of usage, and a few years later she used her real name of 'Liggins' on her marriage certificate. But all concert billings from 1904 onwards were in the name of 'Leginska', and once she went to the United States some years later there was no possible cause for confusion about her name because to United States' citizens she was, and always had been, Leginska.

The period around the turn of the century was one of rapid change in Ethel's life. She had become a seasoned traveller, having gone from Hull to Frankfurt, then on to Vienna, then back to London to audition for concert

---

Footnote from page 47, continued and concluded . . .

Battle Squadron of the Grand Fleet during the Great War, Sir George led a notable action in the North Sea off Scarborough in 1914 which almost succeeded in cutting off the German fleet. Had it done so the duration of the war might have been considerably shortened. In 1915 he was promoted to Commander-in-Chief, Portsmouth, but had to lay down his command in December 1916 owing to illness and he died a month later, on 8th January 1917.

Sir George and Lady Maud had three children; two sons (Sir Victor Warrender who was raised to the Peerage as Lord Bruntisfield in 1942 and Harold Warrender who became a well-known actor) and one daughter, who married Captain A.R. Pym.

Whilst Sir George Warrender was pursuing his naval career, Lady Maud had plenty of time to follow her interests and because of her social standing she was able to move in exalted musical circles. She wrote two autobiographical books which contain statements such as "One day when Paderewski was lunching with me", or, referring to a visit to the opera, "Lady Elgar was with me in my box".[9] Her finger was on the musical pulse of Britain and she knew everyone of importance. In short, she was a person of influence in the British musical scene.

engagements. From London she also returned to Hull occasionally, and a new possibility opened up, of leisure time spent in Hornsea, a village on the Yorkshire coast about 13 miles north of Hull, where the Liggins family had recently purchased a house. This came about as a result of a land agreement in 1902 when land was purchased on which No. 11, Wilton Terrace, later known as 'Wilton House', was built. The site was near the railway station and the purchaser was Ethel's grandmother, Hannah Dawson Liggins, then of 408, Holderness Road, Hull. (It was explained in Chapter 1 that Hannah's husband, Thomas Liggins, was a builder and the house may have been bought in his wife's name to safeguard against the unlikely possibility of his business running into financial difficulties.) On 13th May 1907, Hannah Dawson Liggins bought the house standing on her land for £400. On the death of Hannah in 1918 the house passed into the hands of her daughters Frances Gertrude and Katherine Anne. Frances died in 1920 and the house was sold out of the family in July 1921. [11]

So, from 1902 to 1921, the Liggins family owned the Hornsea property. Being next to the railway station (which closed in the 1960s) it was convenient for travel to and from Hull, and many members of the Liggins family spent holidays there. A map is shown on page 51, drawn by Mr T.P. Langdale (see family tree on page 7). It shows the layout of Wilton Terrace and its relation to the railway station.

Following the acquisition of the Hornsea property the newly-emerged pianist, Ethel Leginska, divided her time between several ports of call following her return from Vienna. Much of her time was spent in the hurly-burly of London, seeking engagements. When she was not doing that she lived with her father in Hull or relaxed in the relative solitude of the quiet Yorkshire village of Hornsea. There were also visits once again to Tranby Croft. * [12]

---

* The Visitors' Book at Tranby Croft records Ethel's signature on the following occasions between 1896 and 1910 (aged 10 to 24):

As Ethel Liggins:	Christmas party 1896	
"	23rd April 1897	
"	9th August 1901	Lady Maud Warrender also there.
"	18th August 1902	Lady Maud Warrender and another of Mary Wilson's protégées, Gwendoline Brogden (see page 13 and ref.12 on page 26) were also there.
"	7th August 1904	Lady Maud Warrender also there.
As Ethel Leginska:	19th August 1906	
"	4th November 1910	Lady Maud Warrender also there.

The Visitors' Book would only have been signed at major social functions – not each time Ethel 'popped in' to see Mary Wilson.

The house in Hornsea where young Ethel Leginska spent part of her youth still stands, and does not look very different today from the photograph taken when Ethel was a young woman (see page 52). She also stayed occasionally in Bridlington, a small coastal resort 12 miles north of Hornsea, where other relatives and friends lived, and where she was always welcome.

It was not long before Ethel Leginska's name started to appear on major concert programmes. Her first real break came in the summer of 1904 when the impresario Percy Harrison invited her and numerous other musicians to an audition at the Royal Albert Hall, where he was making arrangements for concerts.[13] She arrived to find the place crowded with eager pianists, mostly men, and nearly all older than herself. Most of them played before she did and she listened to many impressive performances of the more showy pieces of Liszt and Anton Rubinstein, all of which were very popular at the time. When her turn came she nervously played two salon pieces by her teacher, Leschetizky; miniature, delicate compositions, far removed from the fiery offerings that had just been heard. At the end no one applauded; there was no response of any sort, and she left the hall. Only the doorman made an encouraging remark as she departed: "Cheer up, Missy; your playing's really touching." Evidently his view was also shared by Percy Harrison because, much to her surprise and pleasure, she heard a few days later that he had engaged her for his London and provincial tours of 1904-05.[14]

Percy Harrison was, according to Sir Henry Wood, the "real old type of concert manager". He would run three or four tours a season, visiting many of the larger cities in England and Scotland. Some of them made money, some didn't, but on the whole he succeeded year after year. Henry Wood called him "Daddy" Harrison and as a young man had been a member of some of his tours. He recalled that Harrison "did the thing handsomely" and he never heard an artist say a word against him. Wood remembered Harrison as a "dapper little fellow of uncertain age". He said he (Wood) and his friends used to try to get to know how old he was, but never succeeded.[15]

Thus Ethel Leginska started her adult career. She was now a young professional, ready to vie with the world's greatest pianists in what was a very competitive field. Resourceful, talented and determined, she was not going to let this chance slip, for she knew that the success of these concerts could make or break her. All her energies were put into her preparations for the concerts and recitals, and she was rewarded by success, receiving acclaim from audiences and critics alike. She had at last 'arrived' and could call herself a successful concert pianist.

Metamorphosis: The Emergence of Ethel Leginska

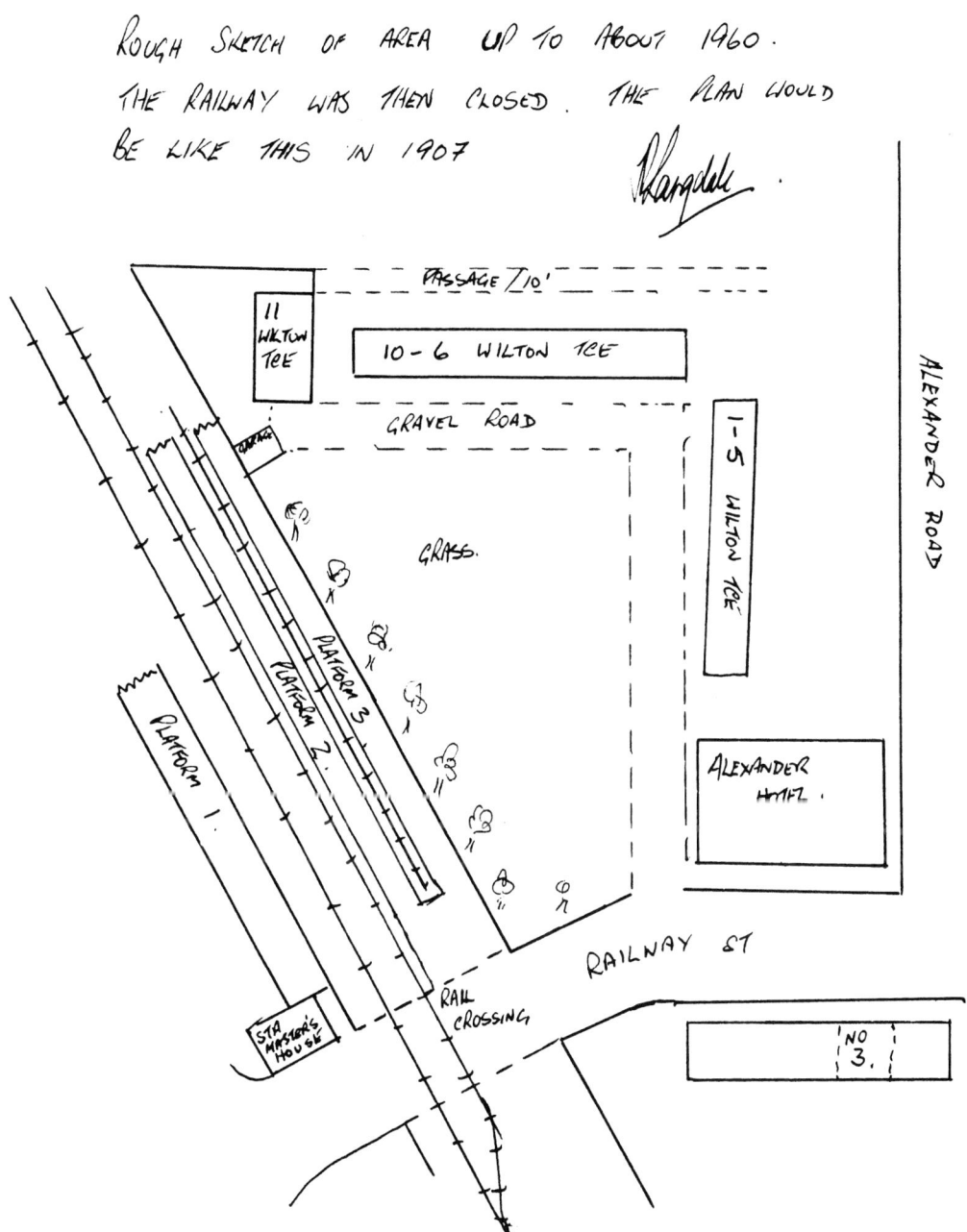

Map of part of Hornsea, Yorkshire, showing the location of her grandparents' house, 11, Wilton Terrace, where Ethel Leginska often stayed as a young woman

11, Wilton Terrace, Hornsea at the time Ethel Leginska used to visit

The adult in the picture is believed by Tom Langdale's sister (see family tree on p. 7) to be Frances Gertrude Liggins and the child is thought to be Vivienne Katherine Witty

Metamorphosis: The Emergence of Ethel Leginska

After this series of concerts of 1904-05, in all of which she used the name 'Leginska', Ethel's London appearances became more frequent. In July 1905, aged 19, she gave a recital at Bechstein Hall, London (which was renamed the Wigmore Hall in 1917). *The Musical Times* wrote: [16]

"Miss Ethel Leginska, sometime a pupil of M. Leschetizky, showed at her recital at Bechstein Hall on July 3 that she is progressing in her art, and she manifestly gave much pleasure to her listeners."

Another recital at the Bechstein Hall took place in January 1906. *The Musical Times* again reported favourably: [17]

"Miss Leginska showed considerable skill as a pianist at her recital on January 17 at Bechstein Hall. Musical perception and good taste prevailed in her readings and she manifestly pleased the audience."

A longer review in another musical periodical of the day was equally favourable: [18]

" . . . her technique has been developed on strong lines. Miss Leginska showed understanding and skill as an interpreter of Beethoven, her performance of the *Sonata Pathétique* being clear, dignified and expressive. The execution was on a high level throughout. There was a lengthy Chopin selection including eight of the preludes, two mazurkas, a nocturne and a valse. Miss Leginska gave most pleasure, perhaps, by her sympathetic and intelligent playing of the preludes in B major and B minor, the mazurkas, and the sentimental valse in E flat. Included in a final group of pieces were a delightful Arabesque by Leschetizky and the exacting Étude in B flat by Rubinstein, the difficulties of which were easily vanquished by this talented artist."

Two months later Ethel took part in a concert in her home town of Hull, sharing the programme with the cellist Boris Hambourg (brother of pianist Mark and son of piano teacher Michael) and the mezzo-soprano Antonia Dolores, daughter of the celebrated Victorian mezzo-soprano Zelia Trebelli. Ethel would have already known Boris as they had been students together at Frankfurt. The programme included Beethoven's sonata, Op. 69, for piano and cello. As soloist she played three pieces by Paderewski and three (unspecified) by Leschetizky, followed by Anton Rubinstein's Étude in E flat. Her playing was praised in the *Hull Times'* report: [19]

"Our gifted townswoman [was] heard as the artist in the truest sense . . . her playing was of delicacy and polished refinement."

By now the young pianist had attracted the attention of the conductor Henry Wood and he invited her to appear as soloist in one of his concerts at the Queen's Hall in June 1906 when she was 20. *The Musical Times* reported: [20]

"Miss Ethel Leginska increased the number of her admirers by her vivacious and clever pianoforte playing at her orchestral concert, conducted by Henry J. Wood at Queen's Hall on June 14. She is to be commended for having revived Henselt's Concerto in G minor; in this and in Rubinstein's Concerto in D minor the young artist played with great brilliance and intelligence."

Leginska must have impressed Henry Wood for he promptly engaged her to play in one of his forthcoming Promenade Concerts at Queen's Hall. Henry Wood (he was plain 'Mr Wood' then; his knighthood was not conferred until 1911) had instituted the 'London Proms' in 1895 under the managership of Robert Newman and in the ten years or so they had been running the concerts had already become something of an institution. Moreover, they were used as a platform not only for well-known artists, but also for many aspiring young musicians to display their talents. Each had to be auditioned by Wood himself, and only the most gifted overcame this hurdle. Leginska's Prom debut was announced in a notice on the front page of *The Times,* first on Friday, 17th August 1906, and again on the day of the concert. The latter notice read as follows:

Wednesday, 22nd August 1906
QUEEN'S HALL
TONIGHT at 8

Symphony No. 39 in E flat	Mozart
The Wanderer	Schubert
Piano Concerto in F minor	Henselt
Serenade from the *Childhood of Christ*	Berlioz
Dream Pantomime from *Hänsel & Gretal*	Humperdinck
Ocean, Thou Mighty Monster (*Oberon*)	Weber
Symphony No. 8 in B minor (Unfinished)	Schubert
March (*Les Troyens*)	Berlioz
Overture, *Patri*	Bizet
Overture, *Il Barbiere di Siviglia*	Rossini

Miss PERCEVAL ALLEN
Mr CHARLES KNOWLES
Solo Pianoforte   —   Miss ETHEL LEGINSKA

The programme actually given differed slightly from that advertised in *The Times* (see contents of the official concert programme on pages 57 and 58) and there were two Leginska contributions, not one as the programme implies – she played Liszt's *Hungarian Rhapsody* No. 2, as well as the Henselt Concerto. [21] Britain at that time was basking in a heat wave and the concert was played in a stifling, almost tropical, temperature. *The Times*, in its report two days later, remarked that the performance was handicapped by the piano being slightly out of tune with the orchestra and organ, which was used in the first movement of the concerto. The orchestra tuned to the piano, but nothing could be done about the tuning of the organ, which led to an imperfect musical result. The problem with the piano was attributed to the intense heat, and could hardly have helped Leginska in what to her was a vitally important occasion. But she soldiered on in true professional style and gave an impressive performance – allowing for the deficiencies of the instrument. *The Times*' critic referred to her playing as "delicate and beautiful in piano scales and passages". He reserved his acid comments for Maud Perceval Allen, the soprano, who appeared on the same programme: [22]

"Miss Perceval Allen, for some unknown reason, sang Weber's *Ocean, Thou Mighty Monster*, again. The performance on Saturday had not been sufficiently distinctive to make us wish for so speedy a repetition."

Leginska's performance in the Henselt Concerto impressed Henry Wood. He described her in his autobiography, published in 1938, as "a pianist of tremendous power. She was an artistic person and undoubtedly talented". [23]

The London Promenade Concert revealed Leginska as a young pianist of stature and outstanding promise, and she was promptly engaged to appear in the forthcoming season of Sunday afternoon concerts at the Royal Albert Hall (which lasted from 7th October 1906 to 30th June 1907), along with such other well-known pianists in the same season as Harold Bauer, Teresa Carreño, Mark Hambourg, Emil Sauer and Irene Scharrer.

Leginska, still only 20, gratefully accepted whatever other reputable concert invitations that came along. On 11th November 1906, for example she appeared in one of the impresario Henry Bernhardt's "Popular Sunday Concerts" held in the concert hall of the Palace Pier, Brighton, sharing the programme with, amongst others, the actress Marie Tempest who, at 42, was at the height of her fame, the Hungarian violinist Joska Szigeti (then a 14-year-old prodigy but later to become world-famous), and a 22-year-old Irish tenor billed as J.F. McCormack who was just starting out on his career. (Soon afterwards he dropped the 'J.F.' (John Francis) and became just 'John McCormack'.) This series of concerts was graced during the 1906-07 season by the appearance of many established and up-and-coming artists including, in addition to those named above, Lily Langtry (who was then 53), Gertie Millar (27), Peter Dawson (24) and Zena Dare (19). [24] Leginska appeared, as did the others, as one 'turn' in a mixed programme. Many musicians took part in concerts such as this. The pianist Mark Hambourg, for example, must have appeared at every major seaside resort in Britain.

Appearances at popular holiday venues such as this one at Brighton, together with the more conventional concert and recital engagements that were coming Leginska's way, all helped her to gain valuable experience and to become more widely known. Her career was beginning to prosper.

Front cover of the programme of Leginska's Promenade Concert debut under Henry Wood. It is much reduced in size in this reproduction. The actual programme was a single folder of 12" x 9½", a format used from the foundation of the 'Proms' in 1895 until 1926

Smoking is permitted at these Concerts, excepting in the seats between doors E and F in the Grand Circle, which are reserved for Non-Smokers. Gentlemen are politely requested to refrain from striking matches during the performance of the various items.

The Analytical and Historical Notes by PERCY PITT and A. KALISCH.

PART I.

1. SYMPHONY No. 39, in E flat - - - - *Mozart*

1. Adagio—Allegro.
2. Andante.
3. Minuet and Trio.
4. Finale.

The last three Symphonies of Mozart—the one now to be played, the one in G minor, and the "Jupiter"— were composed in about six weeks, between June 26th and the beginning of August, 1788, when Mozart had just been appointed Chamber Composer to the Austrian Court. The year was one of the most fertile of Mozart's life, but none of the music to which it gave birth can compare with these three Symphonies, which, as has often been said, form a sort of trilogy—this Symphony being distinguished by sheer melodic beauty; the one in G minor by a noble pathos; and the "Jupiter" by almost elemental grandeur. In no other works is Mozart's unequalled sense of proportion more triumphantly evident. It is worth remembering that these three masterpieces were composed before Haydn's last Symphonies. They have had no more ardent admirer than Wagner, who extols their deep humanity.

The Symphony opens with an Introduction (*Adagio*) of some length, consisting mainly of full chords interspersed with scale-passages for strings. The first theme of the *Allegro*, which is based on the common chord, is given out by first violins, with an answering phrase for horns. This is repeated in a different shape, and followed by a continuation rhythmically related to it, and then by an episode of alternating scale-passages and chords. The gracefully moving second theme, in B flat, consists of a descending phrase for violins, answered by an ascending figure for 'cellos while horns and basses hold a pedal. Its tributary takes the shape of a charming phrase for clarinet. The *Coda* is of a more or less purely formal character, and concludes with a series of brilliant scale-passages and a previously heard phrase, which also occupies the first few bars of the development, and is frequently heard during its progress. After this phrase follows a discussion of the tributary to the second theme, which monopolizes nearly the whole of this very brief section. The *reprise* very soon begins, and takes a perfectly orthodox course, while the *Coda* is based on the same material as that of the first part.

The haunting melody of the beautiful *Andante* is given out by the violins in thirds. It is several times repeated with varying continuations. An episodical theme of more masculine character, in F minor, leads to treatment of phrases derived from the first subject by the wood-wind; and the second theme is ultimately announced by the bassoons, answered by the clarinets. The first subject is soon repeated, scale-passages in the wood-wind being added to the score; and it is now treated in combination with the episodical theme. The development of the previously heard material which follows is unusually ample for Mozart, but it is as transparently clear as it is beautiful, and in this way the movement continues to the end.

The *Minuet* is one of the best known of all Mozart's symphonic movements. The themes are very clear, and their treatment is a model of lucidity. It is not necessary, however, to refer to anything except the two delicious melodies of the *Trio*—the first given to the clarinet, and the second to the first violins. The usual repetition of the *Minuet* of course takes place after the *Trio*.

The *Finale* (*Allegro*) opens with the joyous first subject stated by the first violins, lightly accompanied by the second. Fragments of this—especially the second and third bars—are treated fully, both singly and in combination, with the most irresistible grace and humour. A statement of one of these phrases by wood-wind overlaps the first presentation of the second subject (also by first violins, with second violins accompanying), and reappears at intervals during its exposition. A short *Coda* with a syncopated rhythm, and fragments of the first theme in imitation towards the end, complete the first section. Harmonic variations of the first theme treated contrapuntally are almost the sole material of the development. In the recapitulation the subjects are presented in due order, and the spirited *Coda* introduces no new matter. Though based on such scanty material, this is one of the most delightful and masterly of Mozart's *Finales*, and the ingenuity of the craftsmanship does not for a moment interfere with the irresistible flow of high spirits.

2. SONG - - The Wanderer - - *Schubert*

MR. CHARLES KNOWLES.

I come here from my mountains lone;
The vale is dim, the sea doth moan.
I wander still with grief and care,
And ever ask, while sighing, "Where?"

The sun to me seems dark and cold,
The flow'rs are pale, and life seems old;
Their speech doth seem but empty sound,
A stranger I on foreign ground!

Where art thou, mine own dearest land?
I seek in vain thy far-off strand.
That land, that land so fresh and green,
Where richest roses may be seen;

Where dwell the friends I long to see;
Where sleep the dead so dear to me;
That land where they my language speak—
O land, where art thou?

I wander still with grief and care,
And ever ask, while sighing, "Where?"
A spirit-voice doth whisper near:
"There, where thou art not, all joy is there."

3. CONCERTO in F minor for Pianoforte and Orchestra - *Hensel*

Solo Pianoforte - MISS ETHEL LEGINSKA.

(Her first appearance at these Concerts.)

Rönisch Grand Pianoforte.

1. Allegro patetico. 2. Larghetto. 3. Allegro agitato.

Adolf von Henselt was born at Schwalbach in Bavaria on May 12th, 1814 and studied under Hummel and Sechter. He occupies an important position in the development of pianoforte technique, and, in particular, he carried to a higher pitch of perfection than any previous master the playing of extended arpeggi: Mendelssohn's saying that "he went on all day stretching his fingers" is well known. In 1838 he went to St. Petersburg and became Court Pianist, teacher of the Czar's children, and Inspector of the Imperial Russian Female Seminaries. He visited England privately in 1852 and 1867, and spent the rest of his artistic life in Russia. He died in Germany in 1889. He composed a good deal, his works including thirty-nine pieces with opus numbers and fourteen without, and he is best known by the Concerto now to be played and several smaller pieces, of which "Si oiseau j'étais" is the most popular.

1. The first movement opens, *Allegro patetico, espressivo*, with a *tutti*, in which the leading themes are, in accordance with established custom, passed in review. After a few prefatory bars we get the principal subject, which is in march-like rhythm, while the second is in the key of A flat (the relative major), and of more sustained character. When this has been enunciated the solo-instrument enters, and deals with the same material in the same order. After this we reach the most original feature of the movement—a hymn-like central theme, marked *Religioso*, allotted first to strings alone, and then repeated by the piano in octaves with wide-stretching *arpeggi*. The alternative strain is dealt with in the same manner, and thus we come directly to a *reprise* of the opening in the accepted way. The first subject is now treated with elaborate ornamentation, while the second subject appears in F major; and in that key the brilliant *Coda*, which here ensues, comes to an end.

2. The second movement is a *Larghetto* in D flat. The orchestra has a few introductory bars, foreshadowing the principal subject, which is given out by the piano, the melody being accompanied by sweeping *arpeggi* in the left hand. In due course we come to a strongly contrasted second section (*misterioso*) in C sharp minor. At its first presentation it is played in octaves by the piano and strings *pizzicato*, and later it is announced *fortissimo* by the solo-instrument and two trombones. A repetition of the first subject with characteristic embellishments is succeeded by a short *Coda* of eight bars, which brings the movement to an end.

3. The *Finale* starts with an orchestral introduction in the tonic. This is followed by another introductory octave passage for the piano, and then the piano states the passionate principal theme. The second subject (which is in A flat) is similarly preceded by an orchestral passage and given out by the piano. The only other feature to be noticed is a counter-subject for the piano, accompanied by strings. The form of the rest of the movement is strictly regular, all the themes recurring in due course. The *bravoura*-writing for the piano is of exceptional brilliancy, but no special passage need be referred to here. In the final *Coda* we have the first subject in the orchestra, while the piano is busy with brilliant octave passages.

4. (*a*) SERENADE (*The Childhood of Christ*) - - *Berlioz*
(*b*) DREAM PANTOMIME (*Hänsel und Gretel*) - *Humperdinck*

(*a*) Berlioz composed his "Childhood of Christ" in 1854. It consists of three parts—the Dream of Herod, the Flight into Egypt, and the Arrival at Sais. The Serenade now to be played occurs in the third part at the point where the Holy Family has been sheltered by a poor shepherd.

"The Childhood of Christ" was the subject of one of the most famous hoaxes in musical history. Berlioz announced that he had discovered the music in the archives of the Sainte-Chapelle, and that it was the work of one Pierre Ducré, a forgotten composer of the seventeenth century. Several well-known connoisseurs said that the music was full of grace and charm, and one went so far as to say that "Berlioz could not write anything so delightful."

Seven introductory bars of *Allegro moderato* (in common time) are followed by the main section, *Andante espressivo* (9-8 time), where, after one bar of accompaniment for the harp, the first flute gives out the pastoral principal theme. Five bars later the second flute enters with attendant semiquaver figures. The alternative melody is announced by the flutes in dialogue, while the harp has flowing semiquavers, and then the opening is repeated. After a short *Coda* we come to an *Allegro vivace* (2-4) in the relative minor. This is also treated as a dialogue between the two flutes, which move principally in thirds and sixths. Later the flutes are occasionally heard alone. The *Andante* is then played again, and the piece gradually dies away.

(*b*) Engelbert Humperdinck was born at Siegburg on the Rhine on September 1st, 1854, and studied at the Cologne Conservatoire. In 1880 he made the acquaintance

PAUL WERNER
Celebrated Dresden Pianofortes.
A HIGH-CLASS PIANOFORTE AT A MODERATE PRICE.
Powerful tone, of a beautiful singing quality.
Elegant designs. All the latest improvements. Perfection of touch and repetition.
SOLE AGENTS:
BREITKOPF & HAERTEL,
54 GREAT MARLBOROUGH STREET, REGENT STREET, LONDON, W.

THE
QUEEN'S HALL
ORCHESTRA
May be engaged for Artists or Private Concerts. Terms and vacant dates on application to the Queen's Hall Orchestra, Ltd., 320 Regent Street, W.
ROBERT NEWMAN, MANAGER.

NATIONAL SUNDAY LEAGUE
SUNDAY EVENING CONCERTS
Every Sunday at 7.
Queen's Hall, commencing 19th August.
Islington Empire, Upper Street, N., commencing 2nd September.
The Alhambra, commencing 23rd September.
For full particulars see bills and advertisements.
Offices: 34 Red Lion Square. W.C.
HENRY MILLS, *Secretary.*

MELBA.
PATTI.
DESTINN.
CARUSO.
DE LUCIA.
SCOTTI.
PLANCON.
JOURNET.
MISCHA ELMAN.
KREISLER.
MARIE HALL.
KUBELIK.
JOACHIM.
SQUIRE.
HOLLMANN.

GRAMOPHONE
The Artists mentioned in this Advertisement have all made Gramophone Records.
The Gramophone of to-day brings all that is best in the world of music to your own home.
There are many Talking Machines, but only ONE GRAMOPHONE.
On receipt of postcard we will send Catalogues and Price List, and name and address of nearest dealer.
THE GRAMOPHONE AND TYPEWRITER, LTD.,
21 CITY ROAD, LONDON, E.C.

EDWARD LLOYD.
JOHN HARRISON.
CHAS. SAUNDERS.
EVAN WILLIAMS.
HIRWEN JONES.
ANDREW BLACK.
PLUNKET GREENE.
CHAS. SANTLEY.
PETER DAWSON.
PERCEVAL ALLEN.
E. PARKINA.
DEWS.
GWLADYS ROBERTS
ALICE ESTY.
&c., &c.

Programme of Leginska's Promenade Concert in 1906 – second page

of Wagner, and became one of the intimates of Wahnfried. He was subsequently appointed a teacher at the Hoch Conservatoire at Frankfurt-am-Main, and musical critic of the *Frankfurter Zeitung*. "Hänsel und Gretel," the first work which made him famous, was preceded by many others, of which the "Wahlfahrt nach Kevlaar" and "Das Glück von Edenhall" are now the best known. Of the music written by him since "Hänsel und Gretel"—the "Moorish Symphony" (produced at the Leeds Festival of 1898) and the incidental music to the fairy-tales "Die Koenigskinder" and the "Sleeping Beauty"—none has obtained any lasting success. A new opera from his pen, "Die Heirat wider Willen" (based on "Le Mariage Forcé" of Molière) was produced in Berlin in January, 1905. The chief claim of "Hänsel und Gretel" to attention lies in the extraordinary skill with which the composer brought to bear profound learning and an unusual mastery of polyphony on the simplest material, and enabled him to write music of the utmost complexity which was yet unfailingly melodious and seemingly spontaneous throughout. The themes of the opera, where they are not actual nursery songs, are mostly adapted from them, and the nature of the subject-matter is due to the fact that the opera was originally composed for private performance by the children of the composer's sister, the idea of elaborating and scoring the music only coming to Humperdinck later. It is, perhaps, unnecessary to point out how great an influence the music of "Hänsel und Gretel" has had on the younger generation of German composers.

"The Dream Pantomime" occurs at the end of the second act or picture of the opera. The two children having lost their way in the wood, and having sung their evening hymn, fall asleep on a mossy bank, and troops of angels guard their slumbers, to the accompaniment of the music we are now to hear. At the beginning the violoncellos give out a flowing melody in the nature of a lullaby, while the flutes play figures derived from the theme of the prayer. The melody is taken up later by the wood-wind, strings, and brass in turn, and is dealt with at some length, this portion of the music ending in a climax where the melody is stated *fortissimo* by the trombones. After this the trumpets and trombones announce a fully harmonized version of the prayer, and with this, developed with the utmost ingenuity and mastery of resource, we are chiefly concerned to the end.

5. ARIA "Ocean, thou mighty monster" (*Oberon*) *Weber*

MISS PERCEVAL ALLEN.

Ocean! thou mighty monster, that liest curled
Like a green serpent round about the world.
To musing eye thou art an awful sight,
When calmly sleeping in the morning light
But when thou risest in thy wrath, as now,
And fling'st thy folds around some fated prow,
Crushing the strong-ribbed bark as 'twere a reed,
Then, Ocean, art thou terrible indeed.

Still I see thy billows flashing,
Through the gloom their white foam flinging;
And the breakers' sullen dashing
In mine ear hope's knell is ringing.
But lo! methinks a light is breaking
Slowly o'er the distant deep,
Like a second morn awaking,
Pale and feeble, from its sleep.

Brighter now behold 'tis beaming
On the storm, whose misty train,
Like some shattered flag, is streaming,
Or a wild steed's flying mane.

And now the sun bursts forth, the wind is lulling fast,
And the broad wave but pants from fury past.

Cloudless o'er the blushing water
Now the setting sun is burning,
Like a victor, red with slaughter,
To his tent in triumph turning.
Ah, perchance these eyes may never
Look upon its light again.
Fare thee well, bright orb, for ever,
Thou for me wilt rise in vain!

But what gleams so white and fair
Heaving with the heaving billow?
'Tis a sea-bird wheeling there
O'er some wretch's watery pillow.
No, it is no bird I mark.
Joy, it is a boat! a sail!
And yonder rides a gallant bark,
Unimpairèd by the gale!

O transport! My Huon! haste down to the shore—
Quick, quick! for a signal this scarf shall be waved.
They see me! they answer! they ply the strong oar!
Huon! my husband! my love! we are saved!

SYMPHONY No. 8, in B minor (Unfinished) - *Schubert*

1. Allegro moderato 2. Andante con moto.

This Symphony was composed by Schubert for the Musical Society of Gratz, which had elected him an honorary member, and the manuscript was lying hidden in that town till it came into the possession of Schubert's friend Anselm Hüttenbrenner. From him it was acquired by Herbeck, who first performed it in Vienna in 1865. The work was written in 1822, six years earlier than the great Symphony in C, which however is, strangely enough, in many respects a less mature work, besides being considerably less modern in feeling. It is not known why Schubert abandoned the Symphony after having completed the first two movements and made the sketches for the *Scherzo* which are in existence. The Symphony was first performed in England at the Crystal Palace in 1867.

1. *Allegro moderato*.—A mysterious phrase in the basses, followed by restlessly throbbing figures in the other strings, acts as prelude to the tragic first theme, which is announced by the clarinet and oboe in unison. We do not continue in this agonized mood; a short bridge-passage (horns and bassoons) very soon leads into the more peaceful atmosphere of the second subject, which is stated by the 'cellos with a pulsating accompaniment of violas and clarinets. Its repetition is given out by violins in octaves. A stormy interruption of crashing chords from the whole orchestra shows that there is but a brief respite. After this outburst the *Coda*, which is based on the first phrases of the second subject—now transformed into a song of dejection—brings the exposition to an end. The development, in which the first subject is wholly left out of sight, begins with the theme of the opening, first given to the basses and then taken up by violas and bassoons in imitation. This is interrupted from time to time by crashes of the full orchestra, and we hear the sobbing rhythm of the accompaniment to the second subject, without the melody itself. Later the opening theme is announced in a *fortissimo* unison passage by the whole orchestra, and this is succeeded by a new passionate figure for semiquavers given out by violins and violas. Then fragments of the opening are further developed, and some use is made of a three-note figure that is an inversion of it. In this way we gradually approach the recapitulation, in which the chief changes from the exposition are modifications of the scoring. The closing bars of the movement are based entirely on the Introduction.

2. *Andante con moto*.—As the opening movement was eloquent of sorrow and strife, so the *Andante* breathes a spirit of peace and resignation, in spite of its moments of heartrending grief. After two preliminary bars, which are frequently heard throughout, and of which the chief characteristic is a scale for *pizzicato* basses, the theme is given out by strings. The opening phrase is then repeated (as it is frequently afterwards) before the repetition of the theme. Then follows an impressive unison for strings, and, after a yearning violin-figure, we come to the second subject—a melody of most poignant expressiveness—allotted first to clarinet and then to oboe, with an accompaniment of sobbing chords, which enhance its tragic significance. This suddenly gives way to an episode instinct with masculine force, in which the weighty phrases of the strings, striding irresistibly onwards, are supported by the harmonies of the wood-wind. It is repeated with scale-passages in the oboes, second violins, and violas, while the rest of the orchestra insist on the theme. Shortly after this the grief-laden phrases of the second subject reappear, slightly modified, in the basses and second violins in imitation. This leads to a recapitulation of the beginning. With the exception of changes of orchestration, everything is repeated as before; and the *Coda* is derived from the opening, the *pizzicato* basses of the first two bars being also employed, as well as the violin-figure which heralded the first appearance of the second subject.

7. MARCHE TROYENNE *Berlioz*

This March is taken from Berlioz's "Prise de Troie"—the first half of his last work, "Les Troyens"—which was not performed till Herr Mottl produced it at Karlsruhe in 1890. The other half of the work, "Les Troyens à Carthage," was produced without success in 1863. The two works are to be heard in their proper order for the first time in French at Brussels this season.

After a series of fanfare-like passages for brass, the principal subject appears also in the brass. It is then repeated by wood-wind and strings. The alternative theme is confided to the bass instruments, against bustling passages for violins and triplets in the cornets. Another new melody is introduced by the strings in unison, combined from time to time with a rhythmical figure for oboes and bassoons, and accompanied by the rest of the orchestra. The opening theme, now more richly scored, recurs in due course, there being no *Trio*. The only feature calling for notice is a theme in even minims given out by the wind heard soon afterwards, which is founded on a portion of the alternative. This then appears in a diminished version (i.e., in notes of smaller value) on the strings, the rest of the orchestra persisting in the rhythm of the Introduction, which works up to a sonorous climax, and the March ends with a glorified version of the opening by way of *Coda*.

This concert arrangement was made by the composer himself. From the autograph in the National Library of Paris it appears that Berlioz had originally intended to write a different close.

Interval of Fifteen Minutes.

PART II.

OVERTURE "Patrie" - - *Bizet*

NEW SONG - Egyptian Love-Song - - *J. Airlie Dix*

MR. CHARLES KNOWLES.

PIANOFORTE SOLO Rhapsody No. 2 - *Liszt*

MISS ETHEL LEGINSKA.

4. SONG - - Song of Greeting - - *Emilie Clarke*

MISS PERCEVAL ALLEN.

5. OVERTURE - Il Barbiere di Seviglia *Rossini*

(Conducted by Mr. HENRI VERBRUGGHEN.)

GRAND PIANOFORTE
by Messrs. CHAPPELL & Co., Ltd.

Wagner, Richard. A Selection of melodies arranged as a fantasia by F. W. Kretschmar. Containing melodies from Lohengrin, The Meistersinger, Walküre, Parsifal, The Flying Dutchman, Tristan und Isolde, Rienzi, Tannhauser, Rheingold, Gotterdämmerung, and Kaisermarsch. *Post free, 20 stamps.*

Tschaikowsky Album. Nine favourite pieces. Contents: 1. The Song of the Lark, Op. 37, No. 3. 2. Chant sans paroles, Op. 2, No. 3. 3. Barcarolle, Op. 37, No. 6. 4. Valse des Fleurs (from the Casse-Noisette Suite). 5. Chanson Triste, Op. 40, No. 2. 6. Romance, Op. 51, No. 5. 7. Nocturne, Op. 10, No. 1. 8. Humoreske, Op. 12, No. 2. 9. Feuillet d'Album, Op. 9, No. 3. *Post free, 20 stamps.*

THE FREDERICK HARRIS COMPANY,
89 NEWMAN STREET, OXFORD STREET, W.
Publishers of Albert Mallinson's Songs.

BLÜTHNER,
Pianoforte Manufacturer
BY SPECIAL APPOINTMENT TO
HER MAJESTY QUEEN ALEXANDRA.
BLÜTHNER HOUSE,
7, 9, 11, and 13 Wigmore Street, W.

CHAPPELL
PIANOS

ESTD. 1808

Messrs. CHAPPELL & Co., LTD.,
London, N.W.

DEAR SIRS.—I feel it both a duty and pleasure to thank you for your two magnificent Concert Grand Pianofortes used by me during my first tour in Great Britain. I cannot speak too highly of the brilliant and sympathetic tone and responsive touch possessed by them. I can confidently say you need fear no rival. Yours faithfully,
WILHELM BACKHAUS.

SMALL BOUDOIR PIANOS, 37 Gns. *UPRIGHT GRANDS, 52 Gns.*
FULL COTTAGES, 45 Gns. *HORIZONTAL GRANDS, 95 Gns.*

Hire-Instalment System, or Liberal Discount for Cash. Illustrated Lists Post Free.

CHAPPELL & CO., LTD., Pianoforte Manufacturers.
50 NEW BOND STREET, LONDON, W.

Programme of Leginska's Promenade Concert in 1906 – third page

References: Chapter 4

1. Beverly Carmen, Hollywood, Los Angeles (personal correspondence).
2. Radie Britain, Hollywood, Los Angeles (personal correspondence).
3. Information about Ethel's physique comes from many different sources, particularly her former students in the USA, and from concert reviews.
4. Information on the smallpox outbreak was communicated to the authors by the late Mrs Marjorie Langdale in 1982 (personal correspondence). The date of death of Ethel's mother was found by Mrs Margaret Stockbridge from local records. She also found references to the outbreak of the disease in copies of local newspapers of the time. One, on 21st November 1899, bore the headline "The Small Pox in Hull".
5. The Evan Fraser Isolation Hospital for smallpox and other infectious diseases opened in 1899, so Ethel's mother must have been one of the first unfortunate people to die there. Situated about three miles north of the town centre in what was then a rural area, it was purchased by Hull Council on 5th June 1908 and closed about 1952-53. This information about the Evan Fraser Hospital was found for the authors from local records by Mrs Stockbridge, whose research assistance is acknowledged with thanks.
6. A certified copy of the death certificate of Anne Liggins, which was purchased by the authors, gave the cause of her death as 'variola', which is another name for smallpox. Three other interesting points are revealed by the death certificate:

    (i) Anne's name was given as Annie Liggins, which is clearly the name that the informant, her father-in-law Thomas Liggins, knew her by; this provides a further indication that she was known as 'Annie', not 'Anne', within the family.

    (ii) Her age was given as 40, though she was actually 42. The reason for the discrepancy will simply be that her father-in-law probably knew that she was 'about 40' but probably never knew, or had forgotten, exactly how old she was.

    (iii) Anne's husband's occupation is stated on the certificate as 'architect', which suggests that the informant, Anne's father-in-law Thomas Liggins, regarded his son Thomas Edward as such, rather than a builder.

7. This information comes from several of her former students.
8. Mme Leginska, as she was known in her later life, did not often talk to her students about her early years, but a few of them were told, during a rare reminiscence, about the circumstances of her mother's illness and death.
9. Lady Maud Warrender: *My First Sixty Years*. Cassell & Co., London, 1933; Lady Maud Warrender: *My Medley*. Cassell &. Co., London, 1941. See also the obituary of Lady Maud Warrender in *The Times*, 4th September 1945.
10. Various postcards hand-written by Leginska in the authors' possession. See pages 66 to 68 for some of them.
11. The authors are indebted to Mr T.P. Langdale, the son of Ethel Liggins' cousin Mrs Marjorie Langdale, for the information about the Liggins' family house in

Hornsea and the possible identification of the people shown in the picture on page 52.
12. The entries from the Tranby Croft Visitors' Book have kindly been supplied to the authors by Mrs Gertrude M. Attwood, author of *The Wilsons of Tranby Croft,* published by Hutton Press, Cherry Burton, 1988.
13. Percy Harrison was a well-known impresario from the 1880s until 1914.
14. *Musical Opinion*, London, 30th September 1930, p. 1062. Leginska said in the interview reported in this article that the audition by Percy Harrison took place when she was 16, but the facts indicate that she must have been at least 17 and possibly just 18, unless the audition took place a year before the proposed tour, which is most unlikely. We have been unable to find a reference anywhere to the dates of birth and death of Percy Harrison, which is consistent with Henry Wood's observation, in his autobiography, that Harrison was 'of uncertain age'. It is believed that Harrison retired from concert promotion during the First World War, and it is known that he was dead by 1930 since the *Musical Opinion* article refers to him as 'the late' Percy Harrison.
15. Sir Henry J. Wood: *My Life of Music.* Gollancz, London, 1938, p. 189.
16. *The Musical Times,* London, 4th August 1905, p. 545.
17. *The Musical Times*, London, 1st February 1906, p. 122.
18. *Philadelphia Record*, 20th February 1906.
19. *Hull Times*, 17th March 1906. (Details communicated by Mr Norman Staveley.)
20. *The Musical Times*, London, 1st July 1906, p. 490.
21. A copy of the programme of this and many other Henry Wood Promenade Concerts is in the possession of the BBC Library, London. The programme of Leginska's concert was found with the help of the late Mr David Cox, author of *The Henry Wood Proms*, published by the BBC in 1980.
22. *The Times*, Friday, 24th August, 1906.
23. As ref. 15, p. 199.
24. John Ward: *McCormack on Brighton Pier*. Article in *The Record Collector* (ed. Larry Lustig)., XXXVII, No. 1, pp. 62-69, January/March 1992. The brothers Henry and Louis Bernhardt ran their concert agency from 82 Regent Street, London. Henry was the one mainly responsible for arranging the concerts. (Acknowledgments to Dr Keith Shipley for drawing attention to this article.)

Chapter 5

Marriage and a Prospering Career

Ethel Leginska was a forceful young woman, determined and highly motivated. She cared little about other people's beliefs or views on life; she knew what she wanted and would go all out to get it. She had been determined to go to Frankfurt, and she did. When things there were not progressing as well as she liked, she decided she would have Leschetizky as her teacher, and she achieved that aim. She told her pupils, years later, that she turned up on Leschetizky's doorstep and wouldn't take 'no' for an answer. She was neither diffident nor quiet, though she was always nervous when about to play in public. But this was the keyed-up type of nervousness of a skilled performer determined to give of her best. She was a spirited woman.

When she was away in Europe it had been study and practice that occupied most of her time, leaving little opportunity for social activity. After her return to England, her formal studies completed, her concert engagements started to take her to many different places and she met all sorts of people. It is not surprising that a romantic attachment soon came her way. Her admirer was Karl Germain, a talented American magician then aged 29. * His real name was Charles Mattmueller, and he was appearing in his stage act in Britain in 1906 and 1907, during a tour which included engagements with the famous Maskelyne and Devant Show at St George's Hall, London, in 1907.[1] Whilst there he and Ethel met and he was immediately entranced by the young pianist, according to Germain's friend and biographer Stuart Cramer.[2] There followed in rapid succession tête-à-têtes, private dinners, romantic motoring through Kensington Gardens and even punting on the Thames. The affair reached whirlwind proportions and during this period Ethel even helped Germain in one of his stage acts. The photograph on the next page shows Ethel posing in one of Germain's cabinets on the stage of St George's Hall in London.[3]

---

* Charles Mattmueller (stage name Karl Germain) was born in Cleveland, Ohio, in 1878. After several years touring as a professional magician with great success, he entered law school in Cleveland in 1911, and whilst still a student he helped to finance his studies by continuing to perform magic professionally on the vaudeville circuits from time to time. He ceased to be a professional practitioner of magic after he had graduated and turned down offers of professional appearances in London and elsewhere. Nevertheless, those interested in magic regard him as a legendary figure, for although his career was short he was a great innovator in the field of magic and illusion. Germain spent the rest of his working life from his late thirties onwards practising law in Cleveland but he developed eye problems and was blind for the last few years of his life. He died in Cleveland in 1959, aged 81.

It seemed that Ethel might marry the magician, but it was not to be. The relationship ended early in 1907 when Ethel acquired another suitor, and Germain returned to the United States. Late in 1912 Karl was in his home town of Cleveland, Ohio, when he noticed a poster advertising a recital to be given at an hotel there by Ethel Leginska. He attended the recital with some trepidation, but after noticing that she had a male companion in attendance he did not re-introduce himself.

Karl Germain on the stage of St George's Hall during his stage act. Ethel Leginska, assisting, is in the cabinet, dressed in operatic costume.

Germain's rival for the affection of Ethel Leginska was another American, Roy Emerson Whittern, a musician. * He rarely used his first name of 'Roy', and published his numerous musical compositions, all written

---

* Roy Emerson Whittern (born Cleveland, Ohio, 6th September 1884, died Lyme, Connecticut, 25th March 1958) was the son of Charles Stroud Whittern, a judge. Showing early musical talent, he studied piano in Cleveland with J.H. Rogers. At 15 he appeared as a pianist in the Chautauqua district and in 1904 went to Vienna for a few lessons with Leschetizky. Whilst in Vienna he also studied composition with Robert Fuchs. Between 1905 and 1907 he took occasional lessons with Artur Schnabel, a fine pianist and former pupil of Leschetizky. From 1907 to 1915 he was based in London where he earned his living as a music teacher and wrote music criticism for *The Pall Mall Gazette* and *Musical America*. He returned to the USA in 1915. From 1920 he devoted himself to composition (see list of works in Appendix 6, page 335). From about 1907-08 he used the name Whithorne, the original name of his paternal grandfather, and later had his name legally changed from Whittern to Whithorne. [4]

in distinctly modernistic style, under the name Emerson Whithorne. In 1918 he changed his name officially to Whithorne, and is generally referred to in reference books under that name. Born into a wealthy family he, like Germain, came from Cleveland, Ohio.

Ethel had first met Emerson in Vienna when he had a few piano lessons with Leschetizky. They renewed their acquaintance in London in 1906 when he was working in the city as a music teacher and critic. Soon he started to take Ethel out (he was 21, she was 20) and notwithstanding the Karl Germain episode the relationship soon blossomed into a romance. At that time Whittern (as he was still known) was living in rented accommodation at 128, Green Lanes, Stoke Newington, North London, and Ethel lived at 30, Biddulph Mansions, Maida Vale, about half a mile west of Lord's cricket ground. Emerson proposed, Ethel accepted, and their marriage took place at Paddington Register Office on Saturday, 13th July 1907 when Ethel was 21 years and three months old.[5] Strangely, Emerson's profession was given on the marriage certificate as 'pattern dealer', perhaps referring to some part-time job which helped him to eke out a living. The occupation of his father was given as 'judge' and Ethel's father's as 'architect'. On her birth certificate 21 years earlier it had been given as 'builder'. Emerson's name was given as 'Roy Emerson Whittern' and Ethel's as 'Ethel Liggins'; she omitted 'Annie'. The certificate was signed by the Registrar, the Deputy Superintendent Registrar, and two witnesses, U.L. Krimer and Marion O'Neill. Their connection with either partner, if any, is unknown. After the marriage the couple lived at Ethel's apartment, 30, Biddulph Mansions.

By an American naturalisation law valid from 1790 to 1922, Ethel became a citizen of the United States on her marriage to an American.[6] At the same time she lost her British nationality through marriage to an 'alien'. However, everyone continued to think and speak of her as English.

It was a time of rapid change for Ethel; as a rising, talented pianist, she had appeared as soloist in a Henry Wood Promenade Concert less than a year earlier and plenty of other professional engagements were coming her way. The affair with Karl Germain had come and gone, and now, at 21, Ethel was married. But throughout the period of upheaval involving the Germain affair and the romance with Emerson and their subsequent marriage, her concerts and recitals continued with ever-increasing success.

One of her recent successful recitals had taken place at the Aeolian Hall, London, on Wednesday, 12th June 1907, a month before her marriage. She played Beethoven's early Sonata in A major from Opus 2, Bach's Prelude and Fugue in E minor from the '48', several études of Chopin, and a miscellaneous group of modern pieces. The music critic of *The Times* remarked again, as he had the previous year, on her smooth and easy scale playing and her delicate touch, especially in light and rapid passages. *The Musical Times* also reported her performance most favourably: [7]

"Among the numerous pianoforte recitals given recently, mention should be made of Miss Ethel Leginska, who played with notable intelligence and brilliance on June 12th at Aeolian Hall."

The only other recent pianoforte recital selected as worthy of mention by the magazine was one by Percy Grainger, also at Aeolian Hall, on 13th June, the day after Ethel's recital. Since their days together at the Hoch Conservatory in Frankfurt a few years earlier their careers had followed a remarkably similar course. Each had reached a similar stage of achievement as a concert pianist, though Leginska was four years younger than Grainger.

Ethel was determined that her marriage should not hinder her professional career. The series of concerts and recitals that she was currently engaged in continued unabated and a year of hectic musical activity followed. Towards the end of 1907 she played for Queen Alexandra and the ladies of the court at the town residence in London (13, Bryanston Square) of Lord and Lady de Grey. [8] The Queen complimented Ethel on her excellent technique and said that if possible she would arrange an audience with the King. (Ethel had in fact already met him, as Prince of Wales, when she had played at Tranby Croft as a child.) However, this renewal of acquaintance with the King proved impossible as Ethel and Emerson had already booked a sailing to the USA on the Cunard liner *Campania* for her first visit to his home in Cleveland, Ohio. [9] Thus, at the end of 1907, Ethel, at 21, saw the USA for the first time.

Whilst in Cleveland the opportunity arose for Ethel to take up a week's engagement at the Cleveland Hippodrome, at which she played Liszt's *Hungarian Rhapsody* No. 2 and a *Valse de Concert* by her husband, amongst other pieces. Her 'act' was sandwiched between one involving clowns with performing dogs, and an acrobatic troupe. [10] It could hardly be regarded as an ideal music-making environment nor, by its nature, could it be described as her official concert 'debut' in the United States. Nevertheless it was the first time she had played in public in the USA and would have provided useful experience. This first visit to the USA was brief, requiring only a very short interruption of her busy schedule of concerts and recitals in Britain.

On 12th September 1908, fifteen months after her marriage, Ethel's career was interrupted when a son, Cedric Villiers Whithorne, was born at their home, 30 Biddulph Mansions. (On the birth certificate Emerson gave his name as 'Whithorne', contrasting with 'Whittern' on his marriage certificate in the previous year, and his occupation as 'Music (composer)').

A rather posed publicity photograph of Ethel hand-dated 13th August 1907 – exactly a month after her marriage

The couple were delighted with their offspring who was to be their only child. About this time several more publicity photographs of Ethel were taken, and were issued as postcards – a popular way of publicising musicians at that time. One of them shows Emerson, Ethel and Cedric in a happy family group. Some of these cards in the authors' possession bear messages on the reverse side in Leginska's bold, forthright hand-writing. (See below and pages 67 - 68.)

Left: A picture-postcard dating from about the time of Leginska's marriage

Right: Leginska with her husband and son, early 1909

Marriage and a Prospering Career

Two more publicity photographs

In the summer of 1909, Leginska spent a holiday in a farmhouse on the Yorkshire coast prior to a tour of the provinces. The two pictures above show her in an old costume which had belonged to the grandmother of the farmer's wife. The costume was then over 100 years old and Leginska was allowed to wear it as a special honour.

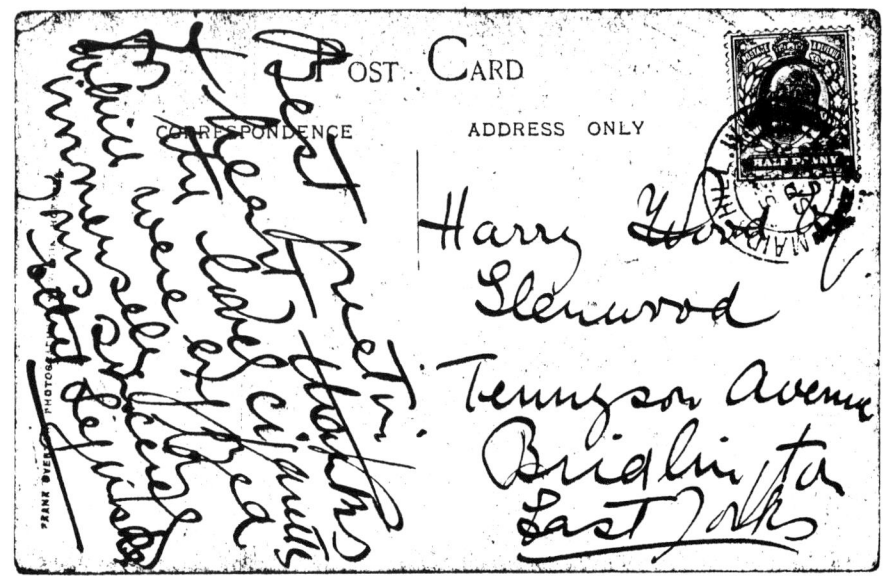

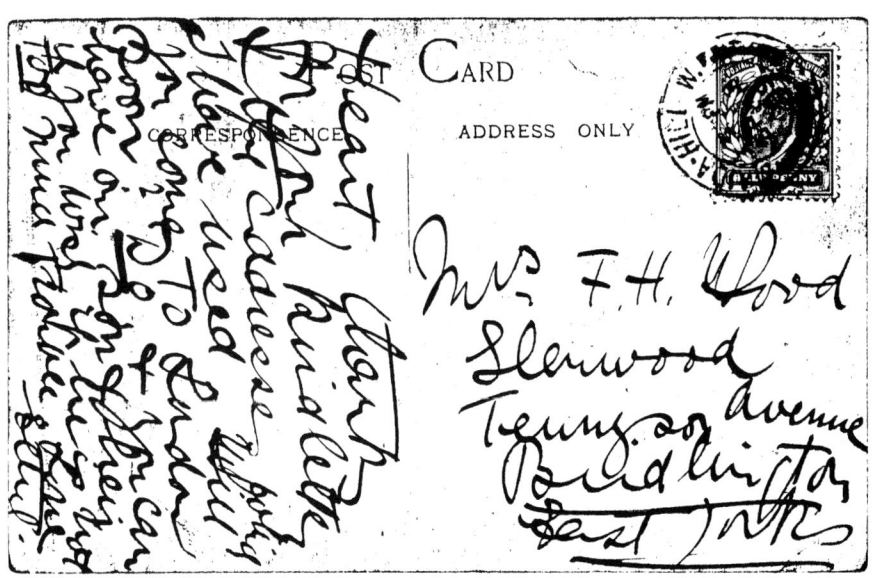

The reverse of the picture postcards shown on the previous page

But music could not be pushed into the background for long as far as Ethel was concerned, and even motherhood was not allowed to interfere with her career any longer than was absolutely necessary. The couple employed someone to look after their son and after a few weeks Ethel reappeared on the concert platform. There was little time for quiet domesticity in the Whithorne household as success in abundance came Ethel's way.

Marriage and a Prospering Career

At the end of 1908, with Cedric only a few weeks old, Ethel embarked on a major musical task. It was arranged that she would give eight recitals in close succession at the Aeolian Hall in London, each devoted to a particular type of music. She was assisted by a supporting artist, the American violinist Marcel Gluck, who was accompanied by Hamilton Harty, later to become one of the most distinguished conductors of the Manchester-based Hallé Orchestra. The subjects of Ethel's recitals included early British music, for which she would play on a spinet made around the year 1663, music of the baroque and classical periods, Polish, Bohemian and Hungarian music, the French piano schools, and American music, in which some of her husband's compositions were represented. Occupying a period of a few weeks at fortnightly intervals from the end of 1908 to the spring of 1909, the preparation of these eight recitals in quick succession was a Herculean task for a young artist, especially one who had given birth only a few weeks earlier. All went well up to and including the third recital (concerned with Bohemian and Hungarian music) in which, according to *The Times*, Leginska played "with genuine romantic feeling" and "with delicious charm and verve".

But the strain of preparing many new pieces, combined with the domestic chores of motherhood, was taking its emotional and physical toll. On the day scheduled for the fourth recital of the series (Friday, 5th February 1909) an event occurred that alarmed Ethel's family and friends. After bidding goodbye to her husband and young son in the morning she disappeared, and failed to turn up for her recital. Let the *Hull Daily Mail* take up the story: [11]

"The mystery of the disappearance of the famous pianist Madame Leginska has caused a sensation in Hull, which is her birthplace. She is better known here as Miss Ethel Liggins, and her many friends and admirers in Hull are deeply concerned as to what might have happened to her. She was to have played at a concert in London on Friday evening, but left her home in Maida Vale that morning and no trace of her has been seen since.

"Some time ago Madame Leginska married a young American composer named Emerson Whithorne. [12] He said today that she was impulsive and erratic by nature, but he could not understand her disappearance. Friends discounted that it is for the purpose of advertisement."

When Ethel left home on the Friday morning there had been no apparent indication of anything amiss. When she failed either to fulfil her Aeolian Hall engagement or to return home, the alarm was raised and a search instituted, even to the extent of telegraph messages being sent to the old haunts of her student days in Frankfurt and Vienna. Throughout the weekend fears for her safety grew as news of her disappearance spread. It was decided to publish her photograph in the newspapers and it was this that led to her discovery on the evening of Tuesday, 9th February after having been missing for four and a half days. She was found in a Birmingham boarding house, where the landlord recognised her from the newspaper photographs and contacted the police. The minds of *Hull Daily Mail* readers were put at rest the next day when the paper reported Leginska's discovery: [13]

"Miss Leginska, the well-known Hull pianist who had been missing from her home in London since Friday morning was discovered last evening. Her husband was informed by the police and made a special journey to Birmingham to fetch her. He said she was suffering from nerves and stage fright."

Ethel's father's view, as reported in the USA which had heard the news, was that his daughter's disappearance was due to "lapse of memory from overwork." [14] Ethel certainly had her hands full in preparing eight programmes containing many works of completely contrasting styles in such a short time, compounded by the fact that she had probably not yet fully recovered from the physical and emotional effects of the birth of her child.

Most pianists would probably have abandoned the series of recitals in these circumstances, regarding the temporary mental lapse as a warning worthy of appropriate action. Not so Ethel Leginska. After a few weeks of enforced rest the remaining recitals were re-scheduled and she resumed where she had left off in January, giving the fourth of the series on Thursday afternoon, 22nd April in a programme devoted to music of the French piano school, from Rameau and Daquin, through to César Franck, d'Indy, Debussy and Ravel. Thereafter Ethel continued her series through to its successful conclusion with no further incident.

The series as a whole widened her experience and repertoire; it attracted many favourable reviews from the national press as well as complimentary reports in at least two American magazines, [15] and further advanced her rapidly-growing reputation as one of the best young pianists of the day.

Following the completion of her Aeolian Hall recitals, Ethel spent a "working holiday" with friends on the Yorkshire coast as she prepared material for an autumn and winter tour of the provinces. It was whilst she was there that the two photographs shown on page 67 were taken, soon to be used as publicity picture postcards with her name printed on the picture.

In the autumn of 1909, her holiday over, Ethel embarked on her tour of Britain. This was followed by three London engagements, after which she set out for Europe where a major tour had been arranged. It was destined to enhance her growing reputation as a pianist very considerably. Emerson went with her. He was an excellent pianist himself, as may be inferred from the fact he was good enough to have had a few lessons with Leschetizky, but he possessed neither his wife's outstanding talent nor her charisma. He therefore took on the role of her manager and assistant during the tour, so playing a useful role. The famous German publishing firm of Breitkopf & Härtel provided publicity material for her.

Leginska's European tour was a great success. Many concerts were given in Berlin and the larger German cities including an excellent debut with the Berlin Philharmonic Orchestra. Wherever she went Leginska's appearances, either with orchestra or in recitals, were well received by the critics and, perhaps even more importantly, she was remarkably popular with audiences. The favourable reports are too numerous to quote in detail but the following brief extracts give a flavour of the impact she made on her tour:

The *Berlin Tageblatt* wrote:

"Leginska, in spite of her youth, stands high above her task. In the runs and trills she showed the splendour of Carreño. Her work is tremendously interesting."

This appraisal was echoed in the other German cities. The *Hamburger Fremdenblatt* remarked:

"Her playing has a thousand nuances . . .",

whilst according to the *Leipziger Tageblatt*:

"The Leginska recital was a huge artistic success."

In Munich the *Münchener Post* was generous in its praise:

"This very young girl has an astonishing technique and a healthy, beautiful touch. Her playing is always interesting and fascinating."

The *Hallesche Zeitung* was no less flattering:

"I never heard an artist with a bigger temperament. Many a pianist could envy her enormous technique, delicious pianissimo and delicate touch."

Leginska's success in Germany was remarkable; in fact she was so well received that re-engagements were offered wherever she went. Her influence on German audiences can be summed up in the words of a Munich music critic:

"Ethel Leginska, although you are English, you are always welcome in Munich; you are one of the greatest of your art."

Following her German triumph Ethel went on to play in Paris, Vienna and Petrograd. The *Echo de Paris* observed:

"Especially admirable were her superb technique and her big musical qualities."

In Vienna the *Vienna Tageblatt* noted:

"She fairly lives for her playing. Quiet, almost dreamily, she renders an andante full of temperament; passionately the parts that call for patterns. Her originality has a charm beyond comparison."

Emerson Whithorne – Ethel Leginska's husband

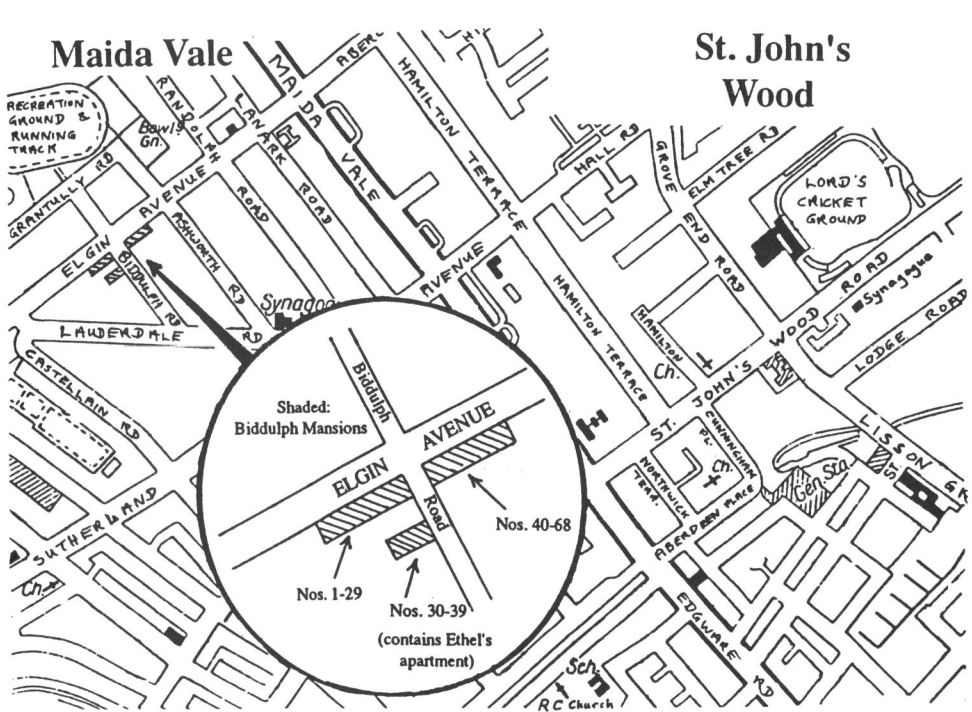

Sketch map of London showing the location of Biddulph Mansions, Maida Vale where Ethel lived from 1906 to 1912. Green Lanes, Stoke Newington, where Emerson lived before the marriage, is five miles to the North East of Biddulph Mansions.

Biddulph Mansions, Maida Vale (London) where Ethel Leginska lived from 1906 to 1912, from which she was married, and where her son Cedric was born in 1908. The photograph was taken on 25th September 2000. This block of apartments will have changed very little externally since the early part of the 20th century. The brickwork has recently been cleaned and the apartments look very smart. This block houses apartments 30 to 39; there are two other larger blocks nearby which also form part of Biddulph Mansions. The block comprises ten apartments; five one above the other on the left and another five on the right. Ethel's (No. 30) was the basement apartment on the left; the window can be seen just to the right of the back of the Range Rover. It was probably necessary for her to have a basement apartment because of her pianos. The apartments are quite large, 'going back' a long way. Maida Vale has always been, and still is, a 'sought after' part of London.

Wherever she went in Europe, Leginska pleased the critics, as the reviews that have been quoted show, and she captivated the audiences, not only through her outstanding musical talent but also through her personality and temperament. Attractive, friendly and unassuming in her private life, on stage she was an artist of remarkable vital force.

Reports of Leginska's triumphs in Europe were not confined to the British and continental press, for word of Ethel's prowess had been reported regularly in America for several years, an example being an account of one of her London recitals which had appeared in *Philadelphia Record* as long ago as February 1906 (see reference 18 of chapter 4). A report early in 1910 in *Musical America* reviewed Ethel's latest successes: [16]

"London, 5th Jan: Ethel Leginska, the pianist, who created somewhat of a ruffle in the musical world last season by her adoption of a sensible stage costume, has been having wonderful success on the continent. Berlin, Leipsic [*sic*] and Paris have all proclaimed her one of the finest of women pianists. Leopold Schmidt, of Berlin, says 'she is one of the most interesting lady pianists of recent years', and even Arthur Smolian, that cautious Leipsic critic, calls Miss Leginska 'a pianist of very great talent'. Dr Niemann writes that 'she is truly a real musical personality, and possesses the power to shape her phrases into a fine structure. Coupled with this is an independent poetic conception and wonderful, even astonishing, technic. Her success is notable.' On the strength of her success Miss Leginska is paying two return engagements in Leipsic, one in January and one in February.

"I have just received a report from Paris, where the young artist gave a recital in the beautiful 'Salle Gaveau', that no such pianistic success had been made for a very long time. Edward Colonne has engaged her for two of his concerts next season, and a tour is being arranged for her in France and Spain for March and April of this year. This will include a symphony concert in Madrid and very probably a performance by command of royalty. The Paris critics commented most flatteringly upon Miss Leginska's highly fascinating personality and superb technic."

It should be noted that this report was signed "E.W." and therefore might possibly have been written by Ethel's husband, Emerson Whithorne, who reported for the magazine. However, if that were in fact the case, although he would have wanted to present Ethel's latest achievements in as favourable a light as possible, he was only citing facts, and the words of established critics on the continent. He would have been careful not to exercise undeserved bias in favour of Ethel since, if he had, his own artistic credibility would have been lost.

It was clearly not for reasons of good fortune that Ethel was making such a name for herself. Her natural talent combined with years of hard work had equipped her with a vast musical knowledge and a formidable technique. It was not necessary to say of her, "She is a very good woman pianist"; she was a very good pianist by *any* standard, regardless of gender. Anything men played, she played, and she could equal the best of them. She was modern in the way she played and would never have adopted the rather genteel approach of many pianists, especially women, of the nineteenth century. Leginska thoroughly understood the technique of piano playing. She had absorbed everything that Mrs Russell Starr, James Kwast and, in particular, Theodor Leschetizky, could tell her about piano playing. Also, she had taught others since she was a small child. She was not like the youthful Yehudi Menuhin who, as a boy, played the violin purely intuitively without really knowing how he did it, and later had to learn how to put his technique on a sound footing. Leginska had intuitive skills in abundance but, with her thorough understanding and mastery of the art and science of piano technique, she did not rely on that alone. Not long after the start of her career as a top-class pianist, she told an interviewer: [17]

"I fancy if Schumann, for instance, could return and play to us, or even Liszt himself, we should not find his playing suited to this age at all. We can imagine the hand position Schumann must have had, the lack of freedom in fingers and arms. It was not the fashion in his time to play with the relaxed freedom and in the broad, deep style which we demand of an artist to-day. In those days relaxation had not received the attention it deserved, and, therefore, we should probably find the playing of the greatest artists of a former generation stiff and angular, in spite of all we have heard about their wonderful performances.

"I believe in absolute freedom of every part of the arm anatomy, from the shoulder down to the finger tips. Stiffness seems to me the most reprehensible thing in piano playing, as well as the most common fault with all kinds of players. When people come to play for me, that is the thing I see first in them – the stiffness.

"While in Berlin [she was referring to the months when she was based in Berlin on her concert tour of Germany] I saw much of Teresa Carreño, and she feels the same as I about relaxation, not only at the keyboard, but when sitting, moving about or walking. She has taught along this line so constantly that sometimes, if carrying something in hand, she will inadvertently let it drop from sheer force of habit without realizing it."

After her successes in Europe, the next logical step was to try her skills in the USA. The brief appearance at the Cleveland Hippodrome in January 1908 could not be regarded as a serious foray into the American market, but she knew, because of the many reports of her musical successes that had appeared in the American press, that she was not unheard of in the United States. She also knew she would not be accepted into the first rank of international pianists until America was conquered. So, in the latter part of 1912, she decided to go to the USA and try to make her mark in the country where musical competition was fiercest.

References: Chapter 5

1. The information concerning Karl Germain and his relationship with Ethel Leginska is described in Cramer's book (ref. 2) and was communicated to the authors by Professor E.A. Dawes of Hull.
2. Stuart Cramer: *Germain the Wizard and his Legerdemain*. Buffum Publishing Corporation, Galeta, California, 1966.
3. Photograph kindly supplied by Professor E.A. Dawes.
4. The biographical details about the musical career of Emerson Whittern (or Whithorne) are from various books, dictionaries and encyclopaedias of music, for example, *A Biographical Dictionary of Composers and Musicians*, Ed. Nicolas Slonimsky, Simon & Schuster, London, 1988; *The New Grove Dictionary of Music and Musicians*, Ed. Stanley Sadie, Macmillan, London, 1980; *Our Contemporary Composers (American Music in the 20th Century)* by John Tasker Howard, Thos. Y. Crowell, New York, 1941; and *Composers of Today* by David Ewen, H.W. Wilson Co., New York, 1934.
5. The certified copy of Ethel Leginska's marriage certificate was purchased from the Supt. Registrar of Births, Deaths and Marriages, London in 1984.
6. The first law regulating naturalisation (date 1790; 1 Stat. 103) included the provision that an alien woman who married a U.S. citizen automatically became a U.S. citizen. As stated in the text, the law was valid until 1922. After that date an alien woman marrying a U.S. citizen was not automatically granted U.S. citizenship status; she would have had to apply for naturalisation.
7. *The Musical Times*, London, 1st July 1907, p. 476.
8. *Cleveland Hippodrome News*, 13th January 1908; the newspaper gave an account of the recent concert at Lady de Grey's home, the news having crossed the Atlantic. A brief biography of Lady de Grey is given on page 42.
9. The *Campania*, a twin-funnel Cunard liner of 18,000 tons, had been plying the North Atlantic route since her completion in 1893, carrying 1700 passengers per crossing. Information about certain sailings of that period, including this one by Leginska, is now available on the Internet (US Immigration Family History Center). In 1915 the *Campania* was pressed into active service as a seaplane carrier but she sank in 1918 after drifting into the battleship *Revenge*.
10. *Cleveland Hippodrome News*, 20th January 1908.
11. *Hull Daily Mail*, 9th February 1909.
12. Emerson Whittern was using the name 'Whithorne' by 1907-08.
13. *Hull Daily Mail*, 10th February 1909.
14. *Musical America*, 27th February 1909.
15. *Musical America*, 25th April 1909 and 1st May 1909; *Musical Standard*, 1st May 1909.
16. *Musical America*, 29th January 1910.
17. *Musical America*, 24th May 1913. (Leginska interviewed by Harriette Brower.)

Chapter 6

Hail – America!

The birth of Cedric Villiers caused only a brief interruption in Leginska's musical career, as is clear from her continuing success in Europe. Unfortunately her musical triumphs were not matched by a corresponding success in her personal life, for her marriage to Emerson was running into difficulties by as early as 1910. It is impossible to know the reason for this with any certainty. Both Ethel and her husband had very active careers which involved a constant whirl of activity: travelling, practising, making arrangements and so on, which cannot have been conducive to a relaxed domestic atmosphere. Emerson wanted to make his own way as a musician and did not wish to continue indefinitely as his wife's manager. He was becoming a proficient composer and had the talent and literary resources to succeed in his own right in music but he was not earning much money, which annoyed Ethel. She was certainly an impulsive, headstrong young woman, and probably not the easiest person in the world to live with. Whatever the whys and wherefores of the situation, the fact is that by 1910 there were periods of separation other than those enforced by Ethel's concert schedule, and by 1912 Ethel and Emerson had officially separated.

At that time Emerson had a number of 'irons in the fire' in London; he had secured engagements as London music correspondent for several periodicals including *The Pall Mall Gazette* and *Musical America*, he studied Chinese and Japanese music from material in the British Museum and, capitalising on these studies, he wrote several compositions based on oriental tunes such as *Adventures of a Samurai*, settings for *The Yellow Jacket* and *The Typhoon*. He also did some private teaching, but none of his work was well paid. By then (1912) Ethel's European tours had temporarily finished and she was again based in Maida Vale in London. Her estranged husband was also still living in London because of the demands of his work; a situation she may have found upsetting. When she received an offer to go to New York later that year she jumped at the idea, for the city was regarded as the mecca for aspiring pianists. The time had come to make a fresh start, to test her skills in the USA amongst the greatest pianists in the world; Godowsky, Hofmann, Paderewski and a host of other great names. Musically her life had gone well in Britain and Europe but domestically it was in ruins and there seemed to be little prospect of reconciliation with Emerson; indeed, after their split they went their separate ways permanently.

According to Leginska, as recounted many years later to one of her students, Ron McFarland,[1] the opportunity to play in the USA arose through the reluctance of the eccentric Russian pianist Vladimir de Pachmann to travel there. Pachmann was worried by the possibility of war, and feared the threat of submarines if he crossed the Atlantic. Consequently he refused, at that time, to honour recitals already arranged for him in the USA; Leginska was offered some of his engagements and seized her chance eagerly.

When Ethel Leginska disembarked in New York late in 1912, reports of her success in Europe having preceded her, it did not take long for engagements to be arranged in hotels and at society functions, which served as a useful 'warm-up' for the more important concerts and recitals that lay ahead. It was recognised that her official debut recital at a big concert hall would be crucial, for it would be at that performance, with the influential New York music critics in attendance, that she would be made or broken as far as the USA was concerned. The date of the debut recital was duly arranged for Tuesday, 20th January 1913 at New York's Aeolian Hall. The programme she chose for the occasion was:

Rondo à Capriccio, Op. 129	Beethoven
Andante Favori	Beethoven
Variations on a Theme of Paganini, Op. 35	Brahms
Sonata in F minor, No. 5	Brahms
A group of pieces	Chopin
'Mazeppa' Étude	Liszt

The next day the critic of *The New York Times*, Richard Aldrich, was enthusiastic about Leginska. His review is reproduced in full here, with due acknowledgment to *The New York Times*, as it is impossible to improve upon the authenticity and spontaneity of a contemporary account.[2]

Mlle Leginska's Recital

Young English Pianist plays with Brilliancy and Poetic Feeling

"Said to be English, notwithstanding her name, Mlle Leginska, a young pianist, appeared yesterday afternoon in Aeolian Hall. She soon showed herself to be an artist of unusual gifts and attainments. She has a fiery temperament and a sweep of style not ordinarily associated with what is English in art or personality; her artistic sympathies are eager, her playing is impetuous and hot-blooded, full of high lights and deep shadows, and yet not lacking in artistic tenderness.

"There are immaturities in her style and a nervous restlessness sometimes obsesses her playing. The repose that comes with a ripe maturity is not yet hers. Mlle Leginska has gifts of inestimable value that come by nature; there are acquirements that she will gain by taking thought. Of what can be learned in her art she already has much. Her technique has great brilliancy and facility, though not yet absolute certainty; but she has mastery of many of the most advanced problems of her instrument. Her strength of arm and of finger, her endurance, are unusual, and it is a controlled strength.

"Mlle Leginska's programme was not cast in the traditional formula. She began with Beethoven's Rondo à Capriccio, Op. 129, 'Wrath over a Lost Farthing', into which she put some unusual changes of expression, and his so-called 'Andante Favori' in F, which he originally intended for the Waldstein sonata but omitted from it on advice of friends. She played a selection from Brahms's variations on a theme of Paganini, Op. 35, which have been, in whole or in part, already twice heard here this season – there is a fashion in Variations as well as in Sonatas and Symphonies and other things. These were given with great dash and power and brilliancy, and such a good deal of the higher musical significance which Brahms put into them but which is not always extracted from them by their performers.

"But Mlle Leginska reached her highest point in her interpretation of Brahms's subtle and poetical Sonata in F minor, No. 5, one of the finest fruits of his early genius, that contains, with some of the rugged austerity of the period, some of the most tenderly elegaic inspiration. The first and last movements she played with commanding power; there were moments of exquisite beauty in her interpretation of the andante and its echo, the intermezzo, a beauty that was expressed in the delivery of the haunting melody, and in many subtle shadowings of the tonal color.

"A group of five pieces by Chopin, and Liszt's noisy Mazeppa Étude, closed the concert."

All this was praise indeed from an important music critic not noted for extravagant acclaim. He could on occasions be brutally damning. But Leginska's performance was a triumph; she had passed her big debut test in the USA. A condensed version of this review was reprinted in *Musical America*. The glowing tribute in *The New York Times* was repeated in the other American newspapers. *The New York Tribune* wrote: [3]

"The player was a lady who chooses to be known as Mlle Leginska. The name has a Polish sound but its bearer is an English woman who was a Miss Liggins when studying with Leschetizky . . . but the name does not matter; what is of real importance is that its bearer is a remarkable sound, a remarkably intelligent and a remarkably finished pianist, a very fine examplar of the characteristic merits of her master's manner of instruction. Her finger technique is facile and finished, her touch elastic and equable, her legato exquisite, her passage playing even, smooth, well accentuated and carried from beginning to end with a fine sense of symmetry, her command of dynamics admirable. She has understanding and a refined and poetical taste. If anything more lovely than her performance of the Andante in Brahms's third Sonata (the one in F minor) has been heard here this season, it cannot be recalled out of hand. There have been more brilliant performances, especially of the Brahms variations on a theme by Paganini, but none in which sheer beauty was more persuasive. In short, she provided one of the aesthetic high lights in the pianoforte recitals of the season."

In the wake of the official 'stamp of approval' from New York's leading newspapers, other engagements followed in quick succession. Leginska was immediately recognised as unique; her impact on audiences immense.

All the New York papers and American music periodicals were agreed that a remarkable new talent had arrived on the scene. *Musical America* observed, after another recital: [4]

"To hear Liszt's La Campanella as played by her, is to hear it for the first time. She does technical stunts without a miss, with utmost nonchalance, and behind it all is a deeply musical nature. The crowd of influential society women and others who surrounded her after her recital, enquiring as to engaging her, etc., was most flattering. Her next important New York appearance is to be March 2, Metropolitan Opera House concert."

At the Metropolitan Opera House concert Leginska played the Rubinstein D minor Concerto and a number of solo pieces. *The New York World* reported: [5]

"From the first few notes the public recognised that a star of great magnitude was before them. Besides a wonderful certainty and bravura, Miss Leginska possesses unlimited fire, temperament, individuality and poetic imagination."

Within weeks of her debut recital at Aeolian Hall, Leginska had endeared herself to the American public. She also added Canada to her list of concert conquests when, immediately after her Metropolitan Opera House concert, she travelled to Toronto where she played chamber music with Jan and Boris Hambourg (violinist and cellist respectively). *Musical America* referred to "their magnificent reading of Tchaikovsky's Trio in A minor." She also gave a recital of solo piano pieces. *The Toronto Globe* reported, under the heading "Leginska's Toronto Success": [6]

"Leginska created a veritable furore. Superb technic, large range of tone color, the pathos of the parts which demand it, the fiery temperament, combined with real poetic feelings, are the characteristic of the young artist."

Saturday Night was equally enthusiastic: [7]

"Though Leginska came to Toronto with little heralding, her recital last Monday night stamped her as one of the very finest artists of the day. Though very petite, she has a beautiful, full-bodied tone and exceptional color in her touch. Her technic is superb, her runs and trills brilliant to a degree, and, in brief, her playing might be described as big in every way. To her remarkable attainments she adds temperament and magnetism."

From the time of Leginska's debut recital in the USA her concert season was a triumph, to the extent that before the year (1913) was half way through, she was established as one of the public's favourite pianists. Her life thus became a whirl of concert and recital engagements and was to remain so for many years.

In the autumn of 1913 Leginska began her second New York season; it was her first full one, as she made her debut half way through the previous season. It included her second recital at Aeolian Hall, on 11th December, her debut recital on 20th January having been her first there. She would return to give a recital at the hall each season for many years to come. It was a 'chronological' recital, in which she began her programme with Scarlatti and Bach and ended with Ravel, Reger, Cyril Scott (with whom she had studied at Frankfurt) and Debussy, covering a broad range of periods, styles and composers in between. *Musical Courier* reported on the recital: [8]

"Leginska knows how to play the calm, pure, Mozart and the Schubert A flat impromptu with a beautiful "floating" tone; it is all a song. She knows how to put virility into the "Waldstein" sonata, and she knows how to trill and work her way through fiercely brilliant effects in the Liszt 'Campanella'. She knows how to do these things, and is able to carry out her definite intentions, hence there is a certain sureness in her playing seldom found. In a man it is called "authority", but in a woman it is more frequently "imitation". Not so with Leginska, whose powers, both physical and emotional, are hers to command. Miss Leginska's attitude towards the music is of the right sort; she will not begin until there is quiet, and accordingly her "pauses" produce an effect of expectation. Several little mannerisms are hers alone; they are not affectations, so do not hinder the enjoyment of the music."

Speaking of the same recital, *Musical America* headed its article "Ethel Leginska wins high praise – English Pianist's Second New York Recital proves a brilliant success". It went on to report: [9]

"Miss Leginska made a strong impression when she played here last season, an impression which she strengthened further by the interesting way she treated her taxing programme on this occasion."

Reviewing each piece in detail, the writer continued:

"Her rhapsodic treatment of the Bach E major Prelude was especially fine and there was a splendid incisiveness in Scarlatti's Capriccio in E, as well as finger work of lovely evenness and clearness. Her tone was most caressing in the Adagio of Mozart's F major Sonata, played with pure Mozartian simplicity. Her performance of the Beethoven Sonata was singularly satisfying. And so one might go through the programme, for Mme Leginska was highly successful in treating the pieces in the many styles represented."

From the start of her American career Leginska was a 'hit' with the popular press as well as the more weighty newspapers and periodicals. Writing about a recital held in Syracuse, New York, held a few days before her second Aeolian Hall success, the *Syracuse Herald* remarked: [10]

"Little Leginska – a "Miss" is absurd before the name of a woman of her artistic stature, a "Mme" to me smacks of years of avoirdupois and I don't know the Russian for "Fraulein" – gave us some of the most artistic piano playing we have heard in my three seasons as a concert goer. She is electric with temperament from the crown of her head to the soles of her slippers, a dizzy drop of some five feet one. From under her hands a noble composition comes as music, not as an excuse for showing off dexterity. She is ardently romantic, but never sentimental. She has a gallant and engaging style. She is her own interpretive artist."

Reporting along similar lines the *Raleigh Times*, observed: [11]

"The recital by Ethel Leginska on Tuesday evening of this week will be long remembered by all who heard it. Leginska was a revelation in the art of piano playing. There was no monotony in Leginska's playing. She held the audience from the beginning to the end of the program. It is difficult to say what impresses one most in her playing, the breadth and sweep of her style, the delicacy of her pianissimos, the beauty of her legato passages, or her faultless rhythm. There is nothing mechanical in her playing. She seems to be thinking every passage. She puts upon her audience something of the spell of an orator who arrests, holds and sweeps his hearers with him."

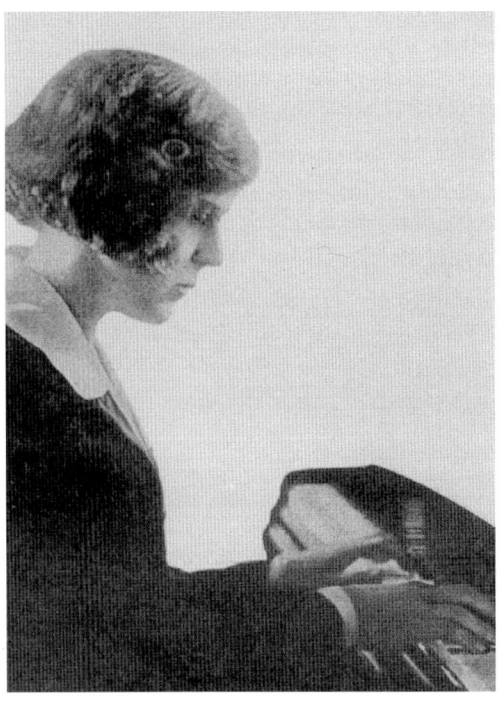

Leginska in 1913, shortly after she achieved prominence in the United States

As her concerts and recitals had been so well received from the start by the American public and critics, numerous offers of well-paid engagements came flooding in. Consequently there was every reason for her to stay in the USA for the time being, living wherever her engagements took her, especially so after August 1914 when war was raging in Europe so that opportunities for concert performances there were severely curtailed. Indeed, so conducive was the atmosphere in the USA to the furtherance of her art that she never felt the urge to return to Britain on a permanent basis and eventually she would make her permanent home in the USA, though she often visited Britain and other European countries and kept in close touch with her family and friends in the Hull, Hornsea and Bridlington areas. During the 1914-1918 war, when she was still young, it is doubtful whether she had any plans about her long-term future.

An event which was said to have pleased Ethel was the re-marriage of her father. (It will be recalled that Ethel's mother had died of smallpox in 1899.) Tom Liggins' new wife, whom he married on 12th November 1913, was his cousin Christina Workman, a spinster (see the family tree in Appendix 1(a)) who until the date of this marriage had been living at Sunny Bank, Hull whilst Tom had lived at Pemberton Street. After the marriage the couple moved into a terraced house at 45, Richmond Street, Bridlington.* He was then 52 and his new bride 38. Ethel was delighted to have a stepmother to visit, as well as her father, on her trips to England. Tom Liggins was very proud of Ethel's success and liked to recount the latest exploits in the career of his famous daughter to members of his family and friends. [12]

On 16th November 1914 Leginska gave an all-Chopin recital at New York's Aeolian Hall, the programme comprising the two sets of études (twelve in each), and the Sonata in B flat minor. *The New York Times* reported: [13]

"Miss Leginska has already shown herself to be an artist of quite unusual quality, a rare and exceptional talent, and in this recital she showed it again. The études and the sonata take a pianist through many moods and emotions, and Miss Leginska did not fail to find significant expression for them. There is a burning intensity in her style, a fiery sweep, her playing is impetuous and hot-blooded, full of high lights and deep shadows, yet it can be exquisitely restrained and is not lacking in artistic reticences. Her tone is of great beauty, whether it is in passages of delicacy or of power or in finely differentiated gradations between these extremes, and the brilliance and facility of her technique rarely failed her in any of the difficulties that Chopin provided in these compositions. The performance of the Sonata was interesting, engrossing. It was cast in a large mold [*sic*] in the first movement, and she avoided pitfalls that lead many to cheapen the funeral march. In the études not all who can set forth the fine spun poetry of some of them can rise to the height of passionate eloquence in others as she did."

---

* Mrs Margaret Stockbridge, who established the details of this marriage following a lead given to the authors in 1982 by the late Mrs Marjorie Langdale (Ethel Liggins' cousin) also discovered from the 1881 Census in Hull that at the time of the census the Workman family numbered eight in all, with Christina being the fifth of six children (see Appendix 1(a)). At that time the family lived at Dansom Lane, which was very close to Pemberton Street where Tom Liggins lived, so the cousins would no doubt have seen a lot of each other over many years.

Musical Courier, writing about the same recital, reviewed the various pieces played and then made a few general observations on Leginska's playing:[14]

"This young English pianist is growing in the favour of New York music lovers. Attractive in personality, she possesses also a distinctive individuality, which characteristic enters her playing and goes far toward making it interesting. Technically she is efficient. Her always dependable fingers, wrists, etc. respond with facility, strength, delicacy, according to the demands of the pianist's interpretations. Add to these requisites an exceptional interpretive talent, and it is not to be wondered at that she should meet the taxing demands of a program of this nature with such distinct success."

It had taken Ethel only a few months from the time of her American debut to establish herself as a firm favourite with New York audiences, and indeed, those in a wider area. So popular had she become that she was attracting large amounts of fan mail of an adulatory nature. The following poem, addressed to "Ethel Leginska, pianist" was sent to her immediately after her Aeolian Hall recital of November 1914 and was typical of many such offerings. Whilst clearly a little 'over the top', it illustrates the impact that Leginska's music, combined with her vital, almost mesmeric, personality, had on members of her audiences:

> *The sacred fire of Genius lights your soul,*
> *And all the elements of Earth and Air,*
> *Fire and Water, rise at your command,*
> *As, summoned by the Magic of your hand,*
> *They rush to do your bidding!*
> *Young and fair,*
> *You lure the lightnings from the purple cloud,*
> *And snatch Jove's thunders from the whelming dark,*
> *Anon, we hear the rapture of the lark*
> *Thronging sun flooded meadows. Loud and clear*
> *Earth calls to Heav'n! 'The Voice of God is here'*
> *Your music lifts us to the stars and sun.*
> *Its ecstacy brings back our vanished youth,*
> *We thrill, we aim, we strive, we hope again,*
> *And for a time, forgetful of our pain,*
> *We dream of all the good we had achieved,*
> *Had but the better self within us lived.*
>
> Isabel Wolfenstein

This one was published in *Musical Courier* in December 1914, as were a number of poetic offerings along similar lines on future occasions. We do not know what moved the author to describe Leginska as "fair" since her hair was dark – unless the reference is to her pale complexion.

Not only had Leginska become the darling of her audiences but even more importantly, perhaps, she had won the attention and admiration of managers and concert directors, to the extent that from her earliest days in the United States she attracted concert engagements and was soon booked up for many months, even years, ahead. Amongst those who admired Leginska's qualities of talent and personality was the influential musician Walter Damrosch, conductor of the New York Symphony Orchestra; after hearing her all-Chopin recital he immediately engaged her for a concert tour with his orchestra. So began a series of concerts with one of the most important orchestras in the United States, which took her to Carnegie Hall and many other major concert venues. Throughout the tour Leginska earned her usual rapturous acclaim from audiences and the plaudits of critics. After one concert, *Musical Courier* wrote: [15]

"The playing of Miss Leginska was marvellous. The youthful pianist fairly carried her audience off their feet by her spectacular and sensational work. Her appearance was the signal for prolonged applause, which would not be stilled until this brilliant young woman had responded with additional selections. It was a shrewd stroke of good judgment which brought Miss Leginska into the Damrosch fold."

A few weeks later *Musical Courier* again reported Leginska's playing with the New York Symphony Orchestra: [16]

"Ethel Leginska, the young English pianist, whose sensational success has attracted widespread attention, played Liszt's Hungarian Fantasy, and captivated the audience, as is usual with her. She has an originality of style, an extraordinary power and a musicianship which place her among the few universally popular and thrilling artists of the day. A slight, emotional, temperamental, romantic little figure, she surprises with her strength and thrills with her daring, unusual, musical effects. It will not be easy to pass on to other pianists and forget her."

Comments such as these were repeated wherever Leginska played. Through her brilliant musicianship, combined with a unique, attractive, personal magnetism, she had well and truly conquered the musical scene in America.

"The phenomenal young English pianist"
('Cleveland Leader', 1915)

References: Chapter 6

1. Radio discussion, KPFK, Los Angeles, April 1986. "Music of America" series. A group of Leginska's former students, including Ron McFarland, recalled Leginska's teaching work and some of the things she had said to them, in a programme commemorating the centenary of her birth.
2. *The New York Times*, 21st January 1913. An abbreviated version was reprinted in *Musical America.*
3. *The New York Tribune*, 21st January 1913.
4. *Musical America*, 29th January 1913.
5. *The New York World*, 16th March 1913.
6. *The Toronto Globe*, 11th March 1913.
7. *Saturday Night*, 11th March 1913.
8. *Musical Courier*, 17th December 1913.
9. *Musical America*, 20th December 1913.
10. *Syracuse Herald*, 5th December 1913.
11. *Raleigh Times*, 10th December 1913.
12. Information about Ethel's relationship with her stepmother was provided in 1982 by the late Mrs Marjorie Langdale (Ethel Leginska's cousin) of Hornsea, East Yorkshire and details of the marriage were found in 1999 by Mrs Margaret Stockbridge (née Liggins) of South Cave, near Hull. (Personal correspondence in each case.) Christina's full maiden name was Christina Bella Workman, as indicated on her marriage certificate to Tom, purchased from the Superintendent Registrar. She seems to have preferred to be called 'Christine' and signed herself as such on letters to Ethel, some of which are in the archives of the International Piano Museum at Maryland. The Curator, Mr Donald Manildi, kindly sent copies to the authors.
13. *The New York Times*, 17th November 1914.
14. *Musical Courier*, 25th November 1914.
15. *Musical Courier*, 27th January 1915.
16. *Musical Courier*, 3rd March 1915.

Chapter 7

The Great Pianist

The years 1913 to 1919 were prolific ones for Leginska. As a concert pianist she had reached the top of her profession and she had no shortage of engagements. She had established herself as one of the leading pianists of the day. Moreover her fire, spirit and magnetic personality had endeared her to the public. By the end of 1914 she had become as famous as any woman pianist; indeed, many regarded her as the foremost woman pianist of her time. During these years she was based in New York, then the centre of the world's musical activity and to which so many of the world's great European-born pianists had migrated, or would do so in the future.

As Leginska's fame as a notable, talented pianist steadily grew, she added to the charisma of her image by her unerring skill in attracting publicity. Some of it was achieved with no effort on her part. The combination of a remarkable musical proficiency and her personal appeal somehow compelled the attention of her audiences wherever she went. As a consequence she was rapidly establishing what was almost a cult following. Added to this was an innate ability to attract publicity in other ways, so her name was never out of the newspapers and music periodicals for long. She was always ready to give interviews and to proclaim views on music which must have appeared radical to many, brought up in the tradition that women pianists should confine themselves to relatively genteel music, whilst never failing to look demure and ladylike.

Leginska was a feminist and never failed to put the case for women in music or to propound the difficulties they experienced. One of her pet themes was the problems women musicians encountered in having to wear the type of concert dress which was then considered to be the norm. She believed it inhibited their freedom of movement. In two interviews reported in *Musical America*, one in 1915 [1] and the other with Harriette Brower in 1916, [2] she discussed the skirt and jacket she had designed for her own concert appearances and her reasons for adopting them. They were designed, she said, to keep her warm but at the same time to allow complete freedom for the arms. Leginska put forward the view that women had not yet achieved the same overall artistic level that some men had because of the many handicaps that had been put in women's way, namely, fashions in clothing, but more importantly, unequal education, and child-bearing.

Leginska had turned her attention in a serious way to the problem of appropriate clothing. In those days concert halls were often very cold, since the heating systems were generally primitive or non-existent. Leginska asserted that the only way a woman could succeed as a concert pianist was to emulate a man in dress. She declared that her choice of dress was not an affectation but her solution to the dress problem for women pianists. She remarked in her interview with Harriette Brower:

"I have contemplated just such an innovation for some time, but it was not until recently, when I played in a hall that was a veritable ice-box, that I arrived at my decision thereafter to wear common-sense clothes, that would keep my arms and shoulders warm and at the same time leave room enough for perfect freedom of the arms. For, at this concert, my fingers were like icicles, and I was forced to leave the platform between the numbers of a group to warm them. To my mind, the nonsensical clothes that women are forced to wear nowadays, on account of the dictates of fashion, have been one of the chief factors in preventing women from attaining the same heights artistically as men. A feminine artist must acquire very much masculinity to become great, just as men must lose much of their masculinity and become to a degree effeminate to be a world artist."

Two more photographs of Leginska published in 1913
Left, *Musical America*, 24th May; Right, *Musical Courier*, 18th June.
The photograph on the left accompanied the interview reported on page 75. The caption read, "Ethel Leginska, the Brilliant English Pianist Now in This Country".

Leginska, believing that the conventional bare-shouldered evening dress of women pianists was a terrible handicap in cold concert halls – a disadvantage she had endured for years – had devised a costume to counter the problem.* It consisted of a white brocade vest and silk shirt with white collar and cuffs. She commented that the attire was "always the same and always comfortable, so that I can forget my appearance and concentrate on my art." Leginska took the comparison with men further, believing that women should also copy men's practical hair styles. Accordingly she effected a hair style resembling that adopted by Paderewski and Liszt.

Leginska's attention to her hair style had begun when she was only 15 years old and was studying with Leschetizky. In an interview recalling those early days in Vienna she explained that her hair was bobbed for comfort, not effect: [3]

"I thought it was time to put my hair up. I used all the hairpins in the world, I think. And then I went to my lesson with Leschetizky. When I finished a Chopin polonaise the piano was buried in a shower of hairpins and my hair was down to its natural position. I tried for a few days to practise and not move my head so vigorously, but it was impossible. So I cut my hair and eliminated the worry.

"It is the same with my clothing. I try for simplicity. I wish women would realise how much time they waste in trying on and worrying about their dress. They should forget the idea that every article they choose must first appear in a fashion magazine. Clothes were made for comfort and warmth primarily, and it is senseless to sit and shiver in a concert hall simply because others wear those thin, sleeveless evening clothes. Men wear a costume which amounts to a uniform."

Leginska extended her thoughts to other relevant matters. She began to speak out about the problems confronting professional women in general, such as arranging child care, and she spoke of the need for women to strike out in new directions. Leginska's unconventional dress and appearance aroused both interest and publicity and heightened her image as the most noteworthy woman pianist of the day.

A vigorous defender of the place of women at the highest level in music, Leginska was not prepared to concede that a woman's place was necessarily in the home. After discussing the matter of dress with an interviewer, Leginska continued: [4]

"Another large obstacle, if not the largest, is tradition. Even today, man considers woman his mental inferior. Why? Because for ages he has been holding her down, believing that her place was in the home and that she was not physically capable of making her way in the world. So that now, when a man marries, he expects his wife to give up everything just to make a home for him and bear his children; expects her to give up her calling, whether it be singer, teacher or actress."

---

* She had devised an early version of a suitable dress for concerts as long ago as 1909 (see page 74, lines 12-13).

Front cover of the programme of a Boston recital, 1914. From her earliest days in America she was usually billed on posters simply as 'Leginska'

NEW YORK

"One of the most remarkable woman pianists now before the public."—**New York Tribune.**

"In her methods there is almost a Paderewski-like impressiveness, a theatrical element which holds the audience in its spell."
—**New York Herald.**

"Miss Leginska by her unfailing musicianship and devotion to the highest ideals of her art has duplicated in America in no small way her vogue and success in Europe. Her share in last evening's programme disclosed a technic that was polished, accurate and brilliant."—**New York American.**

"Leginska's performance of the Rubinstein Concerto proved one of the features of the Sunday night concert at the Metropolitan Opera House. The youthful artist revealed a touch of great power, and she played with a warmth that was surprising."
—**Musical Courier.**

"She played the Rubinstein Concerto in a way that roused the big audience to the utmost enthusiasm."
—**New York Evening Telegram.**

"Leginska played like a young goddess of music. She knows her art inside out. In Chopin's B-minor Scherzo the notes fell like golden drops from her fingers. In 'Mazeppa' she rushed over the keys with tremendous effect. How the notes danced! Never has a soloist at these concerts—good as they have been—received such an ovation."—**New York Staats-Zeitung.**

"She very soon showed herself an artist of unusual gifts and attainments. She has a fiery temperament and a sweep of style; her artistic sympathies are eager; and her playing is impetuous and hot blooded, full of high lights and deep shadows, yet not lacking in artistic reticences."—**New York Times.**

"Her performance had uncommon beauty and variety of tone, a wide range of expressive and well-placed nuances, and an amount of repose rare in a player of not many years."—**New York Sun.**

TORONTO

"Leginska created a veritable furore. Superb technique, large range of tone color, the pathos in the parts that demand it, the fiery temperament combined with real poetic feeling, are the characteristics of this young artist."—**Toronto Globe.**

"She plays as no woman player has ever done in this country—she has characteristics of a genius."—**Toronto Courier.**

SYRACUSE

"A great artist—nothing short of a revelation."
—**Syracuse Standard.**

BUFFALO

"She might justly be termed a female Rosenthal."
—**Buffalo Courier.**

Back cover of the programme – the same recital as opposite

The second of the *Musical America* articles referred to earlier was published under the heading "Are Women Men's Equal as Pianists?" [5] Introducing the article, Harriette Brower (1865-1928, a noted author of the period on musical matters who interviewed all the best pianists of the day) remarked that Leginska "now stands at the summit of achievement", brought about by "great talent, coupled with indomitable will and perseverance". In the interview Leginska spoke about the dress she wore in performance, about technique, and on women's place in music. In direct answer to the question posed in the title of the article she said:

"I do not think women artists the equal of men. This may be different at some future time, but not yet. We don't seem to have the unity of purpose and the endurance to carry it out. It's easy enough to make a single success, a 'hit' so to say, or a few of them. But to keep this up year after year, constantly to strive higher and higher all the time, that's the difficult thing. So many trivial things fill a woman's life."

As the foregoing paragraphs will have indicated, Leginska's views on such matters as dress and the place of women in music were direct, articulate, forceful and uncompromising. As a pianist she was the same; her dynamism and personality, allied to her great talent, set her apart from the general run of women pianists. Her statement about women lacking the unity of purpose and endurance to be the equal of men was directed at her sex in general; she herself possessed in abundance the necessary qualities to be men's equal as a musician, and superior to most of them. No one could ever say she lacked dedication to her art; that was the quality she possessed above all others.

It will come as no surprise to learn that Leginska was seen as a role model by a large number of young women at that time, many of whom were aspiring pianists in an age when a high proportion of them were taught to play the piano. As we have seen, Leginska had very strong views on the place of women in society and was not afraid to express them, which she did very articulately. She also possessed an attractive, engaging personality. Consequently the many young women who saw her as a leader tried to be as similar to her as they could, not only in their opinions but also in their appearance, and many young women adopted a dress and hair style similar to Leginska's. The picture opposite shows Leginska with a group of 'Leginska look-alikes'.

Following Leginska's phenomenal success in the USA in 1913 and 1914, she was snapped up by the Aeolian Company to record piano rolls, and her first titles appeared as early as 1914, only a year after her New York debut. The story of the player piano (an ordinary piano fitted with a special mechanism to enable it to play music automatically from perforated paper

Leginska (left) with a group of admiring followers, all copying her hair style and dress

rolls), is well documented elsewhere [6] and will be described here only in very brief terms. The hey-day of the player piano was the period 1900-1930, when the 'Pianola' (actually a trade name of the Aeolian Company but which became generic to all player pianos) enabled good music to be heard in any home that could afford the instrument. The 'player mechanism' was housed within the piano case, and all the operator (or 'pianolist' as he or she was sometimes called) had to do was to pedal the pneumatic bellows. In the earlier models only the actual notes were recorded and the operator had to put in the 'expression' himself or herself. But from about 1905 onwards an ingenious means of reproducing not only the notes but all the nuances of the expression, including the pedalling, was widely available. This desirable state of affairs was achieved by means of an instrument called the 'reproducing piano' which in effect was the *de luxe* version of the player piano. It enabled piano rolls which had been previously 'recorded' by a celebrity pianist to 'reproduce' the actual performance of the pianist with remarkable accuracy so that, when the system was working correctly, it was difficult to distinguish the performance of the reproducing piano playing the roll from the original performance recorded by the pianist. With this system it was not necessary for the operator to 'interpret' the music by manipulating the hand-controls. Instead, the music was recorded by the pianist using a special piano which detected every nuance of the playing, including the pedalling, and transferred it by means of coded perforations onto a 'master roll'. Numerous paper copies of this were then made and sold to customers. An electric motor was installed in many models of reproducing piano to provide the motive power, so the operator did not even need to pedal. All the listener had to do was switch on; the piano did the rest. Many leading piano manufacturing companies, including such prestigious ones as Steinway and Bechstein, allowed player mechanisms to be fitted into some of their instruments by the player piano companies including, at the top end of the player piano market, the 'reproducing' mechanisms referred to above.

During the 1920s as many as 25 per cent of pianos sold in the United States were fitted with a player mechanism and of these perhaps about a quarter were of the 'reproducing' type, which were able to reproduce accurately the performance of the famous pianist who had recorded the roll. Thus piano rolls, including reproducing piano rolls, were a very important part of the music market and a serious rival to gramophone recordings, the quality of reproduction of which was very poor before the introduction of electric recording in 1925.

Several manufacturing companies introduced reproducing pianos and rolls into their range. The leading systems were as follows:

Duo-Art:	Product of the Aeolian Company, New York and London
Ampico:	" " American Piano Company, New York
Welte:	" " Welte Company, Freiburg and New York
Triphonola:	" " Hupfeld Company, Leipzig
Artrio:	" " Wilcox & White Company, Meriden, Connecticut
Artecho:	" " Apollo Piano Co., De Kalb, Illinois
Duca, Ducartist:	" " J.D. Philipps & Söhne, Frankfurt-am-Main
Pleyela:	" " Pleyel Piano Company, Paris
Virtuola Co:	" " Virtuola Co., Holland or Germany

Of these, the largest share of the market was held by the 'big three' of Duo-Art, Ampico and Welte, with Hupfeld not far behind. In Britain, Duo-Art rolls were the most popular reproducing rolls with Ampico second.

Thus in 1914, after she had been invited to record rolls for the Aeolian Company, Leginska was established as a recording artist. Six of her Duo-Art rolls were issued in November of that year, and may still be heard today, played on Duo-Art pianos. They were Mendelssohn's *Song Without Words*, No. 30, Op. 62, No. 6 (*Spring Song*); Rubinstein's *Valse Caprice* in E flat major; the same composer's *Melody* in F major, Op. 3, No. 1; Schubert's *Hark! Hark! The Lark!* (transcription by Liszt); Schubert's *Marche Militaire* Op. 51, No. 1 (arranged by Tausig); and Schumann's *Kinderszenen*, Op. 15,

The Great Pianist

No. 7 (*Träumerei*). Another recording was issued in May 1915, Chopin's Ballade in G minor, Op. 23.[7] These rolls were probably recorded on an *ad hoc* basis as there is no record of a contract at that time between Leginska and the Aeolian Company, which issued its first Duo-Art roll catalogue in 1915.[8] (The Duo-Art system had been introduced in 1913.) After 1915 the issue of new rolls was suspended, almost certainly due to the intervention of the war in Europe, and did not resume until hostilities ceased.

The period from Leginska's American debut in January 1913 through to 1919-20 were wonderful years for her as a pianist. Reviews of her concerts and recitals were almost unfailingly favourable, and headlines such as "Saratogans held under spell of wonderful playing for two hours" [9] were commonplace, with "Saratogans" replaced by whatever group was appropriate to the venue. She generally included in her programmes, or as an encore, one of the showy 'pot-boilers' that were popular in those days, to augment the more orthodox musical fare and to please those in the audience who liked to hear a few 'fireworks' as a contrast to the more serious offerings comprising the main part of her programmes. A typical example was the Tausig arrangement of Schubert's *March Militaire*, a piece she had recently recorded on a piano roll for Duo-Art. Her ability to conquer the technical difficulties of such convoluted pieces with apparently consummate ease brought comparisons with the leading male pianists of her era in critics' reviews. An example from the *Brooklyn Daily Eagle* read: [10]

"Miss Leginska, the feminine Rosenthal of the piano, played *Blue Danube Arabesque* by Schulz-Evler. It is the sort of thing Miss Leginska does better than anyone else now on the stage, the only question being whether it is worth while to lavish her perfection of technic upon music so little worth while."

Leginska was one of the few pianists able to guarantee a full house at the Carnegie Hall. After one of her recitals there *The New York World* wrote: [11]

"Ethel Leginska, the boyish looking little English pianist, who can evoke from the keyboard thunder as deafening as can any of her male compeers, was the soloist at the first of the People's Symphony Concerts at Carnegie Hall yesterday afternoon. She was heard in Liszt's Fantasie on Hungarian folk melodies, in which she played her part masterfully and brilliantly to the manifest delight of an audience that filled the house from top to bottom. She was recalled many times."

In December 1915, after a concert in Boston, Mass., the *Boston Transcript* published a long article that not only reported on Leginska's recital but also analysed the qualities that made her such a uniquely attractive pianist. [12] Under the heading "Talent and Temperament – the Remarkable Qualities of Ethel Leginska" the article spoke of her "clear and communicating individuality, talent and temperament, her individual personality, rare attributes of technique and tone, concentration, fire and power and the wide range of her abilities." After reviewing her performance in the recital at length and in detail in a most favourable light the writer concluded:

"To play in this fashion through the long course of such a concert is to play with the passion, poetry and power, the range of beauty, resource and style, of a pianist of the first rank. Occasionally these English are surprising."

Reviewing the same recital, the famous music critic Philip Hale wrote in the *Boston Herald*: [13]

"Mme Leginska is a remarkable pianist. Few pianists of the many that have visited Boston of late years have given such unalloyed pleasure. First of all, she has a peculiarly beautiful touch, and admirable mastery over tonal effects, and unusual command of nuances, a poetically musical taste to govern and control. Her fleetness in bravura is never a scramble. The brilliance of her bravura has body and a charming liquidity. She has the gift of caressing the keys so that they in gratitude sing to her. But while her delicacy is fascinating, she has strength, the true strength that is sonorous and euphonious. As a colorist she delights now in broad effects, now in the most delicate tints. It is enough to say that among her rare natural gifts and her acquired accomplishments Mme Leginska has pronounced individuality. We know of no pianist that can be classed with her. She is singularly unique as pianist and interpreter."

It had been less than three years since Leginska's New York debut, yet she was already one of the great attractions of the concert platform. Her hold on her audiences and some of the reasons for it are apparent from *Musical America*'s report of her Carnegie Hall recital of March 1916. [14]

"On Friday evening, March 31, Ethel Leginska gave a piano recital at Carnegie Hall, New York. The clientele which Miss Leginska's playing has won for her was apparent in the size of the audience, one of the largest attracted to the hall this season by any individual artist with the exception of Paderewski, Kreisler and McCormack; and Miss Leginska may well be proud that it is necessary to compare her drawing power with that of such artists. Her program was made up of Busoni's arrangement of Bach's D minor toccata, two Bach inventions, the Beethoven sonata in A, Op. 2, No. 2, Chopin's B minor scherzo, eleven preludes from his Op. 28, an 'Etude Héroique' by Leschetizky, Liszt's 'St. Francis Walking on the Waves' and the same composer's 'Campanella'.

"Miss Leginska's playing was marked as usual by an individualism. Alone on the concert platform, she is extremely interesting before she has played a note. Her knowledge of the possibilities of the piano and her ability to bring out all of these is marvellous. She has a command of tone ranging from the loudest fortissimo to an almost inaudible pianissimo and she employs the various dynamic gradations in between with much intelligence. Her readings are most individual. Her playing demands and wins unceasing attention. The hearer is never jaded and there is always some new interesting turn of phrase to attract and hold the listener. The Bach works were splendidly done. There was much fine playing in the Beethoven sonata. The Leschetizky "Etude Héroique" was played in heroic style, and the pianist was particularly happy in the Liszt numbers.

"Miss Leginska must be ranked very high among the women pianists of today. There is perhaps as strong a note of individuality in her playing as that of any other pianist now before the public, man or woman. The great audience never tired of hearing her play and without doubt she could have kept on well toward midnight. After the Chopin scherzo she played the Beethoven rondo in G in response to numerous recalls, and after completing the program announced, was compelled to add another one nearly complete in itself, playing the eighth Hungarian rhapsody and the 'Rigoletto' paraphrase of Liszt, Leschetizky's 'Two Larks', Schubert's 'Marche Militaire', and ending with the Schulz-Evler transcription of the 'Blue Danube Waltzes'."

The critics were occasionally not as adulatory as this when Leginska played; it would have been remarkable if they had been. On 2nd November 1916 she gave a recital at the Carnegie Hall, the long, difficult programme of which led to adverse criticism in some of the American newspapers. *The New York Times* described the programme, given in front of a big audience, as "severely classical". It consisted of Bach's 'Italian' concerto; Brahms's 16 Waltzes, Op. 39; Beethoven's Écossaises in E flat; the same composer's *Pathétique* sonata, Op. 13; and Brahms's Variations on a theme of Paganini. *The New York Times* expressed some reservations about the recital, not through doubts about Leginska's skill as a pianist, but because of the nature of the programme, on the grounds that it was too long and that the material included was not appropriate to the acoustics of a large concert hall or to Leginska's physique. Again let the newspaper take up the story. Under the heading "Pianist does not appear at her best in a classical programme", the review observed: [15]

"Ethel Leginska, pianist, gave her first recital of the season at Carnegie Hall yesterday before a large audience. Mme Leginska has won a high place among pianists by her gifts. Ordinarily she has been known for a fiery energy, a subtlety and sensitiveness to half shades, and the technical brilliance and refinement necessary to give expression to these qualities. While it would be idle to say these were not in evidence yesterday, or that she did not do some splendid playing, the fact remains that in a programme which might be called severely classical she seemed to be less happy than on some previous occasions.

"It is something of a task to make most Beethoven sonatas sound altogether convincing in a large auditorium like that of Carnegie Hall. In her attempt to make this particular sonata, so much played by piano students, sound 'different', and at the same time make it carry properly, she became less the pianist and more the virtuoso, indulging in a sharp variety of dynamics and devices of expression and a forcing process. The result was neither the best Beethoven nor the best Leginska. The Brahms Variations which followed with no intermission are too long and too much of a matter of displaying the composer's remarkable skill in this form, rather than the feeling he exhibits elsewhere, to fill their place gracefully, even though the player did some of her best work during their course.

"While it may seem ungracious in those who find fault with a program that represents the highest endeavor with no compromise towards the merely 'popular', the preceding might be put in the form of a compliment by saying that Mme Leginska has gifts so unique along certain lines that they should be displayed, even at the expense of things that might be left to 6ft male pianists with heavy arms."

The *Musical Courier*, reporting the same recital, had no such reservations: [16]

"While Bach, Beethoven and Brahms are names that do not necessarily connote femininity, Ethel Leginska gave admirable performances of works by all three composers at a recent Carnegie Hall recital."

Musical America also reviewed the recital favourably: [17]

"Even so severe a program as she offered on this occasion, Bach, Beethoven and Brahms, gained fresh life when subjected to her treatment. There was genuine poetry in the slow movement of Bach's 'Italian' concerto and in parts of the 'Pathétique'. The sixteen Brahms Waltzes were stunning in their rhythmic qualities and buoyancy. The Brahms Variations on a Paganini theme were marvels of virtuosity and fairly sparkled technically."

Leginska's "all-Chopin" recitals had proved so popular that she repeated such programmes many times at numerous venues, including Chicago and Boston. She had become a firm favourite in both these cities, as indeed she was everywhere she went, in recitals and as a soloist with major orchestras. Generally recognised by 1916 as the foremost woman pianist of the day, she was becoming known as "The Paderewski of Women Pianists". The bestowing of this title came about when Leginska was a member of the audience at a Paderewski recital in New York. Paul Morris of the *New York Herald* referred to Leginska by this title during an interval, and it appeared in his review of the concert. The epithet stuck, and was to remain with Leginska for the rest of her concert career. The *Toledo Blade*, in an article published under the headline "Leginska proves herself above the Paderewski Sobriquet", felt the title was misplaced, on the grounds that Paderewski was not generally regarded by musicians as the best concert pianist of the day, though he was undoubtedly the most famous. The paper remarked: [18]

"It isn't fair to call Ethel Leginska "the woman Paderewski". She's entitled to be known as Ethel Leginska, as she proved Thursday night in closing the season for the Toledo Pianoforte Teacher's Association. And, as Ethel Leginska, she must rank with the very best — the top notchers, if you please. This tiny artist (for she is tiny) brought from her piano in the fortissimo passages the Paderewski effect of heavy and sustained thunderous tones, all clearly marked, with no running in of one chord upon another, thanks to her great pedal work. And then when the movements changed, she drew from the instrument those brilliant trills of the birds, the soft murmuring of the brook."

The Great Pianist

Meanwhile, Leginska attracted the attention of more 'fans', as we would call them nowadays, than ever, and continued to receive sackfuls of mail of an adulatory nature. One poem from the hundreds she received from members of the public was quoted in the previous chapter; here is another.

LEGINSKA

Leginska! Thou has plunged deep to the haft
The dagger of thy music in my soul
And no Lethean drug will make me whole.

Thou art bewitched — thy wide-set eyes have read
Beethoven's high and mystic tragedy,
And Bach's rich scroll hath not been hid from thee.

Thou weav'st thy spell about me — and I know
Thou swayest with a rhythm that is not thine:
Thou art afire with ecstacy divine.

Thou art pure disembodied sound — thy hands
Are quick with light, with gesture undesigned
Thou strewest unknown treasures to the wind.

Thou art the shivering reed, that in the dun
And wide morasses where life's water's flow
Doth tell which way the eternal currents blow!

James Fenimore Cooper, Jr.

Two publicity pictures of Leginska, 1916

Through her talent, her personality, and her constant readiness to give interviews, the 'Paderewski of women pianists' remained in the public eye. The unusual and distinctive form of dress she wore in concerts had aroused much interest and helped to establish her image as a unique pianist − "the" woman pianist of the day. Her rather masculine hair style, though effected for purely practical purposes, had established a fashion amongst young women and adorned the heads of thousands of them. And when, in 1916, Leginska caught her finger in the door of a railway carriage she sent a picture of the X-ray of her hand, showing the bruised digit, to *Musical America* which published it. The report alongside the picture explained: [19]

"The accompanying picture is a radiograph of Ethel Leginska's right hand. About ten days previous to her last Carnegie Hall recital, on March 31, she had the misfortune to jam her fourth finger [4th in piano terminology; i.e. ring finger] in the door of a railway train. Despite excruciating pain she insisted upon continual practise, the result being that the finger swelled very badly. Two days before the recital, in the fear that it had been broken, she went to a physician, who ordered a radiograph of the finger in order to determine whether it was really broken or merely a very bad bruise. Happily the latter turned out to be the case. The shadow of the bruise can be seen distinctly on the radiograph, near the top joint of the fourth finger. The finger is very obstinate and persists even now in paining Miss Leginska whenever she has to play or practise."

Fortunately for America's anxious musical public, the finger healed in due course and it was not long before Leginska was restored to her normal effervescent self. Her many followers breathed a sigh of relief.

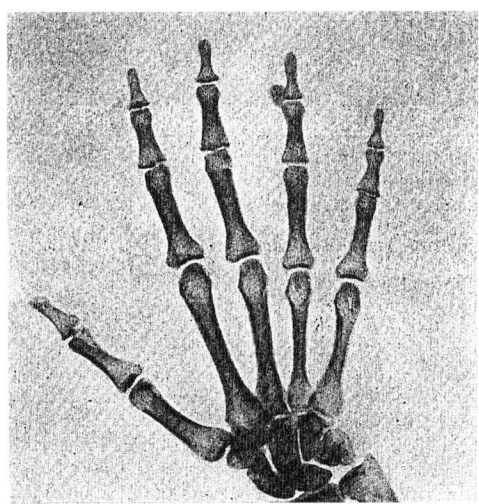

The X-ray photograph of Leginska's right hand, published in "Musical America"
The shadow of the bruise can be seen on the picture,
near the top joint of the fourth (ring) finger.

References: Chapter 7

1. *Musical America*, 20th March 1915.
2. *Musical America*, 16th December 1916.
3. *Kansas City Star*, 21st January 1919.
4. As reference 1.
5. As reference 2.
6. The following references give a comprehensive account of the history and mechanism of the player piano, including the reproducing piano:
   Player Piano Treasury by Harvey N. Roehl, Vestal Press, New York, 1961 (and 2nd Edition, 1973); *Player Piano* by Arthur W.J.G. Ord-Hume, George Allen and Unwin Ltd., London, 1970; *Encyclopaedia of Automatic Musical Instruments* by Q. David Bowers, Vestal Press, New York, 1972; *The New Grove Dictionary of Music and Musicians*, Macmillan, London, 1980, Vol. 14, p. 860 (entry for 'Player Piano', by Frank W. Holland); *Pianola* by Arthur W.J.G. Ord-Hume, George Allen and Unwin Ltd., London, 1984. Welte was the first company, in 1905, to introduce reproducing piano rolls. The Ampico and Duo-Art reproducing systems entered the market in 1913.
7. Information about Leginska's Duo-Art rolls and their dates of issue is from catalogues of the Aeolian Company and various more recent roll catalogues.
8. The authors are indebted to Mr Gerald C. Stonehill of Denham, Bucks, formerly of the Boltons, London, for information about Leginska's contracts with the Aeolian Company.
9. *Musical Courier*, 19th May 1915.
10. *The Brooklyn Daily Eagle*, 3rd May 1915.
11. *The New York World*, 26th October 1915.
12. *Boston Transcript*, 9th December 1915.
13. *Boston Herald*, 9th December 1915.
14. *Musical America*, 6th April 1916.
15. *The New York Times*, 3rd November 1916.
16. *Musical Courier*, 15th November 1916.
17. *Musical America*, 11th November 1916.
18. *Toledo Blade*, 21st February 1916.
19. *Musical America*, 20th April 1916.

Chapter 8

Fame, Fortune – and Divorce

As America's (and probably the world's) foremost woman pianist at the time, Ethel Leginska's schedule was heavy and demanding. Her itinerary involved constant travelling, including frequent visits from her base in New York to such places as Boston, Chicago, Cleveland and Michigan in the United States and there were also visits to Canada. She was often booked in one city for several nights in succession. In those days long-distance travelling had of course to be done by train and her lifestyle conjures up images of the old Hollywood movies in which incessant journeying was depicted on screen by a series of place names against a background of locomotive wheels thundering along a track.

It was an accident on one such journey early in 1917 that could have ended Leginska's career and even her life. The event was widely reported. The following account is from the *Musical Courier*: [1]

"Whilst travelling to Canada and thence to Buffalo, New York [State] on the Michigan Central train, "The Wolverine", to fulfil an engagement with Walter Damrosch and the New York Symphony Orchestra on February 13, an accident befell Ethel Leginska, "the Paderewski of Women Pianists". Just before stopping at St. Thomas near the Canadian border, the first part of the train, containing the sleeping cars, was overtaken by the second section, the force of the resulting collision smashing the dining cars and wrecking a good portion of both trains. Mme Leginska, who was in the sleeper, was struck by a falling partition and severely shaken up. For a time she feared that her shoulder had been dislocated, but Leginska is an extraordinarily loose jointed little lady. On arrival in Buffalo she was driven straight to a surgeon specialist who immediately X-rayed the apparently injured arm and shoulder with the gratifying discovery that no real injury had been done except a severe strain.

"Despite her badly bruised arm and shoulder Leginska decided to appear the day after the accident with the New York Symphony Orchestra in Buffalo, as scheduled, and actually performed a brilliant program as if nothing had happened on the train. There was every reason for an attack of "nerves" on this occasion as not only was she suffering from physical shock, but she was also playing for the first time in America, the extremely difficult Liapounov concerto, * one of the output of the modern Russian School. That she encompassed all these obstacles and scored a sensational success is only one additional proof of the Leginska genius."

---

* Liapounov's name may also be spelt Liapounof(f), Liapunof(f) or (in recent times) Lyapunov. He wrote two piano concertos, No. 1 in E flat, Op. 4 (1890) and No. 2 in E, Op. 38 (1909). All the reports about Leginska's concert say she was playing 'the Liapounov concerto' without specifying which one. It was probably No. 1, which has generally been the more popular of the two and would have been better known in 1917 than the later one.

When interviewed by a reporter after the accident Leginska remarked that figuring in a train wreck was not an event that she would like to experience very often, but said that "at least it varied the monotony of railroad journeys". [2]

Appended to the *Musical Courier* report were brief quotes from various newspaper reviews of her Buffalo concert and another one given in New York two weeks later where she performed the same Liapounov work. All the reviews confirmed Leginska's technical skill and her immense popularity. Here are extracts from a few of them:

Buffalo Courier: [3]

"Ethel Leginska the English pianist who is one of the sensations of the musical world, was soloist for the occasion, playing the concerto for piano with orchestra by Liapounov. This young artist, musically, is a live wire, a perfect dynamo of energy and strength. One of the New York critics writing a few weeks ago said, "Within a few days New York had enjoyed the unusual experience of hearing a man play like a woman and a woman play like a man", Leginska being the woman referred to. Her dazzling fleetness of fingers, her strongly marked technical fluency, make her a notable figure, and in her work with the orchestra she disclosed the great musical growth she has obtained since her last appearance here. Recalled amidst prolonged applause, she played as an encore the prelude by Chopin known as the "Raindrop". Although suffering from an injured arm, Leginska pluckily fulfilled her engagement."

Buffalo Express: [4]

"Mme Leginska has not stood still in her artistic growth since she was last heard in this city and she gave a shining example of modern piano virtuosity in her playing of the concerto. It is marvellous how those little hands can achieve such crashing chords and massive harmonies, and the delicacy and beauty of her touch is no less remarkable than its vigour and power. She played with dazzling brilliance combined with deep poetic feeling, and her playing aroused immense enthusiasm. She was recalled to the footlights many times, and was not permitted to disappear until she had given an encore, the Chopin 'Raindrop' prelude, played with great charm and poetry. Mme Leginska's performance was all the more admirable in view of the fact that she sustained quite a severe injury to her right arm and shoulder in a railroad accident in Canada last Monday."

The New York Times: [5]

"Mme Leginska gave a brilliant and powerful performance of Liapounov's concerto, filled with an intense and nervous energy."

The New York Evening Mail: [6]

"Mme Leginska yesterday dashed through the concerto with splendid spirit and a rousing display of technic."

The New York Evening Journal: [7]

" . . . Mme Leginska attended to all this with immense dash or meticulous delicacies of coloration, as the case happened to be, and she was rewarded with much and freely offered applause."

The New York Evening Sun: [8]
"Ethel Leginska was the soloist and gave a brilliant playing of this concerto. It is one to demand of its interpreter all the resources of modern technic."

The New York Evening Post: [9]
"Leginska was recalled many times after a vigorous and showy performance of a piano concerto by Liapounov, a well constructed piece (after the Liszt model) of considerable interest."

Everywhere she went Leginska's playing received good reviews from the critics, and her status as one of the favourites of the public continued to grow steadily. She played a wide range of music relying on no particular specialities (though her playing of Chopin was often especially praised) and was always ready to introduce pieces that were unfamiliar to the public, such as the Liapounov concerto referred to above. This concerto became one of her great showpieces and she played it all over America. Another very popular piece in her repertoire was the Rubinstein D minor concerto, hardly ever heard nowadays but very popular at that time. Amongst the venues where she played the Rubinstein Concerto was Boston, where she performed it with the Boston Symphony Orchestra on six evenings under the baton of the orchestra's conductor, the German-born Dr Carl Muck, prior to his much-publicised internment, amid a lot of controversy and ill feeling, as a hostile alien when the United States entered the war in April 1917. (Details of this episode are given on page 199). Leginska was as great a favourite in Boston as she was in New York. It is an interesting fact, to which the press frequently drew attention at the time, that Leginska never played with an orchestra that did not immediately want her for a return engagement. This happened with the New York, Boston, and Cincinnati Symphony Orchestras to name but three, and there were many others.

Leginska succeeded as a pianist as much through her personality as through her musicianship, brilliant though that was. Countless numbers of people who attended her performances testified to the personal magnetism that set her apart from so many of her contemporary pianists. Leginska was aware of her ability to thrill audiences and she heightened the effect of her charisma by often playing in a darkened hall, with only the piano keyboard and herself illuminated. This focused attention on Leginska and her music, and it helped to eradicate extraneous distractions. Of these, one of the most irritating to Leginska and to which she took great exception was the audience's coughing and sneezing, which can be enough to distract the most single-minded pianist. Leginska was usually able to quell such disturbances before they took hold; a steely glare from her remarkably hypnotic eyes was generally sufficient.

Off the concert stage, Leginska's exploits and her frequent interviews made constant news. She knew the importance of publicity and seized each suitable opportunity. As early as 1915, only two years after her New York debut, her New York agents, Haensel and Jones, made a movie film of one of Leginska's piano recitals. Even in those days of silent pictures the film, which was shown all over America, must have created quite a stir, because Leginska, petite as she was, with youthful, pallid features, corresponded exactly with the image of the archetypal heroine of the silent film era.

Ethel Leginska in 1917

During these years Ethel was first and foremost a concert pianist of the first rank, but like many musicians she was also interested in composition. As early as 1914 *Musical America*, following an interview with Leginska, had reported on this aspect of her work: [10]

"A diversity of mood is revealed in Miss Leginska's compositions. Two of her songs and the first movement of a sonata furnished a case in point. Of the first was a charming 'Bird song' (dedicated to Frances Alda) and the second had the savour of an old English ballad. The excerpts from the sonata, in contrast, were charged with virile movement. The verve and the clangour of the opening were astonishing, and it was all, in a broad sense, masculine music. The various aspects and manifestations of nature serve as practical lessons for Miss Leginska. She remarks that the sea forms one of her richest sources of inspiration. 'Whether it be a rippling passage to be mastered, or an impetuous outburst such as that in the 'Revolutionary Etude' – the sea will teach me how.' "

Leginska went on to point out, in the interview, the value of conveying impressions of external influences such as the sea into the music of her pupils, and observed: "Only after they have begun to observe can they hope to express."

It is interesting to note that, even at the height of her career as a concert pianist, Leginska found time to teach. She did so because she was good at it, she enjoyed it, she had taught since her earliest years, and for her it was a relaxation. In 1913, shortly after hitting the headlines in America, she had remarked in another interview: [11]

"Yes, I love to teach – children as well as older ones. Whenever I stay in a place for a few weeks or months people come to me for lessons."

So far as Leginska was concerned, learning was an ongoing process which applied not only to her pupils but also to herself. At the height of her powers she still studied the techniques and interpretation of the other great pianists of the day such as Godowsky, Hofmann, Paderewski, Schnabel and others. Brilliant pianist though she was, she knew she could learn still more, and whilst entrancing her audiences all over the American continent she sought out Dr Alberto Jonás. * He was a noted teacher under whom she had studied briefly in Berlin around the year 1909 during her concert tour. She held him in very high regard, and as he was now teaching in New York she went to him once again for further advice and instruction, particularly with regard to interpretation. Leginska, like many other noted performers, was not too proud to take lessons, even when she was enjoying great success on the concert platform.

Shortly before her railway accident Leginska's travels had taken her to Cuba, where, in her usual way, she enraptured her audiences. Francisco Acosta wrote in *Musical America*: [12]

"Had it been possible Mme Leginska could have played ten concerts. Her unique personality, extraordinary tonal production, every sweep and unrestrained vehemence of her playing are quite acknowledged facts which most music lovers of the United States have enjoyed; therefore, further comment seems almost out of place. But who that has heard Mme Leginska and appreciated her art can fail to sing her praises a thousand times over? Singularly characteristic in her interpretations, and colossal in the conception of the musical works, she obtains sounds from the piano which are absolutely marvellous . . . With Mme Leginska (quoting Ysidoro Corzo, the

---

* Dr Alberto Jonás was born in Madrid on 8th June 1868 and died in Philadelphia on 9th November 1943. Initially a piano virtuoso who toured extensively throughout Europe, giving more than 2,000 performances, he later devoted himself to teaching. He taught in Michigan (1894-1904), Berlin (1905-14) and in New York from 1914 with a class one day a week in Philadelphia. He was co-author of *The Master-School of Modern Piano-Virtuosity* with Backhaus, Busoni, Friedman, Ganz, Godowsky, Lhevinne, Rosenthal, Sauer and others.

distinguished critic of *Heraldo de Cuba*) 'There can be no question, no discussion; we have to kneel before her despotic sceptre and acclaim her like a goddess. She is a genius, a pianistic marvel who impresses, without effort on her part, her own strong and wonderful personality into every work she interprets.' "

On a more prosaic level, Leginska gave her services the following month (16th March 1917) in a recital for the benefit of charities. *Musical America* referred to her as "Leginska, warm-hearted artist", in its account of the recital that filled Carnegie Hall. After a glowing tribute to her playing the author noted that Leginska "reached technical heights seldom achieved" and "again made many new friends through her sincere, devoted playing". [13]

Throughout 1917 and 1918, years in which (after April 1917) America was engaged in the war in Europe, Ethel Leginska's career continued to prosper and she appeared across America in recitals and in many concerts with major orchestras, often in aid of the war effort. *The Detroit Times* wrote: "Whatever Leginska does, she does with a touch of genius", whilst, not to be outdone in the quest for superlatives, *The Detroit News* observed: [14]

"Leginska has ceased to be an artist, in the sense that she has mounted to the pinnacle of the artist's view and then has come back down to earth again, back to us poor mortals, to bring us something of her vision and experience."

In March 1918 Leginska gave a recital in Carnegie Hall comprising the Sonata in D by Paradies, The Pastorale and Capriccio by Scarlatti, a new piece, *Angelus,* by Leopold Godowsky, *Islamey* by Balakirev, a Polonaise and Berceuse by Chopin, *Mazeppa* by Liszt, and other pieces. According to the report in *The New York American*: [15]

" . . . Such a diverse list would tax the equipment of any but a competent musician. Mme Leginska possesses amazingly agile fingers, supple and vigorous wrists, a beautiful sense of rhythm and dramatic emphasis and physical force and endurance of almost masculine proportions. She also proved her power to seek and reveal poetic moods and inner voices of the tender and subtle episodes in marked contrast to her vehement and ardent exposition of the bravura passages."

As already explained, Leginska's great gifts as a pianist, combined with her unique personality and propensity for attracting publicity, ensured that her name was never out of the newspapers for long. But the event which produced the most publicity of all at this stage of her career was unfortunately her divorce. Court proceedings were protracted, lasting no less than two and a half years. [16] It will be recalled that Ethel and her husband, Emerson Whittern, had been separated since 1912, and whilst Ethel's career was prospering in America, he had remained in London, earning his living by a variety of musical pursuits including that of music critic. But in 1915 he returned to the United States and became editor for the Art Publication Society of St. Louis, a post he was to hold for five years.

Once settled in the United States, the matter of the broken marriage had to be resolved and Leginska began a divorce action against her husband in August 1915, charging non-support. [17] Their son, Cedric, was six years old at the time. Her husband, Ethel told reporters, had never supported her, and four years previously had deserted her, she alleged, after she suggested to him that "he earn some money". It was shortly after he left her that she arrived in New York. She alleged that after she had recently allowed Cedric to visit him, "he sent the child to his folks in Cleveland", and added, "I am seeking custody of my boy".

Prior to the filing of the divorce suit, few Americans other than Leginska's closest friends appear to have realised that she was even married, let alone that she had a six-year-old son, as she looked younger than her age

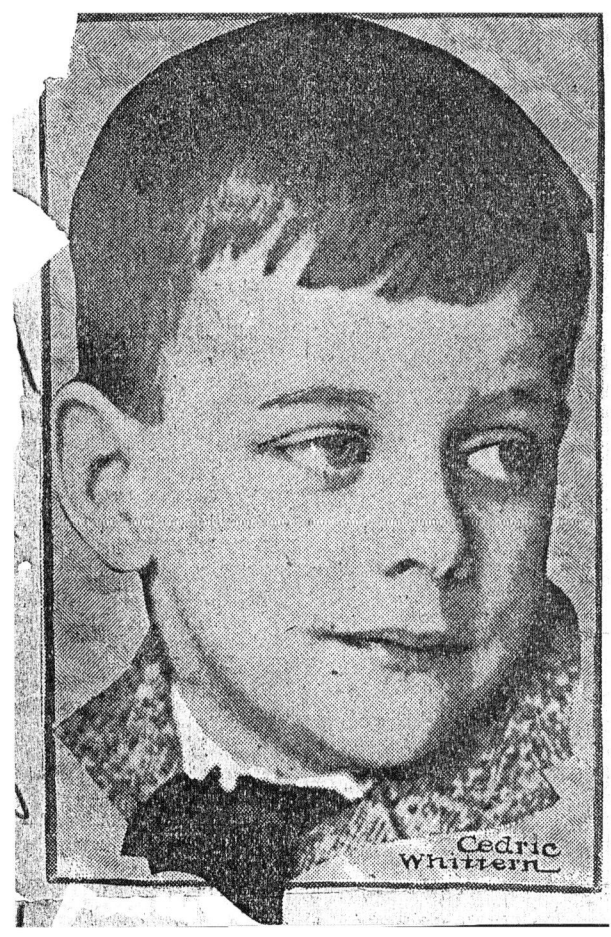

Cedric Whithorne, Ethel Leginska's son, at the time of the divorce proceedings

(29 on 13th April 1915) and her husband had never been with her since her arrival in America. The revelation that she was married, and that she had a son, matters that came to light in all the newspaper reports, astonished the public who had tended to think of her as a kind of prodigiously gifted waif.

The lawsuit became increasingly bitter and Martha Hedman [*] was named in Leginska's suit as "the woman who has caused all the trouble" according to *The Detroit Journal*. [18] Later, Whittern set up a counter-claim for divorce on his own account. Revelling in the unexpected scandal, the same *Detroit Journal* article, in true popular press style, reflected in colourful fashion the general surprise that Leginska was a wife and mother:

"Bang goes another illusion! Ethel Leginska, the marvellous little piano player with the bobbed hair and the plain black frocks and the figure so small that when she's seated at a concert grand piano she always looks like David wading into Goliath, isn't half the child a lot of us imagined she was. No indeed, Miss Leginska not only is not a child, but she is a wife and a mother. And not only is she a wife and a mother, but just now she is a very angry wife and mother, so angry, in fact, that she is suing her husband, Roy Emerson Wittern [*sic*], for divorce and asking that he be made to pay for the education of their son, now six years old.

"Philip Hale, 'H.T.P.', Krehbiel, Henderson [†] – all of the eastern music critics who are supposed to know vaudeville talent from virtuosity, said Ethel was a wonder, and when she finally came to the Arcadia, perched herself on a black bench in front of a black piano, garbed in a black boyish dress, and before a black curtain (with the lights in the auditorium so low that all that was visible on the stage was her face and hands, the keyboard of the piano and one red rose) and flung her whole soul into a program that would have taxed Paderewski, Detroit O.K.'d the verdict of the wise men of the east.

"She played here once later, coored another triumph out at the Ann Arbor Festival, and is scheduled for a concert here next year.

"The impression got abroad on her first visit, and no one took the trouble to correct it, that Miss Leginska was hardly more than a child. Very few people in the town at that time knew that the musical marvel was nearer 30 than 20, and those who did know, of course, didn't say much about it.

"However, the fact remains that Ethel Leginska ranks with the dozen greatest living pianists, and whether her divorce finishes win, lose or draw, she will always be a welcome figure on the concert platform."

As the months dragged on the divorce proceedings continued to make the headlines in all the major American newspapers. The acrimonious bitterness intensified as more charges and counter-charges were filed by both Leginska and Whittern; also by Martha Hedman who filed a $50,000 suit in Chicago

---

[*] Martha Hedman, born Östersund, 12th August 1883 (some sources say 1888); died DeLand, Florida, 20th June 1974. A Swedish-born American actress who enjoyed a successful stage career, mainly in the USA, from 1905 to the 1940s. She also appeared in a few early (silent) films and was on the London stage in two plays at the St. James's Theatre in 1914 when Ethel's husband was working in London. Hedman's picture appeared on a Wills' cigarette card in 1916.

[†] Boston papers: Philip Hale, H.T. Parker; New York papers: W.J. Henderson, H.E. Krehbiel.

against Ethel Leginska for slander. By the middle of 1917 there were five suits and countersuits between Leginska and her husband and the proceedings were complicated by a custody battle between Ethel and Emerson over their son, Cedric, then eight years old. Ethel claimed that Whittern had deserted her. She also insisted that she could earn more than enough to support the child, which was clearly true in view of the great success she was enjoying in the United States. She even offered in court to give up her concert career and instead to become a full-time piano teacher, claiming she could earn $300 a week by her teaching, if the court thought that a career as an itinerant concert pianist was not suitable financially or otherwise for a mother bringing up a child. Whittern's attorney raised every conceivable and seemingly irrelevant reason why Leginska should not have custody; knowing that she smoked, he asked her in court, "Are you addicted to the cigarette habit?" Leginska replied, "If one smokes a cigarette occasionally, is that a habit?"

Whilst all this was going on, Leginska continued her concert career with performances unaffected by the prolonged court case, judging by the glowing reviews she continued to receive. Typical of them are those published by three Detroit newspapers after a concert she gave in the city in May 1917 when she played the Rubinstein D minor concerto:

"Mme Leginska's success was instantaneous and emphatic. In the last ten years no festival audience here has been so tumultuously enthusiastic over an instrumental soloist . . . She put immense physical power into her work, but she put besides this something not gainable in the schools, spiritual force." [19]

"Ethel Leginska received wild applause for her playing of Rubinstein's concerto No. 4, op. 70, in the afternoon concert . . . She is a remarkable young woman, of undoubted musicianship." [20]

"In the afternoon Ethel Leginska was the soloist and huddled over her keyboard and looking for all the world like a tiny elf in the vast auditorium, she swept through Rubinstein's D minor concerto to another of those triumphs which are always hers. Two encores of outstandingly brilliant execution simply served to cement her fast into the hearts of her hearers." [21]

The legal proceedings finally ended early in 1918, and were reported in the *Musical Courier* and other publications, when Leginska was granted a divorce from her husband on 11th February 1918 at Cleveland by Judge Pearson, "on the sole ground of wilful absence on the part of Mr Whithorne", * all other charges having been dropped by both parties. But on the matter of custody, the court ruled against Leginska and she lost custody of her son. Exclusive custody was awarded by Judge Pearson to Emerson Whithorne, "with permission for Ethel Leginska to see him in

---

* He had been using the name Whithorne, instead of Whittern, since 1907-08.

Fame, Fortune – and Divorce

Mr Whithorne's presence or in the presence of someone whom he may appoint". Subsequently Cedric was brought up by her ex-husband's parents. One can only speculate why the judge chose to award custody of Cedric to his father rather than his mother, other than the fact that women had less rights in law, when it was the father who was acknowledged to have deserted, but such was the case. In those days custody was very often given to the father in such circumstances, for no apparent reason.

Back in Hull and Hornsea, Ethel's divorce caused bitterness amongst the more reactionary branches of Ethel's family. 22 This did not make life any easier for Ethel's father. Divorce was then a very rare event indeed in Britain, and by the mores of the country it was socially unacceptable. * There had never been a divorce in the Liggins family before and such an event was seen by some family members (but not all) as a scandal, notwithstanding Ethel's apparent innocence – it was Emerson who deserted.

Ethel's divorce made no difference to her U.S. citizenship which had been granted automatically and unconditionally on her marriage. Having made her home in the USA she remained a United States citizen for the rest of her life. When the divorce was finalised she had already lived in America for five years and had become a great favourite with everyone; she had enormously enriched the cultural scene in the USA. It is surely unthinkable that anyone would have wished to take away her citizenship because of the divorce, and no one did. But the public and critics would always speak and write of her as 'English' because of her birth, upbringing and speech.

With the divorce finalised, Emerson Whithorne passed out of Leginska's life and pursued his own musical career. In 1920 he settled in New York, devoting himself mainly to composition, and was active in the League of Composers. Many compositions appeared, all of modernistic type, several of them in the then-fashionable 'machine music' style. His main musical works are listed in Appendix 6 (page 335). As a result of his compositions, he became a musician of some standing in the United States, and in 1939 he was awarded a public prize by the prestigious Juilliard Foundation for his second symphony. In 1932 at the age of 47, fourteen years after his divorce from Ethel Leginska, he re-married; the maiden name of his wife was Jane Reynolds.† He died aged 73 in Lyme, Connecticut, on 25th March 1958.

With the divorce behind her, a sad chapter in Leginska's life ended. The divorce, and more particularly the loss of custody of her son, were great emotional blows to Ethel. So successful in her career, her personal life was in ruins. But she was a tough campaigner; it was not in her character to let

---

* During 1918 there were less than 1,000 divorces in the whole of Britain.
† Jane Whithorne, born 23rd November 1884, died April 1965 in Connecticut aged 80.

> Cleveland, O., Sept. 27th, 1917.
>
> Dear Mamma:
>
> Thank you for your birthday letter. I certainly did have a happy birthday. I had company, and a large cake with nine pink candles on it and everything nice on a little table in the parlor, flowers, fruit and ice cream etc. I had very nice presents. I have so many toys the folks at home gave me money.
>
> I am now in the high 4th. I skipped six months at school.
>
> 2.
>
> We have a new 1918 Chevrolet machine, and I ride nearly every day.
>
> Love,
>
> Cedric Villiers Whithorne.

This page and opposite: Two poignant letters from Cedric to his mother, written from his paternal grandparents' home in Cleveland. The first was sent during the divorce proceedings and the second after their conclusion when Ethel had lost custody of her son. [23]

> Cleveland, O.
> May, 15, 1918.
>
> Dear Mamma:
>
> I am well and studying my lessons every day.
>
> I go every time the auto goes out of the garage in the day time, but usually go to bed by eight o'clock ever night.
>
> I have an Ingersoll Eclipse watch I can see in the night just as plainly as I can see in the day. I like it very much.
>
> I hope you are well.
>
> Love,
>
> Cedric Williers Whithorne.

the vicissitudes of life get her down. Theodor Leschetizky, her teacher and mentor, had always urged, "Go on! Go on!" when the going got tough in a difficult piece of music. Leginska had been trained to that philosophy and accepted it; it was in her character to do so. She applied it to life as well as to music. Nothing must ruin her career, so life had to go on, and the turmoil and heartaches she had endured must be set aside. The sad events in court would not be allowed to interrupt her march of progress.

Leginska continued her busy programme of concerts and recitals after the trauma of the divorce case just as though nothing had happened and her performances drew excellent reviews as always. A few are printed here as a sample of hundreds of similar ones she was receiving at that time:

In April 1918 *The Washington Post* noted: [24]

"Her playing is electrifying, both in her interpretations and in her technical skill. Mme Leginska is one of the most interesting pianists before the public today. Her interpretations are both bold and original and her technic and tone tremendous."

Later in the year, after appearing at the Maine Music Festivals in Bangor (Maine) and Portland, the *Bangor Daily News* observed: [25]

"Music lovers of eastern Maine again paid tribute to the wonderful pianistic spell of Ethel Leginska. The audience sat spellbound under the sway of what is undoubtedly the greatest woman player of the century. There is a fiery sweep to her playing that carries all before it and her style has burning intensity. The lights and shadows of her first programme number, Liszt's concerto in E flat, were rendered with exquisite grace, and finely differentiated graduations between the extremes. She was recalled many times.

"Among the stars that have blazed across the firmament of eastern Maine, none has made a more powerful appeal, achieved greater triumphs, or shone with more extraordinary luster than Ethel Leginska, the pianistic marvel. She is dynamic in energy, a musical Joan of Arc, a genius moved by unseen powers, and only from inborn inspiration could such restless, dramatic superplaying emanate. Within all her work there is presented the touch of the master. The accurate sense of dramatic values. Energy raised to the nth power. A delicacy of tone, the ease of perfect knowledge, and a power of reflexes that only time and inborn talent combined can ever possibly achieve."

The *Portland Sunday Telegram* reported in similar vein: [26]

"Ethel Leginska, the wonderful young pianist, has visited Maine on several occasions. Since her earlier appearances, her art has grown and her work is more finished, and her perfect assurance is a very convincing factor. The first impression with this unique artist is always amazement at the perfect ease and facility of her technique. Her mastery of the instrument is of course an acknowledged fact and her beautiful liquid tones are a marvel."

Reporting in January 1919 on a Leginska recital, the *Ohio State Journal* summarised her qualities and her position in the world of music: [27]

"Ethel Leginska, a pianist who always arouses admiration, gave a recital in Aeolian Hall last Saturday. I think it is generally acknowledged that Miss Leginska is the greatest woman pianist of the day, and it might be added that she is a much greater artist than many male pianists who are appearing in the concert halls these days. Miss Leginska played last Saturday in a manner to arouse unbounded enthusiasm a program which included Beethoven's sonata, Op. 53, three études by Chopin, Liszt's Rhapsodie No. 8, and a group of compositions by Edward MacDowell. Miss Leginska's playing disclosed the usual brilliancy of style, preponderance of technical ability, and excellence of tone which are hers. Few pianists today arouse more enthusiasm."

The last three reviews, all penned just after the end of the Great War, and others like them confirm Leginska's standing as the foremost woman pianist of the day, her last rival for the accolade, the formidable Teresa Carreño, having died in June 1917. Yet only six years had passed since Leginska's American debut. She had come a long way in a very short time.

All this, of course, had brought considerable financial reward and it is worth noting that, rather can keeping all the money for herself, Ethel made generous financial gifts to some of her relatives back home in war-torn

Britain. In December 1917 a six-page letter to Ethel from her Aunt Lucy in Hull, which gave a moving account of life in Hull at the time, mentioning local young men who had lost their lives in the war, was clearly prompted by a generous Christmas gift from Ethel. Lucy's letter begins: [28]

"I was more than glad to receive your letter dated Dec. 6th this morning. I have been very worried about you; no one seems safe in this war-weary world now-a-days; it is a great comfort to know you are well and prosperous.

Many thanks for your generous gift; you are more than kind to us. What have we ever done for you, to deserve such loving kindness? We can only say "thank you" and promise not to waste and squander your gift. I must ask Tom [Lucy's son, 20, who was fighting in France] if there be anything he would like, and to give him as much pleasure as possible."

Clearly, the sad divorce case had not harmed the affection in which Ethel was held by at least some members of her family.

LEGINSKA

Photo by Underwood & Underwood, N. Y.

"A Pianist of Striking Individuality"

A publicity photograph from around 1918

References: Chapter 8

1. *Musical Courier*, 15th March 1917.
2. *Toledo Blade*, 26th September 1917 (writing about the train crash the previous winter).
3. *Buffalo Courier*, 14th February 1917.
4. *Buffalo Express*, 14th February 1917.
5. *The New York Times*, 26th February 1917.
6. *The New York Evening Mail*, 26th February 1917.
7. *The New York Evening Journal*, 26th February 1917.
8. *The New York Evening Sun*, 26th February 1917.
9. *The New York Evening Post*, 26th February 1917.
10. *Musical America*, 18th July 1914.
11. *Musical America* (interview with Harriette Brower), 24th May 1913.
12. *Musical America*, 15th February 1917.
13. *Musical America*, 28th March 1917.
14. *Musical America*, 3rd January 1918 (quoting extracts from recent issues of *The Detroit Times* and *The Detroit News*).
15. *The New York American*, 12th March 1918.
16. Leginska's divorce proceedings were covered in all the major American newspapers at regular intervals over a lengthy period.
17. *St. Louis Globe*, 11th August 1915.
18. *The Detroit Journal*, 25th May 1917.
19. *The Detroit Free Press*, 5th May 1917.
20. *Detroit News*, 5th May 1917.
21. *The Detroit Journal*, 5th May 1917.
22. Information from the late Mrs Marjorie Langdale (Ethel Leginska's cousin) of Hornsea. Personal correspondence, 1982.
23. The letters are in the Archives of the International Piano Museum at Maryland. Copies were kindly supplied by the Curator, Mr Donald Manildi.
24. *The Washington Post*, 13th April 1918.
25. *Bangor Daily News*, 20th November 1918.
26. *Portland Sunday Telegram*, 24th November 1918.
27. *Ohio State Journal*, 21st January 1919.
28. Letter dated 27th December 1917 from Ethel's Aunt Lucy (Witty) from her home at 20, Albany Street, Hull. Copy of it courtesy of the International Piano Archives at Maryland.

Note that Emerson's and Cedric's surnames were given as 'Whittern' in nearly all the newspaper reports of the divorce case, and Cedric's picture in the press was captioned 'Cedric Villiers Whittern' though Emerson had been using the name Whithorne since around 1907, and Cedric's name was legally Whithorne since that was the name on his birth certificate. However the judge, in granting the divorce and awarding custody of Cedric to his father, used the name 'Whithorne'. As stated earlier, Emerson changed his name legally to Whithorne in 1918.

Chapter 9

Widening Horizons

Leginska's great success as a pianist had clearly not come about solely through her talent and personality, abundantly though she possessed these qualities. A great deal of hard work had been involved. Moreover, she had never been one to rest on her laurels. Throughout her concert career she was always keen to learn all she could from her musical contemporaries. In an interview reported in *The Etude* in May 1919 Leginska described her approach to learning: [1]

"In the matter of personal lessons Leschetizky was an individualist . . . but there it stopped. His idea was to bring his pupils up to a certain standard of excellence and let them develop their own special individualities after leaving his hands. This I have personally sought to do, through self-study, reflection and conferences with my colleagues Mr Godowsky,* Walter Damrosch,** Paul Goldschmidt † of Berlin and, at present with Mr Alberto Jonás †† and many other artists. In this splendid fraternity of art, the workers of the higher type are always glad to co-operate for the benefit of their personal technic and interpretation."

Having in the previous chapter followed Leginska's concert career through to the end of her seventh successful American season in 1919, let us go back in time a few months to the summer of 1918, for it was then that a new facet to her career took shape – composition. Even in the early years of her success as a pianist she had found time to compose a few short musical pieces (see page 105); by 1918 she had completed some songs, a piano sonata and a string quartet. And even before that she was not new to

---

* Leopold Godowsky (1870 - 1938): Polish-born pianist who settled in the USA in 1914. He is generally regarded as one of the greatest pianists of all time, and as a teacher he was much respected and sought-after. His teaching was not restricted to those who were, or aspired to become, concert pianists. The jazz pianists James P. Johnson and Thomas 'Fats' Waller were amongst those who went to him for advice.

** Walter Damrosch (1862 - 1950): German-born American conductor, composer and educator. He was resident conductor of the New York Symphony Orchestra from its reorganisation in 1903 until 1927.

† Paul Goldschmidt (1882 - 1917): German pianist active in the early part of the 20th century; former pupil of Leschetizky and Schnabel. He recorded 22 'Ducartist' piano rolls (serial numbers 1304 to 1325 inclusive) for J.D. Philipps & Söhne, Frankfurt-am-Main.

†† Alberto Jonás (1868 - 1943): A short biography of Alberto Jonás is given on page 106. His famous book on piano playing, written jointly with several other pianists, was a very popular and successful treatise which went through five editions.

composition for, like all professional musicians, she had studied it as part of her training. Nevertheless, like the dedicated professional she was, she would not embark on serious composition without further tuition, and to that end she spent the summer of 1918 studying composition under the guidance of Ernest Bloch, probably the most eminent composer living and working in the USA at that time.* As a composer Bloch knew exactly what he was about, and he had the skill to impart his knowledge to others. Leginska could not have chosen a better teacher; her period of study with him was so successful that it marked a turning point in her career.

Leginska's summer of 1918 was full of invigorating hard work mixed with blissful relaxation. In September *Musical Courier* published a picture of Leginska on the beach 'somewhere on the Jersey coast' with the three children of Ernest Bloch, all of them clad in bathing costumes as they anticipated a dip (see below). [2] One of the children, Lucienne Bloch Dimitroff, recalled "the jolly times" they had in a letter to the authors: [3]

"I remember her very well though I was nine years old. For our family it was the first time we had been on vacation in the USA, near the shores of the Atlantic, and Miss Leginska would join us to play on the beach. She had a remarkable face and was full of gusto."

LEGINSKA SUMMERING

"Far from the subdued lights of concert halls, Ethel Leginska, the brilliant little English pianist, is spending her summer. In this picture, taken somewhere on the Jersey coast, Leginska is anticipating a dip in the brine with the children of Ernest Bloch, the composer. It is no longer a secret that the pianist has been taking lessons from the celebrated Swiss composer, and that some of her work will shortly be published."

Musical Courier, 12th September 1918

---

* Ernest Bloch was born in Switzerland in 1880 and studied in Brussels, at Frankfurt (where he studied under Iwan Knorr, one of Leginska's teachers) and Munich. He lived for a while in Paris but returned to Geneva where he lectured on musical aesthetics. He visited the USA for the first time in 1916 as conductor for the Maud Allan Dance Company and in 1917 he became a teacher of composition at the David Mannes School in New York as well as teaching privately in the city. It was in New York that Leginska went to him for private lessons in composition. In 1920 he became Director of the Cleveland Institute of Music and from 1925 to 1930 was Director of the San Francisco Conservatory before returning to Switzerland in the 1930s. As the political situation worsened in Europe he wisely moved once again, in 1938, to America, settled there, and taught at Berkeley, California. He retired from active musical work in 1952 and died in Portland, Oregon in 1959. In spring 1968 an Ernest Bloch Society was established in the USA, largely through the efforts of the three Bloch children, Suzanne, Lucienne and Ivan.

Bloch is mainly noted for his work as a Jewish composer. The titles of his works bear witness to his deep-rooted preoccupation with Jewish culture – the *Israel* symphony, the *Baal Shem* suite for violin, the *Sacred Service*, and many others. But Bloch's importance does not depend on his Jewish-oriented specialisation, for some of his rhapsodic and colourful composition shows a passionate intensity, especially in a number of his early compositions and in his chamber music.

Leginska's readiness to give interviews has already been remarked on. It gave her the opportunity to make what amounted to statements to the public of her current doings and her plans for the future. In an interview reported in *Musical Courier* in September 1918 she explained to her admiring public why she was not currently giving concerts: [4]

Introducing Ethel Leginska, Composer

Brilliant Pianist Spends Summer in Developing Creative Powers

"There was a strange silence about Ethel Leginska's activities this summer, but to no-one who knows her boundless energy and infinite capacity for work, as well as her vivid, restless spirit, did it seem possible that two whole months could be spent in "just vacation", not even after a concert season that should have exhausted the strongest and most travel hardened of artists.

"However, the secret is out – Leginska has been composing! Under the guidance of Ernest Bloch, whose talent she greatly admires, Leginska composed during the past two months five songs, a piano composition, and partly finished a quartet for strings. Questioned as to how she got started on the path of composer, the little pianist modestly admitted that a year or so ago she wrote a song called "In a Garden", which her friend, Rafael Diaz, the tenor of the Metropolitan Opera Company, heard and immediately asked permission to sing in public. Trying it out in manuscript form, he found it went so well with audiences that he was invariably called upon to repeat it. To date he has sung this song over one hundred times in public.

"From that time, whenever a poem or a bit of verse appealed to her, Leginska put it aside, and this summer, after her concert season was over, she started to set these verses to music. The result – so all who have heard her compositions say – is remarkable, and during this season audiences all over the country will have an opportunity to judge for themselves, as already several prominent singers have placed Leginska songs on their programmes. For instance, Arthur Middleton, the well known baritone, will sing "The Gallows Tree" and "Forgotten", both of which he calls "gems". Marcia van Dresser, the soprano, and Rafael Diaz will give a group of three of them at his Aeolian Hall recital, entitled "At Dawn", "I Have a Rendezvous with Death" and "In a Garden". At her joint recital with Leginska in Detroit, Nina Morgana will sing a group of her songs to the composer-pianist's own accompaniment. *

---

* The singers mentioned in this *Musical Courier* article were all 'top artists' at the time:

Rafael (or Rafaelo) Diaz (1884 - 1943), American tenor who studied in America, Berlin and Italy. Starting out with the Boston Opera Company, he later toured with Luisa Tetrazzini and was a principal with the Metropolitan Opera Company from 1917 until 1936.

Arthur Middleton (1880 - 1929) was an American operatic bass-baritone who joined the 'Met' in 1914. Several years later he gave up opera in favour of recitals and oratorios.

Marcia van Dresser (1880 - 1937) was an American operatic and concert soprano who sang at the 'Met', and in principal roles at Covent Garden and with the Chicago Opera Company.

Nina Morgana, born in Buffalo, 1891 (not 1895 as is often stated), died New York, 1986; sang at La Scala, toured with Caruso in 1919, sang with the Chicago Opera Company in 1919-20 and was with the 'Met' from 1920 to 1936. At the age of nine she had sung at the Buffalo Exposition of 1901 as "The Child Patti". She married Caruso's secretary, Bruno Zirato, in 1921.

"It was after hearing her play some of her own compositions that a very well known musician penned the following "Portrait of Leginska":

> *Blue and white and gold are*
> *   Her colors!*
> *Save where the Rubies of Life stain*
> *   Her lips!*
> *In frail hands, she holds the music of*
> *   Tomorrow –*
> *And upon her lies the grim-black mantle*
> *   Pale Genius! "*

Leginska relaxing at the Ernest Bloch's summer home, 1918
Photograph purchased via Ernest Bloch's daughter Lucienne, and included with her permission

Leginska's new-found enthusiasm for composition was bearing fruit, and in February 1919 *Musical Courier* announced that G. Schirmer had just accepted four of Leginska's songs for publication.[5] They were *At Dawn*, *Spring Song*, *The Gallows Tree* and *Winter*. Two of them had recently been sung at a concert in Detroit by Nina Morgana, soprano, with Leginska accompanying, as anticipated in the interview reported on the previous page. Meanwhile, in the spring of 1919, whilst still engaged in her 1918 - 19 concert tour as a pianist, she had appeared in another role, that of manager, having arranged an engagement for one of her students, Paula Pardee, as piano soloist at one of the Metropolitan Opera Company's Sunday night concerts.[6] This act was entirely typical of Leginska, for whatever her own busy schedule happened to be she was always diligent in promoting the musical careers of her students.

As her interest in composition grew, Leginska announced in June 1919 that she intended to spend the summer in continuing to compose, and to teach. [7] To Leginska teaching was always a joy, never a chore.

In June 1919 Clare Peeler interviewed "The Leonine Little Pianist" for *Musical America* [8] in a wide-ranging discussion encompassing golf, Leginska's future, relaxation (in the usual and in the technical pianistic meaning) and attitudes to music, teaching and composition. Leginska forcefully made the point that the years of constant appearances on the concert platform had been a strain, mentally and physically. Her present lifestyle, with golf high on the list of priorities, had been a tonic. "Now I feel young all over again", she said. Clare Peeler observed:

"Certain it is that the last time I saw Ethel Leginska she was a tense, black-frocked, white-faced little spirit of fire. Yesterday she was a blue-eyed, brown-faced little English girl in a gingham frock. But of course the intensity, the vivid intellectuality of her, the almost too-great force of vitality with which she attacks every subject came to the surface in short order. If the leopard does not change his spots, neither do little lions."

On the subject of how the relaxation she applied to her piano playing helped her to be a better golf player Leginska remarked in the interview:

"It's funny how things are interrelated. They tell me at the golf-club that one reason why I shall some day make a good player is that I don't stiffen up while I play; I am thoroughly relaxed. Now, physical relaxation is just one of the primary requisites, as you know, of the pianist; whole books have been written on the subject. Then, I contend, with the physical relaxation comes the mental ease that one must be pervaded with in order to interpret one's artistic message without self-consciousness. If you are stiff in body you are stiff in mind."

From the start Leginska's compositions were modern in style and were to remain so. A good example is her *Gargoyles of Notre Dame*, written in 1918 and accepted for publication by Schirmer in 1919. Based on Victor Hugo's book, the composition was an imaging of the chimaera,* in the moonlight, with the sounds of the city drifting up. Describing the piece, Leginska explained:

"There is the spirit in the air of many bells, of all the bells that ring in Paris and that have rung; there are the tragedies, the comedies that those stone figures have seen, all condensed into their philosophical sneer. I went over to Paris for days and steeped myself into their pictures of those weird figures."

After playing the piece for Clare Peeler during the interview, "a cigarette between her lips, eyes shut, frowning" as Miss Peeler reported, Leginska remarked:

---

* A fabled fire-spouting monster with a lion's head, a serpent's tail and a goat's body.

"It's awfully modern. I've used D minor in one hand, E flat major in the other, and I'm going to write two signatures. My new song is very modern in style too. Why shouldn't it be? I'm intensely modern. Ernest Bloch, with whom I'm working at composition, doesn't discourage any such tendencies of mine in the slightest."

On the subject of teaching, Leginska explained that grappling with the problems of others provided a fascinating recreation:

"I don't know why teaching is considered by so many to be a drudgery. To me it is most interesting. I find the same joy in diagnosing and prescribing for a pupil's difficulties that a physician finds in prescribing for a patient. I can immediately judge the mental quality of a pupil by the way she* plays, and it is very interesting to observe the gradual development and broadening of her mental powers as exemplified in her piano playing. One gets so tired of his or her own problems that it is really refreshing to get a glimpse of others, and, incidentally, it also helps an artist in his own career – this smoothing out of others' stumbling blocks. In addition to my teaching I also plan to do some more composing this summer and first of all I want to finish a string quartet which I started on last season."

Leginska did in fact spend the summer of 1919 composing and teaching. She took a cottage near the golf club in Staten Island, New York. One day a week she travelled in to New York City to teach in her hired studio near Central Park; the rest of the time she composed and relaxed by pursuing her new-found hobby of golf.

It is hardly surprising that the musical youth of America, particularly the female ones, beat a path to Leginska's door for lessons. She had become so well known through her concert appearances and her unique dress and hair style as to be virtually a cult figure, especially to young women, most of whom wanted to imitate her. The noted critic James Huneker had spoken of the 'numberless little Leginskas' with their bobbed hair and their intensity, scattered through the audiences at piano recitals. Leginska remarked, in her interview with Clare Peeler:

"I can't really laugh at their taking my hair and dress so seriously that they copy it; it's merely the outward expression of an inward loyalty that touches me very much."

A *Cleveland Press* reporter, after calling at Leginska's studio to watch her give a lesson, wrote: [9]

"And right here it must be said that if a pupil does not progress under this artist's guidance, it is only the former's stupidity or carelessness that is to blame, for every word of direction was surprisingly descriptive."

Through the 1919-20 winter season Leginska kept to her promise of abstaining from the concert platform, much to the regret of her many admirers. *Musical Courier* observed: [10]

---

* Most of Leginska's pupils were female, but not all.

"So great, indeed, is Leginska's hold on her admirers that when her health demanded the cancellation of the 1919-20 dates, many of the concerts refused a substitute. 'Leginska or no-one', one manager is said to have declared."

But to compensate, new compositions were coming off the Leginska assembly line. To add to the piano piece *Gargoyles of Notre Dame*, which had been performed twice publicly during the season, came a scherzo on words by Tagore entitled *Oh! Mad, Superbly Drunk*. The latter piece was dedicated to the pianist Rudolph Ganz, whom Leginska admired as an artist and person. Another song, for baritone, with words by Dunsany, was in process of completion and other works were already completed: a symphonic poem *Beyond the Fields We Know*, a quartet for strings, and a chamber work for eleven instruments.

In October 1919 Leginska expanded on her reasons for withdrawing temporarily from the concert platform. After admitting that seven years of incessant concert work had left her tired out and with a great desire to enjoy a little of life, she explained: [11]

"It's a terrible strain, perhaps more than most people realise. The memorizing alone is taxing, and then the travelling about the country, season after season, with always the thought of satisfying your audience. You see, when I concertize, I give up everything else. It is so necessary for one to give his or her audience a definite message. I feel it is a great wrong for an artist to continue to play when he feels his work is not at its best, merely because of the money that is in it. I can't do it! Do you suppose when an overworked artist approaches the piano with a sense of loathing in his heart that he is doing the right thing? No; each time it should be with an intense longing to express what he feels!"

A feature of Leginska's teaching that was to be maintained throughout her life was the 'Leginska evening' or 'Leginska musicale', in which the more talented of her pupils provided a programme of music, open to the public, with Leginska herself in a subsidiary role. One of these took place on 16th January 1920 in Steinway Hall, New York, and featured a number of pupils including two who were to remain Leginska's lifelong friends, Lucille Oliver and Evelione Taglione; their names will crop up again in later chapters. [12] Another took place, again in Steinway Hall, a month later. *Musical Courier* reported: [13]

"On Monday evening the pupils of Ethel Leginska were heard in an unusually interesting recital at Steinway Hall. This season, as is well known, this talented mistress of the keyboard is devoting all her time to composing and teaching, and the results that she is achieving in those who are fortunate enough to be under her guidance were clearly demonstrated in their playing."

The programmes in these musicales were lengthy and featured a range of music from the classical to the modern era. In the latter category were included Leginska's "striking and richly colored" *Gargoyles de Notre Dame* and Leo Ornstein's *Impressions of Chinatown*. The Grieg A major concerto in a two-piano version (the second piano providing the equivalent of the orchestra) was also performed in the programme, with Leginska at the second piano.

Leginska was clearly relishing the teaching role that her absence from the concert platform had allowed. It therefore came as no surprise to her friends and admirers when, in the summer of 1920, she announced an extension to her withdrawal from her role as concert pianist. Her announcement in 1918 that she had taken up composition was only the beginning of her widening interests. In 1919 and the earlier part of 1920 she had let it be known that she wanted to devote her time, at any rate for a few months, to composing, teaching and leisure, but by mid-1920 her ideas had expanded to the extent that she wanted to add the conducting of orchestras to her many skills, and the promotion of concerts at prices that were within the reach of ordinary people.

Leginska had decided to move from New York to Boston, favouring the more rural environment there, and had acquired a small house on a hill top in Malden, a Boston suburb. Her new house was in a quiet area with a friendly atmosphere which she enjoyed, and which she felt suited her requirements of building her more broadly-based artistic pattern. She had employed a companion to help run the house but at the same time she herself enjoyed doing some of the cooking. For extra company she acquired a Persian kitten. There was an English-style garden, and Leginska in frilly blue dress, pottering in the garden, became a familiar sight and was a far cry from her usual image of the intense, black-clad, dynamic figure of the concert stage. Into one small room of her house, next to her living room, she managed to squeeze two grand pianos.

Leginska's decision to withdraw for a while from the concert stage had aroused a lot of comment and not a little speculation from those suspicious of her stated motives. Why should a concert pianist at the summit of her powers want to throw away a wonderfully successful career, albeit temporarily, to concentrate on composing and conducting an orchestra? Few people appear to have realised that to Leginska it was not so much a withdrawal as the opening of new horizons. To her the years as a concert pianist had been merely an intermediate period in her development. She expounded some of her views about her place in the musical scene, about life in general, and the reasons for her temporary withdrawal from the concert stage, in an interview reported in the *Christian Science Monitor* under the headline "Larger Service to Music Sought by Leginska": [14]

"There is an opinion about that I am sulking over something. That's rubbish. I am perfectly happy.

"This hill top", she will say to a visitor, "is a very good place for me indeed. It is spacious. Winds do people good. And – Oh, there's so much before me. I have near neighbors, too. There is the suburban atmosphere. Now I could not live in New York and have that, could I?

"You see, I mean to work in people's music and one must not do that living in a castle by oneself, must one? And, besides the people near me, there are lovely walks – Americans do not walk half enough – and there are bright children to play baseball here with me in my backyard when I need relaxation. You see one does well to choose, so, for a place in which to work."

Leginska's interviewer described her appearance:

"She is small in stature with much unruly dark hair, barely touched with flashes of bronze. Leginska's hands are extraordinarily powerful. They could only belong to an exceptionally trained pianist."

Leginska's sudden expressions and a vigorous, turbulent, habit of thought were also noted by her interviewer:

"She will stare at a rose-striped tulip in her hand and suddenly burst forth: "It isn't knowledge that orders accomplishment in the world. It is imagination. Any fool can buy knowledge, but imagination is that expensive thing that God gives us in the beginning – or does not give us . . . " and then break off and say, "The wind doesn't seem to appreciate that this is my newest and best dress", as her chiffons, blue like the smoke of a mountain lookout, whisper and swirl."

Expanding on her views on music and on her own role, Leginska wanted, she said, to become an ambassador to great audiences on the profundities of music. But she realised she was inexperienced and required schooling. That was why she had gone to Ernest Bloch to learn how to compose well. She had also had advice, she said, from Rubin Goldmark * on harmony, and proposed having further tuition in the future on composition. Nothing was to be left to chance. The job must be done properly.

Outlining her philosophy of music, Leginska explained that she had wanted to "outgrow being a soloist" in order to learn to be of greater artistic service. Her aim, she said, was to be part of a "co-operative design", and the best way a musician could achieve that was by being the conductor of an

---

* Rubin Goldmark (1872 - 1936) was a famous American composer and teacher who in his youth had studied at the Vienna Conservatory with Rafael Joseffy (piano) and Antonin Dvorák (composition). For 20 years from 1902 he gave private lessons in piano and theory and it was in New York that Leginska had consulted him. He also taught at various musical institutions in the USA and in 1924 was appointed Head of Composition at the Juilliard School in New York, where he remained until his death. Aaron Copland and several other American composers studied under him.

Left:

"LEGINSKA
The pianistic marvel"

The photograph and accompanying caption included in the Musical Courier article, 26th September 1918

Right:

Leginska in her Boston garden, 1920

The photograph included in the Christian Science Monitor article, 4th June 1920

orchestra. She had definite views on the prices of admission to orchestral music of good quality, and felt that these were prohibitively high as far as most ordinary people were concerned. She thought that those who appreciated good music and responded to its ennobling influences should be able to hear it at moderate prices. Music should, Leginska explained, be free, ideally, but if that were not to be possible it should be available at an economic price. She added that she would rather present a concert of symphony music to an audience of thousands who came because they could afford the 25 cents or 50 cents charged, than to a few hundred who were able to pay $5 and did so because it was fashionable to attend.

The mercurial, impulsive musical genius, Ethel Leginska, was resolved to seek a new beginning. She felt she could achieve no more if she were to continue working solely as a concert pianist. She would go on playing in concerts, but that would no longer be the *only* facet of her career. She felt that her concert work had become, after 15 years, irksome, and explained:

"One is not required always to remain a concert pianist simply because one has been one. There are thousands of concert pianists, admirable ones, all the world needs. One may learn to play the piano as a parrot learns to use words. But I like to think that I did not play as a parrot talks."

Leginska was aware that some people who had been ardent admirers of her as a concert pianist felt that she had been ungrateful to her audiences for seemingly deserting them. She argued that this was not the case:

"I can give more in a different medium than I have been giving. It will not be 'Leginska is playing today', it will be 'The orchestra Leginska is conducting is playing today'. In the East there are men you know whose lives are spent as musical pilgrims, who go about teaching and singing and playing voluntarily and without charge for those who have no money to spend, because to them it is a matter of pride that simple people shall not lose their ancient heritage of joy that comes from knowing good music."

Leginska then put the whole matter in a nutshell, though, one suspects, with a certain amount of exaggeration to make her point:

"To turn to composing and conducting is for me to turn to a more serious and important work, to unselfish service. Leginska, as a pianist, has disappeared. I am glad. I never liked her."

After Leginska's two sabbatical seasons, from the summer of 1919, it was not long before she re-emerged though, not surprisingly when her recent statements were taken into account, less as a concert pianist only, but more as a combined concert pianist, composer, and later, conductor. Her *Four Poems for String Quartet* were given a semi-public performance in Boston, Massachusetts, on 25th April 1921, after which she sailed to Britain for their "official" first public performance. This took place at the Aeolian Hall,

London on Tuesday 14th June 1921 with Leginska in attendance. The London String Quartet played three of the "poems", and they seem to have made a favourable impression on the London critics. The *Evening Standard* reported: [15]

"She is a composer of excellent technique and ideas. 'Three Poems' for string quartet contained passages that were extremely beautiful, and others that were strikingly effective from other points of view."

In similar vein the *Morning Post* observed: [16]

"There was no fumbling in the expression of Leginska's ideas. Some of her patterns – rhythmic and harmonic – in the first were extremely ingenious. By her independence and skill Leginska is certainly a composer from whom something may be expected."

Whilst in Britain Leginska appeared in several chamber music recitals with the cellist Hans Kindler * during the season of 1921 - 22 and gave a number of solo piano recitals in various cities, including her home city of Hull. She also took the opportunity to study composition further, this time with Eugene Goossens † in London. During her stay in Britain Leginska took an apartment at 52, Tedworth Gardens, Chelsea, as her London base. [17]

Poster of Leginska's recital in London, June 1921

---

* Hans Kindler (1892 - 1949) was a Dutch cellist who became a noted conductor in the USA.
† Eugene Goossens (1893 - 1962) was a gifted English conductor and composer of Belgian extraction, one of a famous family of musicians. He was knighted in 1955.

On her return to the USA, Leginska's *From a Life* for 13 instruments was performed in New York on 9th January 1922 and *Beyond the Fields We Know*, a symphonic poem written in 1921, was first heard at a concert in New York early in 1922. This work was also performed in Germany and became a favourite with audiences there, winning the acclaim of critics in Berlin and Munich. It was regarded in Germany as the work of a composer possessed of abundant original imagination and orchestral talents.

It is interesting and perhaps surprising that Leginska, an outstandingly talented pianist, produced compositions written mostly for instruments other than the piano. Perhaps this was one way of getting away from her image as a concert pianist; it could also have been a way to explore new fields.

During the early 1920s, whilst Leginska was enjoying her new career of combined concert pianist and composer, she often visited her home country of Britain, and when she appeared in concerts and recitals she liked to include some of her own compositions on the programme. In the summer of 1922 she was in London to give a piano recital at Queen's Hall (where she had first appeared as a 10-year-old 26 years earlier) on 8th July, and on 22nd November of the same year she was back there again to give another recital, in a programme displaying her dual skills of pianist and composer. *The Musical Times* reported: [18]

ETHEL LEGINSKA

"This young lady of Hull allowed us, at Queen's Hall, the privilege of considering her both as pianist and composer, a privilege enhanced by the help she had from Mr Goossens's extraordinarily fine orchestra. The public ought to have been more numerous, for Miss Leginska (as she reminded us with her first half dozen bars in a Mozart concerto) is of the race of real pianists. The play was sprightly, fine and feeling. Miss Leginska as composer has sat at the feet of Bloch and Goossens, and we heard her symphonic poem *Beyond the fields we know*, fields where she has diligently planted a lot of little parterres and herbacious borders with quantities of odd little exotics, often pleasing, taken one by one."

In 1922 Leginska composed a lullaby for piano entitled *Cradle Song*, which became quite popular. It is reproduced in full, with the publisher's permission, in the following two pages. A short piece, it was of modern style for its day and was later recorded by Leginska on a Duo-Art piano roll. The roll was issued in December 1924. It is rather similar to some of the preludes of John Ireland in construction. 'Modern' music has of course always been an acquired taste, and there are degrees of modernity. When the authors first heard this piece it seemed a little discordant and unmelodious but on further hearing we came to the conclusion it was rather pleasant – an opinion shared by others who have come to know the composition.

Cradle Song

ETHEL LEGINSKA

Widening Horizons

Cradle Song was dedicated by Leginska to her friends the Russian-born British conductor Albert Coates and his wife Madelon, and was written for their daughter, Tamara. Joseph Enos, a former student of Leginska, has commented on the structure of *Cradle Song* and its value for teaching purposes: [19]

"The piece is a publisher's dream . . . she places accidentals in every measure except the first two lines of page three . . . forcing the student to read the sharps and flats and naturals rather than following easily with a key signature. Also, the piece follows closely Leginska's demand that the student [should] study only works that require dexterity and facility in both hands rather than learning music where the right hand progresses technically while the left hand is left behind. You will notice that the left hand confronts the identical problems of the right hand. Then on the first two lines of page three she introduces wide spread chords without the burden of added accidentals, a problem to solve manually (spread)."

The modern style of *Cradle Song* is echoed in all Leginska's compositions. As a pianist she played all kinds of music but the basis of her repertoire was the classical (in the broad sense) fare represented by Beethoven, Brahms, Mendelssohn, Mozart, Schubert, etc. As a composer her compositions stand very squarely in the modern era, with few hints of classicism. It is perhaps worth noting, in passing, that Artur Schnabel, the arch-specialist in the classical repertoire, composed a few pieces of music – all strictly 'modern' in type. Perhaps classical pianists, in their leisure time, like to break away and do something quite different.

Cradle Song is not too difficult to play and is within the scope of the good amateur pianist. A longer, and much more difficult piece technically, is *Dance of a Puppet,* published in 1924. This is a piece for the professional pianist, and most amateurs to whom the authors have shown it have found it very difficult. It is a composition of character, with a fiery rhythm and long intervals, conjuring up its subject in musical terms with a vivid reality.

The above two pieces, *Cradle Song* and *Dance of a Puppet* were the only published compositions by Leginska written specifically for the piano, at any rate for many years, and probably sold more copies of sheet music (particularly *Cradle Song*) than her other music which required the deployment of several instruments for its performance. But during the 1920s a steady stream of compositions for various instruments and voice appeared. *Two Short Pieces for Orchestra,* written in 1922, was performed by the Boston Symphony Orchestra on 29th February 1924 with Pierre Monteux conducting. *Quatre Sujets Barbares,* written in 1923, was performed in Munich on 13th December 1924 with Leginska herself conducting. It is a four-movement suite for orchestra and was inspired by some of the paintings of Gauguin. The next set of compositions was *Six Nursery Rhymes*, for soprano and small orchestra, written in 1923 and performed regularly from that date. Each of the nursery rhymes was also published in a piano arrangement with a very engaging 1920s-style nursery picture on every front cover (see page 339). The six nursery rhymes are:

Gorgy Porgy; Sleep, Baby, Sleep; Little Boy Blue; Three Mice Went into a Hole; Jack and Jill; Old King Cole.

The music critic Bruno David Ussher described these pieces: [20]

"These 'Six Nursery Songs for Chamber Orchestra and Soprano' are highly original, whimsical, dreamy, wistful, mockingly sad, and grotesque. There is 'Gorgy-Porgy', only nine bars long, but even then Leginska (musical tom-boy that she is) insinuates cleverly how running away does not help pie-eating girl-kissing Gorgy, that fat little coward, who is thrashed in the end. 'Sleep, Baby, Sleep' is more seriously artistic and uncommonly ingenious, based on triads without inter-modulatory chords of other intervallic nature. It is a crooning song which has much of the folk-like.

"Altogether these are songs of characteristic English humor. 'Little Boy Blue' is a shimmering dream picture into which the muted bleating of the trumpet imitating sheep carries a clever touch of realism. 'Three Mice went into a Hole', indeed! But one fairly sees meowing pussy crouch and spring and finally land her prey after the instruments have done their spinning. There is a pseudo-sadness, a crocodile's tear in the closing harmonies when pussy lays out her victims. 'Jack and Jill' is a little holter-polter epic, naïve and drastic. Finally, robust and swashbuckling, 'Old King Cole', syncopating, rollicking, a merry soul is here.

"Leginska has given us here miniatures of exceeding artistry and poetic subtleness. Leginska is a genius who gives herself so wholly that one prays to her guardian angel to take especial care of this generous little body with so big and vivid a heart."

Fantasy for Orchestra and Piano was written at about the same time as the nursery rhyme pieces and was performed on 3rd January 1926, and *Triptych*, for eleven instruments, was premiered in Chicago on 29th April 1928.

Leginska's piano recitals in the 1920s invariably included at least one of her own compositions. A recital she gave in January 1924, billed as her 506th recital, was typical, including music by Beethoven, Chopin, Leginska (two pieces), Goossens, Liszt and Schulz-Evler. Details of the programme are given in the list of references. [21]

The compositions mentioned in this chapter are the main ventures of Ethel Leginska in this field in the 1920s. They put Leginska on the map as a composer worthy of serious consideration. Other compositions were to appear in later years, but from the late 1920s the stream of musical works of the type described here ceased, as Leginska set her sights on music of a larger form – opera. Of that more will be said in Chapter 14.

A list of Leginska's musical compositions is given in Appendix 4 (page 328).

A publicity portrait of Leginska, early 1920s

References: Chapter 9

1. *The Etude*, May 1919, p. 271.
2. *Musical Courier*, 12th September 1918.
3. Lucienne Bloch Dimitroff, Guala, California (personal correspondence).
4. *Musical Courier*, 26th September 1918.
5. *Musical Courier*, 27th February 1919.
6. *Musical Courier*, 3rd April 1919.
7. *Musical Courier*, 19th June 1919.
8. *Musical America*, 28th June 1919.
9. *Cleveland Press*, 7th August 1919.
10. *Musical Courier*, 18th March 1920.
11. *Musical Courier*, 2nd October 1919.
12. The Musicale was reviewed in *Musical America*, 31st January 1920.
13. *Musical Courier*, 26th February 1920.
14. *Christian Science Monitor*, 4th June 1920.
15. *Evening Standard* (London), 16th June 1921.
16. *Morning Post*, 16th June 1921.
17. All Leginska's letters at the time were sent to this address.
18. *The Musical Times*, 1st January 1923.
19. Joseph Enos, Benicia, California (personal correspondence).
20. Article (or concert review) by Bruno David Ussher, late August 1925 (newspaper cutting). The newspaper from which it came and the precise date are unknown, but the author of the article is known to have worked as music critic and writer for the *Evening Express* (Los Angeles) and the *California Graphic* so the article may have come from one of those. He also wrote programme notes for the Hollywood Bowl's symphony concerts. The article is quoted in full in Appendix 7 (pages 336 to 337).
21. The programme of the recital billed as Leginska's 506th, given in Sacramento, California on 24th January 1924, is reproduced in the sleeve notes of the compact disc: *Leginska: The Columbia Masters, 1926-28*, released in 2001 by Ivory Classics.

    The programme comprised:

Beethoven	Sonata in A flat, Op. 26
Chopin	Prelude in A flat major, Op. 28, No. 17
	Ballade in G minor, Op. 23
	Valse in E minor (posthumous)
	Étude in E major, Op. 10, No. 3
	Étude in A minor, Op. 25, No. 5
Leginska	Cradle Song
	Dance of a Puppet
Goossens	The Hurdy Gurdy Man
Liszt	Legende (St Francis Walking on the Water)
Schulz-Evler	Arabesques on the Blue Danube Waltz

Chapter 10

Recording Artist

We have followed Leginska's remarkable career well into the 1920s, and this is perhaps a convenient point to consider her work as a recording artist, for it was during the 1920s that many of her recordings were made.

For a pianist of Leginska's stature her gramophone recordings were relatively sparse. From the date of her London concerts under Henry Wood in 1906 when she was only 20, until 1912, she was more often than not on tour in Britain and Europe and therefore probably not available for recording. From 1913 onwards most of her time was spent in the United States, where, in her ceaseless round of concert and recital giving, her aim in these first few years of her concert career would have been directed primarily towards establishing herself as a pianist of the first rank, an objective she achieved. Far fewer records were made in those days than is now the case and those that were produced had to be made by the relatively primitive acoustic process of the day, which did not give very good results when a piano was being recorded. It is therefore doubtful whether visits to a recording studio would have figured very highly on the list of priorities, at that time, of a young pianist such as Leginska.

In spite of the fact that Leginska had been domiciled in the USA from 1913, her first disc recordings appear to have been a set she made for Pathé on a visit to Britain, around 1920.[1] They were of course acoustic recordings (the electrical process was not introduced until 1925) and were issued on three 12-inch records. The first disc comprised the Liszt Hungarian Rhapsody No. 13 and Moszkowski's Waltz in E major, the second was Leschetizky's *Gavotte* and Chopin's Étude, Op. 25, No. 11 in A minor (*Winter Wind*) and the third consisted of MacDowell's *The Witches' Dance* and *Shadow Dance*, and Arensky's Study in F sharp.

Early Pathé records were unusual in design, compared with most contemporary or later discs. For one thing, they worked on the 'hill and dale' principle, in which the acoustic information on the record was arranged to move the playback needle up and down, rather than side to side. This necessitated the use of a special diaphragm in order to play the records. Secondly, they were designed to be played at 90 to 100 revolutions per minute, instead of the more usual 78 to 80. Thirdly, and this was the most unusual feature, the recording groove started near the centre of the disc and worked outwards – the opposite to the conventional system. This arrangement had probably been adopted to overcome the problem of patents.

But from an engineering point of view it was not ideal. The discs suffered from the disadvantage that the frictional drag of the needle on the disc produced increasing restraining torque on the rotating record as the needle approached the outer edge. As this coincided with the running-down of the spring, the clockwork mechanism driving the turntable was apt to give up the unequal struggle before the needle reached the end (outer edge) of the record unless the listener indulged in a further bout of spring-winding. The need for a mid-record wind would therefore have been more likely with Pathé records than with most of the other records of the day.

Nevertheless, Pathé records sold well, and Leginska's discs established her as a gramophone recording artist. They gave a glimpse of Leginska's ability as a pianist but their technical quality was not very good because of the limitations of the recording process. However in 1926 Leginska was invited by Columbia (USA) to record four 12-inch discs using the then new electric recording process. [2] Each disc was devoted to compositions of a different composer; Chopin, Liszt, Rachmaninov and Schubert, and they provide a much better flavour of Leginska's skill than the Pathé recordings.

The Rachmaninov disc features two Preludes; the famous one in C sharp minor, Op. 3 No. 2, and the one in G minor, Op. 23, No. 5. The Chopin record is of the Polonaise, Op. 40, No. 1 (*Military*) and the Prelude, Op. 28, No. 5; the Schubert is of the *Marche Militaire*, Op. 51, No. 1 in an arrangement by Carl Tausig; and the Liszt record is of the Hungarian Rhapsody No. 8, a work Leginska often played in concerts.

In 1928 another set of Leginska records was issued by Columbia, a fact that suggests the 1926 recordings had sold well. These all featured the piano music of Schubert and were made to commemorate the centenary of the composer's death. They are perhaps the most valuable of Leginska's gramophone recordings, for they enable us to hear her play a number of pieces, in succession, from a set by one composer, whereas her earlier records were merely snippets from the works of various musicians. The 1928 Columbia recordings comprised four Schubert Impromptus (Op. 142, D. 935) on three 12-inch discs, and all six of his *Moments Musicaux* (Op. 94, D. 780) on four 10-inch discs. All were in the dark-blue-label series. They were issued in Britain and in the United States. In Britain the *Moments Musicaux* did not appear in Columbia's catalogues after 1934 but the Impromptus remained until 1938-39. Though the original 78s have not been available from Columbia for many years, good specimens are still to be found occasionally in second-hand record shops or from specialist dealers in old records (the authors have obtained several of Leginska 78s in this way). All of Leginska's Columbia recordings of 1926-28 were re-issued on a single compact disc in 2001 by Ivory Classics, an Ohio-based company which, as its name implies, specialises in re-issuing recordings of historic piano performances. The CD number is 64405-72002.

All of Leginska's disc recordings from the 1920s are listed in Appendix 5(a) (page 330) and re-issues on compact disc in Appendix 5(c) (page 334).

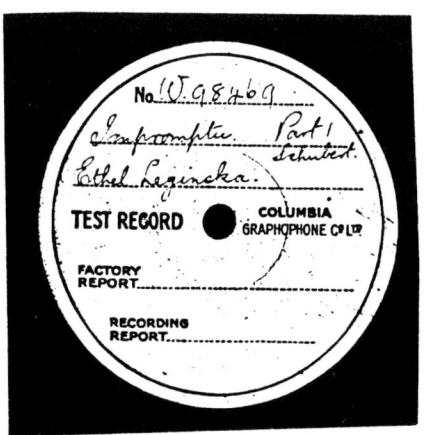 

Labels of one of Leginska's Schubert recordings of 1928 – the 'Rosamunde' Impromptu, Part 1. Test recording (left) and as issued (right)

In November 1928 Leginska's Schubert commemorative recordings were reviewed in *The Musical Times* by "Discus", a writer who never pulled his punches and who in his reviews was often scathing about the performance of some of the most famous and highly-regarded musicians of the day. By his standards Leginska's recordings were well received:

"Ethel Leginska is a gramophone player new to me. She has been recorded in a biggish dose of Schubert – the six 'Moments Musicaux' and four 'Impromptus'. This is good, honest, clean playing, with an unflagging rhythm that is a good off-set against some lack of subtlety. In fact the records are a very good argument for being content with the right notes in their right places (good time and rhythm), plus a reasonable amount of dynamic variety. Any music worth its salt makes a surprisingly good show thus performed; it gains little, and often loses much, by being liberally 'interpreted'. "

No more of Leginska's gramophone recordings were issued after 1928. Her original "78's" are crackly and well below present standards of high fidelity, but with all their technical limitations they succeed in conveying some idea of what a fine pianist she was. The re-issues on CD benefit from the removal of much of the background noise. Also, the need to keep changing the record, as was the case with the original 78s, is eliminated.

It is appropriate to comment on how early gramophone records (pre-1925) compared with the reproducing piano roll, in terms of the fidelity of the replayed performance. Considering the gramophone first, there were very severe problems with the recordings, especially when an orchestra or a piano was being recorded, as summarised here:

a) It was impossible to eradicate the background noise in 78rpm recordings pressed on shellac discs. The 'frying bacon' crackle was inherent in this type of record.

b) In the acoustic process a large recording horn had to be placed over the piano in order to pick up enough sound for the recording. The imperfect acoustics of the horn and the energy required to drive the recording needle caused distortions in the reproduced sounds. Of particular relevance to the piano was the fact that the instrument reproduced in a very 'tinny' manner.

c) In order to achieve enough volume to get a satisfactory recording the pianist was obliged to play in a somewhat fortissimo manner irrespective of the markings on the music, something which is hardly conducive to a correct musical interpretation.

d) It was impossible to use a good quality piano for the recording because it had been found by experiment and experience that such pianos did not record well. As a result, eminent concert pianists would arrive at HMV's or Columbia's studios (taking these major companies as an example) and often would be taken aback to discover they were expected to record using a tinny, poor-quality piano, the technicians having discovered by experience that this gave a better result on record than a superior instrument.

e) A wax disc could only accommodate a maximum of four minutes of music. Consequently, if a longer piece had to be recorded, for example a movement of a sonata, the options were to have a break in the music at some point in order to go on to another track, or to make cuts in the piece, or to play the piece faster than it should be played in order to get it on the disc. Pianists were often asked to do the last of these, and some refused for artistic reasons.

Because of these technical inadequacies, many of the top pianists of those days hated the gramophone recording studio. One very famous pianist, Ferruccio Busoni, complained bitterly about it in a letter to his wife. [3]

Some of these problems were alleviated in 1925 when electrical recording was introduced. Therefore, Leginska's Columbia recordings of 1926 and 1928 were spared the worst of the defects listed above.

Whilst there were undoubtedly problems of a technical nature inherent in the reproducing player piano, in particular the need to ensure that a well-maintained piano is used to play back the piano-roll performance, it can be strongly argued that before about 1925 a pianist's performance from a player piano roll gave a much more authentic impression of the performance than a gramophone record was able to do. This is subject, of course, to the piano roll having been skilfully recorded (which it generally was) and provided the reproducing piano on which the rolls were played (either in a public hall or in a person's home) was properly adjusted. It is therefore fortunate, in Leginska's case, that the relative sparsity of her gramophone recordings is more than outweighed by the large number of player piano rolls she recorded during, and in the few years after, the First World War. They amount to about 74 rolls altogether – quite a substantial output by the standards of the day. *

At that time all the popular tunes of the day were put onto music rolls. In the more 'classical' field, the piano music of Beethoven, Chopin, Liszt, Schumann and many others was admirably suited to the instrument. Music not written for the piano was transcribed for piano rolls, from Bach to Busoni, from Haydn to Elgar. Even symphonies and violin concertos found their way onto music rolls by means of transcriptions. In 'song rolls', words synchronised to the music were printed on the roll. This was the player piano scene when the reproducing piano, able to reproduce a pianist's performance by means of coded perforations on the roll, first appeared. The larger companies were always on the look-out for good pianists to record for them and in keeping with this policy Leginska was invited to record for the Aeolian Company's Duo-Art system in 1914, the year after her United States debut and having had a subsequent year of solid achievement.

The principle of the player piano and the reproducing piano were outlined in Chapter 7 (pages 92 to 95) where it was also stated that between 1914 and 1915 Leginska recorded seven piano rolls for the Aeolian Company's Duo-Art reproducing piano, featuring music by Chopin (1 roll), Mendelssohn (1), Anton Rubinstein (2), Schubert (2) and Schumann (1). All of them were included in the first Duo-Art catalogue issued in 1915. At that time it could truly be said that well-recorded piano rolls played on a good piano were markedly superior to gramophone records of piano music. These early Duo-Art piano rolls therefore provide us with a valuable indication of Leginska's playing when she was young (she was only 28 at the time).

These Duo-Art rolls of 1914-15 were apparently made on an *ad hoc* basis for there is no evidence of a formal contract between Leginska and the Aeolian Company at that time. But in 1919, as she approached the end of a hard six-year slog on the American concert circuit and was beginning to diversify her interests, she signed a contract with the Aeolian Company to run from 1st January of that year for a duration of 10 years. The contract was dated 28th January 1919, just two months after the war ended, and coincided with the company's post-war re-entry into the highly competitive market of piano rolls. The contract called for three recordings

---

* In the earlier part of the 20th century pianists recorded far less than those of the present day, many of the more famous of whom nowadays have vast recorded outputs on disc amounting virtually to the whole of their repertoire. When Leginska was at her peak as a pianist between 1910 and 1930, many famous pianists recorded nothing or very little either on record or on piano roll, their recorded work amounting to only a handful of visits to the recording studio during the whole of their career. Consequently, posterity has to assess their playing, either on record or piano roll or both, on the results of a few days' work.

per year at $200 per recording. To put this figure in perspective, Josef Hofmann, who at the time was one of the world's top two or three pianists, had a fifteen-year contract starting on the same date at $1,000 calling for six to seven rolls per year, Serge Prokofiev received $250, Arthur Friedheim $100 and Percy Grainger $200, the same as Leginska. [4]

The clause in Leginska's contract that called for three rolls a year probably meant three per year on average, for she had many commitments in the 1920s and it would have been convenient for her to record her rolls in batches. She may have recorded some that for one reason or another were not released; this seems to have happened in the case of many famous pianists who recorded for the major companies. All her Duo-Art piano rolls were recorded at the Aeolian Company's premises in New York on one of their special recording pianos. The number of Leginska's rolls that were issued (as opposed to recorded) as part of her contract varied year by year as follows: 1919 (2), 1921 (1), 1922 (2), 1923 (1), 1924 (4), 1925 (1), 1926 (3), 1927 (1), 1929 (2) and 1930 (1). [5] No Leginska rolls were issued in 1920 or 1928. The composers represented in her complete list of Duo-Art recordings (excluding special ones but including the pre-contract rolls of 1914-15) were Bach (1 roll), Beethoven (2), Chopin (3), Leginska (1), Leschetizky (2), Liadov (1), Liszt (1), Mendelssohn (2), Moszkowski (1), Rameau (1), Rimsky-Korsakov (1), Rubinstein (2), Schubert (2), Schumann (1), J. Strauss (younger) (1), Tchaikovsky (2) and Weber (1). *

It will be seen from this list that Leginska's 'ordinary' Duo-Art rolls number 25 in all when the seven from 1914-1915 are included. There were also some special ones, which are described later in the chapter.

During the 1920s it was not uncommon for piano rolls made by the famous pianists of the day to be used as part of orchestral concerts, usually organised by the major player-piano companies for advertising purposes. In these a piano concerto would be performed with the piano part played by a reproducing roll recorded by the particular artist. Sometimes the piano part of just one movement of a concerto would be played by the player piano using a roll 'cut' by the pianist in question (the orchestra accompanying under the conductor's baton in the normal way) whilst the other movements were played by the same pianist in the conventional manner. In concerts such as this, whilst the player piano was doing its work the pianist would

---

* The large number of piano rolls issued in the 1920s, not just by Leginska but by many other pianists, is a reflection of the popularity of the player piano at that time. Of 1,217,035 pianos manufactured in the United States between 1919 and 1925 (both years included), 705,729 (58% of the total) were fitted with player actions. [6] Of these, perhaps 25% were reproducing pianos, able to re-enact the playing of the pianist who recorded the roll. The years 1920 to 1926 marked the hey-day of the player piano.

Left: Ampico catalogue, 1925

Right: Duo-Art catalogue, 1927

Photographs of Ethel Leginska in music roll catalogues of the 1920s

generally be prominently visible, placed in one of the best seats or boxes in the concert hall. Leginska sometimes took part in concerts such as this. [7] Rolls used during these performances were recorded by the pianist beforehand especially for the occasion; they were not the normal rolls available for purchase in the shops. The practice was revived at a BBC Promenade Concert in 1988 when Percy Grainger 'played' the Grieg Concerto by means of a piano roll, the orchestra accompanying. [8]

Similarly, recitals were sometimes given in which an artist played a particular item, which would then be repeated by a Duo-Art piano playing the same piece as recorded on roll by the same pianist. In this case the roll would be a normal one as available to the general public. Another type of light-hearted 'stunt' sometimes employed by the major player piano companies to promote their wares was to invite a number of musical celebrities to a special performance at which a reproducing player piano was set up behind a curtain, with the panel of musical 'experts' in front. The piano would then play and the audience would be invited to guess whether the piano was being played by a particular celebrity pianist, who had also been invited, or by one of his or her piano rolls of the same piece. For each item played, the assessors would make their judgment before the piece ended as to whether it was being played by the pianist in person or by his or her piano roll. After they had decided, and whilst the performance was still in progress, a curtain would rise to reveal the truth. It is a measure of the faithfulness of reproduction of reproducing pianos in the 1920s that the assessors' guess was wrong as often as it was correct.

Leginska's first two post-war recordings for the Duo-Art system were issued in 1919 soon after she signed her contract. They were Valse, Op. 34, No. 1 in A by Moszkowski and Gavotte and Variations (a transcription by Leginska) by Rameau, a piece she often played on the concert stage. In 1921 came Arabesque en Forme d'Étude, Op. 45, No. 1 by her former teacher, Leschetizky, followed in 1922 by *The Two Larks* (Impromptu), Op. 2, No. 1, also by Leschetizky and *Hymn to the Sun God* from *The Golden Cockerel* by Rimsky-Korsakov. In 1923 one Leginska roll was issued, the Concert Arabesques on Motives from *By the Beautiful Blue Danube* transcribed by the Polish pianist and composer Andrei Schulz-Evler from the waltz by Johann Strauss, further arranged by Leginska herself. This pianistic *tour de force* was one of Leginska's favourite *encore* pieces in recitals.

In 1924 four of Leginska's Duo-Art rolls were released. They were the well-known Minuet in G by Beethoven, a piece so often played that it took a pianist of Leginska's skill to make it sound fresh and a delight to the ear, Valse in E minor (posthumous) by Chopin, *The Music Box* (*Une Tabatière à*

Musique), Op. 32, by Liadov, and *Cradle Song*, composed by Leginska herself, the music of which is given on pages 130 and 131. *Cradle Song* is the only one of Leginska's compositions that was recorded for Duo-Art. It was listed in the 1925 and 1927 catalogues of the Aeolian Company but did not appear in the 1932 catalogue so was evidently not a steady seller. The market for modern compositions has always been limited.

In 1925 the Prelude and Fugue (No. 3 in C) from Bach's *Well Tempered Clavier*, was issued, followed in 1926 by Eight Variations on the theme *Tändeln und Scherzen* by Beethoven, Nocturne in E major, Op. 9, No. 2 by Chopin, and the overture *Oberon* by Weber. In 1927 two of Mendelssohn's *Songs Without Words* were released, both on the same roll; they were No. 44 (Op. 102, No. 2) and No. 10 (Op. 30, No. 4). To complete the picture of Leginska's 10-year contract with the Aeolian Company, though this takes us a little ahead of our story, two Leginska rolls were issued in 1929; they were *1812 Overture* by Tchaikovsky (as noisy a piece of music as the title would suggest) and *The Seasons*, No. 10 (*October*) by the same composer, and finally, in May 1930 came Leginska's last Duo-Art roll, Liszt's Hungarian Rhapsody No. 8, another piece she often played on the concert stage.

EIGHT VARIATIONS ON THE THEME "TANDELN UND SCHERZEN"
Composed by Ludwig van Beethoven   'Duo-Art' Roll recorded by Ethel Leginska
6957 .. 12/-

ETHEL LEGINSKA

BEETHOVEN composed many sets of variations, for he was especially fond of the form, and more than any of his predecessors saw in that form its great possibilities as a musical illustration of the natural, logical process of evolution or growth. The simple, vital germ of thought or feeling inherent in a given theme, as the life principle inheres in the germ of a grain of wheat, is seen in the master's treatment of it to expand gradually and develop through the successive variations into new and changing forms of ever-increasing beauty and suggestiveness until its latent possibilities of expression have been matured and exhausted; just as the growing wheat passes through gradual and continuous changes of form and hue until the influences of the sun and soil, air and wind and rain and dew have ripened it to complete maturity.

The Eight Variations here very beautifully played by Ethel Leginska were composed in Vienna in 1799, the year that Beethoven wrote his first symphony. The simple and pretty Theme, "Tändeln und Scherzen" (*Tändeln* means 'to dawdle,' trifle, or flirt; *Scherzen*, 'to joke') was taken from F. X. Süssmayr's operetta "Solyman II., or the Three Sultanas," produced at Vienna on October 1, 1799. The Variations are beautifully fresh, healthful, peaceful, appealing and solacing music—a joy and a delight to hear. Karl Czerny recorded the interesting fact that these Variations were the first of Beethoven's compositions which the master gave him to study when he became his pupil.

An extract from 'Duo-Art Monthly', magazine of the Aeolian Company, January 1926

Some of Leginska's piano rolls, and those of other pianists, were also issued as 'annotated' rolls with different identification numbers. They were introduced mainly for educational purposes, in the hope that people would buy the rolls to enhance their own musical appreciation or, more commonly, to try to educate their children musically. The actual recording (i.e. the perforations in the paper) was the same as in the 'normal' rolls, but these special rolls would often feature a photograph of the recording artist on the leader (the initial part of the roll which precedes the perforations) and a written commentary was provided at the beginning and along the roll, which of course unfurled as the roll played. It explained, with the help of pictures where necessary, what the music was all about. Some were also issued in annotated pictorial form as children's rolls. Consequently, some of Leginska's rolls could be purchased in alternative guises; 'normal' which included just the music in the form of coded perforations, and various types of 'annotated' roll with pictures of the composer and pianist, and illustrations and running commentary throughout the roll. These rolls were more costly.

Leginska also recorded the second piano part only, on three rolls, of Mozart's Sonata for two pianos, K. 448 (issued in 1923). Rolls such as this were intended to help aspiring pianists as they attempted to play the other part. Gramophone records or CDs were later available to do the same job, but the player piano had, and still has, the advantage over them because both contributors play their parts simultaneously on the same instrument. In the mid- to late- 1920s the Aeolian Company introduced all sorts of special rolls in an attempt to bolster flagging sales, amongst them biographical rolls devoted to a particular composer, comprising many appropriate musical illustrations. Leginska contributed with Harold Bauer, Josef Hofmann and the American pianist Albert Stoessel to two special biographical rolls of Beethoven where the various pianists played passages, to illustrate particular points, with written annotations on the roll. All the Duo-Art rolls recorded by Leginska are listed in Appendix 5(b) (pages 332-333).

Ethel Leginska was a participant in another special Duo-Art enterprise, a novelty roll made by the Aeolian Company comprising a set of variations on a particular version of *Chopsticks*. The idea of these variations came from Borodin in 1877; he wrote three, and others were contributed by his friends Cui, Liadov and Rimsky-Korsakov. Later they were heard by Liszt who wrote an *Andante*. In 1925 the Aeolian Company, makers of the Duo-Art system, decided to have ten of their most prominent recording artists make a reproducing roll recording of ten of these paraphrases including the one by Liszt. They made only one copy of the roll and packaged it in a fancy box, all the artists having autographed the roll. It was then auctioned at a concert in the Metropolitan Opera House for a charity benefit. It appears that the highest bidder was a Mr Cornelius Bliss who paid $8,000 for the roll. In the 1970s the master roll from which the auctioned roll was made was found and the roll has been re-issued. The following list identifies each of the ten paraphrases by composer and performer.

1. Valse by César Cui — Rudolph Ganz
2. Polka by Borodin — Josef Hofmann
3. Tarantella by Rimsky-Korsakov — Harold Bauer
4. Valse by Liadov — Ernest Hutcheson
5. Andante by Liszt — Yolanda Mérö
6. Grotesque Fugue by Rimsky-Korsakov — Alexander Siloti
7. Polka by Borodin — Ernest Schelling
8. Galop by Liadov — Ethel Leginska
9. Gigue by Liadov — Myra Hess
10. Mazurka by Borodin — Guiomar Novaës

The Aeolian Company spent vast amounts of money on advertising. A magazine was issued (*The Duo-Art Monthly*) detailing new recordings, commenting on the current musical scene, etc. Leginska often appeared in these monthly bulletins (see example on page 144) which described the latest releases. She was featured on the front cover of the April 1927 magazine.

Copies of most of Leginska's Duo-Art rolls are in the authors' possession and we can vouch for the quality of her playing, some of which, in our opinion is quite brilliant, a view shared by numerous members of the North West Player Piano Association who have regular opportunities to compare the capabilities of Leginska with those of the other great pianists of her era. A member of the Association who had spent a long time restoring his player piano to perfect working order wrote as follows: [9]

"After two years I succeeded in bringing our Weber Duo-Art back to life. The turning point came when I heard Chopin's Ballade in G played with breathtaking facility by Ethel Leginska. This was the first time that I found music played on a player piano quite moving. It seemed for an instant that Ethel Leginska was actually sitting before the piano, on loan from a better world, and utterly oblivious of the turmoil of roll boxes, pneumatic cloth, tools, etc. surrounding her. It was after this performance that I came to recognise the absolute supremacy of the reproducing piano among mechanical musical instruments."

In the list quoted on page 94 of companies which manufactured reproducing pianos and recorded rolls to go with them, the Aeolian Company which manufactured Duo-Art rolls is placed at the top for two reasons. First, it was the largest and probably the most successful company, and second, there are still relatively large numbers of Duo-Art pianos and rolls around at the present time in Britain and elsewhere, so there is no difficulty in hearing the piano rolls of Leginska and others.

Recording Artist

A page from an Aeolian Company publicity leaflet, 1924, showing photographs of Leginska and other famous pianists of the day

Perhaps the next most important company is the one placed second on the list, Ampico (the American Piano Company) of New York whose products, like those of the Aeolian Company, are still to be found in relatively large numbers, though less commonly than Duo-Art. Leginska recorded just three rolls for Ampico: *Le Coucou* by Daquin, the *Blue Danube Concert Arabesque*, (Schulz-Evler's arrangement of Johann Strauss's music) and Liszt's Hungarian Rhapsody No. 8. All three were amongst her specialities which she often played in concerts, and two of these rolls — the *Blue Danube* arrangement and the Hungarian Rhapsody — also appeared in her list of Duo-Art recordings. Leginska's recording of *Le Coucou* for Ampico is the only Ampico recording of the piece.

As Duo-Art and Ampico instruments are still relatively commonplace, which means that there is no difficulty finding and hearing Leginska's rolls for these systems, her Duo-Art and Ampico rolls have been quoted here in some detail. Leginska never recorded for Hupfeld or Welte, two important German-based companies, but she recorded 34 rolls for the American company Wilcox & White of Meriden, Connecticut, whose products were known as 'Artrio-Angelus', or just 'Artrio'. Their products are now rarely to be found, at any rate in Britain. This is probably because the system was technically difficult to adjust and maintain. Thus, specimens able to give a good authentic performance at the present time are rare, though, when the system *is* working properly, the results are comparable in quality with Duo-Art and Ampico. The dates of Leginska's Artrio recordings are not known but they were probably recorded between about 1916 and 1922. All 34 of them appeared in the company's 1922 catalogue. Artrio prices ranged from 11/- (11 shillings) to 16/- per roll in Britain according to the length of the roll and in the United States the corresponding price range was $2.00 to $3.00. Prices of Duo-Art and Ampico rolls were about the same.

Because of the fact that there is so little opportunity to hear any of Leginska's Artrio rolls in Britain full details will not be given in the text, but the rolls are all listed in Appendix 5(b). However, a few points are worthy of special mention. Nineteen different composers were represented covering the whole gamut of music from Beethoven and Chopin to the modern compositions (when Leginska recorded them) of Granados, Moszkowski, Nevin (*Narcissus*) and Leginska herself. The Wilcox & White Company evidently felt they had to satisfy the musical needs of a wide variety of potential customers with fewer pianists at their disposal than the larger companies of Aeolian, Ampico or Welte, and Leginska may have had to be prepared to play anything she was asked to. She was probably allowed, or insisted upon, some preferences nevertheless, for it is interesting to note that seven of the compositions on the list were by her former teacher, Leschetizky, whom she greatly admired, and one was composed by herself (*Moment Musical*, Op. 5, No. 1 (*Love*)). This piece, and her *Cradle Song* which she recorded for Duo-Art, are the only two Leginska compositions ever recorded on piano rolls. Leschetizky's *The Two Larks* which appears on the list was also recorded by Leginska for Duo-Art. The other six Leschetizky rolls she recorded for Artrio were his six *Souvenirs d'Italie* Op. 39. This six-roll set make an important contribution to recorded sound because they are the only recordings of this set of pieces on piano roll, and it is most unlikely they were ever recorded for the gramophone either – they do not appear in any of our pre- second world war gramophone catalogues.

The only other piano rolls recorded by Leginska that have not already been mentioned were seven rolls issued by the Recordo Company. Since the Recordo system was relatively primitive compared with, say, Duo-Art and Ampico, it might be argued that Recordo rolls were not true 'reproducing' rolls that re-enacted the whole performance, but were merely 'expression' rolls that reproduced only some of the dynamics. Nevertheless, they were recorded by pianists whose names appeared on the rolls as recording artists,

Leginska's certification on the 'leader' of an Artrio-Angelus music roll. Similar authentication appeared on the rolls of all the other major companies. Most companies used a stamp for the signature but Leginska hand-signed some of her Artrio rolls and their boxes. The music-roll paper used in nearly all player pianos of whatever make was 11¼ inches wide.

Photograph of Leginska in the Wilcox & White (Artrio rolls) catalogue, 1922

and so must represent, albeit perhaps to a limited extent, the performance of the pianist. There were various kinds of Recordo rolls. The first (System I) were produced by the Imperial Company of the USA, beginning in 1915 or 1916. System II was the product of the Recordo Company founded from the dying embers of the declining parent company, and System III came into being when the QRS company (a long-lived piano roll company that has been in existence throughout the whole history of player pianos and is still in business today) bought out Recordo. The same roll-numbering system was preserved throughout these changes. Recordo did not make instruments, only rolls, and QRS stopped issuing Recordo rolls in 1930. The dates of issue of Leginska's Recordo rolls is unknown but clearly they must all have been produced between about 1916 and 1930 — the lifespan of Recordo rolls. Because of the declining fortunes of the player piano industry towards the end of the 1920s it is likely that the rolls were issued before 1925. Leginska's seven Recordo rolls are listed at the end of Appendix 5(b). The composers represented were Chaminade, Chopin, Leschetizky, MacDowell, Moszkowski, Nevin and a composition by the Dutch pianist Martinus Sieveking (1867 - 1950) — one roll per composer.

Recording Artist

The last of Ethel Leginska's piano rolls to be issued was, as stated earlier, her 1930 Duo-Art recording of Liszt's Hungarian Rhapsody No. 8. Her 1919 Aeolian Company contract having then expired, it appears no new contract was signed. This is not at all surprising. By 1930 the advent of radio and the recent much-improved quality of gramophone records, coupled with the fact that the gramophone does not limit itself to piano music, was sounding the death-knell of the player piano industry, a process hastened by the economic depression and the introduction of 'the talkies' in films. By the early 1930s the decline of the player piano industry was well advanced. Although the major companies struggled on in a limited way until the end of the thirties, few player pianos were sold and the output of new rolls in the 1930s was restricted almost entirely to the popular tunes of the day – by Irving Berlin, George Gershwin, Cole Porter and so on. Hardly any 'classical' compositions were recorded at that time by any artist, and the rolls of this type of music that were sold were merely re-issues of the same recordings that had been released originally in the 1920s.

The fact that Leginska made so many piano roll recordings is indeed fortunate to anyone interested in pianists of the past. As already noted, some of the gramophone records of the early days of recording leave a lot to be desired technically and provide no more than a crackly impression of bygone glories – a ghostly image from the past. But a Leginska piano roll recording, for example a Duo-Art roll played on a Steinway reproducing piano that has been fully restored to its original specification, is a unique and sometimes moving experience and is the only way to fully appreciate her talents. It is as though she were sitting there playing, in one's own home.

When listening to Leginska's recordings, whether her piano roll performances or her disc recordings, it must be borne in mind that fashions change, in music as in everything else, and musical interpretations of the 1920s were sometimes very different from those of today. This is very apparent when we listen to the recordings of Cortot, Godowsky, Hofmann, Lhevinne and all the other great pianists of that bygone era, and especially the more eccentric ones such as Pachmann and compare them with present-day interpretations. It is not that they were right in the way they interpreted a composer's wishes and the present day masters of the keyboard are wrong, or *vice versa*. It is just that in certain ways musical interpretations have altered. Leginska's recordings must therefore be judged by the fashions of three quarters of a century ago.

However, having drawn attention to this, it is also fair to make a seemingly contradictory point, that in the authors' view Leginska's interpretations seem to be surprisingly modern and may be listened to with a great deal of pleasure. As mentioned on page 138, the review in *The Musical Times* of Leginska's Schubert recordings drew attention to " . . . good, honest, clean playing with an unflagging rhythm". We agree, and the facts that these Schubert recordings have now been transferred to CD, that much of the surface noise that was present on the original 78s has been removed, and that it is no longer necessary to keep changing the record as was the case with the original 78s, adds greatly to the listener's pleasure. In our own compact disc collection we have the Schubert Impromptus played by Alfred Brendel and by Clifford Curzon and three versions of *Moments Musicaux*; by Claudio Arrau, Radu Lupu and Andras Schiff. And – dare it be said – we prefer Leginska's interpretation to any of them.

The Columbia discs of 1926 to 1928, which were recorded at the company's studios at Union Square, Manhattan, New York City, comprise the greater part of Leginska's issued recordings on disc. As stated earlier the Schubert works were recorded for the Schubert Centenary in 1928; the other works (recorded in 1926) were part of the Columbia 'Celebrity' series. It is interesting to note, from the Matrix details provided with the Ivory Classics compact discs, that all of the six *Moments Musicaux* were recorded on the same day, Thursday 8th March 1928. Impromptu No. 1 in F minor was recorded the following day, 9th March, and No 4 was recorded the following month (on 5th April). Impromptus Nos. 2 and 3 had been recorded earlier, each of them on 20th February 1928.

Not all recorded work is issued. This may be for technical, artistic or other reasons. In this last category, it may be judged by the record company, after the recordings were made, that the likely return on sales would be insufficient to justify the outlay of production. In the case of Ignaz Friedman (another top-class pianist who was four years older than Leginska) for example who also recorded for Columbia, it appears that much of his volume of recorded work was never issued, possibly because of technical problems concerning surface noise that the company was experiencing at the time. Leginska, in her turn, made a number of recordings for Columbia that remained unissued according to Marina A. Ledin who wrote the booklet notes for the Ivory Classics 'Leginska' compact disc. [10] She states that Leginska's unreleased recordings include two earlier takes of the Schubert-Tausig *Marche Militaire* (on 21st December 1926 and 18th February 1927), a later re-make of the Liszt Hungarian Rhapsody No. 8 (on 21st December 1926), Paderewski's Minuet (on 3rd June 1927), Mendelssohn's Rondo Capriccioso (On 18th February 1927) and three encore pieces on 18th June 1926: *The Hurdy-Gurdy Man* by Eugene Goossens and two of Leginska's own pieces – *Cradle Song* and *Dance of a Puppet*. Not only were they never issued but the masters no longer exist, having apparently been melted down for scrap during World War II. A tragedy!

Leginska was probably a reluctant recording artist. As we saw in Chapter 9, she did not wish to be thought of as a pianist only but as a musician with wider interests. Fortunately, between the years 1914 and 1930 (when her age span was 28 to 44) during which period all her recordings, either on disc or piano roll, were made, she was at her peak as a pianist in spite of her widening interests. Her recordings therefore give a glimpse, albeit brief, of her considerable skills.

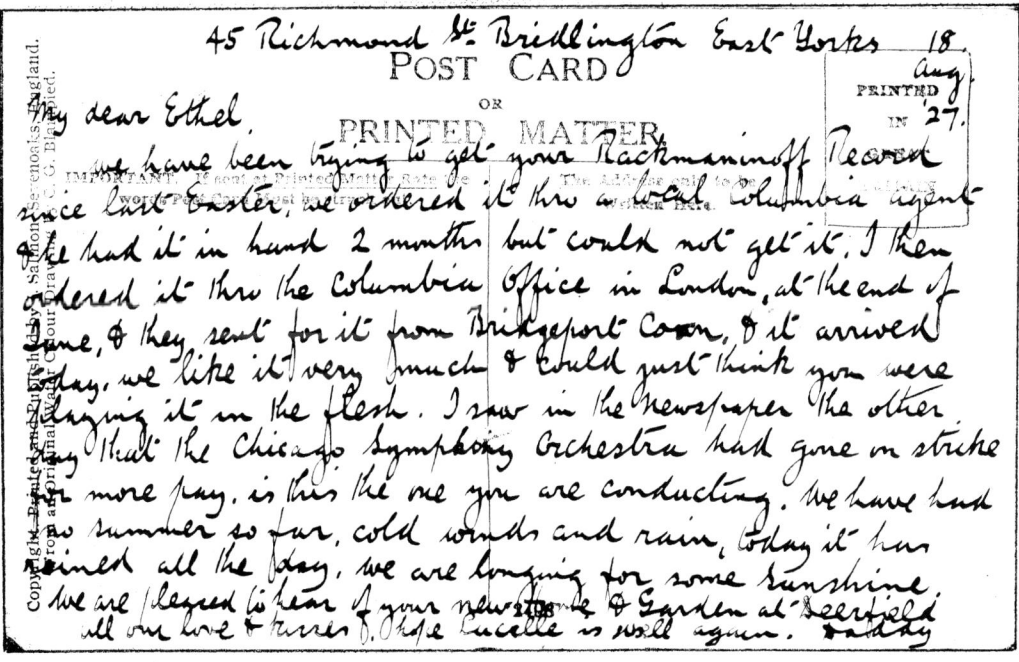

Postcard from Ethel's father to his daughter dated 18th August 1927, describing his difficulty in obtaining her Rachmaninov record. This is because Ethel's Columbia recordings of 1926 were issued in the USA but not in Britain, so they had to be obtained from the USA. (Copy of postcard courtesy of International Piano Archives at Maryland)

References: Chapter 10

1. Some of the information about Leginska's list of gramophone recordings was provided by Ruth Edge, Archives Department, E.M.I., Middlesex. Additional material is from old Columbia and other catalogues of the period 1926 to 1940. The authors have all of Leginska's Columbia recordings of Schubert (original 78s) and the National Sound Archive (part of the British Library) has others. The Columbia records are now available on compact disc (see ref. 10).

2. In the acoustic recording process a large horn is placed in front of the source of sound, serving to focus the sound vibrations onto a diaphragm on which is mounted a needle, the movement of which marks out a track on a rotating wax cylinder or disc, thus giving a record of the music. The energy required to move the needle is extracted directly from the sound source, inevitably resulting in a certain amount of distortion.

   In electric recording the sound is detected by means of a microphone, the output of which is amplified by externally-powered electronic circuits so that much less power is extracted directly from the sound source. This results in a higher fidelity of recording than the acoustic process is able to provide.

   Once electric recording was adopted by the major record companies in 1925 the acoustic recording process fell into disuse within months.

3. Busoni hated making gramophone records and for good reason. Some idea of the deficiencies of the recording process at that time is indicated in a letter he wrote to his wife in 1919:

   "My suffering over the toil of making gramophone records came to an end yesterday, after playing for three and a half hours! I feel rather battered today, but it is over . . . Here is an example of what happens. They wanted the *Faust* Waltz (which takes a good ten minutes), *but it was only to take four minutes.* This meant quickly cutting, patching and improvising, so that there should still be some sense left in it, watching the pedal (because it sounds bad); thinking of certain notes which had to be stronger or weaker to please this devilish machine; not letting one's self go for fear of inaccuracies; and being conscious the whole time that every note was going to be there for eternity; how can there be any question of inspiration, freedom, swing or poetry? Enough that yesterday for nine pieces all of four minutes each (half an hour in all) I worked for three and a half hours."

   These observations by Busoni make it very obvious why he so hated recording for the gramophone, and may explain why his piano roll recordings outnumbered his gramophone discs.

4. This information has been provided by Mr Gerald Stonehill, who is in possession of many of the Aeolian Company's archives.

5. Information about the dates of issue of Leginska's piano roll recordings is from:
   (i) The Aeolian Company's Duo-Art roll catalogues of various years, the same company's monthly news bulletins, and from *Catalogue of Duo-Art Piano Rolls* by Charles Davis Smith, published by The Player Shop, Monrovia,

California, 1987.

(ii) The American Piano Company's roll catalogues for various years and the company's monthly bulletins; also *The Complete Catalogue of Ampico Reproducing Rolls* by Elaine Obenchain. Wm. H. Edgerton, New York, 1977.

(iii) Wilcox & White Company's *Catalogue of Rolls for the Artrio-Angelus Reproducing Piano*, Meriden, Connecticut, 1922.

(iv) *The Classical Reproducing Piano Roll: A Catalogue Index* by Larry Sitsky (in two volumes). Greenwood Press, Westport, Connecticut and London, 1990.

6. Production figures quoted in *Player Piano Treasury* by Harvey N. Roehl, Vestal Press, New York, 1964.
7. One example in which a Leginska piano roll was used in the first movement of a piano concerto whilst she herself played the other movements was in one of her concerts with her own Boston Philharmonic Orchestra, on 10th April 1927. This series of concerts is described in Chapter 13.
8. This concert took place on 17th September 1988 when the piano part of the Grieg Piano Concerto in A was 'played' by Percy Grainger using reproducing piano rolls recorded by Grainger. The rolls were prepared and the system operated during the performance by Denis Hall and Rex Lawson.
9. The late Dr J. Akhtar. Journal of the North West Player Piano Association, Christmas issue, 1982.
10. Ivory Classics compact disc: "Ethel Leginska, The Complete Columbia Masters". Disc No. 64405-72002, 2001. The booklet supplied with the disc is by Marina A. Ledin.

Chapter 11

Pianist, Composer, Conductor, Teacher

When Ethel Leginska decided at the age of about 32 that there was more to life than being a concert pianist, she had to school herself for the disciplines that lay ahead. When she was interviewed by the *Christian Science Monitor* in 1920 [1] (she was then 34) she had spoken of the opportunity to find "new horizons of service"; concert playing had merely marked an intermediate period in her development. Paramount in her plans for the future had been, she explained, the wish to conduct orchestras, and thereby to bring good music to the general public. Already she had become a composer; she had been helped in the attainment of this objective by her periods of study with Ernest Bloch and Eugene Goossens. In the same way, it was necessary for her to become proficient in the art of conducting if she was to achieve any success in that field. So a teacher had to be found.

As a young woman in her early twenties (1906 - 1912) when she was establishing herself as a concert pianist, Leginska had travelled widely in Europe. She had been particularly well received in Germany where, in such cities as Berlin, Frankfurt and Munich, she had encountered many well-known musicians on a professional and social basis. One of the men she had met and worked with in Munich was Robert Heger *, a German conductor who was an associate of Bruno Walter, and a musical rapport had been established between the two talented young musicians. Consequently, in

---

* The German conductor Robert Heger was born in Strasbourg in 1886, four months after Leginska. (Strasbourg was then in Germany). He was destined to become a major figure on the musical scene and remained so for most of his long life. He studied with Lothar Kempter (1844 - 1918, German conductor and composer) in Zurich and later with Julius Schillinger (1895 - 1943, Russian composer) in Munich where, as a young man, he first met Leginska. He began to conduct in 1907 in Strasbourg and later continued, via various orchestral appointments, in Nuremberg (1913 - 21), Vienna (1925 - 33), the Berlin State Opera (1933 - 50) and London (various occasions between 1926 and 1936). In 1953 (Coronation year) he was in London again at the age of 67 to conduct the first British performance of Richard Strauss's *Capriccio*.

Heger never achieved the fame of some of his illustrious compatriots, such as Furtwängler or Walter, but he was nevertheless a conductor of the first rank who was as well known for his recording work as his concert performances. He continued this facet of his work until he was well past 80, thereby demonstrating, as many other musicians have done, that conducting and longevity seem to go hand in hand. Although Heger lacked the charisma of some of the more flamboyant conductors, he could always be depended upon to give an excellent account of himself in whatever he happened to be conducting. Consequently he won the respect, admiration and confidence of his fellow conductors, including those same flamboyant ones who were always the public's favourites. Although Heger was primarily a conductor he also composed quite a lot of musical works of various types. He died in Munich in 1978 aged 91.

1920 when Leginska was looking for instruction in the art of conducting, Heger was the man she sought out. Leginska also studied conducting under Gennaro Papi, an Italian who was working in the United States.* With both these well-known musicians she studied symphonic and operatic conducting. This period of her musical education took place on a part-time basis between 1920 and 1922, and set Leginska on course to become a conductor. At that time her career as a concert pianist was continuing but, as noted earlier, she was also spending time on composition, and her work was being introduced into her own concert and recital programmes and those of other performers.

It was appropriate previously to consider Leginska's recordings all together, in the same chapter. That took us to 1930 when she made her last recording, which is a little ahead of our story. So let us return now to 1924, which is the year we had reached at the end of Chapter 9, because it was in that year that Leginska's career as a conductor began in earnest.

There is no doubt that Leginska had been harbouring thoughts of conducting for some time, and certainly during much of her period of great success as a pianist in the United States before, during and for a couple of years after the First World War. It was not long before she brought her new-found skills as a conductor, honed under Heger's and Papi's vigilant eyes, into practice, beginning with relatively small concerts in which she usually included some of her own compositions. But impresarios insisted on a balanced programme to encourage a good attendance at concerts, so Leginska's own musical compositions had to be introduced discreetly, whether she happened to be conducting or not. She capitalised on her reputation as a top-class pianist in securing conducting engagements by usually agreeing to perform a piano concerto in the programme. Having a conductor-pianist suited the management because, in effect, they got two performers for the price of one.

In October 1924 Leginska conducted the Paris Conservatory Orchestra, her first major conducting assignment. In November of the same year she conducted the London Symphony, the Berlin Philharmonic and the Munich Konzertverein orchestras. Always on the look-out for good publicity, Leginska gave a number of newspaper interviews after each of these concerts, and claimed to have been the first woman to have conducted all

---

* Gennaro Papi (1886 - 1941) was an Italian conductor who had studied in Italy and then conducted at several opera houses, also in Italy. He conducted at Covent Garden in the 1911-12 season and went to the USA in 1913 (shortly after Leginska went there) and became assistant conductor to Toscanini at the Metropolitan Opera House, New York, serving in that capacity until 1916. Later he became chief conductor at the Metropolitan and also guest-conducted at venues worldwide.

of these orchestras. These claims did not pass unchallenged; The Dutch-born American musician Antonia Brica (1902-89) later asserted that she had been the first woman to conduct the Berlin Philharmonic, but as she did not start conducting in a serious way until 1930 it is difficult to see how this could have been true. Catherine Contos [2] said Brica was the second woman to conduct it. But whether Leginska was the first or one of the first is of little importance; the point is that she was a pioneer. At that time women conductors able to conduct major orchestras were a rare breed indeed.

Leginska almost certainly knew, before she started to conduct, that she would run into prejudices, and so it turned out. Samuel Johnson once said: "A woman's preaching is like a dog's walking on his hinder legs. It is not done well; but you are surprised to find it done at all." [3] In the same way, many men, down the years, had been unable to take seriously the prospect of a woman conducting an orchestra; on the rare occasions women had done so, their efforts were generally regarded with a mixture of disbelief, hilarity, and sometimes, contempt. It had long been a strange fact that women pianists were regarded as 'acceptable', musically, and such distinguished practitioners of the keyboard as Clara Schumann, Annette Essipoff and Teresa Carreño, who preceded Leginska, had been accepted for what they were – fine pianists. But somehow women conductors were a different matter. They were a curiosity; an oddity. The prejudice was of long standing. Samuel Pepys reported rather patronisingly in his diary, with apparent amusement, that he had observed, at the Globe in Greenwich, "a woman with a rod in her hand keeping time to the musique while it plays".[4] In 1739 a Frenchman visiting Venice was surprised but captivated by the sight of "a young pretty nun in a white habit, with a bunch of pomegranate blossoms over her ear, conducting the orchestra and beating time with all the grace and precision imaginable".[5] In the middle of the 19th century Josephine Weinlich formed the Vienna Ladies' Orchestra, consisting of 20 members, and in 1871 they visited the USA and gave two concerts under her direction in New York. Towards the end of the 19th century several ladies' orchestras were formed in America and elsewhere but in the main they consisted of only a few players and their activities were confined to the playing of light and popular music in parks and summer resorts.

The situation had not changed much when Ethel Leginska began conducting major orchestras in the early 1920s. [6] If she had accomplished no other feat in music, if she had never played a note on the piano, composed a tune or taught a student, she ought to have achieved a place in musical history for her work as a conductor. *Who's Who in America* credited her with being "the first woman to conduct the principal symphony orchestras of Europe and America, among them the Berlin Philharmonic, the London Symphony, Paris Conservatory and New York Symphony".

When Leginska toured Britain and the continent as a conductor in 1924 her appearances seem to have been very successful artistically and financially. Her talents and unique personality are confirmed by the contemporary accounts of some of her concerts. After appearing in Munich with the Konzertverein Orchestra a critic wrote: [7]

"Leginska created a justified sensation – and the artistic impression of her conducting ranks higher than many of her male colleagues."

Another observed: [8]

Leginska was a sensation – a musician of great assurance and technical skill."

A third reviewer remarked: [9]

"She played and conducted with taste, delicacy and mastery."

When Leginska travelled to Berlin and appeared with the Berlin Philharmonic Orchestra the critics were no less enthusiastic. The *Boessen Courier* reported: [10]

"Leginska proved her ability to conduct. She led with skill and assurance and the orchestra followed her with interest. She makes use of the most modern orchestral effects."

The music critic of the *Deutsche Allgemeine Zeitung*, a prestigious newspaper, remarked: [11]

"Leginska does her work well. She possesses unusual ability. She has thoroughly mastered her orchestral scores, and she understands how to impart her will to the orchestra with energy. Beethoven's A major symphony was very beautifully performed."

In similar vein, the *Berlin Tageblatt* noted: [12]

"She appears as if charged with music, manifesting itself from an inner urge, which gives her the precedence of genuineness."

The *National Zeitung*, equally enthusiastic, observed: [13]

"Leginska dominated the orchestra completely by the storm of her tremendous temperament and aroused the audience to tumultuous applause."

Leginska had conducted the London Symphony Orchestra at about the same time as her German triumphs and had been very favourably received:

The Daily Telegraph critic wrote: [14]

"Leginska conducts with freedom and élan, and her expressive gestures are eloquent of the effects at which she was aiming."

The Observer also reported favourably: [15]

"Her movements are free and apt – she is as ambidextrous as a conductor as she necessarily has to be as a pianist."

Publicity picture from about 1925. It also appeared on the front cover of the Aeolian Company's 'Duo-Art Monthly', April 1927.

Another publicity picture from around 1925

Leginska the conductor

According to another London newspaper, *The Star*: [16]

"She knows the score thoroughly. Leginska knows, in short, what she wants, and has learned how to get it."

The *Daily News* noted: [17]

"Her beat is clear and all her gestures mean something."

The *Daily Mail* observed: [18]

"There was no tentativeness or half-measures about this conducting. She had the orchestra well strung up – everyone on the *qui vive*, and working."

Unwilling to rest on her laurels as a distinguished pianist, Leginska had declared her wish to become a professional symphonic conductor, a role for which she had prepared carefully. And yet, in spite of her outstanding well-documented brilliance as a musician, she had to put up with hostility from some of the male orchestral players who could not accept the concept that a woman could conduct an orchestra, and sometimes with condescending reviews from the critics. After her series of concerts in Paris, Berlin, Munich and London in 1924 she returned to America and on 9th January 1925 appeared with the New York Symphony Orchestra at Carnegie Hall as both conductor and piano soloist in the same concert, as she had in many of those in Europe. This concert, Leginska's conducting debut in the USA, was the first time a woman had appeared on the Carnegie Hall podium, an event recognised by the critics – grudgingly in some cases – as a milestone in American musical life. She conducted Beethoven's Symphony No. 7 in A minor, Op. 92 and then played the Bach Concerto in F, conducting from the piano. This practice, which had been common in Mozart's day, had become rare by the 20th century. Leginska was a pioneer of its revival.

Leginska was well aware that not only were many of the male orchestral members hostile; some of the music critics, almost all of whom were male, could be downright patronising, and the supercilious tone of some of their remarks after this concert proved that women still had a long way to go before they would be accepted as conductors, however proficient they might be. The *New York Herald Tribune* reported the next day that it was "to Leginska's credit that nothing serious occurred to mar the performance". The *New York American* observed that Leginska's debut "occasioned curiosity, scepticism and even some hardly suppressed merriment". Nevertheless, the same critic conceded that "she displayed a thorough knowledge of the scores and got the effects she wanted from the orchestra".

By now Leginska was not only the foremost woman pianist of her day, but she was the foremost woman conductor as well and within a very short time many invitations were extended to her to appear as guest conductor of several major orchestras. In April 1925 she conducted the People's Symphony Orchestra of Boston and gave her usual skilled performance. Again Leginska's appearance as conductor was a significant historical event. The *Boston Post* reported: [19]

"History, musically speaking, was made at the Symphony Hall last night when Ethel Leginska led the orchestra through its 21st and final concert of the season. It was a triumph both for the band itself and for its doughty guest conductor."

The *Boston Transcript* critic wrote: [20]

"She controlled and inspired her orchestra, disclosed and vitalised the music in hand, and now and then laid upon it a vivid, personal touch."

The *Telegram* observed: [21]

"The first symphony concert ever conducted by a woman in this city was a triumph both for the band and for the woman."

The *Christian Science Monitor* remarked: [22]

"She knew what she was about and had definite notions of what she wanted, as well as the means to impress her desires on the players."

Finally, *The Traveller* reported: [23]

"A large enthusiastic audience called Leginska out again and again."

In August of the same year (1925) Leginska travelled to California to conduct the Los Angeles Philharmonic Orchestra at the Hollywood Bowl, a vast amphitheatre. Her performance there drew an enthusiastic response from the critics. The remarks reported in the various newspapers include:

"She afforded readings that brought back memories of famous leaders abroad." [24]

"Both orchestra and audience were completely won by the magnetic personality of Leginska." [25]

The *Daily Times*, in an ecstatic account, observed: [26]

"The popular triumph of triumphs in the Hollywood Bowl belongs to Ethel Leginska. Thirty thousand persons found their way to the great amphitheatre and the applause grew into a veritable ovation culminating with cheers and bravos."

The *Examiner*, not to be outdone, remarked: [27]

"An artist who can attract 30,000 people! That's Ethel Leginska! A greater tribute still was that her performance held the crowd until the very end of the concert."

The respected Californian music critic Bruno David Ussher also wrote a long review of Leginska's concert at the Hollywood Bowl. An extract from it (the section dealing with Leginska's compositions 'Six Nursery Rhymes' that were performed during the concert) was quoted in Chapter 9 (page 133). The review is quoted in full in Appendix 7 (page 336), since it gives a very carefully constructed and unbiased account not only of Leginska's skills as a musician and the particular force of her personality, but also of

Pianist, Composer, Conductor, Teacher

Leginska on board ship, possibly the 'Leviathan', during one of her transatlantic crossings. This picture was taken on 30th June 1925.

some of the prejudices she had to face when conducting a male-dominated orchestra.

The successes of Leginska as a newly-established conductor that have been described so far were just the beginning; many more were to come and their story will be told in Chapter 13. Meanwhile, Leginska's appearances as a piano soloist were continuing. She was happy enough to appear in that capacity, knowing that the other musical facets of her career were enabling her to achieve musical fulfilment. Her musical compositions were being presented regularly, not merely in her own concerts but in those of other musicians, whilst she also still found time to teach a talented succession of pupils. Thus, in the mid-1920s, Leginska was established as a concert pianist, composer, conductor and teacher, and her life was a hectic whirl. It is perhaps hardly surprising that something had to give; she was more than burning the candle at both ends.

It was the fragility of Leginska's physique in conjunction with massive overwork that led to an incident, albeit of short duration, that alarmed her friends and aroused much publicity. Chapter 12 explains.

References: Chapter 11

1. *Christian Science Monitor*, 4th June 1920.
2. Catherine Contos: *Brava, Maestra!* Article in HI-FI / Musical America, May 1971, p. MA 7.
3. Samuel Johnson (1709 - 1784), English poet, critic and lexicographer. Quoted in *Boswell, Life*, Vol. I, p. 463 (31st July 1763).
4. Diary of Samuel Pepys (available in various editions). Entry for 16th June 1661.
5. Same article as quoted in reference 2.
6. It was not until 20th August 1984 that a woman (Cuban-born Odaline de la Martinez, then aged 35) conducted an entire BBC Henry Wood Promenade Concert in London. In the late 1920s Dame Ethel Smyth, who had received the honour of DBE in 1922, had conducted part of a 'Prom'.
7. *Augsburger Neuste Nachtrichten*, 4th November 1924.
8. *Deutsche Allgemeine Zeitung*, 11th October 1924.
9. *Staatszeitung*, 22nd October 1924.
10. *Boessen Courier*, 19th November 1924.
11. *Deutsche Allgemeine Zeitung*, 14th November 1924. (This was a review of a different concert from the one reported in reference 8.)
12. *Berlin Tageblatt*, 21st November 1924.
13. *National Zeitung*, 14th November 1924.
14. *The Daily Telegraph*, 7th November 1924.
15. *The Observer*, 9th November 1924.
16. *The Star*, 4th November 1924.
17. *Daily News*, 6th November 1924.
18. *Daily Mail*, 6th November 1924.
19. *Boston Post*, 6th April 1925.
20. *Boston Transcript*, 6th April 1925.
21. *Telegram*, 6th April 1925.
22. *Christian Science Monitor*, 6th April 1925.
23. *The Traveller*, 6th April 1925.
24. *Los Angeles Evening Express*, 6th August 1925.
25. *Los Angeles Herald*, 6th August 1925.
26. *Los Angeles Daily Times*, 6th August 1925.
27. *Los Angeles Examiner*, 6th August 1925.

Chapter 12

The Disappearing Pianist: An Enigma

In January 1925, a curious episode occurred which attracted much attention in the American newspapers. Leginska failed to appear for a piano recital at Carnegie Hall in New York and 2,000 people were kept waiting. Not only did she not arrive for the recital – she disappeared, and was missing for nearly a week. It will be recalled from Chapter 5 (pages 69 - 70) that a somewhat similar occurrence had taken place in London in 1909 when Leginska 'went missing' before a recital. But at that time there were extenuating circumstances; she was only 22 years old, her marriage was in difficulties and she was having to cope with the care of a young son (he was less than five months old) whilst at the same time facing a demanding schedule of concert engagements that required the preparation of a huge amount of new material. According to the American musician Radie Britain there had also been an incident in Munich, at around the same year as the one in London, when Leginska had failed to arrive for a recital, though no corroborative reports have been found. [1]

Although these events of 1909 had aroused speculation and comment at the time they were soon forgotten, and in the years that followed, up to 1925, there had been no repetitions. Leginska had been very reliable, even punctilious, in fulfilling her engagements, always appearing as scheduled. By 1925, not only was she one of the foremost pianists of the day, she was also an established composer and conductor. Often she was pianist and conductor in the same concert and sometimes her name was on the programme as a composer as well. Endowed with huge personal charisma, she was a personality – always in the public eye. She had also attracted a large clientele of private students. One of these was Lucille Oliver (already referred to in Chapter 9, page 123) who is mentioned again here because she played a part in the story that is to follow. Leginska liked her, and had engaged her as secretary and companion. She was to remain with Leginska in this capacity for the remainder of her (Lucille's) life and, as well as being a friend, became assistant teacher, cook, housekeeper and general factotum.

This, then, was the scene at the beginning of 1925. Leginska and Miss Oliver were living at that time in an apartment at 313, West 27th Street, New York, a location convenient for Carnegie Hall (at 57th Street/7th Avenue) and several other New York musical venues. Leginska had just got back from her successful tour of France, Germany and Britain where she had appeared in a pioneering role as a woman conductor, and had already made

The Disappearing Pianist: An Enigma

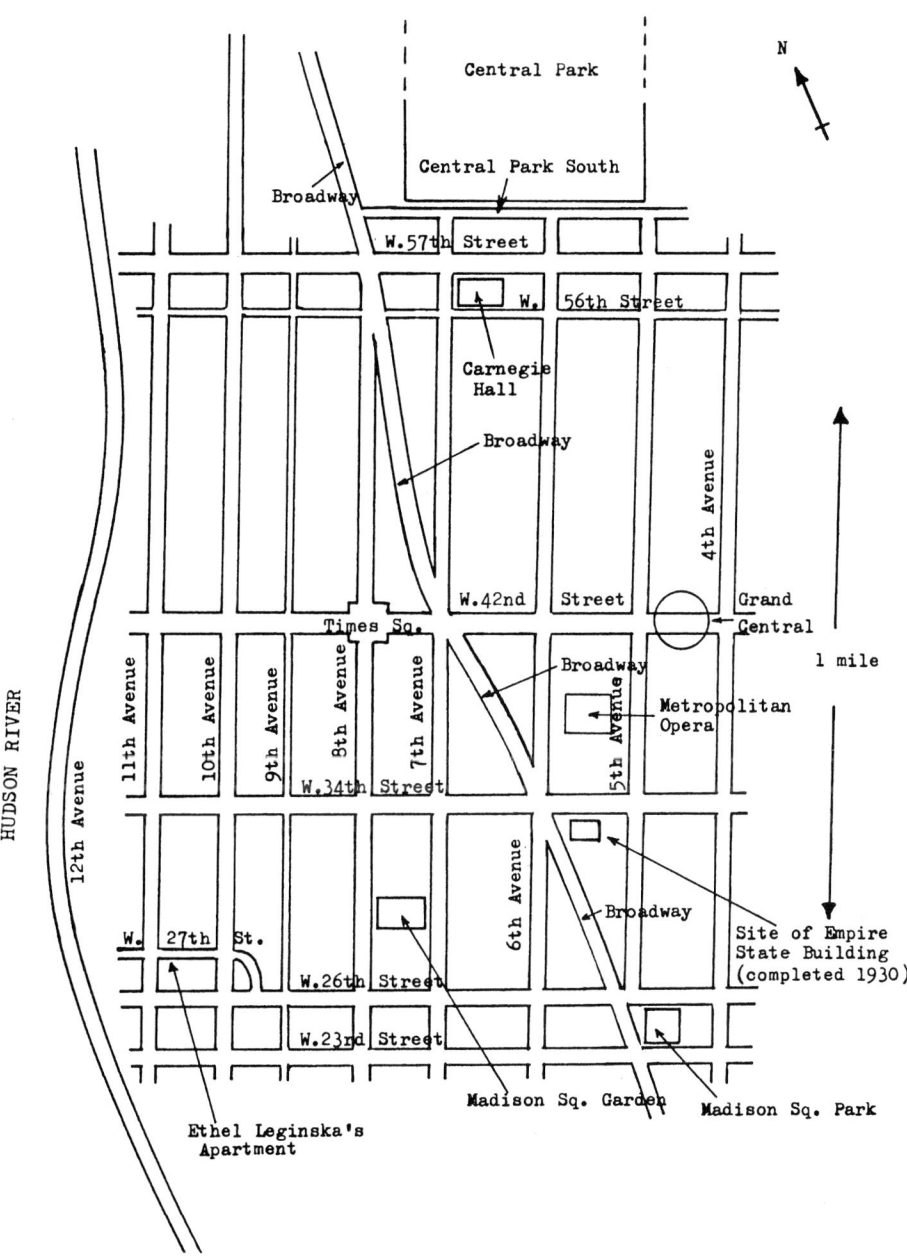

Sketch of part of Manhatten Island, New York as it was in the 1920s, showing the location of Ethel Leginska's apartment, Carnegie Hall, and relevant major roads

her New York debut as a conductor at Carnegie Hall on 9th January (see page 161). Many more such appearances were already scheduled in the USA. Leginska was booked for Carnegie Hall again seventeen days later, Monday 26th January, this time not to conduct but to give a piano recital. *The New York Times* of that day announced in its 'Concerts' section: [2]

Carnegie Hall. Tonight at 8.15:
PIANO RECITAL BY
ETHEL LEGINSKA
CHOPIN-LISZT PROGRAM
mgt. Haensel & Jones. Knabe Piano

The story of what happened can be pieced together from subsequent reports in the newspapers, in particular *The New York Times*. The following account is based on a lengthy report in that newspaper. [3]

Ethel Leginska and Lucille Oliver had left their apartment at 8 o'clock. They were late; they should have set off earlier because the recital was scheduled to start at 8.15. Why they had been delayed is not known. No taxicab was in sight, so Miss Oliver left Leginska outside their apartment whilst she herself hurried to 8th Avenue, the nearest major road (see map on the previous page) knowing it would be crowded with theatre-bound traffic at that hour, and believing she would find an empty cab there. To her dismay the cabs were all full, but after 10 minutes an empty cab did appear which she hastily summoned. On her instructions they drove back down 27th Street to their apartment where she had left Leginska, expecting to find her there. But she had gone. Checking that Leginska was not in the apartment, Miss Oliver concluded that she must have found some other conveyance and preceded her to Carnegie Hall. Consequently, with a feeling of some relief, she asked the driver to take her along 56th Street to the stage door of Carnegie Hall. To her horror she found the hall attendants, managers and audience all waiting. Leginska had not arrived. Miss Oliver explained what had happened, and hurried off to seek the advice of some of Leginska's friends who were in the hall. After a while, when there was still no sign of the pianist, she summoned the police.

By this time it was approaching 9 o'clock and the 2,000-strong audience was naturally very restive. News of the strange situation was eventually conveyed to the audience by the management and at the same time Mr Haensel, the Carnegie Hall Manager, searched the Hall for an emergency performer. As luck would have it there was one such person present, the Polish pianist Mieczyslaw Munz, just off the train from the Pacific coast. He went onto the stage, after a few minutes' preparation, and gave a complete programme. To some extent he followed the programme Leginska had been due to give, playing the pieces by Chopin that were on the programme, but the Liszt items that Leginska had intended to play were replaced by a Beethoven Sonata. Munz's success was instantaneous, demonstrating in spectacular manner the truth of the old adage that it is an ill wind that blows no good. Not surprisingly in view of the circumstances, he received a very sympathetic hearing from the vast audience. Hardly a person left before the end, and Munz was recalled many times. In addition to the pieces he had volunteered he was called upon to play three encores.

To anyone *au fait* with the musical scene in America his triumph would not have come as a surprise. He was far from being a gifted amateur called upon in true story-book fashion, like 'the volunteer organist' of the old song, to replace a famous musician at short notice; he was a young professional pianist with a large repertoire at his fingertips – one who was rapidly rising in the musical world. Nevertheless, this un-anticipated triumph resulted in a spectacular advance, at a stroke, to his developing career. *

And so Leginska's disaster turned out to be an unexpected day of glory for Munz. But it is with Leginska that this account is concerned, so let us take up the story as it continued to unfold. Leginska's friends were naturally alarmed at her uncharacteristic failure to appear, fearing something had happened to her, and they persuaded the police to send out a general alarm. The appeal was made by the officer in charge of the West 30th Street Police Station. He announced that "when last seen she is believed to have been about to enter a taxicab; at least, her secretary left her in front of the house, and supposed, when she returned to find the pianist gone, that she had entered another." *The New York Times* reported on the day after the recital that "although police throughout the city had received a description of Leginska, and were told to keep a sharp look-out for her, no trace of her had been gained at a late hour last night". The newspaper also put forward its own speculations about the reason for Leginska's disappearance, after brief introductory remarks, as follows.

"Miss Leginska is the English pianist, composer and conductor who directed the New York Symphony Orchestra at Carnegie Hall recently. She was one of the pianists who took part in the piano carneval [*sic*] which was staged at the Metropolitan. She had appeared in the dual role of pianist and conductor and aspired also to be known as a

---

* Mieczyslaw Munz (1900 - 1976) was born in Cracow, Poland and studied at the Academy of Music in Vienna and later in Berlin where he had private lessons from Busoni. Later (mainly in the 1930s) he toured much of the world as a concert pianist and in 1941 was appointed Professor of Piano at the Curtis Institute of Music in Philadelphia where Josef Hofmann had for many years, until his retirement in 1938, been Director. He recorded 17 piano rolls for Ampico. He married, but was later divorced from, Aniela Mlynarska, who after their divorce married the famous pianist Artur Rubinstein at Caxton Hall in London.

composer. She was known to be an exceedingly nervous person, and it was suggested by her secretary that while waiting for the taxi she may have wandered away in a fit of absentmindedness."

A description of Leginska followed, in which it was stated that she wore an evening gown, black patent leather pumps, black silk stockings and a three-quarter length caracul * coat. She wore no hat, and, as far as the police were able to find out, no jewellery. Not having carried a purse, it was believed she had neither money nor door key, according to Mr John Gordon from whom Leginska and Lucille Oliver rented the apartment.

At the dawn of the next day (28th January) Leginska was still missing after 36 hours and the story figured again prominently in *The New York Times* under the heading: [4]

Leginska not found: Nerves are blamed

According to this report in *The New York Times*, Lucille Oliver knew about the incident of 1909 when Leginska failed to appear for a recital in Britain. She had no personal knowledge of the event because she had not known Leginska then and had never asked her about it. But she told reporters that, according to the stories she had heard, the pianist had failed to turn up for a concert in England "about 15 years ago". She said she did not know whether it had been due to amnesia or 'temperament', but thought it might have been caused by "lack of memory". "It may have been a case of temporary illness or something of that sort", explained Miss Oliver, who was said to have spent the whole of the previous day communicating with the pianist's friends in an attempt to shed light on the situation. But they had been unable to provide any clues. Miss Oliver added that Miss Leginska was of a very nervous temperament and added, rightly, that she had been overworked during the last few weeks. But she was unable to provide any information that would help clear up the mystery.

The New York Times suspected that there were people around who knew Leginska's whereabouts, and suggested that she was "not definitely missing, nor had she been definitely found". The reason for this view was that the paper had received information, it said, that Leginska might be staying with friends. "Miss Leginska has not been officially found", reported the paper, "and the police are still seeking her. But there was fairly definite information that she had been at the home of friends here while the hunt was on and no great alarm seemed to be felt by those most interested in her." The paper believed that Leginska had fled "in a fit of what was once known as artistic temperament but by modern psychologists would no doubt be

---

* Caracul is a type of fur, or cloth imitating it.

known as a 'fear complex'." The paper then reported 'rumors' that the pianist's hands had not been in good condition of late, and she had fears regarding her ability to cope with the intricate technical requirements of the programme. The newspaper suggested that she feared criticism, "and so, taking advantage of her companion, she became a little girl again and just ran away." Credence was lent to the theory, it was said, by two pieces of information. One was the story of her disappearance in London, 15 years previously, which had just come to general attention. The other was that Leginska had recently complained, so it was said, that the cold weather had injured her hands and made her unfit to play.

The theory that Leginska was staying with friends came about as a result of undenied speculation that she was staying at the home of Miss Evelione Taglione, a pupil and friend of Leginska (already mentioned in Chapter 9, page 123) to whom Leginska's composition *Dance of a Puppet* had been dedicated. When reporters had called at Miss Taglione's rented apartment they had apparently formed the impression, for reasons not stated, that Leginska was, or had been, there since her disappearance. The owners of the property were said to be away, so efforts to procure an admission or denial of the suggestion failed. A newspaper sent a telegram to Leginska at the apartment to see if she accepted delivery; it was reported by the Telegraph Company that it had been unable to effect delivery because the addressee "had been there but had left".

Meanwhile Lucille Oliver, Leginska's secretary and companion, was becoming chief spokeswoman on behalf of Leginska. [5] "I think it is a shame that some of the papers are inferring that the whole thing is a publicity story. She certainly doesn't want publicity of that sort, for it makes it appear that she is unreliable and does not keep faith with her audiences." Miss Oliver explained that she had discussed Leginska's disappearance with the pianist's friends in the audience on the evening of the recital before reporting the matter to the police. "I tried to keep it from the newspapers. Mme Leginska is too well known and too well liked to go in for that kind of sensationalism." She went on to insist that Leginska's friends were "frantic" over her disappearance. One, she said, Mrs Frank Smith, whose husband was said to be an official of the Consolidated Gas Company, had sent word that Mr Smith had put a private detective on the case.

Lucille Oliver cast doubt on the theory that Leginska was or had been staying at the home of Miss Taglione. She said her friend and employer would probably lose $1,000 by having failed to appear for the recital. She asserted that Leginska's career was prospering and pointed out that Leginska had just learned that she had been selected to conduct the People's Symphony Orchestra in Boston in March, just a few weeks hence.

The police still had nothing further to report in their hunt for the missing pianist except that the last person definitely known to have seen her was Mrs Charles Roschore, who lived next door. She said she had watched Leginska "running towards 9th Avenue through 27th Street" whilst Miss Oliver was hunting a taxicab to take the pianist to Carnegie Hall.

By Thursday 29th January, when Leginska had been missing for two and a half days, the feelings of the previous day that she was safe, lying low in someone's home, were beginning to evaporate, to be replaced by ominous signs of alarm. *The New York Times* reported [6] that police had found "a clue", but went on to say that they would not divulge what it was. The case was again reported prominently in detail under the sub-heading "May have lost her memory". Police believed that Leginska had called on "an acquaintance" at about the time her disappearance had become known at Carnegie Hall. "All thought that the mystery had been created for publicity purposes was discounted yesterday by the police and an effort was made to find the missing woman."

The police were worried by the fact that Leginska had no money with her; the only item of value she had with her when she disappeared, in those pre-'plastic card' days, was the caracul coat she was wearing. A search of pawnshops was made in New York in case she had pawned it to get some money, but no trace was found. All Leginska's friends believed that her disappearance was due to "a nervous breakdown". Lucille Oliver was by this time distraught. "I am convinced that something must have snapped in her mind causing her to forget her identity", she said. Lucille had been brooding about Leginska's earlier disappearance in London and told reporters:

"Just such an experience occurred in London some years ago. I never knew what she did, but we found out that she got on a train and went to the Midlands. There she regained her memory when she heard a pianoforte. If she is alive now, it will probably be through the playing of a pianoforte that she will realise who she is. For the last few hours I have been fearing that something tragic might develop. I cannot believe that she has ended her life. If she had done so, it is in a moment of unreason. The statement of the police that they have a clue is encouraging and I hope it leads to her recovery."

The New York Times, in its report, was of the opinion that Lucille Oliver herself was breaking under the strain of Leginska's disappearance:

"She had to call a physician yesterday and she was warned that unless she took a rest she was in danger of collapse."

Whilst the case was reported reasonably objectively in *The New York Times* there was no shortage of speculation in some of the other American newspapers. The popular press – the nearest equivalent in the 1920s to the present-day tabloids – worked on the principle that if no reason was known for Leginska's disappearance then one must be made up. Under the headline "Leginska Case Laid to Love" one of these newspapers wrote:

> "Unrequited love may be the reason for the disappearance of Ethel Leginska, pianiste, [sic] who dropped from sight while 2,000 music lovers awaited her arrival for a concert at Carnegie Hall Monday night. Continuing their search today, police of the Missing Persons Bureau have made discoveries that they say point definitely to that conclusion. They are attempting to locate and question a man whom the artist is said to have told friends she has loved for nine years with 'A love I cannot down, though I know it to be hopeless'. There are said to be reasons why this man cannot return her affection. Questioned today, Mieczyslaw Munz, who took Leginska's place on her failure to appear for the concert, said he scarcely knew the pianiste. He had met her only three times, he said. He denied ever having been a guest at her apartment."

A less fanciful, more plausible, viewpoint was put forward by Mr Frederick Peck, one of Leginska's two uncles who were living in New York (both were her late mother's brothers). In the issue of *The New York Times* of 29th January he spoke up for her and was reported as saying that he believed a nervous breakdown was responsible for Ethel's disappearance:

> "Ethel always was highly strung and had a highly nervous temperament. Lately the amount of work she has been doing may have been too much for her. There is no other explanation short of foul play that I can give for her disappearance. She always kept her word, and if she was engaged to play that night I'm sure she would have unless prevented by means beyond her control."

By Saturday, 31st January the police were very apprehensive for Leginska's safety and her friends were distinctly alarmed. [7] The 'clue' which the police had referred to earlier in the week turned out to be only that Leginska had been seen, so it was thought, in a restaurant at about the time of her disappearance. But it had later transpired that this person was in fact someone else. So the enquiry was getting nowhere. Telegrams had been sent to all Leginska's known friends but none of them knew where she was and none had seen her since she disappeared. The situation was not at all good.

Then, as suddenly as she had vanished, Ethel Leginska re-appeared, on Sunday, 1st February. She had been missing for six days. The next day *The New York Times* reported, "Leginska is found, her mind a blank. Reported in Boston". [8] Full details were being kept secret, but Leginska was said to be "in a sanitarium" and friends who had seen her said she had suffered a breakdown and was in an "awful condition". It was reported that "she had suffered a complete lapse of memory from Monday until Saturday, but that her mind had cleared." "She is in an awful state", said Miss Oliver. "Her mind is a blank on what happened to her from the time she disappeared until she was found." Miss Oliver immediately packed her suitcase and headed for Boston to be with her friend.

Later Leginska was said to be "staying with friends." She had, according to *The New York Times* of 2nd February, been located by the police. "The fact that the musician had been found was confirmed by Capt John Ayers, Commander of the Bureau of Missing Persons, who declined to say where or how she had been found or where she was." His statement was as follows:

"Ethel Leginska was located yesterday at a place outside the city where she is staying with friends. Her disappearance appeared to have been the direct result of a nervous breakdown caused by overwork. Her location was brought about by the work of the Bureau of Missing Persons. Leginska remembers nothing from the time she left her secretary, Miss Lucille Oliver, until she was located. On request of Miss Leginska, the location of her friends is withheld. Her friends have also asked that no further statement be made by the police. So far as this case is concerned, the case is closed."

After giving out this statement, Captain Ayers "disappeared himself" according to *The New York Times*, leaving word that it would be impossible to reach him and that he would have nothing more to say on the matter.

Lucille Oliver was reported as saying, in a telephone call from Boston to New York, that Leginska was found "in a town in Pennsylvania and that her friends had taken her to a sanitarium in Boston." She said Leginska had had a "partial loss of consciousness", and wandered for several days before being found. Another friend said she ". . . habitually and incessantly overworked, and it was not in the least remarkable that her health had broken down".

The final comment from *The New York Times* on the matter was that neither of her two uncles, Frederick W. Peck of 342 Emerson Street and George W. Peck of 61 Norris Street, knew anything of the circumstances of her discovery; they had heard nothing from her since her reappearance and did not know where she was staying. Leginska had no other relatives in the United States apart from themselves, they said. *

Meanwhile, news of the disappearance had filtered back to Leginska's home-city of Hull. A month after the event, the following headline and sub-headings appeared in the *Hull News*, following earlier news stories: [9]

HULL PIANIST'S ADVENTURE
MISS ETHEL LEGINSKA
TELLS HER STORY
WANDERING PENNILESS

"Miss Ethel Leginska, the famous English pianist, made her reappearance last Monday at Joplin, Missouri, where she will give a piano recital (writes the "Daily

---

* Except, presumably, for her son, Cedric, who was 16 at the time.

The Disappearing Pianist: An Enigma

Express" New York correspondent). When interviewed on her mysterious disappearance, she said: "I remember starting to look for a taxicab to go to the Carnegie Hall" (where she was due to perform before an audience of 2,000), "but the world grew hazy. I slipped through one dark street after another for about two hours. I have no recollection of becoming unconscious. It was like being intensely pre-occupied and then coming to, without the ability to recall what I was pre-occupied about.

Realisation

"The thing that brought me up with a shock was the realisation that the concert must be over. I felt desperate. I had walked far down Manhattan Island without a penny. I remembered some friends near, and walked miserably to their house, and told them everything about my career, my work and my life.

"I must have been badly hysterical, for I told them that the one thing I could not bear was to be found. They gave me their word not to tell anybody – and kept it. Music sang in my ears, and I asked for paper and sat at the piano and wrote.

Food at the piano

"My friend's wife, who had been a nurse, understood my condition. Nobody spoke to me. Food was brought to me at the piano and I ate it with one hand. At last much of the music in my head was set down, and I felt better. I knew then that I could face people again.

"The second day I remembered that people must be worried and searching for me. I telephoned my secretary, Miss Lucille Oliver, and I was persuaded to go to another friend near Boston, where there was good air and sunshine, and while I was there I finished my concerto.

"I think it is going to be very nice. I am sorry I disappointed the audience at the Carnegie Hall, and I ask for their forgiveness. I also ask them to remember that I have kept faith with my audiences for ten years, but I have had an utter nervous breakdown."

What do we make of Leginska's statement, as reported? Was it the truth as she saw it, or was it an account prepared and offered for public consumption? No-one can really be sure. One thing that is certain is that the concerto, the creation of which Leginska so romantically described in true Hollywood style, seems to have disappeared. There does not appear to be any record of its having been performed.

And so the episode of the disappearing pianist came to an end. Not quite a nine-day wonder, it was at least a six-day one. What was the reason? The authors have sought the views of several of her former students on this matter and various factors emerged. Let us consider them.

For one thing, Leginska undoubtedly was of a highly-strung, nervous disposition. Furthermore, although she was a brilliant pianist, there is plenty of evidence that she did not really enjoy playing in public as the 'centre of attention' – something her teacher, Mrs Russell Starr, had noticed when little Ethel Liggins was ten. Nor did she really enjoy playing music from memory. On one occasion when a certain performer suffered a loss of memory

Leginska said to Radie Britain, "Why must one memorise all those notes? It is the music from the composer that is important." [10]

Joseph Enos, a former student of Leginska, was once brave enough to ask Leginska about the 'disappearing pianist' incident and said she herself had put it down to 'nerves'. [11] She had remarked that so many of her recitals had met with such excellent reviews from the critics that she dare not repeat the same programme at a later date without detriment to her career; she could not match the earlier performances without days of re-study, which she might not have time for, and she could not bear the thought of giving a sub-standard performance, by her standards. It must be remembered that only a fortnight previously Leginska had conducted the New York Symphony Orchestra at a packed Carnegie Hall and played a Bach concerto – an occasion which had also marked her debut as the conductor of a major orchestra in America. It must have required great preparation and been mentally stressful. Her future as a conductor rested on the success of that concert and her mental and physical resources must inevitably have been drained.

It is interesting to note that Ethel Leginska and her companion Lucille Oliver were late setting out for Carnegie Hall. Possibly something stressful had happened earlier, or the lateness might have had something to do with her general emotional state at the time. Whatever the reason, the resulting frantic rush cannot have helped Leginska to approach the recital calmly. Add all these things together – the dread of not giving her best, her nervousness, her impulsive personality, the fact that her hands were apparently not in their best condition, physical and mental fatigue due to months of overwork, and we see here a glimmer of the truth – do these factors perhaps add up to a recipe for calamity? Temporarily it might all have been too much for Leginska, and, on the spur of the moment when Lucille Oliver's back was turned, she 'blew a fuse' and ran away.

Another of Leginska's pupils, Beverly Carmen, has written to the authors with her views about the incident: [12]

> "Leginska once said to us, 'You cannot do it all (daily cares) and be a great artist too. I once tried; I rented myself a flat in Greenwich Village and tried to do all my cooking and cleaning, and it was a fiasco.' Another time, 'Don't ever play if you are not ready!' Still another, 'Don't give a damn' (this, to a child) 'what THEY say about you – except if they say you played badly. Anything else doesn't count!'
>
> "Put all this together and you may get what I did: Leginska trying to 'do it all' in her Greenwich Village apartment; not being sufficiently ready to play her best; and simply not showing up. Carnegie Hall be damned, audience be damned. But they never got a chance to say she played badly!"

The Disappearing Pianist: An Enigma

Leginska's disappearance in 1925: A few contemporary headlines

Because of this incident, which created so much publicity, Leginska was sometimes thereafter tagged 'the disappearing pianist'. It is impossible to say how much the event harmed her career, if at all. On the one hand, the incident brought her name to the forefront of the minds of the public. On the other, it gave the erroneous impression she was unreliable. The 'disappearing pianist' jibe was perhaps unfair. Between 1909 and 1925 Leginska had always given her recitals with the utmost reliability and great flair. Following this incident, after two or three weeks' rest, she was back in circulation as teacher, pianist, recording artist, composer and teacher, and was once again her usual effervescent self. The event described in this chapter was a wholly uncharacteristic 'blip'. Her isolated lapse was not to be compared with, say, those of Vladimir Horowitz, whose frequent letting-down of audiences at the last minute was well known.

There were to be no more instances in the future of Leginska failing to appear for recitals or concerts. The Carnegie Hall incident was but a brief interlude in a distinguished career.

As a tailpiece to this story, it is interesting to compare Ethel Leginska's disappearance with an astonishingly parallel case which occurred in England the following year when Agatha Christie, the famous English crime writer, disappeared and was missing for eleven days. Like Leginska, she quickly returned to her normal routine after the event and the incident was never repeated in her long and remarkably successful career as a writer. *

---

* On 3rd December 1926 Christie had set out alone from her south of England home in her Morris Cowley car which was later found abandoned at the bottom of a nearby slope. No-one knew where she was and the British papers followed the story of her disappearance day by day just as the American papers followed the Leginska case. The story even appeared in *The New York Times*. Christie was missing for 11 days and was finally tracked down at the Harrogate Hydro Hotel, Yorkshire, having been spotted and recognised by a keen-eyed chambermaid. She claimed to have had a memory loss so complete that she had no recollection of what had happened during the intervening period. Many theories abounded. It is now believed that she knew exactly what she was doing and the incident was 'staged' to spite her unfaithful husband. But Christie never admitted this, always claiming the disappearance was due to amnesia. One wonders whether she had read about the Leginska case! In Christie's autobiography the episode of her disappearance is not even mentioned. [13]

References: Chapter 12

1. Information contained in letters to the authors from Radie Britain (see page 194 for biographical note on Radie Britain).
2. *The New York Times*, Monday, 26th January 1925.
3. *The New York Times*, Tuesday, 27th January 1925 (the day after the recital which Leginska should have given).
4. *The New York Times*, news update, Wednesday, 28th January 1925.
5. *The New York Times*, Wednesday, 28th January 1925. (Lucille Oliver's statement.)
6. *The New York Times*, Thursday, 29th January 1925.
7. *The New York Times*, Saturday, 31st January 1925.
8. *The New York Times*, Monday, 2nd February 1925.
9. *Hull News*, Saturday, 28th February 1925.
10. Radie Britain, Hollywood, Los Angeles (correspondence with the authors).
11. Joseph Enos, Benicia, California (correspondence with the authors).
12. Beverly Carmen, formerly of Los Angeles, California and now residing at Los Alamos, New Mexico (correspondence with the authors).
13. Jared Cade: *Agatha Christie and the Missing Eleven Days*. Peter Owen, London, November 1998. There is a good shorter account of the events surrounding Agatha Christie's disappearance and the explanation of the event that is currently thought to be the most likely, in *The Daily Telegraph*, 'Weekend' supplement, 24th October 1998. See also *Agatha Christie – an Autobiography*, William Collins Sons & Co Ltd, London, 1977.

Radie Britain (references 1 and 10) worked professionally with Leginska.
Joseph Enos and Beverly Carmen (references 11 and 12) are two of Leginska's former students.

Chapter 13

Leginska's Orchestras

We have seen in Chapters 9 and 11 how Leginska the pianist had transformed herself into Leginska the musician of many talents. In particular, she had become a proficient conductor, having already conducted, by invitation, the Berlin Philharmonic Orchestra, London Symphony Orchestra, New York Symphony Orchestra, Boston Symphony Orcestra, and the Los Angeles Symphony Orchestra. She had aroused enough interest to fill the Carnegie Hall and the Hollywood Bowl. But her work as a conductor was only just beginning. Her avowed intent was to make good music available to the masses by charging low prices for admission to concerts, an aim she had proposed in a newspaper interview in 1920. [1] So far, the critics' reviews of her work as a conductor had varied from patronising to enthusiastic. Without doubt there were prejudices in what was essentially a male-dominated preserve. To many critics and orchestral players the idea of a woman conductor was, for some reason, indescribably funny.

Mr Joseph Enos, who was formerly a piano student of Leginska, has told the authors of the prejudice against women conductors that Leginska experienced, as told to him by Leginska herself. [2] His story refers to her appearance as the conductor of an all-male orchestra at the Hollywood Bowl in August 1925. Mr Enos recalls:

"Summer in the Bowl was slanted towards stunts more than high art — and [the orchestra] would have considered a woman conductor as a stunt. She told me that the concertmaster [the 'leader' in Britain] began to "cut-up" while she was conducting, (changing the bowing, no doubt), and she leaned over to him and said that she would stop the orchestra and announce to the audience exactly what he was doing! She told me this when I enquired about her appearance there and how the men received her."

Not one to be put off by such hostility, the veracity of which is confirmed in Bruno Ussher's review of the concert on page 336, Leginska took up residence in Boston in 1926 (it will be recalled that she had lived there briefly a few years earlier, around 1920) and founded the Boston Philharmonic Orchestra. She was to be based in Boston for the next five years and would remain, as she had always had been, a vital figure and a firm favourite in the eyes of the musical public of that city. The setting-up of the new orchestra was no mean feat; it required huge qualities of organisation as well as energy and drive. Leginska set about her task with her usual vigour and assembled an ensemble whose basis was initially a total of 84 players, plus the conductor, as follows:

16 first violins	2 clarinets
14 second violins	4 horns
10 violas	3 trumpets
10 'cellos	3 trombones
7 double basses	1 tuba
2 flutes	1 tympani
2 oboes	3 percussion
2 bassoons	1 harp
2 contra-bassoons	1 piano

All the members of the orchestra, which was a quite separate organisation from the long-established Boston Symphony Orchestra with which Leginska had often appeared as piano soloist, were men except for the harpist and pianist. Naturally enough the setting-up of the orchestra was followed with interest by the Boston press. Photographs of Leginska, baton in hand, appeared in the newspapers [3, 4] shortly before the orchestra's first concert, with Leginska depicted as 'Founder and Conductor of the New Boston Philharmonic Orchestra', whilst a week later the *Boston Herald* published two photographs side by side of Leginska, one showing her in formal concert garb, baton in hand, as 'Director', whilst the other showed her wearing slacks and a cap, carrying a bucket in one hand and a mop in the other, captioned 'An Enthusiast in the Interest of Her Work'. [5] Leginska's ability to hold the attention of the public was as great as ever. As always, her name was never out of the newspapers for long.

Leginska remained true to her promise about low admission prices for her concerts. For the forthcoming series of concerts it was set at 25 cents, and seats cost 50 cents upwards.

The orchestra gave its first performance on 24th October 1926, with a programme consisting of overtures by Weber and Wagner, Beethoven's Fifth Symphony, the premiere of Rudolph Peterka's *The Triumph of Life*, and Liszt's *Hungarian Fantasie* for piano and orchestra, in which Leginska played the piano solo as well as conducting the orchestra. By all accounts the orchestra got off to a fine start in its inaugural concert. The *Boston Transcript*, in a lengthy and detailed review, observed: [6]

"From beginning to end, in every aspect, it was Miss Leginska's concert. The audience, yesterday afternoon, filled a substantial part of the huge Mechanics Hall – and she had assembled it. The Boston Philharmonic Orchestra played for the first time in public – and she was the conductor. The programme arrayed Weber, Beethoven, Liszt, Wagner, a youngish Münchener, Peterka by name – and she was their several mouthpiece. The proof ran manifest. Loud applause greeted Miss Leginska's appearance on the conductor's stand. A few roses in salutation. The plaudits were renewed whenever she entered or departed. A wreath and bulbous bunches of autumn flowers were borne to the stage at the pause for intermission. Most, however, the Leginskans released themselves at the end of Liszt's Hungarian Fantasia, since therein their divinity had double share. A piano replaced the conductor's stand. Seated before it, she played the solo-part. Rising above it, when the other employ permitted, she also led the orchestra. At the end, uproar coursed the hall. The pianist-conductor was clapped and clapped again; cheers topped the din; imposing ladies, not in their youngest years, rose to wave handkerchiefs. Had not Leginska, their Leginska, done a stunt almost unknown to present concert-rooms. Once more, the evidence was unassailable. Audiences hereabouts now go to symphony concerts to hear neither composers nor orchestra. The conductor is the magnet."

One senses here a touch of cynicism. But the same writer had to admit that the results were creditable, for he continued:

"The quality of the new orchestra surprised expectations. It assembled for the first time on Thursday last; being under strict union rules, the subsequent rehearsals were only two hours long; say six or eight at most. For the most part conductor and band were making each other's acquaintance. Yet the playing was often both spirited and precise, as accurate as may be; hardly ever dry or plodding, rarely uncertain and hesitant."

Under the heading "Miss Leginska Makes Auspicious Beginning" the *Boston Herald*'s music critic reported: [7]

"Miss Leginska has gathered some 85 players about her. Although they are of varying worth, some being far superior to others, she has been fortunate in finding a body of musicians capable of playing music to a very considerable extent as she would probably have it. She draws from her orchestra very good tone, including a soft pianissimo and a fortissimo amazingly sonorous, with many gradations between the two extremes. She has taught them already to follow closely her comfortably decisive beat, and to do her will in matters of phrasing, dynamics and rhythm.

"Although her first concert proved over-long, Miss Leginska laid out her program wisely. An overture to begin with, with the symphony to follow; then, not too late in the day, the new work of the occasion, with a solo piece next, and an overture to close – what could be more judicious?"

Speaking of the 'new work' in the programme, the 'Prelude' by Peterka (born 1894 in Austria, died in Berlin, 1933) the *Herald* continued:

"The orchestra played it exceedingly well. They sang its melodies expressively, they revelled in its surges of sound; up and on they swept to a climax truly imposing. The audience was enormous yesterday, and gratifyingly enthusiastic. And so, congratulations on an auspicious beginning."

The *Boston Globe* appeared to have had no reservations: [8]

"Yesterday she won her first great triumph. She and the Boston Philharmonic Orchestra gave 5,000 people a brilliant and enjoyable concert. If ever a wreath of laurel publicly bestowed was deserved, Leginska deserved the one she got in the intermission yesterday."

The *Christian Science Monitor* (whose headquarters was, and is still, in Boston), whilst not exactly calling for three cheers, at least called for two. [9]

Leginska helping prepare for the first concert of the Boston Philharmonic Orchestra

"An enthusiast in the interest of her work"
(Boston Herald)

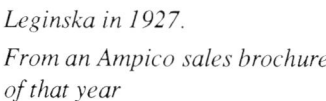

Leginska in 1927.
From an Ampico sales brochure of that year

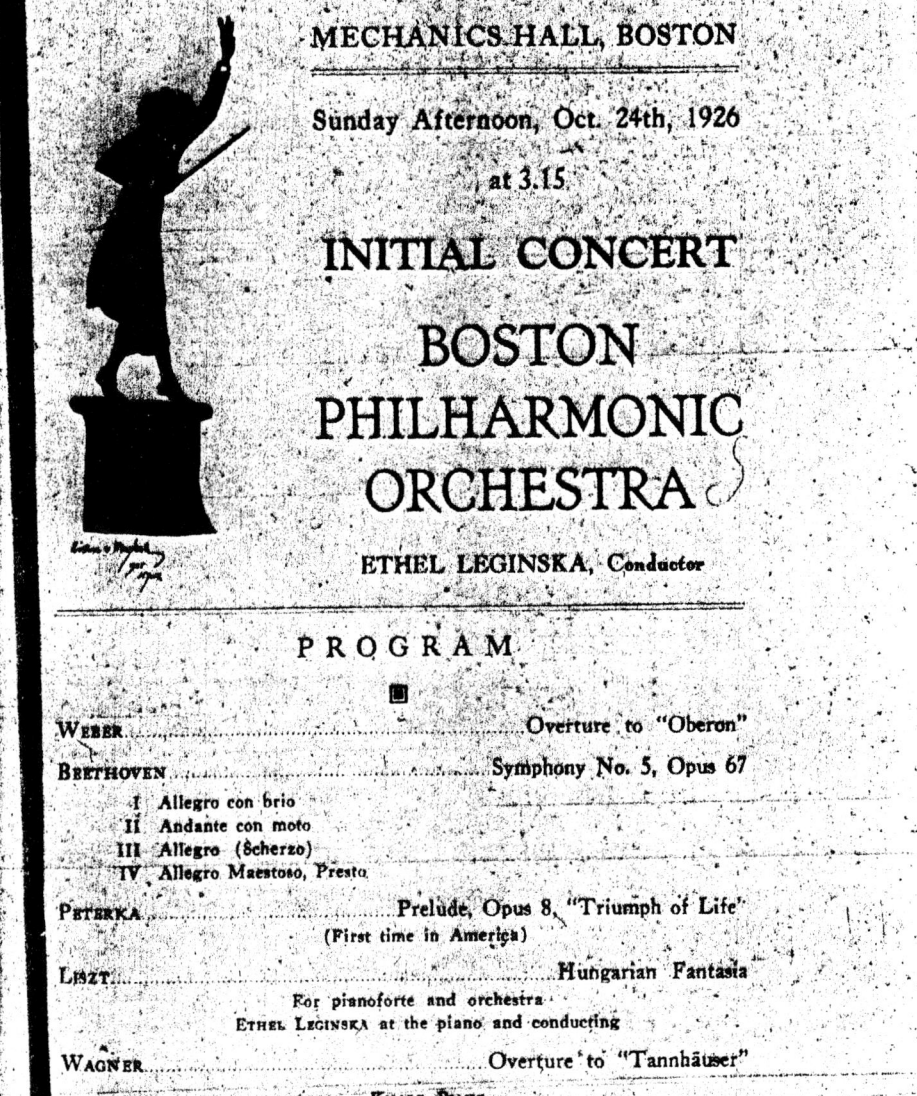

Programme of the first concert of the Boston Philharmonic Orchestra, instituted and conducted by Ethel Leginska. The programme included Liszt's Hungarian Fantasia in which Leginska was soloist in the piano part.

A poster used by Leginska to promote the concerts of her new orchestra

The new orchestra's second concert of the season followed a week after the first. * This time the programme consisted of a Wagner prelude, some Mahler songs, three of Leginska's own *Nursery Songs*, and Dvorak's *New World* symphony. Amongst the musical descriptions of the various pieces being played, as given in the 'programme notes' of the concert, were the following accounts of Leginska's songs:

1. *Sleep, baby, sleep.*
A quiet, soothing melody for voice is supported by a gentle, rocking rhythm in the orchestra. Sustained chords in the strings, obligato voices in the winds.
2. *Three mice went into a hole to spin.*
The melody is simple and piquant. Both words and orchestra are given humorous treatment. The accompaniment is full of unusual figures and characteristic orchestral effects.
3. *Old King Cole.*
An active, rhythmic figure in the orchestra, and an aggressive vocal part, together form the basis for this story.

The Mahler songs were sung by Madame Charles Cahier, a very well-known opera singer whose career had been mainly European. † She had been a friend of Mahler who had engaged her for the Imperial Opera in Vienna in 1906.

It was the practice in the programme notes of the Boston Philharmonic Orchestra's concerts to quote the birth date of the composers represented in the particular pieces being played. It is interesting to note that Leginska's birth date was given as 13th April 1890 (four years later than the true date), a fact that may have led some reference books published in later years to quote this incorrect date. Leginska must have known the information was wrong; indeed, she probably supplied it herself, but like many female (and some male) artists before and since she was never averse to telling a small fib by knocking a few years off her age. When Leginska formed her orchestra she was just 40 but looked younger; she obviously thought 36 sounded better, and more in keeping with her still-youthful image.

---

* A summary of the programmes of the season's concerts is given in Appendix 3 (page 326).

† The distinguished American contralto, Madame Charles Cahier, née Sara Jane Layton Walker (1870 [some sources say 1875] - 1951), was born in Nashville, Tennessee. She studied in Paris with the celebrated Polish tenor Jean de Reszke, and later in Vienna. She made her operatic debut in Nice in 1904 and married Charles Cahier, a Swede, the following year, after earlier being married to Morris Black. Thereafter she appeared as Mme Charles Cahier. She sang leading contralto roles at the Vienna Opera and toured Europe and America, singing oratorio and opera in concert versions and also appeared as a guest singer at the Metropolitan Opera in New York. Later she taught for several seasons at the Curtis Institute of Music in Philadelphia where Josef Hofmann was Director. Her repertoire included *Carmen* and several Wagnerian contralto roles.

It was obvious that funds would be a problem in the setting up and running of a large orchestra. Eighty-odd musicians had to be paid, to say nothing of the administrative costs, and Leginska had to make a living herself. Consequently the official printed programme of the second concert contained a personal appeal from Ethel Leginska:

"The success achieved by the Boston Philharmonic Orchestra in its first concert at the Mechanics Hall last Sunday was tremendous. The Boston P.O. has been founded and established to provide concerts each week for the "man in the street", the musical student, the children who love music, and the music lover in general. To furnish this music for the "masses" it is necessary to pay the musicians for rehearsals and performances, the hall rent, printing of programs, music, and newspaper advertising. There are no overhead expenses for manager or treasurer. I am giving my entire time to this great work.

"In order to furnish admission at 25 cents and seats at 50 cents up, it is necessary to appeal to the more fortunate music lover to assist. Mechanics Hall has proven to be a splendid place for such concerts. With its great seating capacity, fine acoustic properties, accessibility from all parts of Greater Boston, more than 7,000 can hear these concerts at one time. Just think – as many people can hear the Boston P.O. at one concert in Mechanics Hall as now hear the Boston S.O. at not only its Friday afternoon and Saturday evening concerts, but with an extra concert thrown in for good measure. Boston S.O. concerts are entirely subscribed for. There is not a single seat for sale for any of the series of concerts by that organisation.

"Ours is certainly a laudably ambitious movement – the providing of a new orchestra to fill the demand of the people for an opportunity to hear the world's finest music at prices they can afford to pay. We are anxious for subscriptions of any amount – large or small." Signed: Ethel Leginska

An address to which contributions should be sent was then given.

The third concert in the series took place, again in Mechanics Hall, on Sunday afternoon, 21st November 1926. It was Leginska's practice to include one new work in each concert. This time it was Korngold's 'Suite for Orchestra' (incidental music from *Much Ado about Nothing*), the work's first performance in orchestral form. Also included in the programme was a piece for piano and orchestra, Mendelssohn's *Capriccio Brillante*. The soloist was not Leginska but Justin Sandridge, a young pianist who was almost certainly one of her students. In the fourth concert, on 28th November, Leginska appeared as soloist, composer and conductor, playing the Mozart A major Piano Concerto, conducting from the keyboard. The new work on this occasion was Leginska's own *Marche Funèbre* from *Quatre Sujets Barbares*, a composition that had been performed previously by the Konzertverein Orchestra in Munich and by the London Symphony Orchestra.

For its fifth and penultimate concert of the season the venue was changed from the vast Mechanics Hall to the Boston Opera House, a hall of smaller size but greater comfort than the Mechanics Hall. Again meaty fare was offered, the concert starting with Schubert's Symphony in B minor (the 'Unfinished') and continuing with a number of other items including the overture *Susanna's Secret* by Wolf-Ferrari (a performance described as 'delightful' by one listener and which received such tumultuous applause that it had to be repeated) and a group of songs by Richard Strauss.

The sixth and final concert of the 1926-27 season took place on Sunday 10th April 1927 at the Boston Opera House. It consisted of a Weber overture, Beethoven's Piano Concerto No. 3 in C minor, Op. 37, a piece by Malipiero, and a Berlioz march. The Malipiero composition was for soloists, a chorus of mixed voices, and orchestra. Leginska was soloist in the Beethoven concerto, as well as conducting throughout the concerto, but the performance was 'different' in a manner not too uncommon in the 1920s. In the first movement (*Allegro con brio*) the piano part was played by a Duo-Art reproducing piano using a roll recorded specially for the occasion by Leginska herself, with Beethoven's own cadenzas. The second movement (*Largo*) and third (*Rondo*) were played in person by Leginska in the normal way. It is interesting to note that the programme notes for the concert stated that Walter Damrosch, conductor of the New York Symphony Orchestra, Leopold Stokowski, conductor of the Philadelphia Symphony Orchestra and the pianist Rudolph Ganz, currently the conductor of the St Louis Symphony Orchestra, had all included the Duo-Art piano as soloist in their regular programmes. It is certain that the Aeolian Company would have sent technicians to set up and adjust the reproducing piano beforehand and would have sponsored the concert. Such performances were invaluable to the player piano companies from the point of view of advertising their products, as were statements from the great pianists of the day, such as Leginska, extolling the virtues of the Duo-Art system.

Prior to this particular performance the *Duo-Art Monthly*, keen to achieve maximum publicity from the event, published the following news item:

Duo-Art Piano to be Soloist with Leginska's Orchestra

Ethel Leginska, Conductor of the Boston Philharmonic Orchestra, has recorded for the Duo-Art the piano part of Beethoven's Concerto in C minor, Op. 37; and in compliance with her request in the following letter, the Duo-Art Piano will be her soloist at the orchestra's sixth concert, on April 10.

Boston, Mass, Feb. 19, 1927

The Aeolian Company, New York
Gentlemen;

At its sixth concert to be given at the Boston Opera House on April 10th, the Boston Philharmonic Orchestra, of which, as you know, I am the conductor, will perform Beethoven's C Minor Concerto for piano and orchestra, and I should like very much to use the Duo-Art Piano (playing my record) as the soloist for the first movement. The second and third movements I will play personally in addition to leading the orchestra.

I have no hesitancy in requesting you to permit the Duo-Art to play the first movement of this magnificent concerto, for its reproduction of my playing is absolutely perfect.

Ethel Leginska

After the performance the Aeolian Company, wishing to derive as much publicity as possible from the concert, published the following letter (probably drafted by the company) in its *Duo-Art Monthly* magazine:

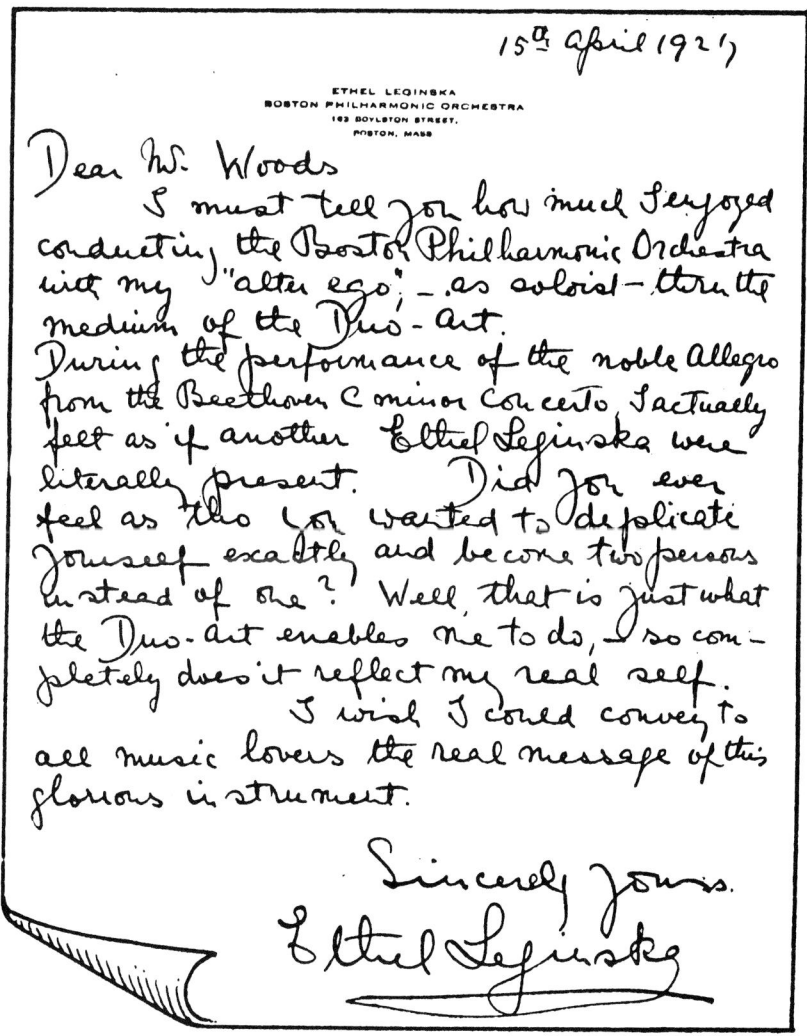

Letter published in the Aeolian Company's magazine 'Duo-Art Monthly', August 1927, under the heading 'Leginska Finds her "Alter Ego" in the Duo-Art Piano'

So ended the first season of Leginska's career as a regular conductor. Artistically her venture had been a success; good music had been presented, it had been performed well, and the critics, allowing in some cases for their prejudices, had written favourable reviews. But financially the picture was not so rosy. After the nearly-full hall in the first couple of concerts the novelty of Leginska's orchestra had begun to wear off; the less-than-capacity attendances thereafter, coupled with the low admission prices, had not brought in enough income to maintain the orchestra on a sound financial footing, even though the six concerts had attracted a total audience of 18,000 people. Nor were there sufficient financial guarantees to secure the future of the orchestra. (One might equally well ask how many orchestras at the present time could survive without external grants to keep them going?) Leginska therefore decided, in the uncertain financial climate, to disband the orchestra less than a year after it had been founded, instead of embarking on a second season; indeed, she had taken the decision some weeks earlier when it had become obvious that the orchestra was not going to be financially viable in the long term.

This setback would have deterred many a less-dedicated musician, but not Leginska. Early in 1927 she founded the Boston Women's Symphony Orchestra, offering to conduct and to train its members without a fee, thus fulfilling her ambition of running her own, top-class, women's orchestra. The orchestra made what was described as an 'introductory appearance' in March 1927, three weeks before the final concert of the Boston Philharmonic Orchestra. The event took place at Jordan Hall, Boston (where Leginska had often appeared as a solo pianist in recital ten or more years earlier) on Wednesday evening, 23rd March. The programme consisted of Mozart's Symphony No. 35 in D major (the *Haffner*) followed by Liszt's Piano Concerto in E flat major, with Lucille Oliver, Leginska's companion, pupil and friend as soloist. (It will be recalled that she was a key figure in the story of Leginska's mysterious disappearance in New York two years earlier, as told in the previous chapter.) The programme continued with *La Pisanella*, a suite for orchestra by the Italian composer Ildebrando Pizzetti (1880 - 1968) (first Boston performance), Leginska's *Six Nursery Rhymes* for voice and small orchestra, with Lydia M. Gray as soloist, and concluded with Tchaikovsky's *Marche Slav*. But this was really little more than a trial performance, a public rehearsal, to allow the orchestra and conductor to get to know each other and to allow Leginska the opportunity to assess what talent was available. Much hard work and many rehearsals were to follow before the orchestra would be ready to make its official debut; that event would not take place until December of the same year.

Meanwhile, Leginska made several guest appearances as the conductor of other orchestras whilst she was training the Boston Women's Orchestra, including the newly-formed 'Women's Symphony Orchestra of Chicago'. The *Musical Courier*, announcing her conducting debut there, described Leginska as "the dynamic conductor of the Boston Philharmonic Orchestra and the only woman director to command international attention."[10] Leginska's first appearance as conductor for this orchestra was at its last concert of the 1926-27 season on 19th April 1927, just nine days after her own Boston Philharmonic Orchestra's final concert. She played Mozart's Piano Concerto No. 23 in A major, K.488, conducting from the keyboard during this work and from the conductor's rostrum for the rest of the concert. Of this concert, Rene Devries, writing in the *Musical Courier*, observed:[11]

"Ethel Leginska's debut with the Women's Symphony Orchestra of Chicago on 19 April was a much heralded event and a great success."

Devries also noted that the orchestra held a special place in Chicago's musical life because its members were women, and suggested that an emphasis on the performance of works by American composers would give the orchestra still another special role. Although Leginska did not live in Chicago she was soon afterwards appointed officially as the orchestra's conductor and director, and in that capacity conducted many more concerts of the Women's Symphony Orchestra of Chicago over the next three years, though she was present in Chicago only on a part-time basis. Under Leginska's leadership the orchestra was rewarded by good artistic success but moderate financial reward. After a performance in January 1928 the *Musical Courier* reported:[12]

"Under the guidance of Ethel Leginska as conductor, the orchestra is forging its way to the foremost rank of symphonic ensembles."

But the orchestra nearest to Leginska's heart at this time was not the Chicago Orchestra but her own newly-formed Boston Women's Symphony Orchestra, whose members she had personally selected and trained. The orchestra consisted of about 65 performers, all women, and it was Leginska's declared policy to introduce works by women composers as far as possible. The first 'unofficial' concert has already been described. At the first 'real' concert held at 8.15pm on Monday 12th December 1927, the programme consisted of a Weber overture (*Oberon*), a Beethoven symphony (No. 5), the piano concerto in C minor by Delius and a suite (Tchaikovsky's *Nutcracker*). The pianist was a man, Reginald Boardman – probably another Leginska student. The next day the *Boston Transcript* reported:[13]

"Last season Miss Ethel Leginska organised an orchestra of women players, termed it the Boston Women's Symphony Orchestra, and led it through an introductory appearance. Last evening in Jordan Hall, Miss Leginska again conducted the new ensemble, but the occasion this time was designated by the unqualified and prophetic title "First concert". She had assembled, as before, an orchestra of about 70 players, each of whom wore a black gown trimmed with a white collar, a costume not unlike her own. At the beginning of the concert, Miss Leginska was ceremoniously greeted by her players, who stood in a body when she appeared. Her large audience likewise gladly welcomed her on this return to the musical life of Boston. The result was commendable and entirely pleasing."

The *Boston Post*, after noting the presence of an appreciative audience of good size, continued:[14]

"Those whose sense of the congruous is disturbed by the sight of Ethel Leginska leading an orchestra of men or presiding over a performance of opera must admit that, when she conducts the Boston Women's Symphony Orchestra, as she did last evening in Jordan Hall, she is wholly within the picture, a pleasing as well as an effective figure. In their Leginskan black and whites its players make a seemly array."

Future concerts were announced for Sunday evening, 19th February 1928 at the Boston Repertory Theatre, and for two Saturday evenings, 25th February and 14th April 1928, both at Jordan Hall. At the Boston Repertory Theatre concert the programme opened with Bach's Prelude and Fugue No. 22, arranged for strings by Mabel Mill Wood (first Boston performance) and continued with a Mozart aria (*Voi che Septe*) from *The Marriage of Figaro*, Liszt's Symphonic Poem *Les Préludes*, Schubert's Symphony No. 8 (the 'Unfinished'), Leginska's *Six Nursery Rhymes*, Radie Britain's *Symphonic Intermezzo* (first Boston performance), and concluded with Wagner's *Flying Dutchman* overture. The April concert's programme consisted of Mozart's Symphony No. 5 in D minor, Glinka's overture *Russlan and Ludmilla*, Leginska's *Fantasie* for Orchestra and Piano (first Boston performance) and Wagner's overture *Rienzi*. Ruth Shubow, a Leginska pupil, was soloist in the *Fantasie*, a piece which the *Boston Herald* described as "not old-fashioned, for it had fascinating discords and modern rhythms." [15]

Other concert performances took place outside Boston and the orchestra was quickly recognised as not a mere novelty but one to be taken seriously. The composition of the orchestra was given in the concert programmes as:

22 violins	2 bassoons
8 violas	4 horns
6 'cellos	4 trumpets
2 double basses	3 trombones
4 flutes and piccolos	1 tuba
2 oboes	2 percussion/tympani
2 clarinets and bass clarinets	1 harp

The costs of running the ensemble were substantial, generating the same kind of financial problems for Leginska as she had experienced with the Boston Philharmonic Orchestra. In an effort to bring in funds Leginska once again appealed to Boston's musical public in her concert programmes:

"The Boston Women's Symphony Orchestra is, so far as we can learn, the first orchestra in this country, the complete personnel of which, including the conductor, is entirely composed of women. Lovers of music in Boston watched with increasing interest the initial performances of the orchestra. These were most successful and showed a women's orchestra of symphonic size and calibre – an orchestra worthy in every way of the support of all music lovers, worthy of comparison with any symphony orchestra in the land – every instrument of the orchestral family is represented by women players. Throughout the season regular rehearsals are held and concert engagements are sought for. Several engagements have already been filled, with highly creditable results.

"Those in charge of this splendid step forward in music by women have given much time, effort and money for the new movement and feel the time has now come when they may conscientiously ask others to help. Orchestral music, even by the largest and most successful orchestras, is not yet self-supporting. To maintain successfully the Boston Women's Symphony Orchestra it is necessary that the musical public of Boston give them support. Contributions received are used only to pay the running expenses of the orchestra – there are no managerial or executive salaries of any kind. The entire movement of the Boston Women's Symphony Orchestra is educational."

A list of subscription prices was then given: Founder, $500; Patron, $100; Associate Member, $50; Annual Subscription, $25 (which offered the purchaser two personally selected seats for each of the season's Boston concerts).

In its second season, 1928-29, Leginska took the Boston Women's Symphony Orchestra on a six-week tour of the eastern states, playing at Chicago, St. Louis, Milwaukee, Buffalo, Cleveland and Washington, D.C., presenting 52 programmes in 38 cities in 43 days. Returning to Boston after what was described by the promoters as "A triumphal return from the Grand Tour", the orchestra presented a concert at Boston's Jordan Hall on Sunday afternoon, at 3.30 on 17th February 1929. The programme of the concert was Mozart's overture *The Magic Flute*, the Mendelssohn Concerto for Piano and Orchestra in G minor, Op. 25 (played and conducted by Leginska), Leginska's own *Triptych* for 11 instruments (first Boston performance; it had been played by the orchestra in Chicago the previous year) and Dvořák's Symphony No. 5 in E minor, Op. 95, *From the New World*. The *Boston Transcript* was enthusiastic: [16]

"Of Mendelssohn's concerto Miss Leginska gave a high-powered reading. Mendelssohn's suave melodies, his quasi-brilliant passages, orchestral tuttis and punctuating chords, interplay between piano and orchestra, all came in character, plus the effects of Miss Leginska's galvanising personality. And audiences 'go wild' about her energetic combining of functions of soloist and conductor, One may add that by the signs of yesterday afternoon Miss Leginska is still an able pianist."

The orchestra's last Boston performance of the season took place on 15th April 1929, with less than 100 seats unsold. The music comprised works by Schumann, Berlioz, Bruch (the Violin Concerto in G minor with Irma Seydel * as soloist), Mabel Hill Wood ** and Powell Weaver †.

A flavour of the lively and exhilarating atmosphere of rehearsals and concerts conducted by Leginska, and some of the difficulties she encountered, is evoked by the recollections of Radie Britain †† : [17]

"She was totally dedicated to music. I have known her since 1928 when she performed my first orchestral work, 'Symphonic Intermezzo', with the Chicago Women's Symphony Orchestra. After rehearsals we would lunch together. She was so distressed about a horn player who was not too far advanced technically. I told Madame, 'Try not to look at the horn player when you direct her entrance'. It worked — it eased the tension — for Leginska was merciless with the orchestral players. She strived for perfection. Even when I was a student in Munich, where I made my debut as a composer, Madame Leginska was conducting the Munich Symphony Orchestra — she would hurl sarcastic remarks at the German musicians, which they were unaccustomed to hear. [‡] I attended the concert; she was about the first woman to conduct an all-male orchestra — and they showed their dislike, even though the performance went well.

"Now back to my performance, which she conducted superbly at the Goodman

---

* Irma Seydel (b. 1896) was born in Boston, the daughter of a violinist in the Boston Symphony Orchestra. She was well known as a violinist in the USA, appearing several times as invited soloist with the Boston Symphony Orchestra and she also played as soloist with orchestras in Europe.

** Mabel Hill Wood (1891 - 1954) was an American composer born in Brooklyn. She helped found the Brooklyn Music School Settlement and the Hudson River Music School. Her best known composition is *The Adventures of Pinocchio*, first performed in New York in 1931.

† Powell Weaver (1890 - 1951) was an American composer, born in Clearfield, Pennsylvania. He was also well known in the United States as an accompanist and organist.

†† Radie Britain, one of America's most distinguished women composers of the 20th century, was born on a ranch near Amarillo, Texas on 17th March 1899. After graduating from the American Conservatory in Chicago, she made her debut as a composer in Munich in 1925. Leopold Godowsky was one of her piano teachers while a gold medal in organ led her to further study with Pietro Yon and Marcel Dupré. Her compositions have been performed throughout America. In 1945 she became the first woman composer to receive the Juilliard Public Award for *Heroic Poem*. She died at Palm Springs, California on 23rd May 1994 aged 95.

The Radie Britain Musical Endowment Fund is sponsored by the Aid Foundation, Inc., to assist talented and deserving music students.

A list of some of Radie Britain's compositions is given in *The Grove Dictionary of Women Composers*, first edition, Macmillan, 1994, p. 87.

‡ It is safe to assume that Leginska was fluent in German, having lived and studied for several years in Frankfurt, Vienna and Berlin and having played in many concerts there from 1909-1912.

Theatre. The next day she called me – asking me to join the percussion department – on her Boston Women's Symphony Orchestra tour. She said 'I will perform your Symphonic Intermezzo if you will join us in the orchestral tour.' 'But Madame! I have never played a percussion instrument.' She exclaimed, 'You write for these instruments – you should be able to play them!'

"Hurriedly I engaged the services of the Chicago Symphony Percussionist – learning some of the techniques for the bass drum, triangle and cymbals. She kept her promise, performing my work in Boston and on tour. At every performance, before she played my work, she would speak with the audience in very complimentary terms about my brainchild.

"In one composition I had only one sforzando note in the bass drum – measure after measure I counted in apprehension – for I believe that if I had entered at the wrong time she would have hurled her baton at me!

"Later, she asked me if I would play the harpsichord in the orchestra in Chicago. 'But Madame, you will scold me unmercifully if I make the wrong entrance.' 'My dear, please do me a favor, and help out with this number'.

"We really respected each other musically. I treasure her friendship – and her faith in my compositions. I have never known a musician more dedicated to her craft. It was one of the highlights of my career to have been associated with Madame Leginska so closely. She was an inspiration to me.

"She had a gift as a conductor, but she lacked diplomacy with her players. Even at a rehearsal in Munich she stormed at the German players. The Women's Symphony in Boston had many amateur performers and their inadequacy exasperated her. But when she took the Boston Women's Symphony on tour the performances were excellent, and very successful with the audience.

"Although she was so small she conducted with assurance. Her strong point was her complete dedication to music and she was one of the top musicians of her day. She knew the value of advertising and I'm sure she used a great deal of her funds for advertising, realising its value. I have known many musicians but I have never known any so dedicated. Her lack of diplomacy in correcting a musician publicly could have hurt her as a conductor. However, I understand Toscanini was brutal with his criticism, even falling on his knees to a player, begging him to understand and perform correctly, so it is difficult to fault Leginska – but to recognise that she was walking on a tight rope seeking perfection in the performance."

These memories bring to life Leginska's appearances as a conductor, and re-enforce her image as a dynamic, tough, forthright, uncompromising and vigorous musician, determined to overcome prejudices. As Radie Britain indicated, the Boston Women's Symphony Orchestra was well received, both in Boston and on tour.

The final concert of the 1928-29 season of the Boston Women's Symphony Orchestra had taken place in April 1929; within a month Leginska had achieved another notable distinction, having conducted a performance of Bizet's opera *Carmen*, sung in English, with a full cast of singers and her own orchestra in support. The event took place on 11th May 1929 at Boston's

*Two programmes of the Boston Women's Symphony Orchestra:
14th April 1928 and 17th February 1929*

Ethel Leginska — conductor. One of her favourite publicity pictures from the late 1920s

Jordan Hall. Marvelling at the feat, the *Boston Herald* reported in favourable terms:[18]

> "Here was an interesting experiment. Miss Leginska conceived the idea that she would like to train an opera company. Done! Though, so far as information goes, she has never dealt exhaustively with the singing voice, though she can scarcely, away from her many activities, have devoted much time to the preparing and conducting of opera performances, Miss Leginska is not the person to let herself be put off by trifles. She determined, evidently, to make a good shift with such assets as she had at hand.
>
> "The most valuable of them was a well-trained orchestra of women players, an orchestra exceedingly competent at a symphonic program, but surely not experienced at opera. Miss Leginska made little of their lack of operatic routine; she, an orchestra conductor of rare ability, could show them the way.
>
> "Building, therefore, on her orchestra, or so it appears to a person uninformed, Miss Leginska gathered a cast about her. In most cases, though perhaps not all, she selected singers of no long experience before the public and no operatic experience whatsoever.
>
> "Yesterday she demonstrated to the world what one woman's genius, combined with hard work, can achieve."

In July 1929 the Boston Women's Symphony Orchestra provided the music for the Great Mid-West Summer Festival in Conneaut Lake, Pennsylvania. In one week 13 different programmes were presented including two choral works, Gounod's *Faust* and Handel's *Messiah*.

Leginska's orchestra was now well established. It began its 1929-30 season with a concert at Jordan Hall, Boston, on 13th October 1929 in which Leginska again appeared as conductor and soloist. The programme consisted of Schubert's Symphony in B minor ('Unfinished'), Liapounov's Concerto, Op. 4, for Piano and Orchestra, Leginska's *Six Nursery Rhymes* in an orchestral version (the voice part eliminated) and Liszt's Symphonic Poem No. 3, *Les Preludes*. The *Boston Herald,* in spite of minor criticisms, was generally full of praise:[19]

> "Once more, yesterday afternoon, Ethel Leginska and her orchestra played before Jordan Hall sold-out. Whether the public went to the hall in support of feminism, out of personal regard for Miss Leginska, or, let us hope, in the mere wish to hear good music, does not matter. A large company did at all events hear an excellent programme, admirably performed, and derived therefrom it was plain to see, rare pleasure. Thus was the cause of music in Boston advanced – even as every dull performance sets back the musical clock.
>
> "The time has come when it is no longer necessary to comment on Miss Leginska's orchestra in terms suitable to an organisation at its beginning. Still less to the purpose is it to stress the point that all her players are women. Miss Leginska has at her command an able body of players, competent now, in every choir, notably strong in some. Her basses, especially, she has bettered, so much so that their tone is at times of a genuine loveliness; only in loud passages for full orchestra do they still tend towards harshness. Her string players have always been so excellent that it seems curious that Miss

Leginska should tolerate the dry quality which, twice yesterday, dulled their tone before the close of the final chord.

"Nobly Miss Leginska began the afternoon with a noble performance of the 'Meistersinger' Prelude. Here was the splendor of rhythm and tone, a plasticity in the treatment of the melody, furthermore, of the greatest significance, that caused a listener to forget, for the moment, his wish that the subsidiary melody in the closing pages might be heard something more clearly.

"With similar perfection of rhythm and of melody-shaping, Miss Leginska dealt with Schubert's Unfinished Symphony. Though avoiding unerringly the pitfall of extravagance, not for one instant did she slip with the even more irritating error of turning Schubert into a Viennese Simple Simon sort of person who knew no more than to sing and dance in the sun. To those first romantically mysterious pages, on the contrary, of the working out, she did full justice. To the dramatic passage, too, that follows, she gave a full force. From a genius, indeed, who is blessed with fine taste, much may be expected.

"She played a piano concerto, Liapounov's Op. 4. She played it superbly, with the technical mastery which tells her how to let every note of unforced tone be heard above a heavy orchestra.

"After the concerto, Miss Leginska brought forward her new orchestral version of 'Old King Cole'. Not missing the loss of a voice, it sounded well, mighty brisk and jovial, humorous in the stout way that fits the title. Then, eager for wild romance, Miss Leginska closed her afternoon with Liszt's 'Les Préludes'.

"If she is a proud woman today, she has a right to be. She has brought her orchestra to a pass when they can do work technically, musically, and emotionally admirable. And she has developed a public eager to hear her. Congratulations!"

The *Boston Transcript* singled out the Liapounov concerto for special mention: [20]

"The concerto of Liapounov yesterday was both played and conducted by Miss Leginska. In the past with this orchestra as well as with the People's Symphony and her own Philharmonic Orchestra of brief career, Miss Leginska has simultaneously played piano concertos and conducted them, but for the most part the vehicles for this dual virtuosity have been compositions less exacting than this concerto of Liapounov. Incidentally, the piece itself, reminiscent of other and greater Russians, has been heard in this city but once before, and then Miss Leginska also played it but with the Symphony Orchestra under Dr. Muck. " *

This initial performance of the 1929 - 30 season preceded another tour by the orchestra, this time of 10 weeks' duration during October, November and December in the East and Middle-West. By January 1930 the orchestra was

---

* The German-born conductor Dr Carl (sometimes spelt Karl) Muck (1859 - 1940) had been appointed permanent conductor of the Boston Symphony Orchestra in 1912. During World War I feelings against him ran high when he failed to temper his German nationalism. In consequence he was arrested at his home on 25th March 1918, sacked from his post, and interned as an enemy alien until the end of the war. Sir Henry Wood was offered the post in his place but declined it. Henri Rabaud took over for one season before Pierre Monteux was appointed. In 1919 Muck returned to Germany, where he spent the rest of his career and life.

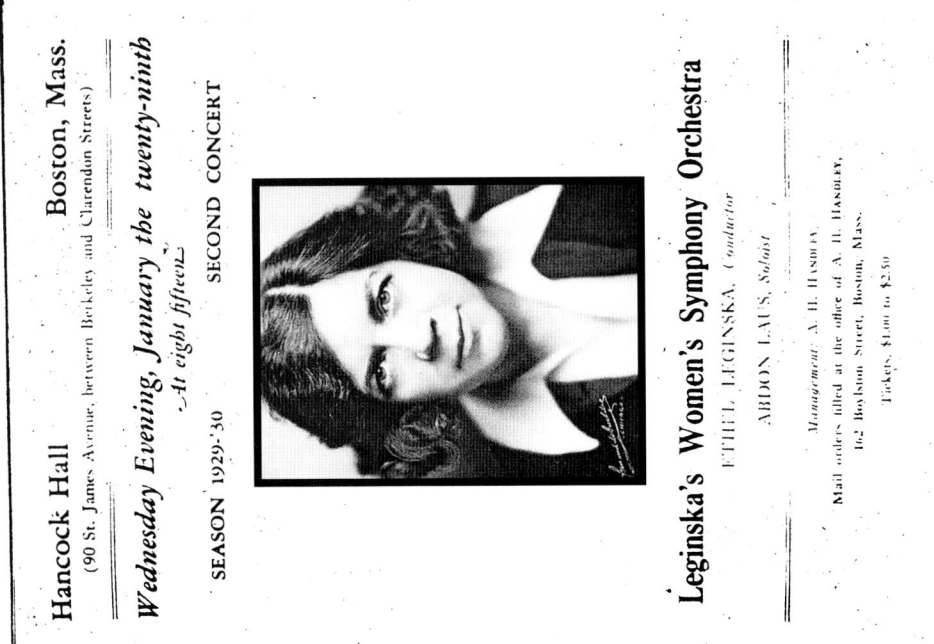

Front cover and another page from the programme of a concert of the Leginska's Women's Symphony Orchestra, 29th January 1930

back in Boston to give a concert at Hancock Hall, the programme comprising Mozart's Overture to *The Marriage of Figaro*, Weber's Concerto in F for Bassoon and Orchestra, Tchaikovsky's Symphony No. 5 in E minor, Op. 64, Debussy's *Cortège* and *Air de Danse* (first Boston performance) and Sibelius's Symphonic Poem *Finlandia*. In this concert a few men appeared as members of the orchestra and the orchestra's name had been changed to Leginska's Women's Symphony Orchestra. Leginska accounted for the presence of the men by explaining that when Boston women could not be found for certain parts, she could not afford to import women players from other cities and simply had to substitute local male instrumentalists.

At the end of the 1920s and the beginning of the 1930s the economy of the United States was precarious, to say the least, after the Wall Street Crash of 1929 and thereafter it proved impossible to maintain the financial viability of Leginska's Women's Symphony Orchestra. The concert of 29th January 1930, referred to above, turned out to be the last one it gave. Nevertheless, the venture could hardly be written off as a failure, for the orchestra, in various guises, had given more than 200 symphonic concerts in 21 states during its three years of existence. It had kept its head above water financially for these three years, and but for the unforeseen, unprecedented and unique national economic problems of the day it would probably have continued to do so. Very few poorly-paid people could spare the money to go to orchestral concerts at a time when they often did not know where the next meal was coming from. The long-established orchestras, fortunate enough to possess deep financial reserves and regular financial backing, were able to continue since they drew their audiences from a richer clientele, but even they found life difficult.

Artistically, Leginska's orchestras of the 1920s had earned consistently good reviews though, from the start of her conducting career, Leginska had been forced to put up with reactions ranging from patronising condescension to downright hostility from male critics and orchestral players who found it difficult to take seriously the concept of either a woman conductor or a woman orchestral member. The *Boston Post*, for example, when reviewing the final concert of a 10-week tour by the Boston Women's Symphony Orchestra, reported that when the orchestra was first created by Leginska it had been treated with polite condescension, but conceded that the situation had since changed. But having made that concession the writer went on to dig a hole for himself by revealing his own prejudices: [21]

"Granted that women performers are not likely to attain masculine proficiencies with such unfeminine instruments as the double bass, French horns, trombones and tuba, the players of these instruments in Miss Leginska's present orchestra are at least adequate to

CHARACTERISTIC POSES OF ETHEL LEGINSKA —THE CONDUCTOR, who scored a brilliant success on May 25 at the Keene, N. H., Festival as guest-conductor and pianist. The Evening Sentinel, in reviewing the concert, said: "The far-famed vivacious artist more than lived up to her reputation as a conductor and piano soloist. She was wonderful in both capacities. Of this there was no doubt else the many hundred persons in the audience would not have come to its feet and wildly applauded her. Critic and layman marvelled alike at Leginska's energy and ability as a conductor. The orchestral group was never heard in a better concert here and the responsiveness of the musicians to every single move of her baton was remarkable. The great Leginska seemed to be directing each instrument singly instead of collectively." After one of the works played the whole audience arose and applauded Leginska for about five minutes. Leginska and the Boston Women's Symphony Orchestra will make an extended tour of the country next fall.

Leginska as seen by her audiences — as pianist and as conductor: late 1920s

any ordinary demands that may be placed on them. The band as a whole plays with a gratifying, even a surprising, effectiveness."

This rather patronising viewpoint ignored the facts of the situation. The critic Deems Taylor once wrote, " . . . the average woman is not likely to possess sufficient lung power and sheer muscle strength to play the tuba just as the average woman's hands are not likely to be large enough to finger the double bass satisfactorily". These assertions rather miss the point, for the "average woman", or the "average man" for that matter, would be unlikely to choose such instruments. Also, as Antonia Brica pointed out, " . . . if a woman can rush all over the stage bellowing 'Isolde', she can blow a tuba". Continuing this theme, Catherine Contos remarked, "Likewise, it might be reasoned that if a woman can play Stravinsky on the piano – not to mention scrub a house, lug groceries, and get small children into snowsuits – a double bass should be a cinch, as it has since proved to be".

But before moving on to the 1930s, and as a tailpiece to this chapter which has focused on Leginska's career as a conductor and conductor-pianist between 1926 and 1930, two non-related events must be mentioned; they have been left to the end so as not to break up the flow of the story of Leginska's conducting career. The first is that although Leginska had become primarily a conductor, rather than a pianist, during these years, it was in this period that she made a number of recordings for solo piano for Columbia including the 'Impromptus' and 'Moments Musicaux' of Schubert as part of the Schubert centenary celebrations. The Schubert recordings (described in Chapter 10) were released by Columbia in the autumn of 1928. They were recorded at sessions in February, March and April of that year (the dates of all the recordings are quoted on page 334) whilst Leginska's conducting season of 1927-28 was still in progress.* She was 41 when she made the Schubert records – and at the height of her powers.

The second event that occurred in 1928 was a sad one – the death of Ethel's father, Tom Liggins, in October of that year at the age of 67. It will be recalled that in 1913, fourteen years after the death of Ethel's mother, he had married his cousin, Christina Bella Workman, whilst still engaged in his work variously described as builder, architect and surveyor. But soon afterwards he retired at the age of 53 and he and his new wife went to live at 45, Richmond Street, Bridlington, a coastal town a few miles north of Hull. [22] His retirement at an age which in those days would have been considered very early might have been due to his poor eyesight, from which

---

* Her recordings of Schubert's Impromptus No. 2 in A flat and No. 3 in B flat (from Op. 142, D.935) were made in New York on 20th February 1928, the day after her Boston Repertory Theatre Concert described on page 192. This demonstrates the busy life she lived at that time.

he is said to have suffered in his later years. [23] Tom Liggins had lived long enough to have seen his daughter achieve tremendous success in Britain, Europe (including Russia) and the United States, which must have given him immense pleasure, and he is said to have enjoyed playing his daughter's records to friends. [24] (These would have been the Pathé records of 1920 and the Columbias of 1926.) It is certain that Ethel would have visited 'home' whenever she was in Britain but the most recent such visit prior to Tom's death appears to have been in 1925.*

Tom had been suffering from a chronic duodenal ulcer and he died at home on 17th October 1928 from complications (haematemesis) arising from the condition [25] whilst his daughter was preparing to embark on a tour with her orchestra. His death occurred on a Wednesday and the funeral took place on the following Saturday, 20th October, followed by interment at the local cemetery. The newspaper report of the funeral, which was conducted by The Rev J. Vivian Davies, listed 24 mourners, chief of whom was Tom's widow, Christina. [26] Ethel was not present. Indeed, it would have been impossible for her to have been there since the funeral took place only three days after the death and in 1928 the only way of crossing the Atlantic was by steamer. By coincidence one of Tom's next-door neighbours, a Mr Charles Dawson who lived at No. 43, had died four days before Tom, aged 72. He was buried the day before Tom died. Several mourners, probably neighbours, were present at both funerals, as reported in the local press.

The circumstances of Tom's death, which occurred seven days after a sudden, unexpected collapse caused by a haemorrhage, were conveyed to Ethel by a distraught Christina in a very emotional 4-page letter (beginning 'Dearest Ethel') dated 28th October. The collapse occurred as the couple were resting following a pleasant summer's evening walk. Earlier, on 6th October, only four days before his collapse, Tom had sent Ethel a cheerfully-worded note wishing his daughter great success (he underlined the words) on her forthcoming tour with her Boston orchestra. [27]

Tom Liggins' will was published on 12th January 1929: [28]

"Mr Thomas Edward Liggins, of 45 Richmond Street, Bridlington, architect, who died October 17th, left £11,425/5/9 with net personalty £10,653/14/2. Probate is granted to the National Provincial Bank, of 15 Bishopsgate, London, and Christina Bella Liggins, the widow. He leaves 51 per cent of the property to his wife for life and 49 per cent to his daughter for her life, with ultimate remainder to his daughter's children."

---

* After professional appearances in Britain and the continent in the mid-1920s, which were referred to in Chapter 9, no evidence can be found of Leginska having visited Britain again until February 1930 when she began another tour of the UK. This 5-year absence is hardly surprising since, in that period, she was fully engaged in establishing, running, conducting and playing in (as soloist) her own orchestras in the USA.

With the death of her father, Ethel's closest family link with Yorkshire ended, though her stepmother would live on, at the same family house in Bridlington, for another 27 years. Tom's estate was quite substantial by 1928 values, amounting to the equivalent of about £350,000 (about $500,000) in present-day money.[29] Of this, as the will stated, Ethel inherited nearly half.

Note: The help of Mrs Margaret Stockbridge in visiting libraries in the Hull and Bridlington districts, to assist the preparation of this book by finding information about the Liggins and Peck families, is gratefully acknowledged. Especially, in regard to this chapter, in discovering details of the newspaper reports of the funeral and the will of Thomas Edward Liggins.

No. 45, Richmond Street, Bridlington, to which Tom Liggins and his new wife retired in 1913. He lived there until his death in 1928 and Christina until her death in 1955. Ethel would have stayed here whilst her father was still alive, and possibly later.

(Photo: Margaret Stockbridge)

References: Chapter 13

1. *Christian Science Monitor*, 4th June 1920.
2. Correspondence with the authors (several letters exchanged) during 1984.
3. *Boston Herald*, 23rd October 1926.
4. *Boston Transcript*, 23rd October 1926.
5. *Boston Herald*, 31st October 1926.
6. *Boston Transcript*, 25th October 1926.
7. *Boston Herald*, 25th October 1926.
8. *Boston Globe*, 25th October 1926.
9. *Christian Science Monitor*, 25th October 1926.
10. *Musical Courier*, 14th April 1927.
11. *Musical Courier*, 28th April 1927.
12. *Musical Courier*, 19th January 1928.
13. *Boston Transcript*, 13th December 1927.
14. *Boston Post*, 13th December 1927.
15. *Boston Herald*, 15th April 1928.
16. *Boston Transcript*, 18th February 1929.
17. Radie Britain, musician. Information in letters to the authors in 1984.
18. *Boston Herald*, 12th May 1929.
19. *Boston Herald*, 14th October 1929.
20. *Boston Transcript*, 14th October 1929.
21. *Boston Post*, 14th October 1929.
22. The *Bridlington Free Press* of Saturday, 27th October 1928, in reporting the death of "the late Mr T. E. Liggins", stated:
    "The deceased gentleman, who was 67 years of age, was a native of Hull and he came to reside in Bridlington on his retirement fourteen years ago. He leaves a widow and a daughter, the latter being Miss Ethel Leginska, the noted musician, who is at present touring America with her own orchestra."
    This information, if accurate, fixes the year of Tom's retirement and his taking up residence in Bridlington as around 1913 to 1914.
23. Information from the late Mrs Marjorie Langdale of Hornsea (Ethel's cousin).
24. Ibid.
25. Certified copy of the death certificate of Thomas Edward Liggins obtained from the Superintendent Registrar at Bridlington. Tom's occupation was given on the certificate as 'Retired architect and surveyor'.
26. Tom Liggins's death was announced in the *Bridlington Free Press* on 20th October 1928 (the day of the funeral) and the funeral, with a list of mourners, was reported in the same newspaper in its issues of 24th and 27th October.
27. Copies of the letters courtesy of International Piano Archives at Maryland.
28. *Bridlington Free Press*, Saturday 12th January 1929.
29. *Whitaker's Almanack* (London): "The purchasing power of the £". Each annual edition gives a year-by-year table of the £'s value.

Chapter 14

The Complete Musician

At this point in our narrative – the dawn of the 1930s – let us stand back for a moment and review Leginska's achievements since she set up home in the United States. During the period 1913 to 1930, Leginska had achieved international renown as a pianist and had travelled the world giving recitals and concerts. Music critics of national newspapers and musical magazines were lavish in their praise of her talent. The authors are fortunate to possess many hundreds of press clippings of critics' reviews of her concerts and recitals, which abound with phrases such as 'Leginska Triumphs', 'Leginska Held Her Audience Spellbound', 'Audience is Captivated by Leginska's Recital', and so on. Headlines such as these were repeated with uniform regularity wherever Leginska toured. Her personal charisma and magnetic personality, qualities only given to a select few, induced a near-hypnotic effect over her audiences. Always newsworthy, Leginska attracted attention wherever she went, and frequent pictures appeared in the newspapers of her playing golf, on holiday on the beach, mending her automobile (tinkering with the engine, or emerging from under the car), climbing a tree, etc., quite apart from the formal reviews of her concerts. Leginska, accorded the accolade "The Paderewski of Women Pianists" by the *New York Herald*, was generally accepted as one of the top few pianists of the day and unsurpassed by any woman pianist.

Leginska had also made her mark in other ways. As we have seen, she had recorded on disc for Pathé and Columbia and had made more than 70 piano rolls under contract to four different companies, the last of her rolls appearing in 1930. A number of her musical compositions had been published and performed all over America and Europe, and she had established a reputation as a creator, organiser and conductor of top-class orchestras, one of the very few women to achieve success or even to be taken seriously in this field. In the setting up of women's orchestras of full symphony orchestra size she had blazed a pioneer trail. The various landmarks in Leginska's life as a conductor were just as successful in attracting public attention as were her exploits as a pianist, and possibly more so. The sight of the dynamic, diminutive figure on the rostrum was always guaranteed to provide interest and excitement.

Moreover, amidst all her busy schedules, which involved a great deal of travelling, she had found time to build up a large clientele of piano pupils, not only in New York but also in London whenever she had visited, and elsewhere. The only setbacks, if they can be regarded as such, in a very successful career since her arrival in America, were the 'disappearing pianist' incident of 1925 and the anti-female prejudices she had encountered as a conductor. When she appeared anywhere as a guest conductor, her problem had always been to win the acceptance of male orchestral players and critics. When she formed her own orchestra, the difficulties were mainly financial, because running a large orchestra requires vast financial resources. But Leginska, determined and purposeful, was not one to be put off by difficulties such as these. So, throughout the 1920s, she had battled on and maintained her prominent place in the musical scene.

In winning acceptance by male orchestral players Leginska had been generally successful. Anecdotes included in an article written in 1929 by the well-known Boston writer on musical matters Laning Humphrey (1896-1988) illustrated Leginska's personality and self-confidence: [1]

"When Leginska first conducted in Munich in 1924 an enthusiastic reception was bestowed by the critical German public upon the young woman conductor – a dubious-seeming phenomenon to them before the concert. At the end of the program there was a great hubbub outside the hall. A great crowd was cheering and waiting for her. Inside the hall, she was surrounded by members of the orchestra, showering compliments on her splendid conducting. 'You must have had great experience leading orchestras in America', one player said to her. 'This is the first conducting I have ever done', she returned frankly. The crowd made a triumphal procession of her journey to the hotel.

"Since then she has won higher and higher recognition as a leader. With the baton, her style is decidedly interesting. She is impetuous, often ecstatic, in her personal approach to the orchestral music in hand. She escapes being bombastic, melodramatic. Always she is musicianly. She exerts a real magnetism over her players and evokes a 'singing tone' from her orchestra. In the matter of interpretation, she does not attempt decided innovations, but manages to put the stamp of her personality on a performance."

In the same article, Laning Humphrey illustrates how demanding of orchestral players, including male ones, Leginska could be as a conductor:

" 'Hang that Leginska woman! Two men conductors couldn't make us work as hard as she makes us. She's playing this orchestra off its feet.'

"So blurted a musician with hair sopping wet, collar limp, as he dabbed a bedraggled handkerchief across his glistening face and neck during the promenade [rehearsal] of a concert by a large male symphony orchestra which was being conducted by Ethel Leginska, the brilliant English pianist, composer and orchestra leader now living in Boston. Then the rueful expression of the man gave way to a big smile.

" 'Say', he added, 'did you ever hear us sound so good before?'

"Now he was proud of the results obtained from having a woman wave commands over himself and his surprised fellow musicians. She exerts an unmistakable authority over them."

To Leginska, the music was everything. Never particularly noted for her tact, she demanded excellence from her players. Leginska also expected co-operation and attention from her audiences. A bout of coughing from the audience, as she played the piano, was usually silenced by a steely, penetrating stare. Laning Humphrey added, in the article quoted above, that Leginska once made history in concert annals by stopping in the midst of playing a piano composition and rebuking a Boston audience for whispering as she played.

When the 1930s began, ten years had elapsed since Leginska's declared intention of widening her interests. She had kept to her word and was now the complete musician. Although she had often appeared in public purely as a concert pianist in the 1920s, this being a profitable source of income because of the high fees she commanded, she always preferred to appear, if possible, in the dual role of composer-pianist or conductor-pianist. Often she combined the three roles of composer, conductor and pianist in the same concert. During the 1920s the accent had steadily shifted from pianist to conductor and by 1930 there were hardly any appearances as concert pianist alone. In this chapter we will look at Leginska's career in the 1930s.

At the dawn of the decade engagements as conductor-pianist abounded. In February 1930 she made another appearance with the Chicago Women's Symphony Orchestra, with which she had been closely associated during the previous three years. The *Transcript* reported the concert, albeit using part of a report from the *Evening Post* (newspapers often had an arrangement to use each other's material so that the 'local man' could write the review): [2]

"Miss Leginska was guest-conductor the other day at a concert of the Chicagoan [sic] Women's Symphony Orchestra. On the program were Chaikovsky's [sic] Fifth Symphony and the Concerto by Lyapunov, in which she is both pianist and conductor. In the 'Evening Post' Mr Hackett set down these impressions:

"Miss Leginska is a striking personality and one who always succeeds in making things interesting.

"In certain episodes she produced effects of great beauty and of power. Her feeling for the melodic line was keen and in the more quiet passages, where things moved along steadily, the players followed her well. Rich colorings and forceful dynamics. Striking, and made an impression on the public.

"In Lyapunov's Concerto she conducted at the piano while playing the solo part, and made a brilliant display. She has the pianistic gift, and when both hands were on the keyboard she kept the players in time with her head, which she did in style to the vast delight of her audience. And now she goes back to London, 'where', she says, 'life is simpler and easier'."

The reference to London related to a forthcoming tour. Europe had heard about Leginska's recent successful exploits as a conductor and soon after the Chicago concert of February 1930, in response to an invitation, she left the

United States for a lengthy tour of Britain and the continent which occupied much of that year, during which she conducted as a guest at a number of important concerts and opera houses in many cities including some appearances in London. The performances were very successful and further raised her standing as a conductor. After one performance Leginska received the following telegram, addressed to her at the Carl Rosa Opera Company, and dated 17th July 1930:

CONGRATULATIONS YOUR BRILLIANT PIONEER ACHIEVEMENT
– AMY JOHNSON –

Praise from one pioneering woman to another! [3]

Whilst in Britain Leginska was interviewed by the long-established periodical *Musical Opinion*, which is still alive and well at the present time. In its "Personal and Otherwise" column, Leginska was introduced as "Composer, Teacher and Conductor". [4] The article began:

"Ethel Leginska has led a charmed life: all the fairies attended her birth and gave her gifts and smiles. Only a determined and happy personality could have accomplished so much and made so world-wide a reputation at so early an age. Although she has had many successes in America and Germany, Miss Leginska remains a simple, unaffected and unassuming Yorkshire maid.

"Miss Leginska was born in Hull and possesses Yorkshire grit. Still very young [she was actually 44] she has already had four careers – piano virtuoso, conductor, composer and teacher. In America she is regarded as the Paderewski among women players. She has played concertos and given concerts throughout the country."

A list of the many orchestras Leginska had conducted in the USA, including her own, and some of those in Berlin, Munich and Paris, was then given, her performances "leaving behind an impression everywhere of possessing profound musical culture and vitality". Before paying tribute to Leginska in its closing remarks, the article continued:

"She has recently conducted [in 1930] the London Symphony Orchestra at the Albert Hall, and a number of guest performances for the Carl Rosa Opera Company. The big outlines usually revealed in her orchestral interpretations appear at strange variance with the slight figure from which they proceed.

"The preceding sketch, though brief, reveals a highly successful career built on determination and ambition. Miss Leginska has made a succession of conquests in America; and though she has now made her [temporary] home in London, it is America which continues to encourage this indomitable little English woman. And in America she is soon to have her first opera produced."

The success of Leginska's presentation of Bizet's *Carmen* in English at Jordan Hall, Boston, on 11th May 1929, followed by her direction of subsequent operatic enterprises in Britain and the continent, had certainly heightened her interest in presenting operatic performances. On her return to the United States, Leginska focused her attention for a time on this field of music and in 1931 she was invited to conduct Charles L. Wagner's production of von Suppé's 3-act light opera *Boccaccio* at the 'New Yorker' theatre on Broadway. The opera opened on 28th November 1931 in an English version, thus continuing Leginska's declared policy of bringing good music to the ordinary public in a form people could understand.

Photograph of Leginska published in 'Musical Opinion' in September 1930. The same picture had also been used in the USA in the late 1920s in concert programmes such as the example shown on page 200.

Allan Jones appeared in the title role as Giovanni Boccaccio. The performance was evidently as successful as *Carmen* had been two years earlier, judging by the reviews. The next day the following report appeared: [5]

Leginska Triumphs with 'Boccaccio'
Her Conducting is a Feature of
Production of New English Text

"In Charles L. Wagner's production which opened at the New Yorker Theatre last night, the chief innovation apart from the Bonnell Bennett new English text, was a change in genders. So far as is known there has never before been a male Boccaccio in any American production, and certainly there has never been a woman at the conductor's desk. Apparently there should have been. For, despite the popular acclaim of the principals, notably Allen Jones as Boccaccio, the outstanding fact of last night's production was Ethel Leginska's performance as director, and the revelation, under her baton, of what a light orchestra can be. Undisturbed by many late arrivals and some unwonted backstage overtones, she produced a crisp and authentic overture which forecast, to those who listened, the virtues that were to come. These were chiefly two — a command of orchestra, soloists and chorus that many a conductor might envy and almost uniform maintenance of balance between them. There is some very charming music in the orchestral score.

"Her second and more conspicuous excellence was the lifting of chorus and orchestra into climaxes which for mass and quality were truly astonishing to hear from a relatively small ensemble. This was largely achieved by keeping most of the reading on a level of lucidity and restraint wherein the solo voices and chorus could display, as they did with commendable frequency, a nice capacity for pianissimo, and for the variety of melodic color with which the tuneful score provides them. Thus, in its broad musical aspects, vocally and orchestrally, the production was so vivid and sure that hereafter one need not heed the excuses which have been made for productions of a similar nature. This company has shown what can be done.

"Youth, good looks, and grace were added to a fine voice in Allen Jones's playing of the leading role. His tenor is capable of charming pianissimo and of ringing bravura, and with this assembly of gifts one may forsee for him a brilliant light opera future." *

The *Musical Courier* also reviewed the performance. Describing Leginska as "an able conductor" the report continued, under the heading "Leginska Enlivens *Boccaccio*": [6]

"She achieved a far more successful ensemble of soloists and chorus than is usual in light opera."

Thus, Leginska was beginning to get a foothold in the world of opera. But in spite of her new-found enthusiasm for this branch of music, her

---

*Although the spelling of the principal tenor's first name is given as 'Allen' in the review, the authors suspected, in view of what was said about him, that he was in fact Allan Jones (1908 - 1992) who established himself on Broadway in the early 1930s (e.g. in *Roberta*, 1933) before going into films. The book *Hollywood Songsters* by J.R. Parish and M.R. Pitts (Garland, New York, 1991) confirms that this was indeed the case. In the film *The Firefly* (1937), co-starring Jeanette MacDonald, Jones sang *Donkey Serenade* which became his signature tune.

aspirations as a conductor of women's orchestras were not yet over. Following the demise of the Boston Women's Symphony Orchestra (latterly re-named Leginska's Women's Symphony Orchestra) she had moved in 1931, after returning from her tour of Europe, from Boston to New York, in order to prepare for and conduct *Boccaccio*, and she decided to settle there for a while. In 1932 Leginska founded another women's orchestra, based in New York City, this time called the National Woman's [*sic*] Symphony Orchestra. * In February 1932 the New York newspapers published photographs of Leginska conducting the new orchestra in rehearsal in New York. The first concert of the orchestra was given in Carnegie Hall at 8.30 on Saturday evening, 12th March 1932. The programme comprised:

Overture, Russlan and Ludmilla	Glinka
"Spring Symphony" in B Flat Major	Schumann
Concerto in A Major for Piano and Orchestra, K. 488	Mozart
(Played and conducted by Ethel Leginska)	
Russian Easter	Rimsky-Korsakov
Cortège et Air de Danse (from the Cantate "L'Enfant Prodigue")	Debussy
Overture, Rienzi	Wagner

STEINWAY PIANO
PRICES: $1.00, $1.50, $2.00, $2.50
Management:
CHARLES L. WAGNER, 511 FIFTH AVENUE, NEW YORK

The concert was reviewed the next day in *The New York Times*: [7]

Ethel Leginska Conducts

"Ethel Leginska last night conducted the initial concert of the Woman's Symphony Orchestra in Carnegie Hall; the first time, so far as is known, that an orchestra entirely feminine has appeared there under a woman director.

"Those of the audience who remember Miss Leginska's deft ability with the orchestra and chorus of the late "Boccaccio" revival were not altogether surprised at the cleanness and vivacity of the orchestra's attack upon Glinka's "Russlan and Ludmilla". It is a good warhorse on which to ride into the symphonic arena, as it is merely bright and tuneful music to whom subtlety is unknown. Nevertheless, it must prance bravely and sparkle becomingly and this it did, with the orchestra rising to applause and the little conductor – the desk comes to Miss Leginska's chin – bowing to them."

The review went on to pay tribute to the "generally creditable performance of the new ensemble" and remarked that the audience was enthusiastic.

---

* The orchestra's name was printed on the programme, and in the previous press releases announcing the concert, as the 'National Woman's Symphony Orchestra' but one wonders why – was it a printing misunderstanding? Most, but not all, of the contemporary reviewers referred to it in their reports as the 'National Women's Symphony Orchestra' which one would have thought was more correct, including the *Boston Transcript*'s music correspondent and the famous critic W.J. Henderson of the *New York Sun*.

"I am firmly convinced that
the Steinway Piano has no rival.
Today, as always, it is the greatest
of them all."

ETHEL LEGINSKA

ETHEL LEGINSKA, *Conductor-Composer-Pianist will appear with the National Woman's Symphony Orchestra in Carnegie Hall on March 12, evening.*

Top: Announcement of Leginska's forthcoming Carnegie Hall concert of March 1932 (see pages 213 and 215) complete with Steinway endorsement. Lower: Cover of the concert programme.

The *Boston Transcript* carried a lengthy account, with assistance from the *New York Sun*'s veteran critic, W.J. Henderson *: [8]

Leginska's Dream Stands Fulfilled
To New York She Introduces Her Women's Orchestra; One Hundred Strong

"What Miss Leginska attempted in her latter days at Boston, she has now brought to pass in New York. Last Saturday at Carnegie Hall, her National Women's Symphony Orchestra – "one hundred musicians, one hundred per cent women" – gave a first and fairly successful concert. They marched ceremoniously to the stage, all attired in black with white collars, after the fashion of their conductor. They made a sober, even Puritan, picture. In the *Sun*, Mr Henderson continues the report:"

"Where Miss Leginska found them all can only be conjecture. She had eight double basses, all women, and evidently no novices. Only one of them used an Italian bow; the others went at it full-fisted. There were five horns. Where, when and why do women take up the horn? 'Cellos can be obtained by scores, but where do you get a female tuba player? Whence comes the lady tympanist?

"No matter. There they all were, and it was demonstrated early in the concert that by far the larger number were not new to orchestral performance. There was too much knowledge of routine for that. There were technical slips, to be sure, and in Schumann's Symphony in B flat there was considerable exposure of the rawness of the organisation. Some of the long-drawn phrases of the slow movement were separated from one another by pauses more than rhetorical. One felt that some of the charming wind players needed time to get breath.

"But, on the whole, the first concert of the new orchestra was distinctly worth while. The girls knew how to count their rests. The strings delivered a fairly good quality of tone and played with assurance and spirit. The trumpets and trombones were somewhat rough, but that is a fault which will undoubtedly be corrected soon.

"The opening number, Glinka's overture 'Russlan and Ludmilla', went off well. There was plenty of snap and fire in the performance. After the symphony Miss Leginska played the solo part in Mozart's Piano Concerto in A major, directing the orchestra at the same time. She might possibly have got on as well without quite so much conducting – leaping to her feet after every piano passage, even beating time with one hand while she was playing with the other. However, if she likes to work so hard it is her affair. She had our sympathy and admiration. In spite of the manifest anxiety of the occasion she gave a pretty smooth keyboard performance.

"Miss Leginska is a clever conductor. Why should we not have women conductors and orchestras? The National Women's Symphony Orchestra had a very businesslike appearance and went at its programme in a workmanlike manner. This music-lover hopes that these musicians will find favor with the public and not be regarded merely as a passing curiosity."

---

* W.J. Henderson (1855 - 1937) was a well-read and highly respected music critic. He had been a reporter with the *New York Times* but was with the *Sun* from 1902 until his death by suicide 35 years later at the age of 81. He was an authority not only on music but also naval affairs, having been an expert yachtsman, an officer in the Naval Militia, and an instructor in navigation.

Clearly, Leginska's National Women's Symphony Orchestra (which we will call it) based in New York had had a reasonably good start, with potential for early improvement. Unfortunately, the economic depression then gripping the USA showed no sign of abating. Consequently the financial problems that had caused the collapse of Leginska's Boston-based women's orchestra still prevailed and in spite of its artistic success the new orchestra stood no chance of surviving in the economic climate of 1932; the costs of running such a large, new ensemble were far too high at a time when few people were in a position to spend their money on concerts. Leginska reluctantly decided, therefore, to disband the orchestra only a few months after its establishment. It was singularly unfortunate that Leginska's best efforts to run women's orchestras had finally been defeated not by artistic deficiencies but by a severe national economic depression entirely beyond her control. In retrospect, she had done very well to keep her orchestras going for as long as she did, in particular her Boston Women's Symphony Orchestra which had given over 200 concerts all over the eastern part of the United States, its eventual demise being due solely to the economic depression following the Wall Street crash of 1929. *

The niche that Leginska had carved for herself was an important one. Initially conducting male orchestras, she had conducted women's orchestras with great artistic success from 1927 to 1932. (Boston Women's Symphony, Chicago Women's Symphony, National Women's Symphony.) When she made her extensive tours with the Boston orchestra between 1927 and 1929 her orchestra might have attracted attention initially because of its all-female membership. But in featuring women as orchestral members she had proved a great champion of women in this capacity. She had set out to prove a point – to show that a woman could be a top-class conductor and that women could be first-rate orchestral players. On both counts she had succeeded. She had introduced many new works to her audiences and in presenting such music as Beethoven's Fifth Symphony in out-of-the-way locations that had rarely, if ever, heard music on this scale, she had been a true pioneer.

After the National Women's Symphony Orchestra had given its final performance, Leginska withdrew from this particular fray and founded no more orchestras of her own. She was then 46 years old and it seems entirely reasonable that, having shown the way, she should leave it to others to continue the work she had begun. From 1933 onwards her appearances on the

---

* The whole of the music business in the United States was affected in this *Brother, Can You Spare a Dime* era until things started gradually to recover when Franklin D. Roosevelt's 'New Deal' began to take effect some years later. For example, in the early 1930s the famous Steinway piano factory in New York was virtually shut down, the workers being laid off. If an occasional order for a piano came in, some of the laid-off workers were called in to make it.

The Complete Musician

rostrum in concerts were either as a guest conductor with major orchestras or on an *ad hoc* basis for performances of her own compositions.

But Leginska still had plenty to do − other worlds to conquer. Her new interest in opera had channelled her energies into this area. Her principles dictated that she must aim to bring good music to the ordinary music lover in a form that could be easily understood; that was why she had presented both *Carmen* and *Boccaccio* in English versions. Their success must have contributed to Leginska's desire to write her own opera.

Ethel Leginska was a cultured woman and from childhood had possessed a thorough knowledge and love of English literature, valuable assets for a composer of opera. In the years 1930 to 1935 she put her gifts to good effect and used what spare time she could muster amidst her numerous other duties to compose two operas.

The first of these was *The Rose and the Ring*, based on a satire by William Makepeace Thackeray, which she composed in the years 1930 to 1932. In the earlier part of this period she had time only to sketch out the outline of the opera, but in the summer of 1932, taking a break from her conducting, she travelled to England and rented a cottage in a quiet rural locality so that she could work undisturbed. The cottage, 'Elm Lea', was in Withersfield, a village of about 300 inhabitants near Haverhill in the east-coast county of Suffolk.[9] (Due to boundary changes the village is now in Essex.) It was there that she completed the opera. Leginska always enjoyed her visits to England. She used them to 'unwind' from her hectic life in the United States and this visit was no exception. She revelled in the tranquil, rural surroundings of Suffolk, a location not dissimilar to the haunts of her youth in East Yorkshire, particularly at a family home in Hornsea. The contrast with life in New York could not have been more complete, providing conditions entirely conducive to the swift completion of her opera. No publisher or concert manager expressed any interest in the completed work, however, once she had returned to America, and it was to lie unperformed until 25 years later when it received its premiere in Los Angeles (23rd February 1957) with Leginska conducting. This event will be described in Chapter 16, which covers that period of Leginska's life.

After completing *The Rose and the Ring* Leginska went to Cuba, where in 1933 she conducted the Havana Philharmonic Orchestra in a performance of Beethoven's Ninth (Choral) Symphony. Afterwards she spent several more months there, training a chorus and orchestra for a season of Italian opera which duly took place under her conductorship.

Seemingly undaunted by the music establishment's indifference to *The Rose and the Ring*, Leginska set about writing her second opera; its title was

A publicity picture used by Leginska in the early 1930s. This one was sent by Ethel to her Aunt Lucy (Witty, née Liggins) and her family in Hull (see family tree)
(Picture courtesy of Tom Langdale, Lucy Witty's grandson)

Gale, subtitled *The Haunting*. This time she fared better, the opera being accepted for presentation. It was staged at the Chicago Opera House, one of the premier venues in the United States, on 23rd November 1935, Leginska conducting.

The story on which the opera is based was supplied by Mrs C.A. Dawson-Scott in a novel entitled *The Haunting*. The scene is a village in Cornwall where Gale (the hero of the opera) and his young sailor brother, Pascoe, quarrel over a hoard of gold hidden in an ancient chest. The beginning is happy, dominated by bright folk tunes, but later the music reflects the macabre plot. Gale murders his brother and hides his body in a cave near the sea. However, he never succeeds in escaping his brother's ghost, and Leginska's dramatic music reflects this fact.

John Charles Thomas took the title role.* The presentation was a huge success, being well-received by both press and public. The event made musical history – the first time anywhere in the world that a woman had conducted her own opera in a major opera house. Here are a few of the press reviews, starting with the *Chicago Times*: [10]

"A thin, middle-aged woman stood in the darkened pit at the Chicago Opera House last week waving a baton as if she believed it possessed some superhuman power. Her eyes blazed. She tossed her bushy head this way and that, pointed vigorous commands to the singers on the stage. Ethel Leginska had good reason to make much of the music, because she had written it. Hers was the distinction of being the world's first woman to conduct her own opera in an important opera house.

"Well-knit and melodious, the music often gives a real feeling of the sea as it beats against the chalk cliffs of the Cornwall coast. Leginska worked like fury at rehearsals and got telling results from orchestramen."

The complimentary remarks of this critic were endorsed by others. For the *Chicago Sunday Tribune*, under the heading 'Chicago Enjoys World premiere of Opera 'Gale' ', Edward Barry wrote: [11]

"The world premiere of Ethel Leginska's 'Gale' was the high point of a crowded Saturday at the Civic Opera House. For the first time in history a woman composer of opera appeared in a major house to conduct her own work. Besides hanging up an operatic first, the Chicago City Opera Company managed to provide a performance for its patrons that was remarkable in several ways.

---

* The American baritone John Charles Thomas (1891-1960) was very well known in the USA between the two world wars. He was born in Pennsylvania and studied in Baltimore, his first appearance on stage being as the Judge in a conservatory performance of *Trial by Jury*. He sang in musical comedy in New York from 1913, later in opera in Brussels, and made his debut at Covent Garden in 1928 as Valentin in Gounod's *Faust*. He appeared with the Chicago Opera from 1930 and in 1934 made his first appearance with the Metropolitan Opera in New York as the elder Germont in *La Traviata*. He continued to appear from time to time with the 'Met' until 1943 when he settled in California.

"In the first place John Charles Thomas created the name part. His characterization of the repressed and moody but outwardly respectable Cornish townsman had the usual Thomas power and conviction about it; the music lies well for his admirable voice.

"Leginska's conducting was fiery and exciting. Also, it was most certainly authoritative. In at least two departments, the direction and the title role, last night's performance set a mark which future producers of the work will find it hard to better . . .

"I will not presume to pass judgment on the music after one hearing. Its melodies have an impressive lyric beauty and a certain sustained nobility of line. Leginska is mistress of a very flexible technique and is successful in the task of making the music mirror admirably the lights and shadows of the drama's thought and action.

Laurels for the Composer

"She writes richly and idiomatically for orchestra. Her use of dramatic device is skilled and modern. She has wed the grim story to music without subcontracting a mite of its grimness, but has been clever enough to take full advantage of the opportunities it offers for lyric exposition."

Herman Devries* writing in the *Chicago American* reported, under the heading 'World Premiere of 'Gale' Well Received': [12]

"A world premiere. "Gale", by Ethel Leginska, composer-conductor, was given in English with an all-American cast at the Civic Opera House last Saturday evening . . . We must credit Miss Leginska with some excellent ideas of orchestration and we must, in all sincerity, state that there were moments of dramatic import heightened by some very original and fitting orchestral sonorities."

Robert Pollak in the *Daily Times* noted: [13]

"Week-end activities at the Chicago City Opera House included the startling world premiere of "Gale", a short opera by Ethel Leginska, the talented and tempestuous woman, who conducted her own work on its first hearing Saturday night. The name part, that of Gale Corlyon, a Cornish tradesman, was taken by John Charles Thomas, who won himself a huge ovation for his operatic study of remorse. Miss Leginska's score is melodious, and she is acquainted with all the best modernistic tricks. "Gale" can be counted one of the hits of the season."

The *Brooklyn Daily Eagle*, publishing an account written on the night of the performance, demonstrated that New York had not forgotten Leginska's premiere. In a lengthy review the paper reported: [14]

Operatic History Made as Leginska conducts
Becomes First Woman to Write and Lead Major Production
As She Wields Baton Before Full House in Chicago

"Ethel Leginska became tonight the first woman in history to write and conduct an opera in a major opera house. Wielding the baton, the internationally known conductor directed the world premiere of her opera, 'Gale', as sung by the Chicago City Opera company with John Charles Thomas, noted baritone, in the title role.

---

* Herman Devries (1858-1949) was a well-known American operatic bass before becoming a teacher and music critic for *Chicago American* when his singing days were over.

The Complete Musician

"Con Spirito, I Told You"
Ethel Leginska, Conductor
As the Orchestra Sees her

*(Boston Evening Transcript,
11th October 1929)*

*Woman Leads Opera:
Operatic History Made
as Leginska Conducts.*

*(Brooklyn Daily Eagle
24th November 1935)*

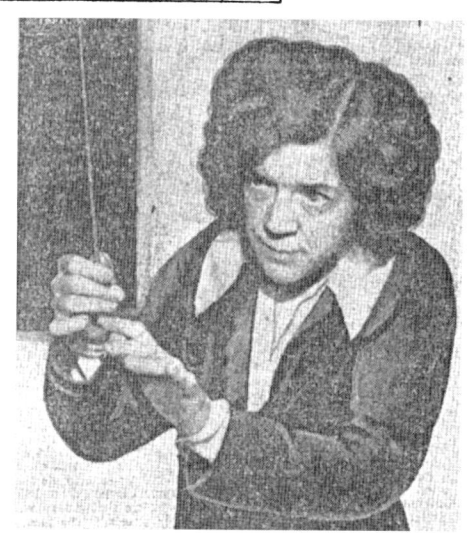

Two more studies of Leginska the conductor
Top: As seen by the artist Lydia Hess with the accompanying newspaper caption
Bottom: Photograph published the day after 'Gale' was presented

"The interest of opera lovers and musical circles in Europe and America was focused on this small, friendly woman. Greetings from afar were delivered and heavy box office receipts recorded unusual local attention.

"Her black velvet frocked-coated figure, heavy head of dark hair, and her strong hands are familiar to the world's great symphony orchestras, for she has appeared as guest conductor before most of them – the first woman to achieve such an honor."

Rene Devries, reviewing the occasion two weeks later for the magazine *Musical Courier*, observed: [15]

Leginska Opera in Premiere
Dramatic One-Act Score by Woman Composer Wins Warm Success, Under Her Baton, for John Charles Thomas and Co-artists

"Gale (The Haunting), a one-act opera in three scenes by the conductor-composer, Ethel Leginska, found much favour with our opera-goers when it saw the footlights for the first time at the Civic Opera House . . .

A Spirited Score

"Miss Leginska is as good a composer as a conductor and this means much. For the first scene, the marketplace of Stowe, Cornwall, in 1830, she has written music reminiscent of folklore of Cornwall – highly spirited, bubbling with humour, and joyful, and which well prefaces the second episode, which also begins gaily. In the third scene, after Gale has murdered his sailor brother, Pascoe, and is haunted by the living spirit of the dead, the music suddenly becomes tragic and here we find Leginska at her best, even though our ears caught strains of Tchaikowsky, Wagner and even Gruenberg. But for all that, Miss Leginska's music is original, well conceived and interesting and, to be quite candid, it is one of the best short operas produced here in many a year.

"The work was well received and Leginska and the interpreters were recalled time after time by an audience that showed unmistakably its pleasure towards the composer and the principal protagonists."

Leginska's conducting of *Gale* made a lasting impression on those fortunate enough to be present. Herbert Donaldson, who became a music critic for the *Los Angeles Examiner* and music editor of the *Hollywood Citizen News*, attended the performance of *Gale* and wrote to the authors: [16]

"I recall her agile, youthful self and the spirit she evoked from that score. Then she had a large amount of black hair which she tossed about in the enthusiasm of conducting."

Mr Donaldson's remarks testify to the youthful image still projected by Ethel Leginska, though at the time of the Chicago performance she was within five months of her 50th birthday, a fact that would have surprised most of the audience had they known. Those who were curious as to her age would most probably have been misled by her tendency, shared with many others then and now, to understate her years in printed literature.

The production of Leginska's opera at the Chicago Opera House was perhaps the highlight of her career as composer/conductor. But there were many other occasions to remember in her musical life of the 1930s, judged as a conductor alone, in both the operatic and symphonic realms. She had forced the music critics to take her seriously by her musicianship, vitality and dedication. Consequently she had no shortage of engagements to appear as guest conductor and notched up numerous successes apart from those already quoted. Some of the occasions on which she conducted operas are worthy of particular mention. She conducted the San Carlo Opera Company in Puccini's *Madame Butterfly* in Boston, Tchaikovsky's *Eugen Onegin* in Russian at the Manhattan Opera House, New York, and Debussy's *Pelleas et Melisande* during a season devoted to opera in Montreal, Canada. Other highlights included performances in various large opera houses of Puccini's *Tosca*, Verdi's *Rigoletto*, Bizet's *Carmen*, and Charpentier's *Louise*. Leginska also travelled to Austria and conducted *Madame Butterfly* in Salzburg.

In the symphonic field Leginska furthered her reputation as a musical pioneer in her second appearance as guest conductor of the Dallas Symphony Orchestra by conducting, with a 200-strong chorus, the first performance in Texas of Beethoven's Ninth (Choral) Symphony. Her appearance in Cuba, conducting the same symphony, has already been noted; she had also presented it on tour with her orchestra in the late 1920s.

The list of Leginska's achievements in these years of maturity seems endless. She was still one of the busiest musicians in the United States – a human dynamo, as she had been all her life. As pianist, composer and conductor she had become one of the best and most famous musicians of her era and had followed this up by pioneering the role of women as orchestral conductors, a role almost unheard of previously. Moreover, by forming and running women's orchestras she had championed the cause of women instrumentalists. Perhaps more than any woman before, she had put women 'on the musical map'. They had much to thank her for.

In 1936 Leginska celebrated her 50th birthday, marking the event by embarking on a lengthy visit to Europe, and it was there that most of her time was spent during the next three years. She continued to make guest conducting appearances, but increasingly she devoted herself to teaching, a facet of her career in which she had been engaged ever since she taught music to her dolls at the age of six, but which had of necessity been pushed into the background while she was in peak demand as a performer. During these years she lived in London and made occasional visits to Paris. In both cities she operated with great success as a piano teacher. In 1936 and through to April 1937 Leginska lived at 26, Oakley Crescent, Chelsea. In May 1937 she moved to 38, Glebe Place, and soon afterwards to 4, Oakley Gardens. All these Chelsea premises, consisting of apartment blocks, were within a stone's throw of each other, close to the Albert Bridge over the Thames. They were near Tedworth Gardens, where she had lived during her British tours of the early 1920s. Leginska obviously liked Chelsea.

In the late 1930s in London Leginska taught piano very successfully, and made efforts to have *Gale* presented in London. But here she was beset by difficulties. It is clear, from correspondence between Leginska and eminent British conductors and concert managers such as Adrian Boult* at the BBC, Landon Ronald** at the Guildhall School of Music and Drama and Lilian Baylis † at the Old Vic, that there was little chance of an opera such as Leginska's *Gale* being presented by a professional company in Britain in the current climate. The following extracts from two letters from Lilian Baylis, Manager of the Old Vic, sent in reply to Leginska's soundings as to the possibility of *Gale* being presented at the theatre, explained the position: [17]

11th December 1935:
Dear Madame Leginska,
 Thank you for your letter. Our arrangements for the present season are completed, so that there could be no immediate prospect of the production of Gale, but if you got in touch with us in April we would gladly try to arrange to hear it.
 It is only fair, however, to warn you that the chances are heavily against the production of English operas here, because they empty the house for us! We do one or two each season, as a matter of principle, and have already several awaiting production, but our people are horribly faint-hearted and won't risk the unfamiliar – unless it is in Russian.

19th March 1936:
 ...We will certainly bear it [Gale] in mind when we are considering our programme for next season, but it is only fair to warn you that with the exception of the ever-popular "Cav. and Pag." our audience has shown its distate for one-act operas, and I am terribly afraid that we will not feel justified in incurring the risk the production of another would entail. We added Gianni Schicchi, Savitri and Il Tabarro (the latter for the first time in English) to our repertory this season, and although the press for them was excellent, the

---

* Adrian Boult (born Chester, 1889; died Tunbridge Wells, 1983) was a distinguished British conductor. From 1930 until 1950 he was Musical Director at the BBC and conductor of the BBC Symphony Orchestra; he also conducted many other orchestras during his long life. In 1953 he conducted the music for the Coronation of Queen Elizabeth II at Westminster Abbey. He was knighted in 1937.

** Landon Ronald (real name Landon Ronald Russell) was born in London in 1873 and died there in 1938. He was a distinguished conductor and Principal of the Guildhall School of Music from 1910 until his death. He conducted the New Symphony Orchestra in London, later renamed the Royal Albert Hall Orchestra. He composed an operetta and a ballet. He was knighted in 1922.

† Lilian Baylis (born London in 1874, died there in 1938) was the daughter of musicians and was a musician herself. In the early 1900s she helped manage the Royal Victoria Hall (afterwards the Old Vic) and became its manager in 1912, a post she retained until her death. Under her the theatre became a joint home of Shakespeare and opera. In 1931 she acquired Sadler's Wells Theatre for the exclusive presentation of opera and ballet. She was created Companion of Honour in 1929.

houses they drew were dreadful! We have, before now, tried putting other one-act operas with either Cavalleria or Pagliacci, but people refuse to come to them, preferring to wait until "the twins" are together again! It is very disheartening, especially as, at our prices, we have no margin for loss, and must take no unavoidable risks. I felt it was fairer to explain this, so that, should there be no possibility of our considering your opera, you would understand the reasons for this decision.

The late 1930s were of course dominated by gathering war clouds – plain for all to see. The time had come for Leginska to take stock. The days when she was purely a concert pianist were long gone, by her own choice; they had been superseded by her conducting, with some piano playing 'thrown in' for good measure – a state of affairs that had enabled her to express herself musically as she wished. She had achieved numerous 'firsts' especially regarding the place of women in music. She had proved a point, that women could do these things, and do them well. But she had to look to the future. After the Munich crisis of 1938 it appeared to many that war was inevitable. The only question was, when would it begin? It was also likely that sooner or later the United States, of which she was a citizen and where she had lived for most of the last 25 years, would be drawn in. It was an appropriate time to consider what form her future career should take. Should she continue her existing lifestyle until overtaken by old age, or should she seek a new objective? If, or when, war came in Europe, there would almost certainly be fewer opportunities for her there in the type of role she sought.

Furthermore, the sight of Leginska on the rostrum was no longer a novelty, and though she was a more experienced and proficient conductor than she had been in the mid 1920s when the slight, youthful, energetic and dynamic figure had thrilled concert audiences, there were still plenty of prejudices against women conductors and she could not go on forever being the 'dynamic young conductor' that the public knew and loved. Concert managers had to think in terms of the number of seats sold, and it seemed likely that, as Leginska grew older, conducting opportunities would come less easily, especially in time of war. And clearly, there would be few possibilities for the production of either of her operas in Britain.

As Hitler's machinations grew more menacing by the month, Leginska decided at the end of 1938, following the Munich crisis, to give up her lifelong career as a performer and to earn her living instead as a teacher. She had no desire to continue the tedium of incessant travel, nor was there any point in trying to run orchestras in wartime – it would be an impossible task. So she would confine herself to teaching, combining it with some performing, but only in a subsidiary role, in collaboration with her students.

It will be clear from what has been said in previous chapters that Leginska had always loved teaching. Moreover, she had a great gift for it.

From her childhood in Hull and subsequent early years as a professional pianist in London (from about 1905) she had taught, and when she went to America in 1912 she immediately took pupils, not only to help support herself financially whilst she sought concert engagements, but because she could not imagine life without teaching as part of it. Her forthright personality and her ability to teach by example had immediately established her reputation, and over the years her teaching skills had been maintained and developed. As soon as she first arrived in New York in 1912 (with just $100 in her pocket, so she said) she hired a studio for $25 a month in which to teach, and then taught at $1 a lesson, until she began to make a name for herself and could charge higher fees. [18] Throughout her most prolific years, when she was always in the public eye in one way or another, she had taught as often as her engagements allowed, and had always maintained a private teaching studio, right through to the end of 1938.

In the light of Leginska's 25 years of experience of life in the USA in comparison with her recent experiences in Britain, combined with the likelihood of imminent war in which Britain would clearly be involved, she decided, after due consideration, to return to the USA and set up a teaching studio in Los Angeles, California, a locality rich in prospective students. There was also another reason for selecting Los Angeles. As she later told a student, Ron McFarland, she had been offered the opportunity by MGM in 1938-39 to play the part (acting and playing the piano) of Clara Schumann (née Wieck) in a Hollywood film about Robert and Clara Schumann [19], making residence in the Los Angeles area desirable. With the threat and finally the reality of war, plans for the film were postponed, possibly because the Schumanns were German, which would not have helped its box-office success. But by the time the film was put on hold, Leginska had already settled in Los Angeles and established herself as a very successful teacher there, having built up a large clientele of students, so the city had become her home. After the war plans for the film were revived, but by then Leginska was nearly 60 and considered too old for the part. The acting part of Clara Schumann in the film, entitled *Song of Love*, went to Katharine Hepburn, with the piano played (off-screen) by Artur Rubinstein – not Leginska. What a loss! With all due respect to that fine screen actress Katharine Hepburn, it would have been marvellous to have had a glimpse of Ethel Leginska recorded on film, and playing, for posterity. The film was released in 1947.

And so, in 1939, Leginska embarked on the final but lengthy phase of her remarkable musical life. From that time onwards it would be her students who would benefit from her skills and experience the force of her personality.

References: Chapter 14

1. Leginska interviewed by Laning Humphrey, *Boston Sunday Post*, Boston, Mass., 22nd September 1929.
2. *Boston Transcript*, 19th February 1930.
3. Amy Johnson's telegram was addressed to 'Miss Ethel Leggins', the misspelling being probably attributable to a transcription error at the telegraph office. Since hardly anyone had used Ethel's birth-surname for about 25 years, not even family, the fact that Amy used it suggested she knew her background. This would not really be surprising since Amy was another 'daughter of Hull', having been born in the city 17 years after Ethel (in 1903) and would have known of Ethel's exploits from her earliest years. Amy had only recently (in May 1930) made her epic flight from Britain to Australia in her flimsy single-engined open-cockpit Gipsy Moth biplane *Jason*, which had resulted in her new-found fame. The telegram was sent from the P & O liner *Naldera* whilst she was en-route home, so clearly resulted from her having read press reports of Ethel's conducting.
4. *Musical Opinion*, September 1930, p. 1062.
5. Review from an unknown newspaper (acquired as an unattributed press cutting), the date of which is 29th November 1931. Signed "H.H."
6. *Musical Courier*, 12th December 1931.
7. *The New York Times*, 13th March 1932.
8. *Boston Transcript*, 16th March 1932.
9. The address of Leginska's rented cottage was given in a news item in *Musical Courier*, 16th July 1932. Also, letters at that time were sent to her there.
10. *Chicago Times*, 2nd December 1935.
11. *Chicago Sunday Tribune*, 24th November 1935.
12. *Chicago American*, 24th November 1935.
13. *Chicago Daily Times*, 25th November 1935.
14. *Brooklyn Daily Eagle*, 24th November 1935.
15. *Musical Courier*, 7th December 1935.
16. Letters to the authors from Mr Herbert Donaldson of Sherman Oaks, California, dated 26th June and 16th October 1984.
17. Copies of these and other letters, the later ones of which (from 1936) were sent to Leginska at the addresses listed on page 223, were kindly supplied by International Piano Archives at Maryland.
18. Reported in an interview Leginska gave with *Musical Courier*, 2nd October 1919.
19. One of Leginska's former students, the composer Ron McFarland, contributing to a discussion about Ethel Leginska marking her centenary in 1986. It was broadcast by the radio station KPFK Los Angeles in the "Music of the Americas" series on 6th April 1986 (a week before Leginska's centenary).

Chapter 15

Madame Leginska – Teacher

When Ethel Leginska decided to give up the ceaseless itinerant round of the performer and become a full-time teacher she was nearly 53 years old. The date was late 1938 and the Second World War was soon to start in Europe. Always a woman of vision, Leginska's aim was to be more than just a piano teacher; she intended to produce finished musicians, skilled in the art of public performance. With this in mind, she quickly established a large clientele of talented students after settling in Los Angeles.

Leginska's first Los Angeles studio, which she set up early in 1939, was on South Ardmore Avenue but it was not long before she moved to premises about one and a half miles further north, at 254, South Hobart Boulevard, Los Angeles 4, and it was here that she made her permanent home. The house was a two-storey wooden-framed building of imposing appearance built about 1925, and situated in a middle-class area.[1] It was a family type of home duplicated throughout the district, but since the Second World War most of the houses have been demolished to make way for large apartment buildings. Leginska's house and adjacent ones were in fact demolished in the late 1970s or early 1980s to make room for 'condominium' development. The studio room where the teaching took place was about 35ft long and 25ft wide at the piano positions. The room could not accommodate more that 35 or 40 people, so during Sunday afternoon recitals the overflow sat in the porch and on the outside stairs listening to the playing through open windows. The room was sparsely furnished, with nothing of value except the pianos and the contents of book cases.

A vivid account of piano lessons with Ethel Leginska has been written for the authors by the concert pianist Marilyn Neeley, Professor of Music at the Catholic University of America. It will be quoted at length here, along with other first-hand accounts, since it is impossible to improve on the recollections of those who were there:[2]

"Since I studied with her for 14 years, 5 to 19, I can certainly say that she is responsible for a great part of my playing today – particularly the technical equipment.

"Since I was so young when I began studying with Mme Leginska, I really do not remember my first impressions. Indeed, I have powerful overall impressions, unchanging over the years, of a very strong-willed woman, with positive, unequivocal ideas, a drive for technical perfection and a regimen for achieving this.

"It is only now, as I teach and play, more and more, that I appreciate what her technical approach meant: super-strong fingers, constant and total relaxation of the wrist and elsewhere, playing with back and shoulder strength for big works and sound without

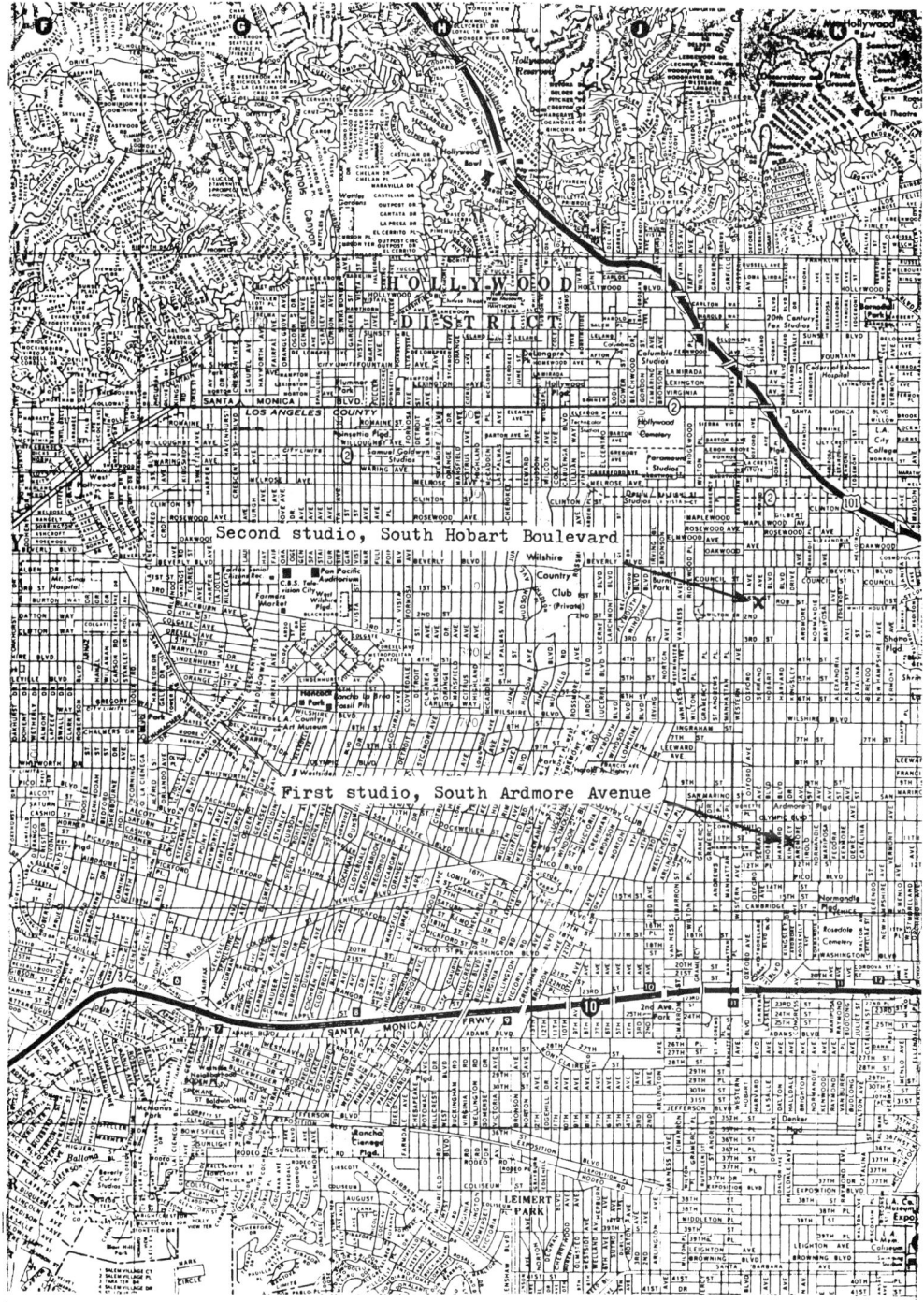

Street plan showing the location of Leginska's first and second homes (and studios) in Los Angeles

tiring, unwavering attention to producing a beautiful (singing, warm, rich – never harsh or edgy, even when loud) tone.

"Mme Leginska stressed technical perfection in all matters, musical and technical. Needless to say, this created great tension when playing for her. Nearly every lesson proceeded by the student playing one beat – on rare occasions a complete measure or two – and Mme Leginska shouting 'No!'. She demonstrated, constantly, and we would copy until the correct effect was achieved. She did refer to the printed music for her reasons, so it was not only rote learning, although for the younger student this result was inevitable. Her culminating remark was always, 'You must always try to play something better than anyone has ever played it!'

"Of course, not knowing how everyone has ever played anything or even what 'better' is, such advice could be construed as objectively meaningless. However, the impact that it made, then, and still makes, now, is the desire to strive, continually, for a still-more-beautiful result.

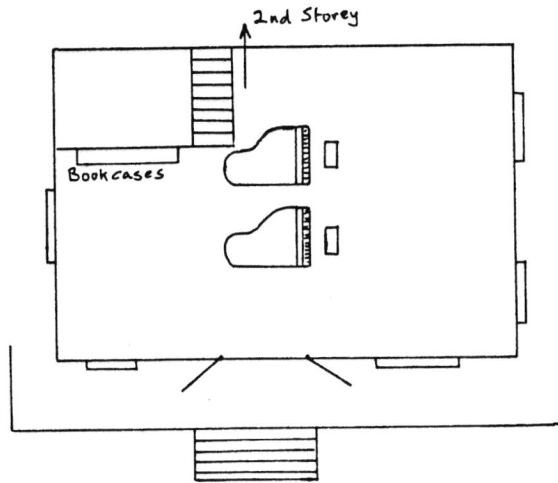

Ethel Leginska's teaching studio at South Hobart Boulevard, Los Angeles

(From a sketch by Mr Joseph Enos, a former student)

"To return, briefly, to the technical side, we had a regimen of one to two hours, daily, of technique. (She was not interested in young students who practised less than four to six hours a day – a requirement my parents had to work out with the public school system.) Now, when I see my 18 - 20 year old university students struggling with standard pianistic patterns – scales, arpeggios, chord figures, etc., – I realize what those daily one to two hours accomplished. They gave me a technical-muscular-mental 'vocabulary' of patterns, which serve as the groundwork for most music I learn, today, or will ever learn. (I realize that this kind of training is standard for the Russians and many Europeans, but it is generally not part of the curriculum for the younger students in America, today or in the past. I credit much of my success in international competitions to having been fortunate enough to have had such a background.)

"Another advantage Mme Leginska provided was the monthly recital. Many teachers do have occasional studio recitals throughout the year, but few that I know make them the kind of 'professional event' that Mme Leginska did. Although they were held in her living room, we were expected to behave and play as if it were in the Carnegie Hall. To add to the tension, Mme Leginska sat several feet away and shouted, 'Go on! Go on!' if a student stumbled. Many people wince when I relate this and say that that takes the 'fun' out of learning and performing. That may well be true, but Mme Leginska was not teaching the average music-lover 'to have fun and relax with music'. She was preparing professionals, in every sense of the word, who must, indeed, 'Go on!', no matter what happens on stage.

"(She has, in fact, been criticized for frightening so many students out of music, but I think she felt her mission was to train potential artists; the rest could always find teachers who would encourage them to enjoy themselves at the piano. Frankly, I find that I enjoy myself on stage considerably more due to the experience of preparation, technically and psychologically, than I would had lesser demands been made upon me in the formative years.)

"In addition to the monthly recitals, her unflagging energy and dedication provided two more experiences for us:
(i) Orchestral (concerto) performances, and
(ii) The 'all the works of one composer' series.

"Since Mme Leginska loved conducting, she would, at least once a year, hire and conduct an orchestra [known as the 'Leginska Little Symphony'] for accompaniments to student concerto performances (from Mozart to Tchaikovsky) in a large public hall. Also, nearly every year, she would have a series featuring all the works of a given composer, played by her students. In fact, my first major public appearance was at age five, playing the E flat major Prelude and Fugue of the second volume of the *Well-Tempered Clavier* in her series covering all the keyboard works of Bach. The chance to hear all these works was an enormous heritage, in itself.

"I was lucky that my 14 years of merciless attention to detail and expectations of perfection (plus some rather old-fashioned musical ideas, particularly in the Baroque and Classical periods) were counter-balanced by seven years of study with Muriel Kerr, the marvellous Canadian pianist, who stressed line and direction, the musical whole. However, the older I get, the more I am aware of the tremendous debt I owe to Ethel Leginska in truly preparing me for every aspect of the musical and pianistic art."

Further accounts of Ethel Leginska's methods of instruction were sent to the authors by Joseph Enos, another Leginska student; a 'mature' one in his case, not a child:[3]

"Two procedures represent the ultimate in the Leginska lessons that guaranteed the pupil's certified progress in their musical endeavour. Two grand pianos, side by side, were used and the pupil (of whatever age) sat at Leginska's left. She demonstrated every hand position, tone control, dynamics, tempi; in other words every essence of piano performance, study and illumination . . .

"Nothing can surpass or restore the pupils' awareness of the musical moment at hand than the capacity to witness a player with perfect control of performance acuity tied in with a superior intellection toward the art; displaying the full competence of her art for the pupil's ear as well as his eye. I have talked to many students, professional and otherwise, and never have I heard of a teacher who followed this process. Most teachers sit through their hour with boredom and some encouragement and a little musical knowledge offered, or correction. Leginska felt that most students perfected their bad technique with years of study and hours-per-day of practice. She claimed that a half-hour of correct practice would suffice as a total gauge for their progress as the bad habits would have to be unrehearsed as four hours of faulty work would take four hours of a more correct session at the piano.

"The second procedure, for her beginners, was her demand that the mothers of the students attend the lessons and witness and be able to recall every event in the lesson . . . many a mother could have become pianists in their own right if following this procedure over several years of study. Also, Leginska demanded that the mothers supervise all practice at home . . . this takes a militant mother with real interest in the musical education of her child, not to accept it as another 'cultural' process in their child's development.

"To attend a Leginska recital and see 8-year-olds playing with perfect confidence and ability, some in brief concerti with Leginska at the second piano; this was a total joy and delight, also an elevating experience; not just cute and precious . . . the real thing . . .

"I once asked or rather commented on the fact that the young people showed such a lack of nervousness . . . Leginska's forceful answer was, 'We don't allow the word NERVOUS in this studio' . . . To her, the sense of nervousness implied incompetence, unprepared content and poor teaching and learning devices.

"I was forty at the time I studied with Leginska and within a 12-year stretch as staff pianist and organist at the NBC Studios in Hollywood. Nerves were a constant problem when the red light went on. You played the right notes, gave the right directions and cues or else went home and stayed there. One joke was that a producer (radio director) of a program was 'an ulcer with a stop-watch'. With a time spread of six to eight hours at the studio and unused studios all during the day with fine Steinway pianos, I decided to use up free time with study and practice, hence the transition to Leginska.

"The first few lessons with Leginska were ego-shattering. She stopped me after a few bars of my introduction to her (of my playing) which she was able to analyse with one glance . . . She said, 'You learned to play, but didn't learn how to study'!!! She proceeded to prove this in subsequent sessions. However, she had to prove that I had not had the first 10 lessons every student should have before touching a piano. She required a pupil to place his five fingers on top of the c-d-e-f-g in both hands but not depressing the keys. Fingers should not tremble and not the slightest indentation of the keys permissible . . . then the wrist must be dropped slowly then raised to its highest arc still without any finger movement or accidental depressing of any key. An extreme display of control during movement of the wrist and hand.

"I was of course in awe of this procedure as it was entirely new to me. A child with his mother's attendance could complain and the mother would ask; 'When will my child play 'The Blue Danube'?' and leave the studio. Leginska also displayed a two-hand 4th- and-5th finger exercise which she said she did for ten minutes beginning every practice session and demanded that pupils (who could acquire the exercise) do it 10 minutes a day also. She said it strengthened the 4th and 5th fingers but really it meant to drive the

Madame Leginska – Teacher

A publicity picture used by Leginska in the early 1940s

4th and 5th to a spread in all positions that could be required in any sequence of playing and in all black-and-white-key or black-or-white-only positions. Try reaching (playing middle C with the 3rd finger and holding on to stretch 4th finger up a third to E ... do the same with 4th finger on E-flat holding it to strike a G with the 5th finger. This exercise progresses through all scales, major and minor) ... To see Leginska do it was a gleaming experience ... Don't know it to be original or some device she acquired in her study ...

"In every music store and every student music-rack in U.S. there is displayed the 'Leschetizky Method' volume, a handsome book with slick paper and fine illustrations which comprised the essence of the Leschetizky piano method and teaching ideas. Leschetizky had been highly publicized as the teacher of Paderewski who dominated the concert stage in U.S. from perhaps 1910 until 1930.

"This star pupil [Paderewski] was the commercial value of the book and although purchased widely it WAS NEVER USED. The reason: It is a difficult method, it must be delineated by a fine super teacher and sincere advocate of the methods described in the book. Leginska must have studied the method and mastered its difficult exercises and reading material.

"A teacher, in my teens, who taught me little, but could declaim and expound on his abilities for the entire lesson, claimed the only use for the Leschetizky method was to elevate the piano bench-pad to assist the younger pupils to reach the keyboard ... and he took great delight in demonstrating this device for me ... a disgrace!!! He could not do the work in the book, either in his head or on the keyboard. Leginska could do the exercises and astound you with her steady tone control and perfection in the performance of them. EVERY NOTE PLAYED HAD TO BE PERFECT AND UP TO HER STANDARD OF PERFORMANCE ...

"One session, we spent the total time on the FIRST BAR of the D Minor Sonata of Beethoven ... to acquire the correct tone control, hand position dynamics and with no reason to proceed to the second bar until the first was perfect. If the pupil accepted the first bar with less than the needed style, then the next bar could suffer from the same confusion. Leginska needed to restore the pupil's disaffection to something near her concepts if possible. Music can easily delude the performer, but not an ear that has resulted from a lifetime of listening for the murky offences and artless results of poor training and unsound bewilderment as to what music is really all about!!!

"At one session two women outside Leginska's open window were into a rattling, rasping conversation that disturbed the lesson; probably the neighbor and a friend ... lasting only a few brief sentences ... Leginska said: 'How can sound like that be permitted in the world when there are beautiful sounds like music that should replace them.'!?

"The procedure for study was as follows ... learning new music that is: Play the total bar or measure to and including the downbeat of the next measure ... then commence at the first beat of the next measure and proceed in the same way ... in a four-four bar one would be practising five beats as a section only ... the progress would be beat five of the previous section converted to beat one of the next five-beat section. This method cannot be improved!"

Madame Leginska — Teacher

LEGINSKA

"The Paderewski of Women Pianists"
—*New York Herald Tribune*

presents the following highly talented American pianists from her
Los Angeles Studio
Now booking for Season 1941-1942

RALPH PIERCE
"A young pianist far above the average."
—Eugene Stinson, Daily News.
—CHICAGO DEBUT RECITAL, March 2nd, 1941.

"One of the finest of the younger American pianists." —Florence Lawrence, Examiner.
—LOS ANGELES DEBUT, April 4th, 1941.

ENGAGED TO APPEAR ON THE ARTIST SERIES AT U. C. L. A. SEASON 1941-42. (Engagement won in competition.)

ELAINE WIGHTMAN
Six-year-old WONDER CHILD delighted and amazed more than four thousand listeners in three concerts this season—two being as soloist with symphony Orchestras.
"Elaine, a tiny tot of six years, could barely reach the piano pedals, but played with a surety and aplomb that brought her a real ovation."
—R. D. Saunders, Hollywood Citizen News, Feb. 22nd, 1941.

"Little six-year-old Elaine made a profound impression with her surprisingly good performance of the Concerto in A-major by Mozart. The audience re-called her again and again. She finally responded with two encores."
San Bernardino Daily Sun, May 7th, 1941.

ARMANDO LOREDO
"An effective presentation of the difficult Prokofieff Third Concerto, Op. 26, showed to advantage Armando Loredo's musicianship, firm tone and technical facility. He displayed the work's wit and humor, as well as its loveliness in the discursive Andantino, and built to a pyrotechnical climax."
—R. D. Saunders, Citizen News.

". . . Showed musical vitality and brilliant technique." —Bruno David Ussher, Daily News.
LOS ANGELES SYMPHONY ENGAGEMENT, January 21st, 1941.

GLORIA GREENE
"A highly talented child." Boston Globe.
". . . . She has considerable technical equipment and signs of real individual talent." —Herald.
—BOSTON DEBUT RECITAL, January 18th, 1941.

"Played with beautiful tone and fleet technique, fine memory and a remarkable sense of construction." —Los Angeles Herald and Express, March 21st, 1941.

"Little Gloria proved to have a perfect technic, and the soul of a great artist."
—L'Avenir National, Manchester, N. H., January 20th, 1941.

THREE APPEARANCES AS SOLOIST WITH SYMPHONY ORCHESTRAS, SEASON 1940-1941.

ETHEL LEGINSKA'S
3rd Season (1941-42)
in Los Angeles where she is permanently located training a large group of Concert Pianists, Teachers, etc.
For Further Information Address
Secretary, 254 So. Hobart Blvd.
Los Angeles, Calif.
Tel. Fi. 0336

BEVERLY CARMEN
PRESS COMMENTS FOLLOWING LOS ANGELES DEBUT RECITAL OF 11-YEAR-OLD BEVERLY CARMEN—JANUARY 10th, 1941:

"Young Beverly has dynamic strength and strength of purpose. . . . Her tone is big and her playing has breadth." —L. A. Times.

"Played with surprising skill . . . and a lot of musicianship, receiving much applause for many good points of expression and future promise."
—L. A. Herald and Express.

Leginska, who knew the value of good advertising, always made sure that the advertisements for her own studio promoted her students as well, such as this one from 'Musical Courier' in 1941. When her students were due to give public concerts she ensured that first-rate promotional material was prepared on their behalf.

Another pupil, Beverly Carmen, started her studies under Leginska when very young, beginning shortly after Leginska's arrival in Los Angeles in 1939. She has many recollections of her teacher: [4]

"She based her teaching on the Leschetizky method, having studied with this master – according to her, she 'ran away from home and landed on Leschetizky's doorstep'. She encouraged (encouraged? – insisted upon) absolute imitation – she sat at one piano and the student at the other, and the student had to imitate every motion, every position, and every nuance (if possible). The trouble with this is that the students picked up too many of her mannerisms – natural with Leginska but too contrived in another. She always said, 'Thank God for Leschetizky!' But for me, I shall always say, 'Thank God for Leginska' – for with all her irregularities (discussed later), she made music a personal thing for me. She insisted that you 'make it interesting' and go into everything in minute, note-by-note, detail. She encouraged me to read (preferably, I think, literary works that would make me cry and bring out an emotional response). She was one of the last great Romantics. The other side of the coin turned out to be an overly-romantic approach to Bach, but this was quite common among musicians of her early era (early 1900s).

"She told me that Leschetizky had once (at a group lesson) gathered the other students around to see her hands, and said 'I have not seen a hand like this since [Anton] Rubinstein.'

"She also taught by a rather hypnotic influence over students. She had grey eyes that always seemed to be looking out into the future instead of at any close-range thing or person. But when she glared at you with those eyes you remained glared-at.

"She would do ANYTHING to put over her musical idea. One day we arrived at a lesson to find her limping. She had been attempting to illustrate a leap in the musical-line with a ballet-type leap across the floor. Only the floor was carpeted, and Leginska wore shoes with corrugated rubber-type soles; while Leginska leaped, the shoe gripped the carpet. And down went Leginska.

"You always knew 'where you were' with her. My lessons were two or three times a week, and often for two or more hours. She would have high-tea brought in, which she would share with my mother. If my lesson was good, I was invited too. If my lesson was ordinary, no invitation was forthcoming. A fine barometer. Also, she could send you out of the house at the end of your lesson with something akin to Anathema thundering down the walk-way. And then greet you next time with a completely clean slate, as if nothing had happened.

"She would never accept a child for training unless there was a mother, father, aunt, or butler to supervise the practice at home. 'I'm not going to give the same lesson a second time', she thundered. My mother came to every lesson with a note-pad to take down every comment and what page and line was referred to (chapter and verse)!

"However, her teacher-authority tried to enter other parts of her students' lives . . . which to her were not as important as their development of a pianistic career. She tried to break up one student's marriage. I was at the piano, and Leginska spoke to this young man on the phone, 'Why don't you send your little wife home to her parents while you rent a room and spend all your time practising'. I distinctly heard him say, 'Go to Hell', before he hung up.

"As for me, she tried to break up our family: lessons on holiday was one method. Another was to tell my mother to stop coming to the lessons with me. She would then spend part of the lesson talking against my father. Oh, yes . . . she hated the fathers. Also the non-playing siblings of her child-students. 'Ordinary school-brats' was her term for them. She did not much like children – except as budding pianists – and bought me a compact of powder, saying, 'if I ever see your shiny little face again I'll kick you out' . . . she couldn't even stand a child's well-scrubbed face. She really wanted me to finally leave home as <u>she</u> had, and devote myself to piano. She said of me to my mother, 'Beverly ought to have a tragic love-affair' (I was, after all, only 11 at this time – and this makes her sound like Miss Jean Brody). 'Oh, I don't mean a happy one where she'll get married and be all smug and self-satisfied; I mean a tragic one, where she'll finally turn to music and be through with love.' I couldn't wear a pair of socks if Leginska didn't approve them.

"However, through her teaching and her past associations, we got a glimpse of greatness. She simply may have been a bit too strong a potion for most children to take. I remember her trying to evoke emotional playing from a six-year-old: 'Play with passion, Elaine, with passion.' So the six-year-old breathed hard and snorted and attacked the keys . . . when she left Leginska she would never touch the piano again. I, of course, already had a musical and technical background, and even knew (or thought I knew) what she meant by the great, tragic, love affair, having been madly in love secretly with a young violinist four years my senior. So I probably withstood Leginska as well as anyone could, even to the point of walking out on her when that seemed indicated. Neither she nor I would give an inch. She had wanted me to learn a Brahms concerto and finance my part of the concert by giving a studio recital. But since she said nobody would come to hear me play my old pieces, I would have to learn a new program in six weeks. My mother [having been told this by Leginska on the phone, at home] was horrified. 'Harold Bauer wouldn't do it; you wouldn't do it'. Leginska replied, 'No, we wouldn't do it, but Beverly can get away with it!' And then, 'I have no more time for this; send her over at two' . . . and hung up the phone.

"I was sitting at the piano, and said, 'I'm not going. After this conversation she'll only scream at me about you and Daddy.' And I stayed home; and she did not call. And that was the end. To be taught was one thing; to be exploited was another. She had a <u>bit</u> of the Charlatan in her; she was not above telling people that I had never studied before I came to her, thus consigning my background and previous training (that had impressed her in the first place) to oblivion.

"She had an arrogance about her and a way of getting her own way. (Of course, she was born under the "pianists' sign" – Aries – and with me she had a Taurus to deal with in the end.)

"When preparing us for public performance, we were trained within an inch of our lives. Then, as the recital approached, she would use psychology to calm us down: 'Think of the rows of people as rows of cabbage heads – no-one can be afraid of cabbage heads'. She got very angry with me one day when I said, 'But one of the cabbage heads is reviewing for the 'Times' '. . . thus ruining her speech for several other children present.

"But she had success in sending us out on stage 'on a high'. She would whisper, 'Rubinstein doesn't know the right tempo, Horowitz doesn't know the right phrasing, but

YOU know!' Another time she hissed at me, 'Forget everything I ever taught you and go out there and knock 'em dead!!' The great football coaches could have learned from her, on the art of the pep-talk."

Another of Leginska's students of the early 1940s, Esther Lee Kaplan, who described her teacher as "unique and dynamic", sent the authors a post card which Leginska had arranged to be made to help publicise her young student's career: [5]

"Miss Kaplan enjoyed the Saint-Saens G Minor Concerto to the full. She has **outstanding finger technique** and surprising appreciation of the style of this work, sailing through the difficult passages with much fun and no worry."
L. A. Times, June 29, 1943

"The finger facility of little Esther Lee Kaplan had full reign in the scintillant Saint-Saens G minor Concerto. She played with the joy that professionals try so hard to keep."
Shibley Boyes, B'nai B'rith Messenger, July 2, 1943

"She played with considerable brilliance, displaying **an unusual depth of tone** for one of her years, and commendable command of the keyboard."
Richard D. Saunders, Hollywood Citizen-News, June 28, 1943

"Esther Lee Kaplan threw abandon into the Saint Saens Piano Concerto in G-minor, showed much appreciation for required touch and felt the orchestra with a **mature charm**."
Carl Bronson, L. A. Herald, June 28, 1943

"Esther Lee Kaplan played the Saint-Saens G-minor Concerto with very considerable forcefulness of tone and technique." *R. Vernon Steele, Pacific Coast Musician, July 3, 1943*

"puis entendimes Esther Lee Kaplan dans le Concerto in G-Minor de Saint-Saens ou elle se revela parfaitement a l'aise tant au point de vue technique que de l'amplitude du traitement des themes." *Andree Hodel, L'union Nouvelle, 3 Juillet 1943*

ESTHER LEE KAPLAN
Child Pianist
Has highly successful Los Angeles debut with Leginska Little Symphony at Wilshire-Ebell Theatre, June 27, 1943.

Publicity post card, produced under Leginska's supervision in 1943, to promote her young pupil Esther Lee Kaplan. Miss Kaplan has enjoyed a successful career, which still continues, as a teacher and concert pianist.

The recollections of Ethel Leginska's former students give us a graphic insight not only into her teaching system, but also her character and personality – demanding, volatile, impulsive, dynamic – but completely dedicated to music, and never dull. In formal terms she clearly followed Leschetizky's method of teaching and was his ardent disciple. His lessons were based on teaching by example; 'this is how it should be played', with little emphasis on theory. Leschetizky tailored his instruction to the individual needs of each student, taking into account their physique; so did Leginska. Leschetizky also knew that he was teaching only very gifted pianists who would go on to earn their living by public performances; his tuition was therefore appropriate to such students. Nerves were banished and the performance must 'go on' in spite of any stumblings or memory lapses. Leginska's philosophy and teaching was exactly the same.

When Benno Moiseiwitsch was auditioned as a teenage pianist by Leschetizky he was at first rebuffed. After hearing Benno play, the old man remarked, brusquely, "I can play this better with my left foot. There are a hundred delicate nuances in the piece which you've sacrificed for effect. I don't want bravura or exhibitionism. Go and practise for a couple of months until you've mastered real control. Then you can come back and we'll see what progress you've made." Moiseiwitsch did as the Master bade, and when he returned, Leschetizky's assessment was more favourable. "Now you are no longer a 'gifted amateur', young man. You're beginning to hear yourself seriously." Moiseiwitsch later said of Leschetizky, "He taught me, above all, I think, never to stop studying". [6]

This sort of remark tossed out by Leschetizky was mirrored half a century later by Ethel Leginska, as was his insistence on 'control'. The statement made by Leginska to Joseph Enos and other pupils ("You've learned to play, but didn't learn to study") [7] could have been made by Leschetizky himself. In all major respects she followed the precepts of her own teacher. She could hardly be faulted for doing so, since he was indisputably one of the greatest piano pedagogues of all time. His methods suited Leginska's personality and she possessed the exceptional standard of technique necessary to put his teaching system successfully into practice.

It is clear that as a teacher Leginska was very demanding; music always had to come first, over and above her pupils' private lives or any other considerations. But she demanded nothing which she had not willingly given herself as a girl and young woman. To her, music had always been all-important and she had made it her business to leave home and friends to venture to Europe in order to benefit from the best teaching available. She probably felt that her pupils in Los Angeles 'had it easy', and she was therefore never loth to insist on the priority of music in the life of a would-be top-class artist.

Notwithstanding Ethel Leginska's outstanding gifts as a pianist, and her ability to teach by example, it was her dynamic personality that made her into a great teacher. Inevitably the weaker students fell by the wayside (and they were only 'weaker' judged by the very highest standards, for a pianist had to be very talented to be accepted as a pupil by Leginska in the first place). But the best of her students, spurred on by the love-hate relationship with their remarkable teacher, prospered under her demanding regime and stayed under her tutelage for many years. Except, that is, in cases such as Beverly Carmen (a fine child pianist who had done very well under Leginska's expert teaching), where a clash of two sparky personalities finally brought the teacher-pupil relationship to an end. And for all their differences, even Beverly recognised her debt to her tempestuous teacher, retaining a huge respect for her and remembering her with affection, as her remark "Thank God for Leginska!" indicates.

Leginska's vocation was primarily concerned with piano teaching but she sometimes taught other skills. Robert Logan, for example, wrote: [8]

"I spent some time in 1940 studying orchestration with Leginska. She had a vibrant, positive personality and demanded, and obtained, excellence and dedication from her pupils.

"Her attitude towards her students was quite vigorous, almost domineering, but in a kind manner – this was because she knew exactly what she wanted to hear from each pupil. She would demand explicit attention to phrasing, dynamics, and every detail which would meet the intentions of the composer. It was a privilege and a pleasure to have known this dynamic woman."

These are just a few memories of Leginska as recalled by some of her former students; more will be given in Chapter 17. As a teacher of highly talented students Leginska, in her unique way, was very successful, and would remain so for the rest of her days. A large number of students were to pass through her hands in Los Angeles over a thirty-year period, many of whom achieved great success in their musical profession. All her students respected her because of her undisputed technical mastery of the piano. Some feared her, some enjoyed a love-hate relationship with their inspirational teacher, and some, including Marguerite Heller [9] who will be quoted in later chapters, felt nothing but affection and admiration. One thing is certain – all of Leginska's students would remember their lessons with her for the rest of their lives.

References: Chapter 15

1. Information about the house and teaching studio was communicated by Mr Joseph Enos of Benicia, California, a former pupil of Leginska. (Personal correspondence.)
2. Professor Marilyn Neeley, Catholic University of America, formerly of the University of Maryland, Baltimore County. (Personal correspondence.)
3. As reference 1.
4. Beverly Carmen, now of Los Alamos, New Mexico; formerly of Los Angeles. (Personal correspondence.)
5. Esther Lee Kaplan, New York. (Personal correspondence.)
6. Maurice Moiseiwitsch: *Benno Moiseiwitsch*. Frederick Muller Ltd., London, 1965.
7. Joseph Enos. (Personal correspondence (see reference 1).)
8. The late Mr Robert Logan of Sun Valley, California. (Personal correspondence.)
9. Marguerite Heller of Los Angeles, California. (Personal correspondence from 1984 to the present.)

Chapter 16

Years of Fulfilment

By 1943 Leginska's full-time teaching career had met with such success that she embarked on a new project. Jointly with her concert manager, Mary-V Holloway, she founded *The New Venture in Music* series.[1] The purpose of this movement was to introduce talented young pupils to the public through the works of the great composers. During each season a different composer was featured (sometimes more than one) and many of Leginska's pupils gave performances. When piano concertos were scheduled, Leginska hired top-quality players from professional orchestras such as the Los Angeles Philharmonic to form her own orchestra, the 'Leginska Little Symphony', which she conducted herself.[2]

Year by year the series prospered and became an established part of musical life in Los Angeles. Leginska was always alert to the value of publicity and ensured that the *New Venture* series was well advertised. Use was made of any letters of praise that had been received from eminent personalities in the world of music. For example, the venture received letters of support, according to Leginska's brochures, from such important musical luminaries as Albert Coates, Walter Damrosch, Otto Klemperer, Serge Koussevitzky, Darius Milhaud, Pierre Monteux, Fritz Reiner, Artur Rubinstein and Bruno Walter.[3] Leginska was of course well known to all of these from her performing days. She had appeared as a pianist under the baton of most of those in the above list who were conductors.

Leginska's system was an extension of the methods she had used for many years. As early as 1920, and probably earlier, she had arranged for her students to appear before the public in effectively-promoted recitals with critics from the national and local press in attendance.

A list of the composers featured in the first few series of *New Venture in Music* and an indication of the number of pianists taking part is shown in the extract on the opposite page from a brochure of the series, dated 1954. It illustrates the depth of musical content represented by the concerts and recitals. It is quite clear that the demanding nature of the programmes and the intense study required to master them must have prepared Leginska's students well for their impending arduous careers. By featuring all the piano works of a given composer, Leginska instilled a thorough knowledge of their music into the minds of her pupils.

NEW VENTURE IN MUSIC, founded in 1943, by Mme. Ethel Leginska and Mary-V Holloway, concert manager, has brought many stimulating letters of praise and approval for the cultural and educational series from world celebrities in Music, including Bruno Walter, Serge Koussevitsky, Pierre Monteux, Walter Damrosch, Albert Coates, Fritz Reiner, Otto Klemperer, Artur Rubinstein, Alexandre Tansman, John Alden Carpenter, Darius Milhaud.

This series, far reaching in scope, has pioneered in historic recital presentations. It offers a comprehensive study and knowledge of the works of individual composers.

FIRST SERIES, 1943-44: Twenty Pianists, each playing one or more of the 24 Preludes and Fugues from the Well Tempered Clavichord, Vol. 1, by Bach.

SECOND SERIES, 1945-46: Thirty-seven pianists in 10 concerts; 24 Preludes and Fugues from Well Tempered Clavichord, Vol. II, by Bach, and the 32 Sonatas and 21 sets of Variations by Beethoven.

THIRD SERIES, 1946-47: Six recitals devoted to the entire piano works of Chopin.

FOURTH SERIES, 1947-48: Seven recitals devoted to the entire piano works of Robert Schumann.

FIFTH SERIES, 1949: Continuing entire piano works of Schubert and Liszt, in 18 recitals — seven have been given.

SIXTH SERIES, 1952: 18 Suites, Bach; 18 Sonatas, Mozart and the entire piano solo works of Debussy and MacDowell — four recitals have been given.

In 1941 orchestral concerts were inaugurated at the Wilshire-Ebell Theatre by Mme. Leginska and Mary-V Holloway.

In nineteen orchestral concerts, forty-six different concertos have been heard; at least thirteen of these had their first Los Angeles performance.

Twenty public piano recitals have been given — not counting those of the "New Venture in Music." Fifty-eight pianists have made their successful Los Angeles debut at these concerts. Each month there is a studio recital.

This is Mme. Leginska's sixteenth year in Los Angeles, where she is permanently located, training a large group of talented concert pianists, teachers and students of all ages

For further information telephone DUnkirk 4-0336, or write 254 South Hobart Blvd., Los Angeles 4, California

Part of a 1954 brochure of 'The New Venture in Music' series which reviews what had been achieved in the previous few years

Apart from the *New Venture in Music* series, many other public recitals were given by Leginska's students. Again mindful of the value of publicity, Leginska was careful to ensure that all of the concerts or recitals had printed programmes of high quality, usually supported by a photograph of the artist and a string of acclamatory press cuttings resulting from previous performances. Leginska's pupils always received meticulous attention to detail from their teacher when placed before the public in a recital or concert. Leginska's approach in presenting her pupils to best advantage was very professional – the same as if she were appearing on the stage herself.

Leginska taught students of any age: adult, teen-age or children. Amongst the very young ones was Elaine Wightman, six, who featured in the notice on page 235. She had already given "a surprisingly good" performance of "the A major Concerto of Mozart" (which must have been No. 12, K. 414 or No. 23, K. 488) in a public performance so well received that she had responded to the acclaim by playing two encores. One cannot help but wonder whether Leginska, when she taught children such as Elaine, cast her mind back to her own very early years when she had been given the opportunity to display her own prodigious talent at public recitals in Hull, and in front of distinguished visitors at Tranby Croft, including the Prince of Wales – the future Edward VII. She would have been well aware that the sooner talented young children got used to playing quite advanced music before an audience the better. The one thing that all Leginska's students, young or adult, had in common was ability, otherwise she would not have taken them on.

When her 'child stars' were appearing in concerts or recitals, Leginska usually arranged for several of them to share the same programme. The notices shown on pages 245 and 246, for example, are for a concert given on 22nd January 1944, with, as usual, professional orchestral players hired for the occasion and Leginska conducting. The choice of music shows that the four children taking part, whose ages ranged from eight to 12, were clearly able to play very demanding piano compositions. One of these children, Daniel Pollack, will figure again later in this chapter and in the next.

The pattern of Leginska's full-time teaching career which began in 1939 was to continue for most of the remainder of her life. She no longer sought publicity for herself now that she had ceased to be a performing artist, but published glowing reports regarding her former achievements on some of the advertising leaflets devoted to her pupils, knowing that her glories would reflect on them.

Years of Fulfilment

LEGINSKA...
"Paderewski of the women pianists..."
— *N. Y. Herald-Tribune*

Since 1941 has presented an annual series of orchestral concerts in Los Angeles. Twenty-three young pianists have made highly successful debuts. Four of them are making their first New York appearance at this concert.

Program

CONCERTO, OP. 15, C MAJOR................**BEETHOVEN**
   Allegro con brio
     Largo
       Rondo - Allegro scherzando
        Suzanne Gayner

CONCERTSTUCK, OP. 79, F MINOR................**WEBER**
   Larghetto, ma non troppo - Allegro passionato
     Assai presto
       Viana Bey

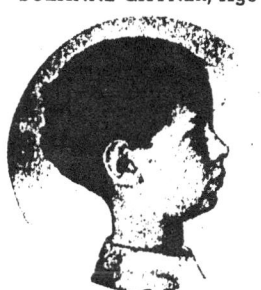
SUZANNE GAYNER, Age 9

VIANA BEY, Age 10

Intermission

CONCERTO, OP. 11, E MINOR................**CHOPIN**
   Daniel Pollack

CONCERTO, OP. 23, D MINOR................**MacDOWELL**
   Larghetto calmato
     Presto giocoso
       Largo - Molto Allegro - Presto
        Sybil Steinberg

DANIEL POLLACK, Age 8

SYBIL STEINBERG, Age 12

Steinway Piano

Management: JOSEPHINE VILA, Inc., 119 W. 57th St., N. Y. C.
Josephine Vila   William A. Taylor

This page and overleaf:
Programme of a concert given by some of Leginska's child students in January 1944

ORCHESTRAL CONCERT

LEGINSKA conducting

Sat. Aft.
JAN. 22
3:00

with following soloists:

SUZANNE GAYNER, Age 9

"Received an ovation for actual musicianship."
—*Los Angeles Herald*

VIANA BEY, Age 10

"Definitely a wonder child."
—*Los Angeles Times*

DANIEL POLLACK, Age 8

"Possesses indubitably the vital spark of artistry."
—*Hollywood Citizen-News*

SYBIL STEINBERG, Age 12

"Delivered the McDowell Second Concerto with vigor and ability of a mature performer."
—*Hollywood Citizen-News*

Years of Fulfilment

Leginska often arranged for her older students to have an entire recital to themselves, for which she would have an attractive programme printed, enhanced by press reviews of the pianist's previous successes. One of Leginska's best pupils in the 1940s was Marguerite Baum. The front cover of one of her recital programmes is reproduced below, and the inside pages (reduced in scale) are shown on pages 248 and 249. This programme is typical of the many prepared by Leginska for her students.

Front cover of one of Marguerite Baum's recital programmes, 1945

What the Critics Say:

Los Angeles Orchestral Debut Leginska Little Symphony

1942

"... Her, playing is brilliant and emphatic. She is gifted and has personality."
—*Isabel Morse Jones, Los Angeles Times, June 8, 1942*

"One of the interesting personalities of the afternoon was Marguerite Baum, who gave a dashing and fluent reading of Henselt's Concerto in its first performance in Los Angeles. Individuality marked the pianist's handling of every movement . . . The effect was of musicianly understanding and sheer delight in the performance."
—*Howard Becker, Los Angeles Examiner, June 13, 1942*

"The young pianist played with resolution, the vehicle serving to display her technical virtuosity and lovely tone, which should lead her to a concert career."
—*Richard D. Saunders, Hollywood Citizen-News, June 8, 1942*

"There were beautiful passages in the old Henselt Concerto in F Minor and Marguerite Baum expressed them with feelingful command of the keyboard."
—*Carl Bronson, Los Angeles Herald-Express, June 8, 1942*

1943

SECOND APPEARANCE WITH LEGINSKA LITTLE SYMPHONY

"Most dynamic . . . displayed excellent technique and fine temperament. Her individuality should make her progress rapid."
—*Shibley Boyes, B'nai B'rith Messenger, July 2, 1943*

"The Grieg Concerto was given exceptional emphasis by Marguerite Baum, who is climbing rapidly, and gave a fine professional atmosphere to her aplomb performance."
—*Carl Bronson, Los Angeles Herald-Express, June 21, 1943*

"Played with great vigor and considerable brilliance."
—*Richard Drake Saunders, Hollywood Citizen-News, June 21, 1943*

" . . . a highly emotional performance of the Grieg A Minor Concerto . . . This young lady possesses a big talent and authoritative musicality . . . A pianist of uncommon attractiveness."
—*R. Vernon Steele, Pacific Coast Musician, June 22, 1943*

"She has a sense of design and sees the work as a whole picture."
—*Isabel Morse Jones, Los Angeles Times, June 22, 1943*

1944

Winning contestant as soloist in Beethoven G-Major Concerto with Glendale Symphony.

1945

"NEW VENTURE IN MUSIC"

"Marguerite Baum . . . impressive artistry."
—*Carl Bronson, Los Angeles Herald-Express, June 4, 1945*

PROGRAM

Two Preludes and Fugues ....Bach
   F Minor, Vol. I
   C Sharp Minor, Vol. II
   (Well-tempered Clavichord)

Sonata, A Flat Major, Opus 110 ....Beethoven
   Moderato cantabile molto espressivo
   Allegro molto
   Adagio ma non troppo
   Fuga: Allegro ma non troppo

Sonata, F Minor, Opus 5 ....Brahms
   Allegro maestoso
   Andante espressivo
   Scherzo: Allegro energico
   Intermezzo: Andante molto
   Allegro moderato ma rubato

INTERMISSION

Scherzo Grotesque ....Lionel Barrymore
(First Public Performance)

Trois Dames Fantastiques ....Shostakovitch

Scherzo after Tagore, "O Mad, Superbly Drunk" ....Leginska

At Dawn ....Leginska

Islamey (Oriental Fantasy) ....Balakireff

---

This page and opposite:
Inside pages of the programme for a recital by Leginska student Marguerite Baum, 1945

Los Angeles Recital Debut
October 19, 1945

☆ ☆ ☆

Marguerite Baum Shows Emotional Spark at Piano Recital

"That Marguerite Baum's piano performance last night at Wilshire-Ebell Theater had at least three virtues is undeniable. There was **great spirit, broad tone,** and a **spark of mature emotion** that a few more years of intensive study will build into a **blaze.** ... a lot of **romantic appeal.**

Miss Baum's interpretation of the Beethoven Sonata in A-flat, Op. 110, and Brahms' Sonata in F minor, Op. 5, was.... tempered by much attention to the sense of climax in the music, to getting somewhere, which is especially necessary in playing Beethoven.

The last half of the program was the well-known dessert, after such a heavy meal. Lionel Barrymore's facile Scherzo Grotesque had its first public performance, while Shostakovitch, Leginska and Balakireff were represented by Three Fantastic Dances, the Scherzo after Tagore, "O Mad, Superbly Drunk," and At Dawn and Islamey (Oriental Fantasy). ... a Chopin encore, which exploited the pianist's singing tone ..."

—G. A., *Hollywood Citizen-News,* October 20, 1945

☆ ☆ ☆

Young Pianist Wins Praise

"Brahms' long Sonata in F-Minor, Opus 5 proved no tax to the resources of the **brilliant young pianist, Marguerite Baum,** who on Friday night was presented in concert at Wilshire-Ebell Theater by Mary-V Holloway.

In the five movements of the Brahms work, Miss Baum gave ample evidence of **remarkable technique** and of an **extraordinary control of her left hand.** This musicianly tour de force was preceded by Two Preludes and Fugues by Bach and by Beethoven's Sonata in A-flat, Opus 110, in which the legato called for in the adagio showed another phase of the pianist's exceptional attainments.

The latter part of the program was in lighter vein, with a charming Scherzo Grotesque by Lionel Barrymore having its first public performance. Delicate and yet vivid, the work consists almost entirely of staccato passages. Three Fantastic Dances by Shostakovitch, two numbers by Ethel Leginska and "Islamey," an Oriental fantasy, concluded the program."

—*Los Angeles Examiner,* October 22, 1945

Baum Recital

"Marguerite Baum, pianist ... was heard in recital at the Ebell Theatre last Friday. Numerous facets of her playing that had to do with the sheer business of playing the instrument deserve praise. She disclosed **facile technic** in passages and octaves, **various touch applications, fine tonal quality,** and **discreet pedal technic.** In Beethoven's Sonata Op. 110, the Scherzo and Adagio movements were impressive ...

In the Brahms' Sonata Op. 5, the second movement and the Retrospect appealed ...

More **freedom, verve and brilliance** was noticeable in the second half of this program. It began with a Scherzo Grotesque by Lionel Barrymore which ... was effective enough. Shorter pieces by Shostakovitch and Leginska were played easily and effectively ...

All in all a **creditable effort.**"

—*Alfred Price Quinn, B'nai B'rith Messenger,* October 26, 1945

☆ ☆

Girl Gives Recital

"... **Fine and well-trained technique** ....
Power of emotional evocation.
Delicately beautiful touch and romantic responsiveness ...
Three Fantastic Dances by Shostakovitch were played with fine facility and humor ..."

—C. S. H., *Los Angeles Times,* October 20, 1945

☆ ☆

"The piano recital of Marguerite Baum, at the Wilshire-Ebell Theater last night, under the Mary-V Holloway direction, drew a representative audience that applauded every number of the **brilliant pianist's performance. Charm of personality and a brilliant grasp** of Bach, Beethoven, and Brahms added a new lustre to old familiars, emphasizing the new angle of refreshing musicianship of this young artiste."

—Carl Bronson, *Los Angeles Herald-Express,* October 20, 1945

NOW BOOKING for SEASON 1945-1946

MARY-V HOLLOWAY
Concert Manager

431 West Seventh Street   Los Angeles 14, California
VAndike 2441

Backstage at the Wilshire Ebell Theatre, Los Angeles, mid 1940s. Ethel Leginska (seated, left), student Marguerite Baum (centre) and Mary-V Holloway, concert manager (standing).
(Photograph taken by Marguerite Baum's husband, Alex Heller; reproduced with Mrs Baum Heller's permission)

When Leginska first established herself as a teacher in Los Angeles she was still well known as a pianist, composer and conductor, but the traumatic years of the war soon put all that out of people's minds. The general public, and even the musical public, soon forgets musical performing artists once they are no longer appearing on stage. In the immediate post-war years she

Leginska, mid 1940s, when she was about 60 (Another photograph by Alex Heller)

was almost forgotten (except by her students) in America, let alone in Great Britain where she had not been a regular performer since the early 1930s. By the end of the 1940s the citizens of Los Angeles were mostly unaware that the once-famous pianist and conductor was living amongst them, and readers of newspapers had to be gently reminded of her presence. Such a reminder appeared in *The South Coast News* (a Californian paper) in 1949: [4]

Mme Ethel Leginska Enjoys Laguna Life

"Living quite unobtrusively in our midst is one of those rare geniuses who have contributed prodigiously to the culture of the world. She is Mme Ethel Leginska, piano virtuoso, orchestral conductor, composer, and piano pedagogue.

"Mme Leginska was a "prodigy child". Her career as a pianist began at the age of six. Eight years later, she became a pupil of the master teacher, Leschetizky. Under the baton of Sir Henry Wood in London, the celebrated artist made her official debut as orchestral soloist at sixteen [*], after which she performed in major cities in Europe, England, the United States and Canada.

"Perhaps the successes that Mme Leginska has attained may be epitomised by the usually conservative German critics. 'She is a master, this splendid genius. She played the Liszt Sonata, that mighty seat of tones, that unique piano symphony. Mind and heart, strength and fire, an absolutely demonical temperament, with immense pianistic skill. All united to make this re-creation of the work a moving artistic experience of unforgettable value.' "

After recalling various other major milestones in Leginska's long and brilliant career, *The South Coast News* brought its readers up to date with what the musician was now doing, and enumerated some of the successes of her pupils:

"Mme Leginska, with manager Mary - V Holloway, has founded 'New Venture in Music'. This movement is designed to introduce talented young pupils through the works of the great composers. This season the complete piano works of Schubert and Liszt will be presented. During the period beginning in 1943, 34 pianists made their successful debuts in Los Angeles as soloists with orchestra.

"In the past six years, Mme Leginska, with the assistance of Lucille Oliver (herself twice soloist with the New York Philharmonic, piano recitals in New York and London) has added to the concert stage more than 50 talented pianists from the Leginska studio at 254 South Hobart [Boulevard] in Los Angeles. On Oct. 2, at 2 p.m., Mme Leginska will conduct an orchestral concert in which five of her pupils will be soloists at the Wilshire Ebell Theater. The program will feature Eugene Hoffman in a Mozart concerto in C major; Richard Ellis playing Beethoven's concerto in B flat; Barbara Dell Culver in a concerto by the American composer Piston; Adrienne Allert in Rachmaninoff's fourth piano concerto; and Charmian Joy in the A major concerto of Liszt. The first four concertos have not yet been publicly performed in Los Angeles.

"Pupils of Mme Leginska have been the recipients of awards sponsored by Occidental College, U.C.L.A., radio station K.F.L. and the Los Angeles and Hollywood Bowl Symphony Orchestras."

This newspaper article reported that Ethel Leginska had been spending many of her weekends and vacations since 1943 in Laguna Beach, a resort a few miles south of Los Angeles (see page 260). She had purchased a cottage at 686, Coast Boulevard North and spent her leisure hours "beautifying the lovely garden that surrounded her cottage".

---

* This is incorrect. She was 20 when she first appeared with Henry Wood.

As the 1940s ended and the 1950s began Ethel Leginska was 63 years old, but as energetic and vigorous as ever. Her work continued with unabated zeal and occasionally she found time to compose.

On 16th March 1955 Leginska's stepmother, Christina Bella Liggins, died at the age of 79 at the Haybourn Nursing Home in Bridlington. It will be recalled from Chapter 6 that she and her husband, Tom, had lived at 45, Richmond Street, Bridlington from 1913. Tom, Ethel's father, had died in 1928 but Christina lived on in the family home until her death. The cause of death was given on the death certificate as coronary thrombosis, exacerbated by cardio-vascular degeneration. [5] Christina, as well as being Ethel's stepmother, was a distant blood relation (Christina and Ethel's father were cousins; see Chapter 6, page 83 and the family tree on pages 316-317).

At the time of Christina's death Ethel, who was only 11 years younger than her stepmother, was herself 68 years old. Christina was the only one of Ethel's close relatives to have lived long enough to have been able to follow her performing career from beginning to end. A table has been prepared (see Appendix 1(c) on page 319) which gives the dates of birth and death of Ethel's four grandparents, her parents and her stepmother, and it also indicates the stage Ethel had reached in her career when each of them died. When her mother died Ethel's career had not even started (though, as a student in Frankfurt, she was recognised as a noted child prodigy) but her father, and even one of her paternal grandparents (Hannah) had lived long enough to see her recognised as a top-class pianist who had already given very successful solo recitals in Carnegie Hall. With the death of Christina, Ethel's close family connections with the East Riding of Yorkshire ended.

However, word of her continuing achievements sometimes filtered back to her home city of Hull through a friend with whom she still corresponded. In 1957 the *Hull Daily Mail* reported: [6]

"Madame Leginska is still composing, and, at a private recital in July, she introduced a new group of Lieder songs [sic]. A critic of the recital said, 'The accompaniments, which were enormously difficult, were played as only a pianist and musician of Leginska's calibre could interpret them.' "

Although Leginska was now approaching seventy years of age, the possibility of retirement, or even cutting down her teaching load, seems never to have entered her mind.

Leginska's pupils continued to do well in their public performances, always supported by the full might of Leginska's genius in presenting them to best advantage. Her publicity material ranged from postcard-type notices in support of individual pupils (for instance, the one shown on page 238 promoting Esther Lee Kaplan) to programmes on art paper, as reproduced on pages 245 to 249, which displayed many press reports of the favourable impression made by Leginska's pupils in previous public performances. Between them, these talented pianists had excelled in the performance of piano concertos by such diverse composers as Arensky, Beethoven, Chopin, Khachaturian, Liszt, MacDowell, Mendelssohn, Mozart, Piston, Prokoviev, Rachmaninov, Saint-Saëns and Schumann, as well as many others. Amongst the glittering array of young pianists was Daniel Pollack, eight (see pages 245 and 246) who played the Chopin E minor Concerto at a concert in New York Town Hall under Leginska's supervision at the age of just nine. A former judge at the Leeds International Pianoforte Competition, he has been for many years, and still is at the time of writing, a distinguished international pianist. He is one of the many former students of Leginska who have been kind enough to recall memories of their teacher in letters to the authors.

In 1957 Leginska achieved what had been denied her in the early 1930s: the production on stage of her opera *The Rose and the Ring*. The opera, it will be recalled from Chapter 14, was written in the years 1930 to 1932. Based on the satirical fairy story by William Makepeace Thackeray, it received its world premiere at the Wilshire Ebell Theatre in Los Angeles on 23rd February 1957 with Leginska herself conducting. The presentation appears to have been a success, judging by the press cuttings. Here is part of a review by Herbert Donaldson for the *Los Angeles Examiner*:[7]

Rose, Ring Premiere Glitters

"Last Saturday night at the Wilshire Ebell Theater there was cause for thanksgiving. Ethel Leginska's opera "The Rose and the Ring", based upon the satirical fairy story by William Makepeace Thackeray was given its world premiere.

"There was a 24-member, gold-plated orchestra, with such gifted persons as Elliott Fisher, Morris Brenner, Ennio Bolognini, Arthur Pabst, Haakon Bergh, Arthur Gault, Dominick Fera, Jack Marsh, Wendell Hoss, Lester and Dorothy Remsen occupying principal chairs; a chorus of 24, a corps de ballet of 21, not to mention the large number of principal singers who made up the cast. Mme Leginska herself conducted with skill and authority.

Success

"It was a success. Henry Reese, the stage director, deserved plaudits for the fact that the opera moved quickly from scene to scene without the delays that often accompany first night performances. Mme Leginska had written singularly appropriate intermezzi to connect scenes, eliminating any possibility of dead spots.

"The score is thoroughly tonal: the composer knows the vocabulary of the orchestra.

"Nor was her orchestration given over to mere ingenious sound effects – though there were many in logical places. For example, there were the wonderful "hiccupping sounds" in the orchestra, devised for the usurping king as he takes to the bottle at breakfast in Scene 2 of Act 1; the wholly fitting, grotesque sounds that invaded the forest scene in Act 2, and that which accompanied the "exchange of crowns" in Act 3.

Sonorous

"Her scoring is economically devised. It is sonorous, without being obtrusively so.

"There are many lovely solos. Amongst those which come to mind are Betsinda's in Scene 2 of Act 2, and the one for Prince Giglio in Scene 1 of Act 2. These were beautifully done by soprano Kristina Kohler and by Steve Stagner, a lyric tenor of great promise.

"Owen Gruber, as Valoroso XXIV, usurping King of Paflagonia, brought real comedy into the theater with his fine portrayal. He has a talent worthy of consideration by a major opera company.

"There were other great moments of comedy in the opera. The monkey and lion bit in the third Act, and the blackface number of the corps de ballet in Act 1, would intrigue the most opera-shy person."

For the *Evening Tribune* Bruno Ussher reported: [8]

Leginska Satire Scores in Debut – Composer-Conductor Applauded
Performance has Humor, Charm

"Ethel Leginska's flair for startling happily a musical public is still hers. The world premiere of her seriously-undertaken opera-parody "The Rose and the Ring" was cordially received by a near-capacity audience Saturday at the Los Angeles Wilshire Ebell Theater.

"Mme Leginska could acknowledge numerous bravos not only as a composer but as her own conductor.

"I enjoyed her frankly humorous and easily atmospheric music for "The Rose and the Ring." In fact she does sustain very well the rather involved plot of the satiric tale for adults as well as young children by William Makepeace Thackeray.

"It is melodious music, simple of harmony and rhythm, adding life to the plot. She has invented charming tunes. Characters and magical effects of the "Rose and the Ring" are well designated by special themes, which of course vary slightly as situations differ. But they give the musical setting coherence and meaning as well as humor."

Alma Gowdy, writing for the *Los Angeles Herald and Express* under the heading 'Leginska's Opera Buffa Given World Premiere Here' observed: [9]

"Thackeray's lofty spoofing of monarchy was the basis for the libretto of Ethel Leginska's opera buffa, "The Rose and the Ring", given its world premiere Saturday night at Wilshire Ebell Theater. The witty satire of Thackeray was transferred brilliantly into the vocal line, orchestration, chorus and ballet by Yorkshire-born Mme Leginska who acted as conductor, composer and sponsor. E.E. Ohlson adapted the libretto.

"Magic inherent in a rose and a ring had the power to make beautiful the possessors. Masks were used to indicate sudden changes in the looks of characters. British understatements made for dry humor in episodes where Valoroso, a usurping king, demanded to know what he was to have for breakfast during an off stage hanging scene. The squat figure of the Queen of Paflagonia on flat heels poked fun at Queen Victoria.

Music Witty

"The spirit of the Thackeray masterpiece was caught by the composer in unusual uses of woodwinds (a wonderful solo for the piccolo), harp and bassoon. Themes for characters and action were skilfully woven into the orchestration and vocal line à la Wagner's leit motif. A mixed cast of professionals and ardent amateurs along with skilled instrumentalists learned their roles and performed from manuscript. The opera was a small masterpiece, and with some editing, could go into the permanent repertoire for the amusement of 'great and small children.' "

The success of the opera must have been very gratifying to Leginska. When she wrote it in the early 1930s she was only 45 years old. Now 70, she had waited a long time for its production.

Meanwhile, year by year, Leginska's students continued to display their considerable talents in the concerts and recitals she arranged for them. Three typical programmes dating from 1957 are shown on pages 257 to 259. They indicate the varied and difficult works performed by the students and also show that Leginska prepared her students in all kinds of music from Bach, through all the classical composers and impressionists, to Copland. Occasionally Leginska appeared on stage in programmes presented by Los Angeles educational bodies, as for example in October 1957 when she took part in the 'Musicale' series organised by the Los Angeles City College Music Departments (programme on page 259). She appeared there as guest composer and accompanist to Steve Stagner, tenor, in four of her songs (*Oh Lovely Moon, Desire, In a Garden, I Have a Rendezvous with Death*) as the programme shows. In her years in Los Angeles she seems only to have appeared on stage as a conductor, or accompanist, or in support of her pupils at the second piano in compositions for, or arranged for, two pianos. She never appeared in public as a solo pianist in her own right.

Throughout Leginska's years in Los Angeles she was predominantly a piano teacher, but she never lost her interest in composing and conducting. In 1959 a set of three of her compositions was published: *Three Victorian Portraits* recalled some of the bygone days of her youth in Yorkshire. It received its first public performance in New York Town Hall on 10th November 1959. The pianist was Joanna Hodges, one of Ethel's students, who evidently performed the composition very well, for according to one critic "her playing had a high degree of musicality and intelligence." The first piece was entitled *Nostalgic Waltz*, the second *Dirge*, and the third *Heroic Impromptu*. They were dedicated to the Wilson family in Hull, and the second of these impressionist pieces represented the funeral procession of Arthur Stanley Wilson. As recounted in Chapter 2 (page 15) the coffin was carried on a horse-drawn cart and the music was intended to suggest the rumbling of the cart being driven over uneven muddy, rutted ground.

Years of Fulfilment

Madam Leginska

Presents

Nineteen Pianists

IN THREE RECITALS

(120th, 121st, 122nd)

AT HER STUDIO

254 South Hobart Boulevard

Los Angeles 4, California

Sunday, 2 p.m., June 30, 1957

Sunday, 2 p.m., August 25, 1957

Sunday, 2 p.m., October 27, 1957

GUEST ARTISTS

Kristina Kohler .... Soprano
Naomi Myrick .... Contralto
Steve Stagner .... Tenor
John Detra .... Bass

THIS PROGRAM WILL ADMIT YOU AND A FRIEND

Program - June 30, 1957

Concerto, D minor, Adagio .... Bach
   ROSEMARIE INTRIERI
Courante I & II (with two Doubles)
   from English Suite, No. 1, A major
   ANNE WARE

Sonata, C major, K. 330 .... Mozart
   Andante cantabile
   Allegretto
   JAMES LYNCH
Menuetto, from Viennese Sonatina, F major
   LEE WARE (Age 6)

Adagio, from Concerto, B flat major .... Beethoven
   AURELIO GALLI
Concerto, B flat major, Op. 83 .... Brahms
   Allegro non troppo
   MARILYN DICKIE

Sonata, G minor, Op. 22 .... Schumann
   As fast as possible.
   ADRIENNE ALLERT

Nocturne, C minor, Op. 48 .... Chopin
   ART PALMER
Valse, F minor, Op. 69
   JIMMIE NEWMAN (Age 8)

Jeux d'eau .... Ravel
   ROSINE NOCERA

Songs: Kälte. Love Song. .... Leginska
   A Song of Knowledge.
   Ode to the West Wind.
   NAOMI MYRICK
Dance of Court Ladies and Courtiers
Dance of the little Blackamoors
   (From Opera "The Rose and the Ring")
   CHARMIAN JOY
Songs: Strictly Germ-Proof. Mumps.
   A Tract for Autos. The Ambiguous Dog.
   A Fable with a Moral.
   NAOMI MYRICK

Scherzo Humoristique "The Cat and the Mouse" .... Copland
   RENEE ZAMBROWICZ
Etude No. 5 "The Hunt" .... Paganini-List
   MITSUE USHIO
Concerto, B flat minor, Op. 23 .... Tschaikowsky
   Andante non troppo e molto maestoso
   JON ROBERTSON

This page and overleaf:
Programmes of recitals given by some of Leginska's students in 1957, when she was 70

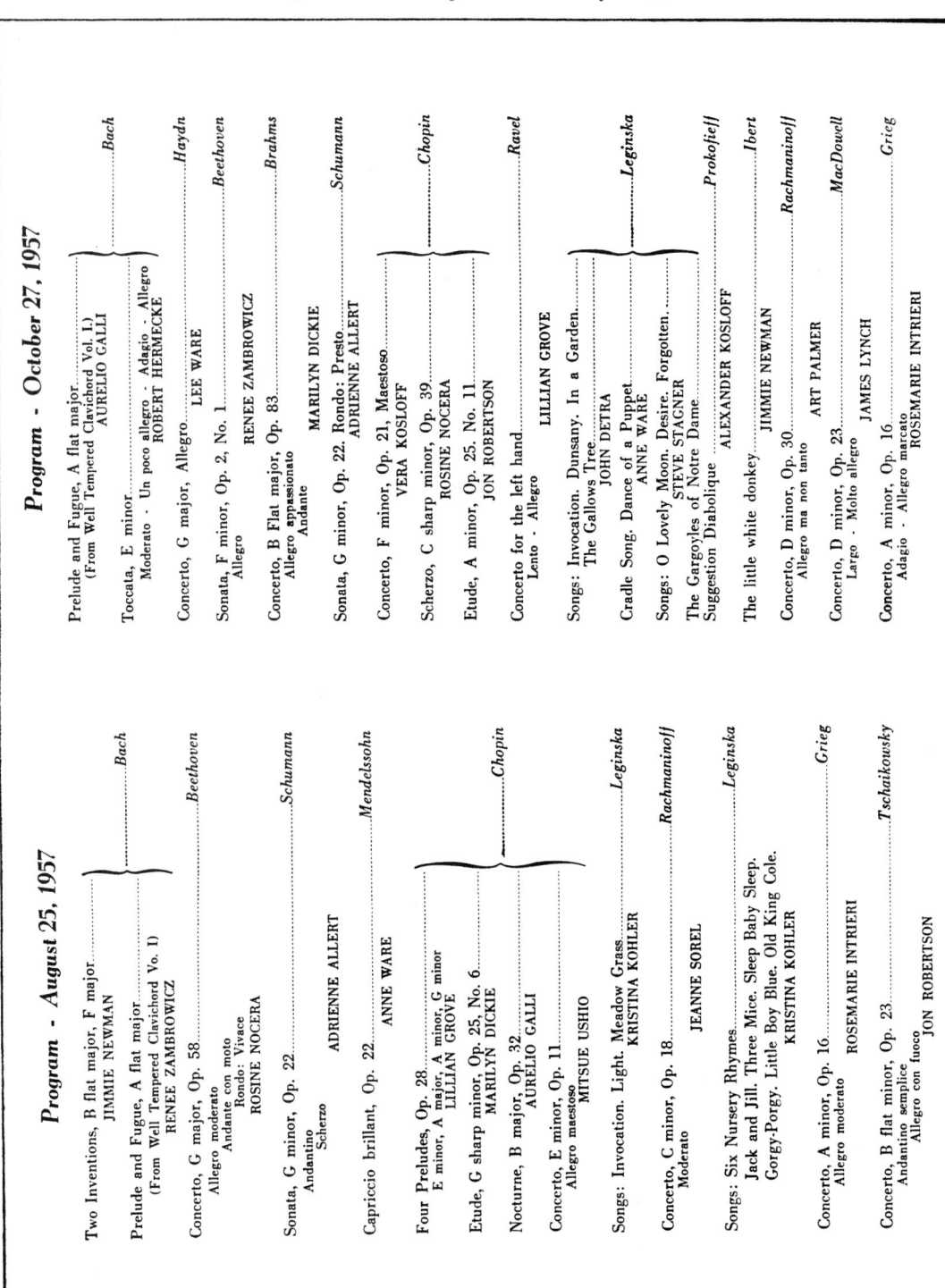

Program - August 25, 1957

Two Inventions, B flat major, F major .... Bach
  JIMMIE NEWMAN
Prelude and Fugue, A flat major.
  (From Well Tempered Clavichord Vo. 1)
  RENEE ZAMBROWICZ
Concerto, G major, Op. 58 .... Beethoven
  Allegro moderato
  Andante con moto
  Rondo: Vivace
  ROSINE NOCERA
Sonata, G minor, Op. 22 .... Schumann
  Andantino
  Scherzo
  ADRIENNE ALLERT
Capriccio brillant, Op. 22 .... Mendelssohn
  ANNE WARE
Four Preludes, Op. 28 .... Chopin
  E minor, A major, A minor, G minor
  LILLIAN GROVE
Etude, G sharp minor, Op. 25, No. 6.
  MARILYN DICKIE
Nocturne, B major, Op. 32
  AURELIO GALLI
Concerto, E minor, Op. 11
  Allegro maestoso
  MITSUE USHIO
Songs: Invocation. Light. Meadow Grass .... Leginska
  KRISTINA KOHLER
Concerto, C minor, Op. 18 .... Rachmaninoff
  Moderato
  JEANNE SOREL
Songs: Six Nursery Rhymes .... Leginska
  Jack and Jill. Three Mice. Sleep Baby Sleep.
  Gorgy-Porgy. Little Boy Blue. Old King Cole.
  KRISTINA KOHLER
Concerto, A minor, Op. 16 .... Grieg
  Allegro moderato
  ROSEMARIE INTRIERI
Concerto, B flat minor, Op. 23 .... Tschaikowsky
  Andantino semplice
  Allegro con fuoco
  JON ROBERTSON

Program - October 27, 1957

Prelude and Fugue, A flat major.
  (From Well Tempered Clavichord Vol. I)
  AURELIO GALLI .... Bach
Toccata, E minor .... Haydn
  Moderato - Un poco allegro - Adagio - Allegro
  ROBERT HERMECKE
Concerto, G major, Allegro .... Beethoven
  LEE WARE
Sonata, F minor, Op. 2, No. 1
  Allegro
  RENEE ZAMBROWICZ
Concerto, B Flat major, Op. 83 .... Brahms
  Allegro appassionato
  Andante
  MARILYN DICKIE
Sonata, G minor, Op. 22. Rondo: Presto .... Schumann
  ADRIENNE ALLERT
Concerto, F minor, Op. 21, Maestoso .... Chopin
  VERA KOSLOFF
Scherzo, C sharp minor, Op. 39
  ROSINE NOCERA
Etude, A minor, Op. 25. No. 11
  JON ROBERTSON
Concerto for the left hand .... Ravel
  Lento - Allegro
  LILLIAN GROVE
Songs: Invocation. Dunsany. In a Garden.
  The Gallows Tree.
  JOHN DETRA
Cradle Song. Dance of a Puppet .... Leginska
  ANNE WARE
Songs: O Lovely Moon. Desire. Forgotten.
  STEVE STAGNER
The Gargoyles of Notre Dame.
Suggestion Diabolique .... Prokofieff
  ALEXANDER KOSLOFF
The little white donkey .... Ibert
  JIMMIE NEWMAN
Concerto, D minor, Op. 30 .... Rachmaninoff
  Allegro ma non tanto
  ART PALMER
Concerto, D minor, Op. 23 .... MacDowell
  Largo - Molto allegro
  JAMES LYNCH
Concerto, A minor, Op. 16 .... Grieg
  Adagio - Allegro marcato
  ROSEMARIE INTRIERI

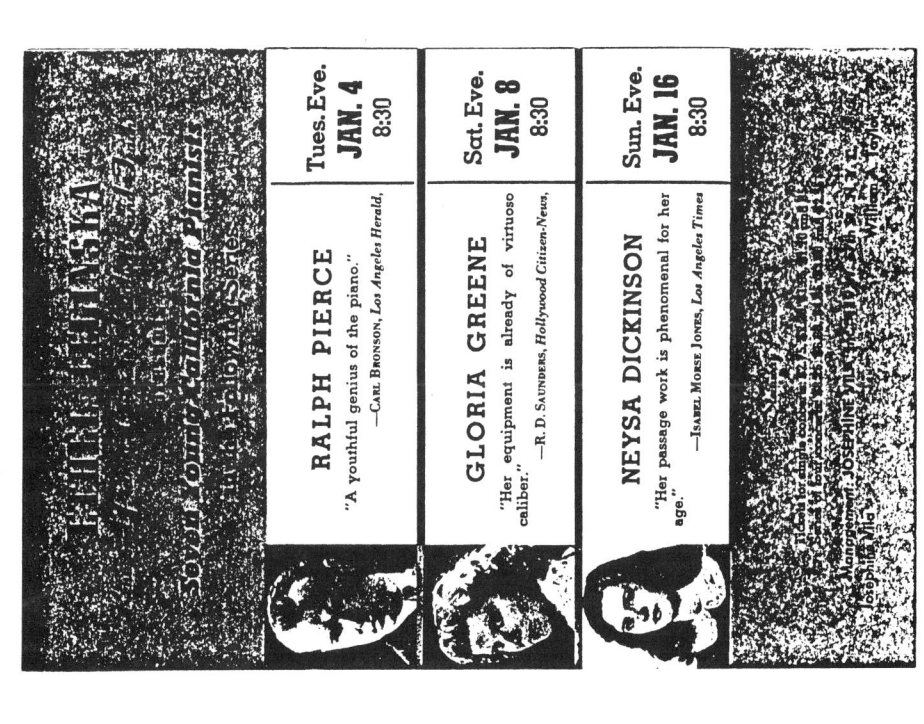

Some of Leginska's students perform in the 'Musicale' series at the Los Angeles City College Music Department, 1957

In the same year (1959) that Leginska's three latest compositions were published, she won the Mu Phi Epsilon Award* for Chamber Music with her musical setting of the song *Americans Are Always Moving On,* composed for mixed chorus, solo voices and piano, to words by Stephen Vincent Benét.

So, as the 1950s gave way to the 1960s, Leginska was still following an active life at the age of 73, having taught very successfully in Los Angeles for the previous 20 years. There were more productive years still to come.

---

* Mu Phi Epsilon is a National Music Honour Sorority [sisterhood; a women's academic society] founded at the Metropolitan College of Music (now closed), Cincinnati, on 13th November 1903. The Sorority awards cash prizes for original compositions by American women composers. (Leginska had been a citizen of the USA since her marriage in 1907.) A settlement school, known as the Mu Phi Epsilon School of Music, is maintained in Chicago.

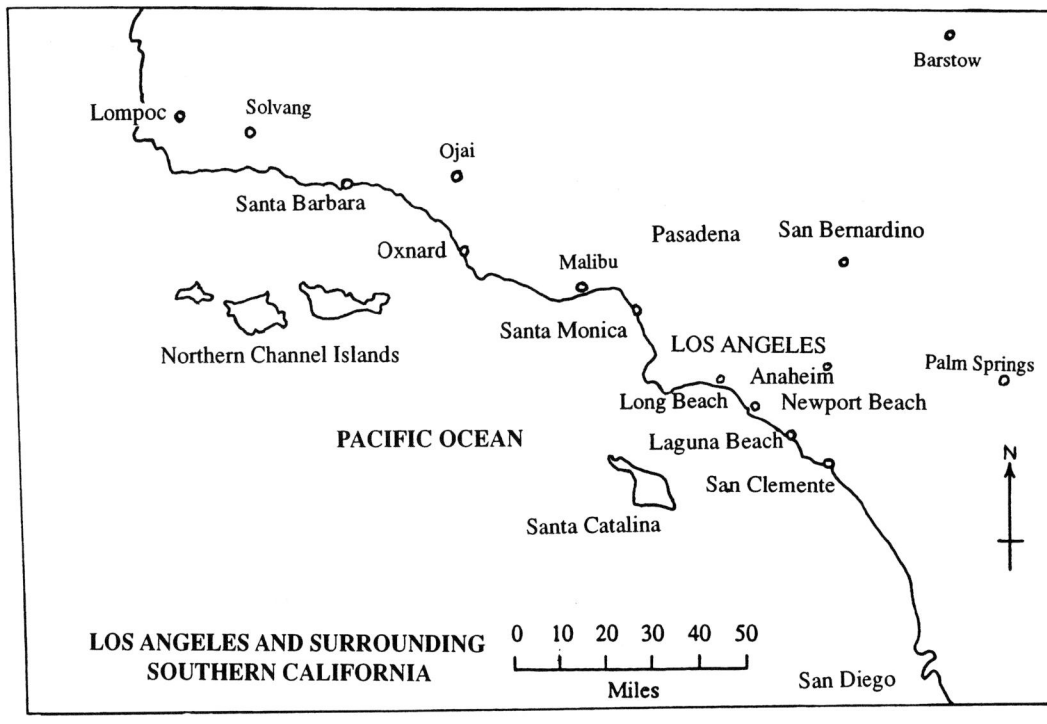

Map of Southern California showing Los Angeles and Laguna Beach, where Leginska used to spend her holidays

References: Chapter 16

1. Information about the "New Venture in Music" series has been compiled from many different sources; in particular, the recollections of Leginska's former students and from printed material (pamphlets, brochures, advertisements, programmes, etc.) sent to the authors by them.
2. Information about the "Leginska Little Symphony" was provided by Marilyn Neeley and other former students and by press reviews.
3. The evidence of support of the various famous musicians listed was stated on some of the advertising items which Leginska produced on behalf of her students.
4. *The South Coast News*, 23rd August 1949.
5. A certified copy of the death certificate of Christina Bella Liggins (née Workman) was purchased from the Superintendent Registrar, Bridlington. The informant was Christina's nephew, J.D. Workman of 42, Washington Street, Hull. The help of Mrs Margaret Stockbridge in finding the date of Christina's death from local records is acknowledged.
6. *Hull Daily Mail,* November 1957. The friend in Hull with whom Leginska still corresponded was Mrs Irene Jackson of Cuthbert Avenue, Airlie Street, Boulevard. (Boulevard is a street in west Hull). Leginska occasionally sent her programmes of recitals such as those of 1957. Mrs Jackson's friendship with Leginska was said to date back to their early youth.
7. *Los Angeles Examiner*, 25th February 1957.
8. *Los Angeles Evening Tribune*, 25th February 1957.
9. *Los Angeles Herald and Express*, 25th February 1957.

Chapter 17

Leginska – Remembered by her Students

The last chapter took our story to the end of the 1950s, when Leginska was aged 73 and still enjoying an active musical life. The book so far will, it is hoped, have built up a picture of Ethel Leginska as a person, as a musician, and as a teacher. Before continuing the account, chronologically, by considering the final years of Leginska's life, it seems appropriate here, at a time when Leginska had already been teaching in Los Angeles for 20 years, to recount a few more of the memories and anecdotes of her students. Some of their recollections have already been quoted, but the length and success of Leginska's teaching years in California and the wealth of first-hand accounts available, enables her students to shed further light on her personality as well as her teaching methods.

This chapter will be devoted to such personal accounts, all of which are additional to the extracts already given. Some of them are taken from letters received by the authors in response to enquiries. They are spontaneous writings which give a vivid insight into Leginska's remarkably forceful personality and supreme talent. Most of the other observations are précised from recollections of some of her students given in a radio programme broadcast in April 1986, a tape of which was kindly sent to us by Tom Curtis, who was one of those who took part. The programme was made to mark the centenary of Leginska's birth.

Many of Leginska's students have drawn attention to a few general facts about their petite, darked-haired teacher with her deeply intense grey-blue eyes. They contrast the vigour and dynamism of her personality, with which she achieved an almost hypnotic effect over her pupils, with the slightness of her physique. [1] All her students agreed that, as a pianist, she possessed a complete mastery of her instrument.

One of the authors' picture postcards of Leginska, hand written by her on the reverse in 1908 (reproduced on page 68), thanks her friend "for the cigarettes" which she said she had enjoyed. Beverly Carmen, a former student who figured prominently in Chapter 15, reported that Leginska, when she knew her, "smoked loads of cigarettes". [2] This observation was corroborated by several other students. As it is known that she smoked in the 1900s, 1910s, 1920s, 1940s and 1950s, it seems a fairly safe assumption that she was a relatively heavy smoker for most of her adult life.

Leginska was not a church-goer but she believed in God, loved nature, and worshipped God through his creations. She was very well-read, and loved the classics of English literature on which she had been brought up. She never completely lost her English accent, and it became more noticeable when she was angry, a fact confirmed by several of her students in letters to the authors.

Though her son lived in Los Angeles during the long period of Leginska's life in which she taught there, contacts with him appear to have been few and far between, and many of her pupils were unaware that he lived in the city until after Leginska's death. Consequently, as far as her students were concerned, she appeared to be a lady with no family connections, whose sole close companion was her live-in friend, secretary and teaching assistant Lucille Oliver, herself a talented pianist.

The breakdown of her marriage and the estrangement from her son must have been a source of great sorrow to Ethel. She resented being called 'grandmother' by her son's children on the rare occasions when they met. [3]

Now let us quote a few extracts from letters received from people who knew Ethel Leginska, to amplify the earlier accounts of Marilyn Neeley, Beverly Carmen (who will be quoted again in this chapter) and others. Some of the letters were written in response to the authors' appeal for information from those who knew her, which was published in *Overture*, the magazine of Local 47 of the Musicians' Union of Los Angeles, during the summer of 1984, and some result from other (earlier and later) correspondence.

Joan Meggett: [4]

"I studied with Mme Leginska from 1940-41, a year, as I remember, with some private lessons but mostly in a master class with several local pianists. My role was an ambitious one: the Beethoven Piano Sonata, Op. 2, No. 3, and the Mozart Piano Concerto, K. 595. She was a knowledgeable and exciting teacher as well as a fine pianist, illustrating points herself from her remarkable memory. I considered it a profitable year."

Joseph Enos (see also Chapter 15): [5]

"I studied a year with Leginska around 1950-52 and unlearned all the bad playing and acquired an improved technique which sustained me another couple of decades, all due to the superb tutelage and enrichment from her abilities. There was never any casual talk . . . all business and music playing with constant demonstration at her second piano.

"I attended recitals of her pupils where she accompanied the students on the second piano in her home. The audience flowed out onto the porch and stairs as space was limited and one heard, as best one could, with street noise, etc."

Lynnore Dagg: [6]

"I studied with her 1944 through 1947 and again 1948-50. I kept in touch with her throughout the intervening years also. I loved and admired her and have tried to teach my pupils everything I learned from her."

Magda Loeb: [7]

"I studied with Ethel Leginska from about 1941 to 1945, beginning at age 13. She had a tremendous influence – good and bad – on many of her students. She was very controlling, often deciding, in collusion with a parent, what the student would wear (in order to appear younger at performances), how many years to deduct from the actual age of a student in order to make the student appear more precocious, what school to attend (the idea being to spend as little time as possible in school and therefore more time practising). As I recall, I liked her but was also afraid of her. I think she taught the Romantics quite well, though of course at that time the interpretation was more exaggerated than it would be today. I think she knew very little about the Baroque period and tended to romanticize it. She tended to limit the repertoire experience (as did many other teachers) because her better students were always preparing for a public performance and therefore spent a great deal of time perfecting a very small number of pieces.

"I also feel she often had her students working on material well beyond their ability – but of course, if one worked long enough (as I did on the Winter Wind Etude of Chopin) eventually it could be played. She certainly had an excitement and an intensity about her and often demonstrated with some very wonderful playing. I don't think she really cared about making her students 'rounded' musicians – there was never any analysis of the music in terms of structure or harmony, etc., no emphasis on sight reading, and often, instead of covering the basic repertoire, we would be working on odd pieces of music – as I did, learning the difficult Liapounov Concerto and playing it with her orchestra.

"A few little asides – she always wore pants [trousers in British terminology] – quite unusual in those days. She had a little waiting room for the students – filled with signed photos of her students – which somehow created a sense of seriousness and excitement for the lesson to follow. I think she was quite generous (though ultimately self serving) in her many partial scholarships and extra free lessons given before performances."

Esther Lee Kaplan (see also page 238): [8]

"I was a student of Leginska's in 1942 - 43 - 44. She was a unique and dynamic teacher as well as a very special personality."

Robert Logan (see also page 240): [9]

"I made several entries in a diary I kept during 1940 wherein I noted that I had taken my mother to her lessons at Mme Leginska's home on South Hobart in Los Angeles. I remember the house was on the east side of the street – a large one-storey home with a large living and dining-room where the piano lessons were given. My mother, Marie Logan, was herself a piano teacher and former President of American Artists Inc.,who felt there was no limit to what a musician could learn so she availed herself of the vast technical knowledge offered by Leginska. My mother did not call her Ethel, but addressed her as Mme Leginska. My mother introduced one of our friends, a very talented pianist, Armando Loredo, to Leginska, and shortly thereafter [she] arranged a concert at a large auditorium where Armando played the Third Piano Concerto of Prokofiev, with Leginska conducting the symphony orchestra. She had been the conductor of the Women's Symphony of Boston and also the Chicago Women's Symphony."

Armando Loredo (see also last paragraph of previous page): [10]

"It made me very happy to know that at last someone was writing a biography of Ethel Leginska. I've always felt that she was great and deserving musically and a humane person."

Beverly Carmen (see also Chapter 15): [11]

"My parents saw Leginska's advertisement in the Los Angeles newspapers, offering a scholarship 'to the most talented pianist' of ten years or younger. It was after the deadline, but she invited me to play for her. Then she said, 'I have already given the scholarship, but there is no law against my giving two'. My father, at this first meeting, told her that he had heard her play in Carnegie Hall in 1922 * while he was a student at The Institute of Musical Art; he mentioned the program, whereupon she went to the piano and played most of that program for us. It was a dark, rainy day and she had High Tea and wine brought in, and invited us to stay. It was the Autumn of 1939.

"This was a vivid day for me, and I remember so much about it, as well as of the subsequent years of constant study with Leginska. It was the beginning for me of a glimpse of greatness. I was at her funeral, too. Another dark, rainy day, somehow forming a symmetry.

"She was in contact with many other musicians and singers, but I believe that I had one of the closest associations with her ... sometimes good, sometimes bad, but always interesting."

The following are further snippets of information from Beverly Carmen's many letters:

"In answer to your question, 'Why did she settle in Los Angeles?' I somehow have the impression that she simply fled the Blitz, settled down in a war-prosperous part of the world, and decided to build up some security and gather some money. As I wrote you, I never paid her but was taught free-of-charge. But she charged a goodly sum (for those days) from others.† She dragged me all over to play, and every time I played, she got more students!

---

* This would probably actually have been 1923 when she gave two recitals at Carnegie Hall, on 20th February and 7th November (see programmes on pages 322 and 323).

† According to Robert L. Watt, [12] a French hornist with the Los Angeles Philharmonic Orchestra, Leginska charged $25 per hour for lessons in the 1940s though, as stated elsewhere, some students paid nothing, having been given 'Leginska scholarships'. At the same period Rosina Lhevinne, another noted teacher, was also paid $25 an hour for her teaching classes at the Juilliard whilst Rosina's husband Josef Lhevinne, one of the 'all-time great' pianists, was paid $40 an hour for his classes at the same music school. The $25 an hour charged by Leginska, assuming the figure to be true, was the equivalent of about £5-10s in British money in the 1940s. To put these figures into some kind of perspective, the average male schoolteacher in Britain at that time was paid about £420 per annum (about £2 per working day). So if Leginska managed to fit in four 2-hour lessons a day (allowing for the fact that her lessons always overran), five days a week (on average) for, say, 40 weeks a year, her income at that time must have been of the order of $40,000 a year, or more than £8,000 a year in British money (at the 1940s exchange rate). All her taxes, expenses and the salaries of people who worked for her in various ways, and the orchestras she hired, would of course have had to be paid out of this.

"In Los Angeles she gave no recitals of her own; she played all the orchestral parts (reduced for piano) for her students, in lessons and in smaller recitals. For larger concerts, she formed the 'Leginska Little Symphony'; mostly peopled by musicians from the [Los Angeles] Philharmonic Orchestra. I was the first child to play a concerto with this orchestra. She was a vigorous and exacting leader.

"Music was, I believe, her religion. (This may work in with her teaching methods.) She believed in controlled, repetitive practice, and to help her, she had some carved ivory beads (six) on the piano. She advised playing a phrase three times with music (moving a bead for each time well-played) and three times by memory (moving a bead till they were all moved over). 'This', she said, 'is how I "tell my beads" '.

"She did not attend Church, and quite often scheduled lessons (at least mine) on Sunday, Christmas, Thanksgiving and New Years! This was to emphasize that she believed Art more important than Family.

"She had a companion for whom she had advertised . . . someone to keep her company and make tea.* At first this lady would open the door for us, and often be seen reading a book or magazine . . . Mrs Guys was her name. She would sit on the sofa or reading-chair and was a most pleasant person. But there was a change . . . first of all apparent in her dress: she had worn street-dresses and sweaters (at that time the Southern California uniform) and her hair was always nicely done. Then, little by little we saw her in the type of uniform worn by a housemaid, [she] never sat in the living room any more, and always looked tired and ill-done whenever we saw her. Soon we didn't see her anymore. Leginska had taken a companion and made a servant of her and the lady finally left.

"Lucille Oliver's 'Uncle Ted' became chief cook and bottle-washer, too. I believe Lucille passed away, as did Lucille's uncle, Ted Naish, whom we ALL called 'uncle'. However, no one ever believed that he was anyone's uncle.

"I believe she had resented being a mother – she had, after all, given the baby to her husband at the time of their divorce – a thing unheard of in those days, even among 'great artists'. † She did not much like children – except as budding pianists.

"Her sense of humor came and went. It was not a creative sense of humor, and it wasn't ALWAYS responsive, but here and there I saw a glimmer. Mostly, she loved irony when the 'joke' was on someone . . . so I believe she loved slapstick. She adored Chaplin, and thought that 'The Great Dictator' was 'the greatest art in the world'. She did love a funny story, but I think that the broad, wild type of humor of American kids remained alien to her.

"Here's a wild remark I remember: 'You'll never be a great artist until you can enjoy a good glass of beer' . . . this shows another side of her character.

"She retained an English accent and English usage, and pronunciation and accentuation. We (at least I, who was a grand mimic) caught some of this from her . . . all part of the imitation process.

---

* This must have been in addition to Lucille Oliver, Leginska's secretary, companion and teaching assistant who had been with her for many years.

† She had not given "the baby" to her husband but it shows what Leginska's students believed to be true at the time. As recorded in Chapter 8, Ethel fought a bitter custody case in court to keep the child, but lost. At that time custody was often given to the husband in such cases.

"She did often poke fun at things American and contrast them very badly with things English. The way we made toast, or buttered it (sloppily, using too much butter), and little things of that sort.

"She never spoke much [about England], but she remained, in many ways, Anglophile. However, in little things she thought freely, as in the remark, 'You know, English frocks are not smart'.

"I hope I have added some detail and some flesh-and-blood. It amazes me how much total-recall I have of those days ... I can see her studio clearly. This was, after all, over forty years ago. But you can see what a profound impression she made."

Forty years on ... Beverly Carmen in the authors' garden in Wilmslow, 11th July 1985

Daniel Pollack (see also Chapter 16, page 244:) [13]

"Madame Leginska was my first teacher. I studied with her from 1941- 44 (ages 6 - 9) and made my debut with her conducting in the Town Hall, New York in '44 (when I was nine years old).

"I visited her shortly before she died, about an article that was going to be written on great pianists (women) who were so influential."

Radie Britain (see also Chapter 13, especially page 194): [14]

"She moved to Los Angeles where I had a studio in Hollywood. She had a huge piano class. On two different programmes she included my 'Rhapsodic Fantasy for Piano and Orchestra' using the talent of one of the male students at the Ebell Theater performances.

"Several times I invited Madame Leginska to a social evening in my home – but she always refused – saying, 'I never accept social engagements – music is my sole interest'. I have never known a musician more dedicated to her craft. She was an inspiration to me.

"Leginska's life dedicated to music was her stronghold. Her life was built around music. I have never known another musician who has no other interests but music. She was totally dedicated to music." *

Marilyn Neeley (see also Chapter 15): [15]

"Leginska spoke very little of her past, except for her years with Leschetizky, whose method she followed quite strictly. The Brée compilation of Leschetizky's exercises, and Hanon, Czerny and I. Philipp comprised her regimen and she quoted Leschetizky frequently. ** She was very fond of quoting English poetry.

"She was very demanding, in all matters, musical and otherwise, and certainly never hesitated to give her opinion.

"She had a good sense of humor, provided the occasion was right and she thought the humor, mostly hers, was appropriate. It was NOT appropriate for a student to joke with her!"

Several of Leginska's former students whose written recollections about Leginska have already been quoted (including some of the above) also contributed to the KPFK programme of 1986 referred to earlier in the chapter. † Some of these verbal comments follow, as do the recollections of other contributors to the programme with whom the authors have not had written contact. [16]

---

* But Leginska also had a well-documented love of literature and the natural world.

** The definitive book of Leschetizky's method and exercises, *The Groundwork of the Leschetizky Method* by Malwine Brée was published by G. Schirmer in 1902. As may be surmised, Brée was a pupil of Leschetizky.

Charles Louis Hanon (1820-1900) – French organist and piano teacher; Carl Czerny (1791-1857) – Viennese piano teacher and composer who was a pupil of Beethoven and teacher of Leschetizky; and Isidor Philipp (1863-1958) – French pianist and teacher, all wrote well-known books of piano studies and exercises.

† A strict transcript of a radio discussion is not always the best means of conveying what was said in a written text such as this because people do not speak as they write. The extracts from

continued at foot of opposite page . . .

Marguerite Heller (formerly Marguerite Baum, see also Chapter 16):

Mrs Heller has provided a great deal of helpful information in letters from 1984 to the present. In the KPFK radio programme, comprising recollections of Leginska by several of her former students, Marguerite Heller quoted several telling phrases relating to Leginska's influence on her as a student, describing Leginska as "a pace-setter, a trail-blazer". Leginska's philosophy was "to create, to achieve a definite purpose, and to justify her existence", qualities she succeeded in imparting to her students.

Mrs Heller admitted that when she first played (very nervously) for Leginska, she was told she played "like an old maid". But under Leginska's guidance there was a rapid improvement and she started to play with emotion. Leginska remarked, "You're like a wild woman – what did your mother feed you on – red meat?" Leginska preferred a racehorse to a plodder who had "no fire or temperament within"; Leginska knew how to bridle and temper her 'racehorses'. She took infinite pains; the process of growth takes time. Mrs Heller (Marguerite Baum as she was when Leginska taught her) said that Leginska, who was very well-read, had introduced her to literature. To Leginska, music and art reflected nature.

When Marguerite Heller asked Leginska how to overcome stage fright she told her, "Any great artist has stage fright – I used to go cold all over before playing". The answer, Leginska said, was in thorough preparation, through concentration and study, because then the performance would hold no terrors. "Music is like a blueprint", said Leginska, and mastery of it is the answer to stage fright.

"In some ways", said Mrs Heller, "Leginska was a showman. If I played a wrong note she would say, 'If you're going to play a wrong note, play it with authority – nobody will know then!' " Leginska felt that it was cruel to encourage a child to continue in music if it didn't have the talent. "A turnip doesn't bear roses", according to Leginska. She was prepared to take infinite pains with the talented ones.

Moreover she would do all she could to promote the musical careers of her students; she would write "beautiful" letters of introduction, help her students in every way possible to succeed in competitions, and so on. Her letters were excellent and she could be a diplomat when she wanted to be. To illustrate this, Marguerite Heller recalled that under Leginska's guidance she had won first prize in a local (Californian) piano contest which offered a recital engagement, and because of the fact that at the same time of month she had to appear at Carnegie Hall for a nationwide competition, the local people wanted to give their prize to someone else. After all, she would be playing at Carnegie Hall, they said, and she didn't need their prize. But Leginska would have none of this and wrote to them explaining that "this young pianist needs the exposure of playing in front of critics" and just because the two events coincided it was neither fair nor just to withhold the prize. Leginska won the day and Marguerite was given the prize. Leginska always acted vigorously on her students' behalf and was as protective as a parent to her many pupils.

Mrs Heller described Leginska as "a towering figure in the music of Los Angeles, and an inspiration to me".

---

continued from foot of opposite page . . .

the radio broadcast which follow are a written account (or précis) of the lengthy discussion, which preserves accurately the gist of the various speakers' remarks. Exact words and phrases used, where quoted, are enclosed by inverted commas.

Daniel Pollack (see also Chapter 16 and page 268):

Daniel Pollack, who became a concert pianist, studied with Leginska from age six to nine, having previously had another teacher from the age of four. Later he studied with Rosina Lhevinne. When he arrived for his first lesson with Leginska he waited outside but within earshot of the previous lesson. Leginska knew he was there. He heard her ask the student she was teaching what a certain note she played at her second piano was, then yelled "Daniel, what's the name of that note?" He correctly answered 'A' (or whatever the note happened to be) and she said "That's good – I'm glad you have perfect pitch". She liked her students to have that gift. That was his introduction!

She took Daniel away from public school ['state' school in Britain] and had him put into a private school. She felt that reading, writing and arithmetic were important but many other time-consuming subjects taught in school were superfluous and were a bar to piano practice; their removal freed more time for music study and practice. He said she gave him an "unbelievable" technical foundation by the age of six; he played double thirds and double sixths at that age, and he knew all about such things as diminished sevenths at six or seven. At that age his sight-reading was poor, he said, but he could play all kinds of music. He played the 13th Hungarian Rhapsody of Liszt and the Chopin E minor concerto well at eight years old. When he went to Rosina Lhevinne for further lessons she was astonished and asked, "Where did you learn this technical equipment?"

He said many of today's pianists have a percussive style; they "bang". Leginska never let her students do that – they had to listen to what they themselves were playing and strive for beauty of sound. She was an enormous influence on the Los Angeles musical scene in her day, an "important musical force". She demanded perfection and her pupils developed "a love/hate relationship" with her.

Leginska adapted her scale of charges to the needs and talents of the individual students, just as Leschetizky had done. Daniel recalled that his parents only paid $5 a week, which was very cheap.

Leginska taught by rote. When a pupil started to play a piece she would not let him move on until the bit being played was mastered. Sometimes he would play the first note of a piece and she would say, "No, I don't like it – play it again." He recalled that he spent months on one of Mendelssohn's 'Songs Without Words', playing bits over and over. "No, there isn't the singing tone I need – no, the pedalling isn't right – the accompaniment is too loud" – and so on. To get it right, she would play a phrase, he would copy, until it was right. He remembered it vividly! She was a perfectionist. But many couldn't handle what she was giving.

She chain-smoked at the piano. Time off was spent with nature. She kept a pet rabbit and the children (her pupils) would play in the garden with her and the rabbit.

Leginska was very professional in all things. Small children were taught how to bow, even how to walk on [to the stage]. Many pupils rebelled, leaving not only the piano, but music totally. Leginska's attitude was 'sink or swim'. In the Sunday recitals the small performers had to be dressed like professionals.

He felt that Leginska was from another era – the 'Golden Age' of pianists – the era of de Pachmann, Josef Lhevinne, Rosenthal, and so on. The pupils of Liszt and Busoni lived with their teacher and no other instruction was deemed by those great pianists to be necessary. He felt Leginska agreed with that philosophy – that was how she would have liked life to have been.

Anyone of Leginska's magnitude, Daniel Pollack believed, "created waves". But Leginska had the ability to draw out what was deepest inside her students and she gave them the ability to achieve great things. But she would not have accepted the 'querying' attitude of today's students who want to know the 'how' or 'why' of everything. Her attitude was, "just do it!".

The disadvantage of Leginska, in his view, was that she shut off the life around her pupils. He felt that a child should be aware of the outside world, "in order to bridge the gap between being a child prodigy and coping with the world". Leginska's pupils had eventually to leave her in order "to get on with their lives". It was like holding on to the umbilical cord, and she didn't understand that. She would have liked all her students to have stayed with her for the rest of their lives, which in his view was not a healthy situation. She gave a wonderful grounding in all aspects of music and was always hurt when any student left her. She was "overwhelming, like a tidal wave."

Ron McFarland:

She was a perfectionist – a tremendous disciplinarian. Everything a student did, she had to approve. She disapproved of the music of Arnold Schoenberg, and said of him "we all know he's gifted but he's lost his mind". She had taught one of her students the Schoenberg Piano Concerto and told McFarland that at rehearsal she "knew Schoenberg was insane because the dogs barked when they heard his music". McFarland, who later became a composer, wanted to have lessons on composition with Schoenberg, who lived in Los Angeles. He did – but said he had to have them on Sunday mornings at Schoenberg's home without Leginska's knowledge.* He felt that in some ways she was a "naive, childlike person" but she dominated the lives of all her pupils and inspired them.

According to Ron McFarland, the local music teachers' associations were upset by Leginska's arrival in Los Angeles. She had told him she had received letters from some of the more small-minded of them saying, "Leginska, we don't want you here", which is not surprising in some ways as she was a great pianist, on a different plane to all but a tiny minority of teachers, and they knew she would take some of their custom. Their fears were well-founded; pupils flocked to her. She set up competitions, which took the best students, and many who auditioned became her pupils.

Ron McFarland studied with Leginska from the age of 4½ until he enrolled at the Juilliard School. She considered four was the right age to start. He agreed with other contributors to the radio tribute about the love/hate relationship between Leginska and her pupils. He said he became a kind of assistant teacher for Leginska [just as Leschetizky had had assistants] and lived at the studio for a time. "It was a marvellous training." She once told him, at that time, that when she decided to study conducting in the early 1920s the person she had most wanted to teach her was Bruno Walter, but he was reluctant to take students. Consequently she sought out his assistant, Robert Heger (see page 156). In Ron McFarland's view, Leginska's life "was total music".

He told the story of an occasion when he was living at the studio and was practising when Leginska was in the garden. She suddenly walked in, said "The octaves are uneven!" and walked out. "She heard everything. She was so accurate."

---

* But strangely, he says on his website that Leginska arranged for him to study privately with Schoenberg. Perhaps she relented.

Highly gifted pianists from the *Leginska*

ETHEL LEGINSKA
Conductor-Composer-Pianist-Teacher

ADRIENNE ALLERT*
"Accomplished technique . . . fleet passage work . . . carefully molded tone production . . . good dynamics . . . strong and articulate left hand . . . perceptive way with musical phrases . . . brought her resounding bravos . . ."—W. A., *Los Angeles Times*.

ALMA BARTHOLOMEW*
"Presented the Mac Dowell Concerto in A-minor brilliantly . . . setting forth the musical jewel with command of all pianistic requirements."—Carl Bronson, *L. A. Herald*.

VIANA BEY*
Two Eastern Tours
"Viana is a well-taught little girl of unusual talent, a definite personality . . . the octaves in the closing Allegro assai were a real triumph."—R. L., *New York Times*.

MARY ANNE BULLOCK*
"Age 12, played the Symphonic Variations by Cesar Franck with fine tone and sureness in its intricate harmonic discourse."—Alfred Price Quinn, *B'nai B'rith Messenger*, April 19, 1946.

JACQUELINE and EUGENE CAMBELL
(Child Duo Pianists)
"It is safe to predict a concert career for those highly gifted and splendidly trained children." — *Hollywood Citizen-News*, April 27, 1942.

BEVERLY CARMEN
". . . showed the results of excellent schooling and a depth of quality and tone surprising in one of her years."—*Hollywood Citizen-News*, Jan. 11, 1941.

GEORGE CASSADY*
Winner, age 10, KFI and Los Angeles Philharmonic Young Artists' Competition, 1944, for children under 14; award, soloist, Philharmonic Orchestra, Alfred Wallenstein conducting. Winner, Young Artist Contest U.C.L.A., awarded two engagements 1946 Artist Series Subscription Course.
* "Headed for important achievement in the world of music."—O. D., *L. A. Examiner*, June 9, 1948.

PEGGY CONSTANCE
"Demonstrated her technique of high order; phrasing and interpretation revealed unusual talent and she gave a splendid reading of Rachmaninoff's F-sharp Minor Concerto, a first Los Angeles performance."—W. G., *Music of the West Magazine*, Nov., 1948.

BARBARA DELL CULVER*
"The Walter Piston Concertino, bristling with rhythmic, harmonic and technical complexities, was so ably projected that it impressed this listener as a brilliant achievement, and probably the most striking performance of the program."—Alfred Price Quinn, *B'nai B'rith Messenger*, Oct. 7, 1949.

MARILYN DICKIE*
Debut recitals in San Francisco, New York and Boston.
"Her performance was excellent . . . achieved results beyond her years in Beethoven's Sonata . . . a rare combination of grace and incisive strength . . . full of charm and individuality . . . very musical."—C. H., *New York Times*, April 15, 1951.

NEYSA DICKINSON*
"Has a good technique and shows undoubted promise. Her tone is good, her readings intelligent, and she possesses an ingratiating personality."—E. MacD. B., *New York Herald-Tribune*.

RICHARD ELLIS*
"Beethoven's Concerto in B-flat was successfully achieved . . . a player of ability. Technically and tonally he was impressive. The Adagio movement was played with astonishing expression and finesse."—Alfred Price Quinn, *B'nai B'rith Messenger*, Oct. 7, 1949.

VIRGINIA FRENCH*
"Her touch was delicately light, the runs being taken both easily and flawlessly . . . one cannot belittle her evident technique and musicianship." — C. S. H., *L. A. Times*, Oct. 21, 1946.

SUZANNE GAYNER*
New York debut, Town Hall, age 9, soloist with orchestra.
"Exhibited astonishing understanding in Beethoven's Concerto in C, only lacking in grown-up power as a full-fledged virtuoso . . . receiving an ovation for actual musicianship."—Carl Bronson, *L. A. Herald-Express*, Feb. 15, 1943.

BONNIE GOLD*
"Performed the Mozart Concerto with mature interpretive aplomb and rippling finger dexterity."—Carl Bronson, *L. A. Herald-Express*, March 9, 1946.

NORMA GORDON*
"Presented the Schumann Concerto and from feathery touches to fortes, performed with a mature aplomb, clear-cut pedaling and distinction of themes that promises a great future."—Carl Bronson, *L. A. Herald-Express*, March 26, 1943.

GLORIA GREENE*
Winner of three Los Angeles contests within one year. Winner Young Artist Contest U.C.L.A., awarded engagement 1945-46 Artists' Series Subscription Course, Bruno Walter was judge. The only first place winner 1944-45 K.F.I. & Los Angeles Philharmonic Young Artists Competition and appeared as soloist with the Orchestra March 23, 1945 at Philharmonic Auditorium, Alfred Wallenstein conductor. Winner Young Artists Competitive Audition, Occidental College Concert Series and presented in an entire piano recital at Thorne Hall Subscription Course, February 2, 1945. Gloria was the unanimous selection of Southern California committee to open San Francisco Gainsborough Music Foundation recitals, October 24, 1946. Five Eastern tours. Soloist, Buffalo Philharmonic Orchestra, William Steinberg, Conductor, Feb. 6, 1948. Kleinhans Music Hall, Buffalo.
"Gloria Greene, assailed a program at Kimball hall last night that would have given pause to a seasoned virtuoso.
Young Gloria has a genuinely prodigious piano talent . . . her command of the piano is on a magnificent scale, of an enormous and unforced technical fluency and a tonal range that encompasses the extremes of velvet limpidity and great depths of power without harshness. There is in her, the makings of a first rank pianist."—Albert Goldberg, *Chicago Daily Tribune*.

LILLIAN GROVE
"Played the Liszt Concerto in A-Major. There was more class and artistry disclosed in her playing than in any of the others."—Alfred Price Quinn, *B'nai B'rith Messenger*, April 9, 1948.

Additional pianists who have received their

Mary Francis Griffin
(Daughter of Irene Dunne)

Janeen Brimley
Eugene Hoffman

This page and opposite: An advertising flyer for Leginska's studio, late 1950s. It was a single large sheet of paper. Here it has been divided vertically to fit on two pages at a (just) readable scale.

Studio who are appearing in public

MARGUERITE HELLER*
California State winner in nationwide piano competition, won an engagement at Carnegie Hall, New York, on March 6, 1948. Through competition was soloist with Glendale Symphony.
"Showed herself to be a well-trained pianist, having considerable speed and dexterity. On occasion she performed feats of great skill."—B. R., *L. A. Times*, Nov. 14, 1949.

SUZANNE JOHNSON*
"With the echoes of De Pachmann still ringing in my ears I attended with misgivings, but departed with the realization that feathery beauty of touch not alone belonged to him . . . an interpretess: one of a new 'Teen dimension' that will demand attention through sensitivity and an equipment at the keyboard that is astonishing."—Carl Bronson, *L. A. Herald-Express*, Dec. 16, 1946.

CHARMIAN JOY
"Young pianist of uncommon talent and ability . . . pianistic achievement . . . technical skill . . . a particularly lovely and sensitive interpretation . . . most dazzling . . . a display of power and technique that had the audience calling for encores."—H. L. C, *Los Angeles Times*, June 4, 1951.

ESTHER LEE KAPLAN*
"Enjoyed the Saint-Saens G Minor Concerto to the full. She has outstanding finger technique and surprising appreciation of the style of this work, sailing through the difficult passages with much fun and no worry."—Shibley Boyes, *L. A. Times*, June 29, 1943.

LYLE KENNEDY
"Displayed admirable pianistic training in the local premiere of Radie Britain's effective Rhapsodic Phantasie."—Richard Drake Saunders, *Musical Courier*, February 15, 1948.

NATALIE KOSCHES*
"Played the Beethoven Concerto Op. 58 in G with great style, and evidenced not only digital proficiency but an amazing sense of rhythm."—F. Lawrence, *L. A. Examiner*, March 26, 1943.

MARGERY LAMB*
"A dependable performance of the Liszt A major Concerto. She has facility and surprising digital strength."—Isabel Morse Jones, *L. A. Times*, June 22, 1943.

MARIANNE LEWIS*
"A notably promising young artist." — Richard Drake Saunders, *Musical Courier*, March 1, 1948.

ARMANDO LOREDO
"An effective presentation of the difficult Prokofieff Third Concerto showed his musicianship, firm tone and technical facility."—*Hollywood Citizen-News*, Jan. 22, 1941.

RONALD McFARLAND
"A first performance in Los Angeles of Arensky's F-Minor Concerto fared exceedingly well under his hands. His tone quality, his emotional directness and his amazing fluent fingers, added to a musical grasp of light and shade, earned for him repeated calls from his listeners."—O. D., *L. A. Examiner*, April 8, 1948.

JACK MOE
"Performed the Beethoven 'Emperor' Concerto creditably, with a clear sustained tone and with power sufficient to give a warm and interesting interpretation."—O. D., *L. A. Examiner*, April 8, 1948.

LUCILLE NAGEL
". . . proved a dynamic figure in the Liszt E flat Concerto, and displayed clear-cut technique and fine rhythm."—*L. A. Examiner*, June 13, 1942.

Fundamental musical training from the Leginska Studio are:
June Lusk   Cash Jeannie Salas
Adrian Ruiz   Evelyn Stolz   Clyde Willson

MARILYN NEELEY*
At age 10 winner of Forest Lawn-Hollywood Bowl competition for instrumentalists up to age 15. Received Hubert Eaton Scholarship Award. Two Eastern Tours. Third New York Recital, Town Hall, Feb. 13, 1955. Twice soloist, Los Angeles Philharmonic Orchestra, Alfred Wallenstein conductor, Philharmonic Auditorium, Los Angeles. Soloist, Buffalo Philharmonic Orchestra, William Steinberg conductor, Kleinhans Music Hall, Buffalo. Twice soloist, Glendale Symphony Orchestra, Scipione Guidi, conductor. N.B.C. engaged Marilyn as featured guest on Arlene Francis "Home" telecast, February 15, 1955.
". . . remarkably talented . . . sensational keyboard progress . . . delicacy and strength that one might more reasonably expect to find in a pianist thrice her years . . ."—Mildred Norton, *Los Angeles Daily News*.

LUCILLE OLIVER*
(Mme. Leginska's Assistant Teacher)—Soloist twice with the New York Philharmonic Orchestra. Piano recitals in New York and London, England, etc., etc. Toured United States several times.
"Lucille Oliver, the third pianist to appear on the 'New Venture in Music' all-Chopin series, was the first to play with a mature artistry and comprehending sense of the composer's romantic style . . . revealed an emotional plasticity which was stimulating . . . her concert was thoroughly satisfying and frequently moving."—C. S. H., *L. A. Times*.

JOHN PFALZGRAFF
"'Clear, sustained tone, along with temperament, good technique and inborn musicianship . . . It was pianism of high promise, and already enjoyable."— O. D., *L. A. Examiner*, Sept. 12, 1947.

RALPH PIERCE*
Winner of first Young Artist Contest, U.C.L.A., awarded an appearance 1941-42 artist series . . . California State winner of Federated Music Clubs 1943 Young Artists Contest. Eight Annual Coast to Coast Tours.
"Third Town Hall recital that featured Beethoven's great 'Hammerklavier' sonata, Opus 106 . . . There was strength and vigor in his performance, a sure technique and a fine clarity of outline."—E. L, *New York Times*, Feb. 22, 1950.

DANIEL POLLACK
New York debut, Town Hall, age 8, soloist with orchestra.
"Hit of the occasion was Daniel Pollack, 7, a lad who possesses indubitably the vital spark of artistry. He showed amazing tone, warm, full and velvety of texture, and of surprising depth; in the Chopin E-minor Concerto, his phrases were well turned and musicianly, and his understanding and delivery were remarkable."—R. D. S., *Hollywood Citizen-News*, Feb. 15, 1943.

ALFRED PURCELL
Winner of So. Calif. Talent Quest in the Daily News-Fox West Coast Contest, age 13.
"Spectacular keyboard renditions brought a thunderous response from the audience as well as the unqualified praise of the judges."—*L. A. Daily News*, April 11, 1949.

JON ROBERTSON*
Winner age 9, Young People's Audition 1952, for artists under 16. Soloist, Glendale Symphony Orchestra, Scipione Guidi conductor. Jon appeared on Eddie Cantor Television Show, May 1953. Redlands Bowl presented him as soloist in August '53. New York Town Hall Recital debut, Oct. '53. Five weeks tour, 17 Celebrity Concerts in Jamaica, Caribbean, and Latin America where he played two entirely different full length programs and a Concerto with several orchestras, July-Aug. '54. The 21st Annual Bach Festival, First Congregational Church, Los Angeles engaged Jon to play an entire Bach program Nov. 13, 1954. Walt Disney Productions had him as soloist for a program filmed at Walt Disney Studios, June '55.
"A formidable program did not daunt 12-year-old Jon Robertson. Though he had surprising command of technique in the opening Mozart Sonata, D major (K311) as well as in the Bach E Flat Major French Suite, it was in the Debussy Six Preludes, Book 2, that his natural feeling for line and color came to fruition.
Here his keen memory, accuracy and fleetness of fingers combined with a lovely tonal coloring to make the Debussy and the succeeding MacDowell 'Woodland Sketches' high points on the program. Master Robertson closed with MacDowell's 'Etude de Concert' and, for encores, played two Bach chorales and a MacDowell sketch."—Alma Gowdy, *Los Angeles Herald and Express*, June 13, 1955.

JOSEPHINE RODRIGUEZ*
Winner, Matinee Musical Club Contest. Soloist, L.A. Philharmonic, Alfred Wallenstein conductor, Philharmonic Auditorium, L.A. Soloist Glendale Symphony, Scipione Guidi conductor.
"A phenomenally gifted girl, and she has a technique which matches many who are twice her age and 20 times as well known." — C. S. Hickman, *B'nai B'rith Messenger*, March 10, 1950.

JUDY ROSS*
"Mendelssohn's D minor Concerto, Op. 40, as played by Miss Ross, was remarkable for tone color and a long phrase line."—*L. A. Times*, June 29, 1943.

JEAN RUSSELL*
". . . played with noble clarity, and with good taste and sensitivity. Very effective, too, was her performance of Charles Wakefield Cadman's vivid and lyrical Sonata in A Major, which had not been played previously in Los Angeles."—*L. A. Examiner*, Feb. 12, 1946.

SYBIL STEINBERG*
New York debut, Town Hall, soloist with Orchestra, Age 12.
"She delivered the difficult Second Concerto of MacDowell with the vigor and ability of a mature performer two or three times her age. She was not only in command of the requisite technique at all times, but interpreted its moods with obvious understanding."—R. D. Saunders, *Hollywood Citizen-News*, March 26, 1943.

PAULINE TURRILL
"A charming touch, technical ease, and a quality of tenderness in tone marked her reading of the Mozart D-minor Concerto."—*Hollywood Citizen-News*, Jan. 22, 1941.

ANNE WARE*
Made her film debut in the Twentieth Century Fox production of "Tonight We Sing" (Life of Manager Sol Hurok) playing the Schubert Sonata in C Major.
"Little Miss Anne Ware drew for her first assignment a little known sonata in C major, which she played with nice fluency and cleanly delineated scale runs. The youngster appears to possess exceptional talent."—Mildred Norton, *Daily News*, L. A., March 23, 1953.

ELAINE WIGHTMAN
"Gave a reading of Mozart's A-major Concerto which created a sensation. Los Angeles has in this talented little girl a rarely endowed personality, capably guided by the experience and wisdom of her teacher."—F. Lawrence, *L. A. Examiner*, Oct. 3, 1941.

LEON ZAMBOWICZ
"Played the Concerto by Khachaturian with commendable spirit and growing virtuosity." — Alfred Price Quinn, *B'nai B'rith Messenger*, Oct. 5, 1948

*These pianists have appeared several times in the "New Venture" concerts, and as soloists with "Leginska Little Symphony", Wilshire Ebell Theatre, Los Angeles.

Leginska used to say, "If you're going to be a concert pianist you put on blinders." ['blinkers' in the UK]. "Don't see anything else." Four hours' practice in the morning and another four hours after a light lunch was considered perfectly normal by Leginska.

Ron McFarland recalled that his finest moment as a student with Leginska was when she told him, when he was about 16 or 17, "You're probably the most gifted person in my studio. Isn't it a pity that I'm sure it's too late!"

Roberta Hamilton:

Leginska was a perfectionist. She touched our lives in such a way we all benefited. She was highly paid for lessons (though she gave some scholarships) but lived frugally. She was a tremendous disciplinarian, and a great influence on all of us. "No-one could play a phrase like Leginska. To watch her at the piano was incredible. The piano was totally dominated by her hands and mind. When she entered the room there was majesty and total energy." She was immensely strong-willed.

Roberta Hamilton said it was she who gave Leginska a copy of Mark Twain's *Joan of Arc*, which Leginska turned into an opera. [See next chapter. However, Leginska was aware of Mark Twain's version of the book as long ago as 1936, having discussed it then with Edith Ohlson, her collaborator in *The Rose and the Ring*, as their correspondence at the time indicates.] Leginska was more impressed by Mark Twain's version of the story than by G.B. Shaw's.

Leginska was always musical. When teaching the César Franck Variations she would give the music words – 'Do You Love Me', with the answering phrase, 'Yes I Love You.' She gave her students "total confidence that anything was possible". In some ways she was "really sweet" and was "very generous with her time. She loved her students."

Jon Robertson:

Dr Robertson started lessons with Leginska at the age of seven, when she told him, "It's almost too late". He regarded her as "a force"; not just in music, but as an astute theologian and philosopher whose references and similes with regard to life were "overwhelming". The greatest body of musical information he possessed had come from Leginska. The lessons were "terribly intense" and would involve two or three hours of very systematic work. She taught her students how to concentrate.

As in the case of several of the other students, Leginska took him out of 'normal' school. As a black child it was impossible for him to enter the type of school which would have benefited him most as they wouldn't take black pupils. Leginska arranged a private tutor for him. She decided how many hours a day he could play with other children; what clothes he should wear. "She ruled your life. She was oppressive – yet there was a magic about her."

When a student was working for a recital she would sit on a couch behind the pianist as he or she practised, taking notes. "After you'd played about three notes you would hear a scratching sound behind you" as she scribbled; she would produce a sheaf of notes on matters requiring attention. She had a deep work ethic. But she "would work a magical trick before you went on [to the stage], and tell you you'd got terrific talent", so the child walked onto the platform full of confidence. "Backstage, before you went on to give a recital, Leginska would make you believe you could play anything, so you always went on stage on a high."

Once he had four lessons in one day. Having been scheduled for two lessons, Leginska phoned after he had just got home from the first and said there had been a cancellation and she wanted him back. Then having got home again from that one she rang to say there had been another cancellation [as an aside, he said he pitied the person who had made the cancellation!] and he had to return yet again. She nearly always had hard feelings when her former students went back to see her − it was difficult, after leaving, to continue a rapport with her, for she was always hurt that they had left her. Jon Robertson said he was "pained he couldn't give the love back that he had received. She always felt she had more to teach you. She was a giant!"

Jon's father would come to the lessons to take notes. (It will be remembered, from pages 232 and 236, that Leginska insisted that an adult be present to do so.) Leginska was a fierce disciplinarian, and Jon came from a home where the same work ethic and outlook regarding discipline applied, so his father loved Leginska's regime − it was food and drink to him. Jon said, "they ganged up on me!".

Leginska "pushed and pushed" Jon as a child, and sometimes, when he was unable to understand what she wanted, she would stop, and say "come with me". Then she would take him by the hand out into the garden to look at the flowers and would say, "Look at these. Touch them − smell them", and would say "these are the colours I want you to find in your playing". She had a wonderful sense of timing and always knew if a child was near to breaking point. She never took a child beyond that point. But sometimes she would spend a week on three bars of music, until it was just right.

She insisted that a student should listen carefully to the sound he made as he played. She could be very emotional. Once, after he had played well in one of the recitals she had arranged for him, she hugged and kissed him after he walked off the stage amid the applause − and he cried!

Although Jon Robertson had studied as a child pianist with Leginska and enjoyed a very successful career as a pianist, in more recent years he has become a conductor. When he had watched her working with an orchestra, young as he was at the time, he had seen how she moulded it into shape. "Her 'ear' was unbelievable." Jon Robertson said it was a source of great regret to him that he had not been able to study conducting with Leginska. But he owed his success as a conductor to what he had learned from her. He added that he had studied and worked all over the world and met "many wonderful people in music", but no-one of greater magnitude than Leginska. He said the life's work of many of today's top musicians is "a drop in the bucket" compared with what Leginska achieved. She was from another age. "If you could throw away the difficult aspects of her personality, she was a saint!"

Thomas Curtis:

Tom Curtis said he was unusual in that he was about 17 when he started lessons with Leginska. When he arrived for his first lesson he knocked on the studio door − which, he discovered, had been a mistake. She was furious. Leginska's lessons always overran, and the correct procedure, he learned, was to quietly turn the latch and tiptoe into the room, sit down, and listen to the end of the previous lesson. Leginska's pupils, he said, learned a lot from the lessons of the previous student!

Leginska liked to receive Christmas cards with pictures of flowers and animals. He added that Leginska had "a beautiful smile − the warmest smile anyone could give. "If she smiled at you, you would walk out of the studio 10 feet off the ground."

Leginska — Forgotten Genius of Music

Daniel Pollack

Marilyn Neeley

Jon Robertson

This page and opposite: Some of the people quoted in Chapters 15 and 17 photographed in recent years, long after their lessons with Leginska. For brief biographies see pages 280 and 281.

Leginska – Remembered by her Students

Ron McFarland

Esther Lee Kaplan

Summarising these recollections of Leginska's students, a remarkable unanimity of opinion emerges. Without exception they regarded her with awe, considering her to be a totally dominant, even domineering, personality, who ruled their lives, decided what school they should go to, how long and in what way they should practise, what they should wear, and so on. But everyone agreed that she was a wonderful pianist with a complete mastery of her instrument. Her musical skills were immense; music was her life and she had the magnetism and dynamism to impart her wishes and skills to her students. The love-hate relationship was very real; her students adored her and yet they were in awe of her. However, they all agreed that her personality was huge and she had about her an aura of magic.

On the other hand, there was a feeling amongst some that she dominated her students' lives too much. She was never happy when any of them "moved on", even to such eminent teaching organisations as the Juilliard School as many of them did. She said to Jon Robertson, "What can they teach you that I can't?", and he felt, in retrospect, she was right. When anyone left, it was never without a sense of hurt that they had done so. Daniel Pollack studied with her from the ages of six to nine and played concertos in public under her auspices before going on to the Juilliard School; subsequently he made an excellent career as a concert pianist and was (and still is) very well known in the USA and elsewhere. When he went to see Leginska, shortly before her death, when he had already enjoyed a successful career as a concert pianist for nearly 20 years, she said, "And what have you been doing since you left me?"

Her pupils were in a sense her possessions. Marguerite Heller remarked that Leginska was a surrogate mother to them. After the failure of Leginska's marriage and the estrangement from her son, music was all that was left in her life, apart from her love of beauty, nature and literature. She was probably a lonely person. Her pupils were her children and she hated ever to lose any of them.

The 'Leginska Little Symphony' orchestra, referred to earlier, comprised mainly musicians hired from the Los Angeles Philharmonic Orchestra. According to Tom Curtis, the Los Angeles Philharmonic at the time Leginska hired its members was a poor, ragged orchestra. But Leginska "knocked them into shape", he said, when they played in the 'Little Symphony' and moulded them into a remarkably effective ensemble. In his view she was an excellent conductor – and an inspiring teacher. "When that power touches you – it's forever. She was the incarnation of music."

References: Chapter 17

1. Information about Leginska's slightness of build is well documented and comes from many sources: former pupils, newspaper articles, reviews, etc.
2. Beverly Carmen, formerly of Los Angeles, now of Los Alamos, New Mexico. Correspondence from 1984 to the present.
3. Marguerite Heller, Los Angeles, California. Correspondence from 1984 to the present. Mrs Heller (then Marguerite Baum) studied with Leginska for seven years and met her from time to time in later years.
4. Joan Meggett, Alhambra, California. Correspondence, 1982-86.
5. Josef Enos, Benicia, California. Correspondence, 1984-86.
6. Lynnore Dagg, Glendale, California. Correspondence, 1984.
7. Magda Loeb, Los Angeles, California. Correspondence, 1984.
8. Esther Lee Kaplan, Northridge, California, now of New York. Correspondence, 1984.
9. The late Robert Logan, Sun Valley, California. Correspondence, 1984-89.
10. Armando Loredo, Los Angeles, California. Correspondence, 1984.
11. Beverly Carmen. As reference 2.
12. Robert L. Watt, Los Angeles, California. (In the 1980s Mr Watt was a French hornist with the Los Angeles Philharmonic Orchestra.) Correspondence, 1984-87. The information about Leginska's fee of $25/hour for lessons was given to him by Bernice Lawson who knew Leginska.
13. Daniel Pollack, concert pianist, Los Angeles, California. Correspondence, 1984.
14. Radie Britain, composer. Hollywood, Los Angeles. Correspondence (several letters), 1984.
15. Marilyn Neeley, concert pianist and university teacher, Baltimore. Correspondence, 1982-86.
16. Two-hour radio programme *Tribute to Ethel Leginska*; part of the 'Music of the Americas' series, broadcast by KPFK, Los Angeles on Sunday, 6th April 1986 in anticipation of the centenary (seven days later) of Leginska's birth. Leginska's former students taking part were Marguerite Heller, Roberta Hamilton, Ron McFarland, Daniel Pollack, Jon Robertson and Tom Curtis. During the programme some of Leginska's recordings were played, listed here in the order in which they were heard:

Duo-Art piano rolls:
6592	Schultz-Evler	Concert Arabesque on Strauss's *Blue Danube* Waltz	Issued 1/23
6217	Rameau	Gavotte and Variations	Issued 12/19
7137	Mendelssohn	Songs Without Words Nos. 44, Op. 102, No. 2 and No. 10, Op. 30, No. 4	Issued 7/27

Gramophone recordings (Columbia 78s, recorded 8th March 1928; issued 1928):
17013D, 17014D Schubert *Moments Musicaux*, No. 1 in C major and part of No. 2 in A flat major

Duo-Art piano roll:
7396	Liszt	Hungarian Rhapsody No. 8 in F sharp minor	Issued 5/30

Brief biographies of some of Leginska's former students quoted in this chapter and chapter 15:

Joseph Enos: Pianist, formerly staff pianist and organist at NBC's studios in Hollywood.

Esther Lee Kaplan: A native of Pennsylvania. At the age of 11 whilst studying with Leginska she performed the Saint-Saëns Piano Concerto No. 2 with the Los Angeles Philharmonic Orchestra, Alfred Wallenstein conducting. Later she attended the Juilliard School where she studied under Rosina Lhevinne and Irwin Freundlich. Subsequently she has performed extensively as a soloist and with chamber musicians throughout the United States. The *Los Angeles Times* has commented on her performances as possessing "a scintillating brilliance, displaying an unusual depth of tone and a commendable command of the keyboard". She records for the Cambria label.

The late Robert Logan: Musician who went to Leginska for lessons in orchestration. His mother, who was a musician and formerly president of American Artists Inc, also had lessons with Leginska.

Beverly Carmen: Pianist who also plays piano in chamber music groups; teacher and writer of musical reviews. One of Leginska's first pupils in Los Angeles.

Daniel Pollack: Concert pianist whose career has taken him across five continents – North America, Europe, Asia, South America and Africa. Major orchestras with which he has appeared include the New York Philharmonic, Los Angeles Philharmonic, Moscow State Philharmonic and London Philharmonic.

After his study with Leginska he studied with Rosina Lhevinne at the Juilliard School and later at the Hochschule für Music in Vienna under a Fulbright Scholarship. He has given solo recitals in most of the world's major music centres including London's Royal Festival Hall, Vienna's Musikverein, Amsterdam's Concertgebouw, New York's Carnegie Hall and has made guest appearances at many important music centres including Tchaikovsky's home in Kline, Russia where he played the composer's piano.

He is in demand on international juries having participated several times on the Tchaikovsky competition in Moscow (in which he was a former prize-winner) and Montreal, Leeds and many others worldwide. He has held many academic positions and is currently in the music faculty of the University of Southern California.

The late Radie Britain: Distinguished American composer whose biography is on page 194. Worked with Leginska and her orchestras in the 1920s.

Marilyn Neeley: Concert pianist and professor of piano and faculty adviser in chamber music and vocal accompanying at The Catholic University of America. At age 10 won the Forest Lawn-Hollywood Bowl competition for instrumentalists up to age 15. As a young teenager was twice soloist with the Los Angeles Philharmonic Orchestra with Alfred Wallenstein conducting. Later was prize-winner in the Van Cliburn, Leventritt, Michaels, and Geneva competitions with solo appearances with over one hundred symphony orchestras including the Chicago Symphony, the Boston Symphony and the Los Angeles Philharmonic. Recipient of the Outstanding Alumna of the School of Music and Distinguished Alumna of the University awards from the University of Southern California. Recent Convention Artist for the Pennsylvania, Tennessee, Georgia, Oregon and Alabama State Music Teachers' Associations, Georgia Music Educators, and the Juilliard School. Recorded the complete Beethoven violin and piano sonatas with her husband Robert Gerle and received an Emmy Award for their videotape of these for public television. Released a compact disc of solo piano music of Brahms, Mozart, Debussy and Liszt. Teaches on the summer faculty of Brevard Music Center in North Carolina. Studied with Leginska for 14 years (age five to nineteen).

Marguerite Heller: California State winner in a nationwide piano competition which won an engagement at Carnegie Hall. Currently pianist and teacher, very well-known in the Los Angeles area.

Ron McFarland: Under Leginska was the first person to perform Arensky's F-minor Concerto in Los Angeles. After his studies with Leginska and lessons on composition with Arnold Schoenberg he started his musical career as a pianist and appeared very successfully in that capacity before moving to New Orleans where he abandoned music for a while and began a career as an artist. Whilst in New Orleans he renewed his piano studies under the Hungarian pianist Istvan Nadas. When Nadas took up a teaching post at San Francisco, McFarland decided to move back to California and his thoughts returned to a piece of music he had worked on with Schoenberg. He soon decided to make the commitment to spend the rest of his life writing music. Many of his compositions have been performed by major orchestras and his recorded work has appeared on a number of compact discs.

Dr Jon Robertson: Jon's career as a concert pianist began at the age of nine with his debut in the Town Hall, New York. At the same age he won a competition for artists under 16. Appeared as a child pianist on the Eddie Cantor Television show the following year (1953) at 10 years of age. Later, as an adult, he played in many concerts in Europe and South America. His degrees were in piano performance but after studying choral conducting under Abraham Kaplan at the Juilliard School and orchestral conducting with Richard Pittman of the New England Conservatory he decided to move from piano playing as his primary work to conducting. As a conductor he has appeared in many countries and is currently Principal Guest Conductor of the Armenian Philharmonic Orchestra. He is now in his 18th year as conductor and music director of the Redlands Symphony Orchestra in California.

Some websites:

Daniel Pollack: http://www.danielpollack.com/bio.htm
Radie Britain: http://www.musicweb.uk.net/classrev/2001/June01/Radie.htm
Marilyn Neeley: http://music.cua.edu/FACULTY/neeley.html
Ron McFarland: http://www.eroica.com/rm-artist.html
Jon Robertson: http://newton.uor.edu/RedlandsSymphony/conductor.htm

Chapter 18

Indian Summer

In 1960 there was another highlight in Ethel Leginska's long and distinguished career – an event which combined her talents of pianist, composer and conductor. A programme of her compositions was presented on 12th May at the Wilshire Ebell Theatre (on Wilshire Boulevard, Los Angeles) by a number of soloists and a small chamber orchestra (see pages 340-343 for the printed programme). Leginska accompanied the singers at the piano in the vocal pieces, as well as conducting the orchestra. At 74, age seems not to have wearied her unduly according to the several reviews that appeared in the press.* Rachel Morton reported on the day after the concert: [1]

Ethel Leginska Performs in Concert of Own Works

"At one time Ethel Leginska was one of the most famous of women pianists. Coming from England she took this country by storm. I can still see her with her shock of curly dark hair and magnetic personality thrilling Carnegie Hall audiences. Thursday night in the Wilshire Ebell Theatre she presented herself as a composer, conductor and accompanist in a program of her own compositions. There was still the heavy shock of curly hair, now graying, and the same vital personality, although time has frailed the lithe figure.

"Mme Leginska has many talents. She assembled a remarkable group of musicians for this concert, several of whom are members of the Los Angeles Philharmonic Orchestra, and there were three vocal soloists.

"A chamber music work, 'From a Life' played by 11 instruments, opened the program. In this number, as in all of her music, there was serious and interesting harmonic treatment, mostly in a minor key.

"Katherine Hilgenberg, contralto, sang five songs by Leginska, with the composer at the piano. These songs were all tragic and sad. Miss Hilgenberg brought out all the dramatic intensity required.

"Steve Stagner, a tenor with a very high voice and a passionate interpretive sense, sang four songs with Mme Leginska accompanying him. Of these, 'Oh Lovely Moon' and 'I have a Rendezvous with Death' were especially fine. Four poems by Tagore were set to music by Mme Leginska and played by the Arioso String Quartet with great artistry and beautiful tonal color.

---

* As far as can be ascertained this was the last occasion at which Leginska appeared in public as a performing artist. In view of the consequent historic nature of the occasion (though this is evident only with the benefit of hindsight) five reviews of the evening's performance are quoted here. Interestingly, in two of them the venue is referred to as the 'Wilshire Ebell Theater', in two as the 'Wilshire Ebell Theatre' (its true name) and in the other merely as the 'Wilshire Ebell'. Wilshire Boulevard where the theatre is located is a 16-mile-long thoroughfare running through Los Angeles to Santa Monica and the Pacific Ocean. It was named after the eccentric, entrepreneurial millionaire Henry Gaylord Wilshire (1852-1927).

"After intermission, the program was enlivened by six gay nursery rhymes sung delightfully by a beautiful blonde soprano, Kristina Kohler. She and the tenor joined in two duets from Mme Leginska's opera buffa, 'The Rose and the Ring'.

"A chamber music work for 11 instruments, 'Triptych', was conducted with vigor and sensitivity."

A complimentary review by Alma Gowdy appeared in *The Los Angeles Herald and Express*, another daily paper: [2]

Leginska Program Well Received

"Ethel Leginska, one of the world's distinguished musicians now resident in Los Angeles, last night presented a program of her compositions at Wilshire Ebell Theater. Acting both as accompanist and conductor, she selected chamber music, songs and opera buffa solos and duets from her long list of creative works.

"Most revealing of her vast musical experience were the chamber music works, all of which had received earlier praise from leading critics when they were performed by famous ensembles in New York and Europe.

"Among the vocal groups were five songs performed by Katherine Hilgenberg, contralto with the San Francisco Opera Company.

"A cycle of Six Nursery Rhymes for Soprano and Chamber Orchestra were full of the rare Leginska humor. Although sung with considerable style by soprano Kristina Kohler, the orchestration made merry with 'Jack and Jill' and 'Old King Cole'.

"Some of the best musicians in Southern California were among the instrumentalists assisting. The Arioso String Quartet and 21 orchestra players were bolstered by members from the Los Angeles Philharmonic Orchestra and such favorites as Abraham Weiss, violist; Natalie Limonick, pianist; Vladimir Drucker, French horn and Arthur Cleghorn, flutist."

A third daily paper, the Los Angeles-based *Citizen News,* also reported on Leginska's concert the following day in a review by Richard D. Saunders. [3]

Leginska's Conducting Has Warmth

"A varied and interesting program of compositions by Ethel Leginska was presented by several excellent soloists and a chamber orchestra of first-rate players conducted by the composer to a warmly approbative audience in the Wilshire Ebell Theater last night.

"The concepts were diverse but always artistic and treated with musicianly skill. The instrumental works held the most breadth, being given thematic development. The songs were mostly brief, with terse moods or else moods so quickly changing that the listener hardly had time to assimilate them.

"Particularly well-knit were 'Four Poems' for string quartet, inspired by Tagore poems. They were admirably interpreted by the Arioso String Quartet of Ralph Schaeffer, Joseph Livoti, Abraham Weiss and Nino Rosso, which gave the lines their obvious intent of simulated vocalism.

"An effective 'Triptych' for 11 instruments held a delightful folk lilt of almost Celtic color in its first movement, followed by a melancholy Lento and a rather angularly dancy Allegretto. For a similar combination was 'From a Life', alternately reflective and energetic movements in the first two movements and ending with an insouciant vivace.

The Wilshire Ebell Theatre where the 'Evening with Leginska' was held. It was, and still is, a popular venue for Californian musical events.

"Katherine Hilgenberg's lovely, warm mezzo-soprano tones made the most of five eloquent art songs that demanded and received the utmost accuracy in delivering difficult intervals with secure intonation. Kristina Kohler enhanced her limpid, pliant soprano with appropriate facial expressions in delivering a cycle of 'Six Nursery Rhymes' with the chamber orchestra.

"A group of four songs, heard for the first time anywhere, was enjoyably proffered by Steve Stagner in an appealing lyric tenor. And two duets from the opera buffa, 'The Rose and the Ring', formed the conclusion with Stagner and Miss Kohler, each of whom had encored with solos from the same work.

"Miss Leginska conducted the ensembles with a firm and knowledgeable hand, as well as providing the piano accompaniment for Miss Kohler and tenor Stagner. And special mention should be made of Natalie Limonick's admirable pianism in the chamber groups."

Writing in the *Los Angeles Examiner* four days after the concert, Patterson Greene not only reviewed the concert of Leginska's music and a performance of 'La Traviata' the next day, but also took a swipe at the citizens of Los Angeles for their apparent lack of interest in the musical scene in their city: [4]

Leginska and 'La Traviata' Admirable Presentations

"Two musical events of the last week filled me with admiration and discouragement:

"Admiration for the interesting compositions of Ethel Leginska, expertly performed at the Wilshire Ebell Thursday night, and for a musically top-notch presentation of 'La Traviata' in the same theater Friday evening.

"Discouragement over this city's indifference to its rich musical potential.

"Many of the Leginska works have won high praise in other music centers but though Mme Leginska has lived here for about twenty years, passing her great musical knowledge to a younger generation, most of the numbers on the program bore the notation "first Los Angeles performance".

"Certainly our several string quartets should explore the Four Poems after Rabindranath Tagore – including an exquisitely graceful portrait of 'a musk-deer in the shadow of the forest'. Her 'Triptych' for 11 instruments is harmonically bold, thematically original and orchestrally knowledgeable.

"Her songs, notably 'In a Garden' and six mischievous 'Nursery Rhymes' were sung skilfully by Steve Stagner and Kristina Kohler respectively. I liked also the charmingly melodious duets from Mme Leginska's comic opera based on Thackeray's 'The Rose and the Ring".

In the month after the concert a review by Evelyn Seifert appeared in the *Music of the West Magazine*: [5]

Leginska

"A highly artistic performance of compositions by Ethel Leginska kept a devoted audience until the last stroke of the baton at the Wilshire Ebell Theatre May 12. A program of art songs, many sung for the first time anywhere, instrumental music for chamber orchestra, and excerpts from the Opera Buffa 'The Rose and the Ring' provided

'An Evening with Leginska', for this musically-gifted woman not only led a hand-picked 26-piece chamber music orchestra but accompanied the soloists at the piano.

"The composer – conductor – pianist was assisted by the Arioso String Quartet, a chamber music orchestra composed of many from the Los Angeles Philharmonic, and three soloists, Katherine Hilgenberg, contralto; Kristina Kohler, soprano, and Steve Stagner, tenor. The programmed works included 'From a Life' for eleven instruments, Four Poems for string quartet (after Tagore), 'Triptych' for eleven instruments, Cycle of Six Nursery Rhymes for soprano and orchestra, and two groups of art songs.

"Miss Leginska proved that she is not only endowed with the gift of composing but is a sensitive and skilful conductor as well as a fine pianist. She provided excellent accompaniments for Miss Hilgenberg and Steve Stagner in their performance of the varied and difficult songs. Everyone, the soloists and players, performed with artistry and obvious warm regard for Miss Leginska."

Clearly, in spite of her age Leginska had lost little if any of her skill in making the most of the limited resources available to her. She seemed as energetic as ever and at 74 was still, as the last review avers, a fine pianist.

Leginska's home had been in the United States (New York, Boston and Los Angeles) ever since she made her remarkable debut as a pianist in New York in 1913 at the age of 26. And, as explained in Chapter 5 (page 63) she had been a citizen of the USA since her marriage in 1907. Having made her home in the USA it would have been pointless for her ever to have applied to become a British citizen once again. Consequently she retained her American nationality from 1907 when she married to the end of her life. But it is doubtful whether her many friends and admirers ever considered the legal aspects of her nationality. They thought of her as 'English' and she is generally referred to in American books and articles as an English musician.

Although she had sometimes visited her Yorkshire home in the earlier years of her American sojourn until her father died, and had performed in Britain and in continental Europe in the 1920s and 1930s, her forays across the Atlantic over the years since 1913 had been relatively few, though, as recorded in Chapter 14 (page 217), she hired a cottage in Suffolk in the early 1930s in order to work on her operas in quiet surroundings, and she lived in London for a while in the late 1930s. After she gave up her performing career in 1939 and settled to the more sedate life of a piano teacher in Los Angeles, contacts with Britain appear to have been sparse. After the death of her father in 1928 the only remaining member of her immediate family, since she had no siblings, was her stepmother, and when she died in 1955 most family contacts appear to have ceased.[6] But she did keep in touch with some old friends in East Yorkshire. In 1961 the *Hull Daily Mail* reported:[7]

"Hull-born pianist Madame Ethel Leginska, who achieved world-wide fame as a teenage prodigy 50 years ago, is still actively pursuing her musical career.

Indian Summer

"Although she has been living in America since 1913, she keeps in touch with relatives and friends, and has sent Mrs Irene Jackson, of Cuthbert Avenue, Airlie Street, Boulevard, * a programme of a concert she presented recently in Los Angeles.**

"For the past 20 years Madame Leginska has made her home on the west coast and her studio at 254, South Hobart, Los Angeles, 4, California, is a venue for artists from all parts of the world.

"Composer, conductor and accompanist, Madame Leginska was once described by a German music critic as achieving 'a place of honour among the modern composers'.

"In addition to being a prolific composer, she has conducted many orchestras, including the Boston Philharmonic and concerts at the Hollywood Bowl.

"At her latest concert in Los Angeles, Madame Leginska not only conducted a hand-picked 26-piece chamber music orchestra, but accompanied three soloists at the piano, in a programme of her own compositions.

"Before adopting a professional name for her musical career Madame Leginska was Miss Ethel Liggins, of Pemberton St, Hull.

"Her father was an architect, the late Mr Thomas E. Liggins who lived in Hull and Hornsea, and Bridlington people may recall her step-mother, the late Mrs C.B. Liggins, who lived in Richmond Street for many years.

"Madame Leginska's friendship with Mrs Jackson dates back to their early youth when they both lived in Bridlington." †

Shortly after the "All Leginska" concert of 1960 that has just been described she became ill. Breast cancer was diagnosed and a mastectomy operation was performed. At 74, after an illustrious professional career of well over half a century, Leginska could have been forgiven had she decided to 'call it a day' and drift into a well-earned retirement. But that was not her style. Her whole life was devoted to music and it is impossible to visualise Leginska ever abandoning her involvement; inactivity was anathema to her. Dedicated and almost as energetic as ever, it was not long before she was back in circulation and resuming her role as a full-time teacher.

And so, as the 1960s unfurled and the music of The Beatles hit Europe and America, Ethel Leginska, who was born three months before Liszt died and had learned her early musical skills in the reign of Queen Victoria, continued quietly and efficiently to pass on some of her vast knowledge to a new generation of musicians. By the mid-1960s Bob Dylan had informed the world that "The times, they are a-changin'", but for Leginska they were not. She celebrated her 80th birthday on 13th April 1966 and even after that

---

* Cuthbert Avenue is in west Hull, about two miles from the city centre.

** This would have been the concert of May 1960, of which the reviews are quoted earlier in the chapter.

† The report does not explain that not only did Ethel's stepmother live at Richmond Street, Bridlington; her father lived there also, with his wife, from 1913 until his death in 1928. To set the record straight, Ethel did not live in Bridlington 'in her early youth' but often visited, and she would have visited her father and stepmother there, and friends, on rare occasions, after 1913.

notable event the regular pattern of her teaching life continued in much the same way as it had for the previous 27 years.

Ethel Leginska in her late 70s and early 80s was still not finished as a composer. It was in these years that she finalised the music of another opera, 'Joan of Arc', based on a libretto by Mark Twain. The work was presented at the same venue as some of her other successes in Los Angeles, the Wilshire Ebell Theatre, with Anne Marie Biggs in the title role. Advance notice of the forthcoming event was given in October 1968: [8]

NEW OPERA ARRIVING:
Anne Marie Biggs Set for
'Joan of Arc' Opera

"Anne Marie Biggs has been signed for the title role of 'Joan of Arc' in a new opera by British-born composer and conductor Ethel Leginska, which will receive its world premiere in a concertized version Sunday afternoon, Oct. 27 at 2.30 p.m. in Wilshire Ebell Theatre.

"Among the more versatile of younger U.S. sopranos, Miss Biggs has sung leading roles in New York, Chicago, Paris and west coast opera houses; Broadway shows, recordings and motion pictures.

"She may currently be heard singing the title music for Warner Bros.' 'The Illustrated Man' and, on the other end of the musical scale, the soprano lead in a new Angel recording of Carl Orff's 'Catulli Carmina' with the Roger Wagner Master Chorale.

The signing of Miss Biggs as the Maid of Orleans has sentimental significance for music history buffs. Her father, the late famed organist Richard Keys Biggs, appeared with Miss Leginska in the 1910s and 1920s when, as one of the very few successful women baton-wielders, she was conducting the New York Symphony, Paris Conservatoire, etc."

The concert version of the work referred to in this announcement was abandoned before it took place in favour of a full stage presentation to be held the following year. Leginska rehearsed the work over a period of several months but, sadly, she was not feeling well in the weeks before the performance and did not conduct it. The work was staged, and billed as 'The Gala World Premiere' on Saturday, 10th May 1969. A poster advertising the opera is shown opposite but there were some changes in personnel for the actual performance. The conductor on the night was in fact Mr Bogidar Avramov and the performance was staged by Mr Henry Reese.

Anne Marie Biggs, who sang the title role of Joan, has written to the authors, recalling the opera and her part in it: [9]

"Regarding my singing the title role in the world première of 'Joan of Arc' by Ethel Leginska: Mme Leginska was an extraordinarily unique personality – completely outspoken when necessary, gentle through her loving nature, (an elfin-like sense of humor with a devilish sparkle in her eye). Her untiring persistence towards perfection (which reminded me of my own teacher) I enjoyed thoroughly, during the months of

Indian Summer

Poster advertising Leginska's opera 'Joan of Arc'

Photograph used by Leginska in the printed programme of Joan of Arc

preparation. She had been searching for years for 'Her Joan', she said to me after my audition, "At last I've found my Joan – a voice and a musician with graceful drama and spirituality!"

"It wasn't until we had been working together on the opera that I remembered my father's association with her early in his career as organist under her orchestral direction. My father, Dr Richard Keys Biggs – celebrated organist, composer, director – made the first commercial organ record in 1916 for Victor Records, which led to a long and brilliant career in the United States and abroad. The fact that my mother was born in Angers, France and that I had always honored the French Saint Joan assisted in my involvement. During a concert tour in France, I had visited her shrines along the route to meet my many relatives. Yes, this role was meant for me.

"The fact that she wanted not a warrior Joan but the Maiden Joan (as portrayed in Mark Twain's writings) caused some critics to complain; but that's what she insisted upon with me and the stage director. Although, she had composed scenes with Joan surely depicted as the strong defender in the familiar armor – which satisfied the director, as well. And so I began the memorizing of the 70 pages allotted to my portrayal of the Maid of Orleans. The music – which I enjoyed very much – I found to be contemporary and yet very lyrically melodious. The entrance passages were not the easiest, and I was grateful to be able to rely upon my pitch and the years of my musical training.

"I believe she knew she had little time left in her life to promote her endeavors. She, at first, scheduled the opera in a concert version which was later replaced by a more elaborate, full stage presentation. Madame Leginska was most assuredly satisfied and overjoyed with the performance, and she proceeded to start working on her "Gale the

Indian Summer

Signed photograph given by Ethel Leginska to Anne Marie Biggs, inscribed "After looking for my Joan over ten years, in Anne Marie Biggs I found my dream. All my love to you, Ethel Leginska."

(Photograph courtesy of Miss Biggs)

Haunting" opera (in which I also sang at the Wilshire Ebell Theatre). * I understand John Charles Thomas sang the original performance.

"I am proud of the tribute/assignment she allowed me, and grateful for the photograph she gave me of her with her baton (see page 291) – and the inscription:

'After looking for my Joan over ten years, in Anne Marie Biggs I found my dream. All my love to you, Ethel Leginska. †"

Miss Biggs also told the authors a touching little story which somehow epitomises Leginska's care, and her love for the piano, even at the age of 82:

"Her piano was her child and love. My youngest son, John, was privileged to have been asked at the age of seven to sit at her piano. She knew he had shown the talent left in him by my late father (who had died shortly after John's birth in 1962). 'Not so hard on those precious keys, if you please, you must caress them', she would say. I too had appreciated those moments, for I had also studied keyboard and other instruments, as well as the ballet."

The performance of Joan of Arc was reviewed in the *Los Angeles Times* but drew only lukewarm praise, partly because, as indicated earlier, the critics would have preferred a 'warrior' Joan, which was contrary to Leginska's wishes. Referring to Leginska, the paper reported: [10]

"Her Joan of Arc with a libretto based on Mark Twain's Personal Recollections of Joan of Arc received a world premiere by the Los Angeles Lyric Opera in Wilshire Ebell Theater Saturday night. The opera in two acts and five scenes is actually more of a series of comparatively brief vignettes, highlighting the events of Joan's turbulent career, than an integrated music drama. Some 20 characters appear in the course of the narrative.

"For this sequence of still-lifes Miss Leginska has provided music of naive and artless simplicity. Only occasionally is the placid surface ruffled by suggestions of conflict or disturbing drama. She does write tunes, and lots of them, singable tunes, mostly of ballad-like character that often display the voices to pleasant advantage."

Complimenting some of the lead singers on their performances, the reviewer noted that Anne Marie Biggs sang "with a lyric soprano of sizable dimensions and agreeable quality, all nicely controlled". Earl Wilkie, in the narrator's role as Le Sieur de Conte, "made it sound impressive", Ray Gagen as the Dauphin "sang in a firm, ringing tenor voice" and Arthur F. Edwards made "a forbidding appearance" as the Bishop of Beauvais. The review noted that the musicians in the orchestra pit comprised members of the Los Angeles Philharmonic Orchestra.

---

* The date of the Los Angeles performance of 'Gale' is not known, but it was probably staged soon after 'Joan of Arc'.

† Clearly the opera had been in Leginska's mind for a number of years. Leginska's correspondence indicates that she had discussed the possibility of an opera based on the story of Joan of Arc with Edith Ohlson as long ago as the mid-1930s (see pages 274 and 329).

Indian Summer

Saturday Evening, May 10, 1969 at 8:30 p.m.

LOS ANGELES LYRIC OPERA
Irwin Parnes, General Director

presents

The World Premiere Performance of

"JOAN OF ARC"

An Opera in Two Acts (Five Scenes) by

ETHEL LEGINSKA

Libretto from MARK TWAIN'S book, "Personal Recollections of Joan of Arc" based upon manuscripts in the National Archives of France.

featuring

ANNE MARIE BIGGS
as the Maid of Lorraine

MEMBERS OF THE LOS ANGELES PHILHARMONIC
Conducted by **BOGIDAR AVRAMOV**

Chorus Director	*Stage Director*
CURTIS STEARNS	**MANFRED ULBRICH**

Ballet Choreography	*Stage Manager*	*Assistant Stage Manager*
KATHRYN ETIENNE	**RICK DAVIS**	**JOE BILLINGS**

This page and pages 294 and 295:
Pages from the printed programme of 'Joan of Arc'
(Courtesy of Anne Marie Biggs)

THE CAST
(in order of appearance)

Le Sieur Louis de Conte, Joan's Page and Secretary	EARL WILKIE
Haumette, Mengette, (Playmates of Joan)	LOUISE PIXA IRENE FUENTES
Pierre, Joan's brother	RICHARD NELSON
Joan	ANNE MARIE BIGGS
Benoist, an escaped madman	RICK DAVIS
St. Michael	MARIO LEONETTI
St. Catherine	ADRIENNE LEONETTI
St. Margaret	MARIA DELORES FERRACIOLI
Robert de Baudricourt, Governor of Vaucouleurs	TED HURWOOD
Jean de Metz, a Cavalier	ALLEN WEST
Court Tailor	RICHARD NELSON
The Dauphin, Disinherited Charles VII	RAY GAGAN
Mistress of the Dauphin's Court	PATTI WINSTON
La Tremouille, Dauphin's Minister	JOHN DYAR
Count of Vendome	JACK VANDER LAAN
D'Arc, Father of Joan	TED HURWOOD
Cauchon, Bishop of Beauvais	ARTHUR F. EDWARDS
Loyseleur, a spy for the English	DOMENIC SUNZERI
Secular Judge	WILLARD BRISTOL

Villagers, Courtiers, Court Dancers, Heralds, Soldiers, Choir Boys, Ecclesiastics

TIME and PLACE: Fifteenth Century France (1428-1431)

ACT ONE

Scene One: A clearing in the forest of Domremy.
Scene Two: Throne Room, Castle of Chinon.

INTERMISSION

ACT TWO

Scene One: Rheims Cathedral, Coronation Day.
Scene Two: Court of Justice, Chapel of Fortress at Rouen.
Scene Three: Rouen, in the Old Market Square.

CHORUS PERSONNEL

Sopranos: Linda Cole, Virginia Gagan, Joyce Jodon, Louise Pixa, Linda Shue, Frances Weiss

Altos: Betty Bruce, Irene Fuentes, Martha Marty, Joan Zatac

Tenors: Eldon Chown, John Radic, Domenic Sunzeri, Lionel West

Basses: Willard Bristol, John Dyar, James Mirachi, Eugene Reise

CREDITS

Blessed Sacrament Church Boy's Choir directed by Frank C. Brownstead.
Publicity by Joy Parnes.
Banners executed by Belinda Hannick and the Villa Cabrini High School Art Department.
Exploitation Art by Allen Tench.
Joan's costumes designed by Miss Biggs.
Costumes designed and executed by Logan Costume Company.

THE ARTISTS

ETHEL LEGINSKA began her extraordinary career – virtuoso pianist, conductor and composer – over seventy-five years ago as a child prodigy of six. At fourteen, she became a pupil of the master pedagogue, Leschetizky; at sixteen, she made her official debut as orchestral soloist under the baton of Sir Henry Wood in London. Hailed as "a great pianist" in London, "an artist of distinction . . . a master" in New York, and "a splendid genius" in Munich, she was soon engaged as recitalist and as soloist with practically all of the prominent orchestras in Europe and America, attracting record-breaking audiences.

She became well known as a composer, her orchestral works being performed by such prominent organizations as the Boston Symphony Orchestra, Pierre Monteux conducting; New York Symphony, Albert Coates conducting; Berlin Philharmonic, etc.

Leginska was the first woman in musical history to be invited to conduct most of the world's great orchestras – the Boston Symphony, New York Philharmonic, London Symphony Orchestra, Paris Conservatoire Orchestra, Hollywood Bowl Orchestra, Koncertverein Orchestra of Munich, etc. She was also the first of her sex to be engaged as grand opera conductor, appearing with the San Carlo Opera, Chicago City Opera Company, Paris Opera, Salzburg and her own Opera in English Company.

ANNE MARIE BIGGS (Joan) made her stage debut at the age of eight – as a ballet dancer – having won a scholarship with a pupil of Pavlova. After studying piano and organ with her celebrated father, composer Richard Keys Biggs, she was awarded a violin study scholarship, which was cut short by her theatre debut, as a dramatic actress.

Growing up in Hollywood, singing in the choirs of her father and mother, she often substituted as director for her busy parents. Her debut on the "musical" stage was in *The Waltz King* at the Chicago City Opera House before going on to Broadway's *Music in My Heart*. She has sung leading roles in light and grand opera – including Marguerite in Faust, Susanna in *The Marriage of Figaro*, Rosina in *The Barber of Seville* and Violetta in *La Traviata* in Los Angeles, Chicago, Laguna Beach, New York and France. She has been soloist with the Valley Symphony, Los Angeles Philharmonic, Beverly Hills and Hollywood Orchestras.

Her folk songs from European concerts have been broadcast throughout France. She was chosen by director King Vidor for MGM's *American Romance*, and her voice has been featured in such solo sound tracks as *Out of the Tiger's Mouth*, filmed in Hong Kong and Maceo, *The Sound of Music*, *The Illustrated Man* and a forthcoming Elvis Presley film based on the historic Chautauqua Circuit.

Miss Biggs has made appearances at the Los Angeles Music Center with the Roger Wagner Master Chorale in Carl Orff's "Catulli Carmina", which she has since recorded for Angel Records.

Biographical details of Ethel Leginska and Anne Marie Biggs, as given in the printed programme of 'Joan of Arc'

References: Chapter 18

1. *Press Telegram*, Long Beach, California, 13th May 1960.
2. *Los Angeles Herald and Express*, 13th May 1960.
3. *Citizen News*, 13th May 1960.
4. *Los Angeles Examiner*, 16th May 1960.
5. *Music of the West Magazine*, June 1960.
6. The late Mrs Margorie Langdale, Ethel Leginska's cousin, informed the authors in 1982 that family attempts to contact Leginska in the post-World War II years met with no response. This rather contradicts the report in the *Hull Daily Mail* (reference 7) that Leginska kept in touch with 'relatives' as well as friends. But Leginska had corresponded with her Aunt Lucy (Witty) in the 1930s, and presumably with her stepmother until her death in 1955.
7. *Hull Daily Mail*, 6th January 1961.
8. *Citizen News*, 21st October 1968.
9. Information sent to the authors by Anne Marie Biggs in April 1985. Note that Miss Biggs's father, the celebrated organist Richard Keys Biggs, is not to be confused with the well-known English-born organist, E. Power Biggs (1906 - 1977) who spent most of his career in the United States and became an American citizen in 1937.
10. *Los Angeles Times*, 12th May 1969.

Chapter 19

Journey's End

The production of *Joan of Arc* at the Wilshire Ebell Theatre in 1969 proved to be the highlight of Leginska's final years. Shortly before it was staged she had been put on medication to alleviate the effects of arteriosclerotic heart disease (hardening of the arteries of the heart), a natural process of ageing but probably aggravated in her case by a near-lifetime of smoking. It was this that had prevented her conducting her opera. Even Leginska could not retain her seemingly endless health and vigour for ever. Nevertheless she continued to teach, albeit on a reduced scale compared with former years, and to work on revisions of her operas. Life continued as normally as her advancing years would allow.

On 22nd February 1970, nine months after the Los Angeles production of *Joan of Arc*, Leginska was playing the piano at her studio when she suffered a stroke and collapsed to the ground.[1] She was taken to the Queen of Angels Hospital in Los Angeles but the stroke, caused by cerebral arteriosclerosis, had been massive and there was little that medical science could do to help. She died peacefully at 5.15a.m. on Thursday, 26th February, four days after her admission to hospital.[2] The vigorous, vibrant spirit that had given so much to the world of music was at last stilled.

Leginska's death was registered by her attorney, John W. Erpelding of 1100 Glendon Avenue, Los Angeles. The death certificate is shown on page 300. Cremation was arranged and the funeral took place at Forest Lawn Memorial Park Cemetery at Glendale, California on 4th March 1970, preceded by a service at the Wee Kirk o' Heather Chapel.[3] A number of Leginska's former students, friends, and several of the musicians who had appeared in *Joan of Arc* were there. According to Leginska's former pupil Beverly Carmen it was a gloomy, wet day, in keeping with the sadness of the occasion.

The funeral was also attended by Leginska's son, Cedric, with whom she appears to have had little contact over the years; some of those present believed he had paid for the funeral. * Leginska's many friends and pupils (past and present) were amazed, meeting him there, to discover that he had evidently been in Los Angeles all the time Leginska had lived in the city. In all those years he had never been present at a studio recital and whenever

---

* The fact that Cedric might have paid for the funeral is not at all surprising. He was the only relative Leginska had in the USA, apart from her grandchildren, and until Leginska's estate was wound up and probate obtained, the funeral would have had to have been paid for by someone.

she had spoken of him it had always been in terms of events of the distant past. It has recently been established that Cedric died in 1988. *

Marguerite Heller (Marguerite Baum in the days when she had studied with Leginska) wrote a brief eulogy on her teacher, consisting of a few random thoughts, and sent it to the Minister officiating at the funeral, who read it out. It is reproduced here with her permission:

TRIBUTE TO ETHEL LEGINSKA
By Marguerite Heller

"Emerson said, 'All great men find eternity affirmed in the very promise of their faculties'. Ethel Leginska continued to the very last moment to realize her promise.

"Although she has passed our physical scene, her unswerving and all-encompassing dedication and devotion to music as pianist, conductor, composer and piano pedagogue remain a musical melody that will linger on.

"Her life's pulse was music and she literally breathed music all the days of her years.

"An everlasting, incandescent musical fire continued to ignite young people who met her. She was selfless in her inspiration to share with you without any reservation her vast musical knowledge. She lost herself always in music which was greater than herself and therefore found herself more fully.

"She was a severe musical taskmaster and highly disciplined herself. She had the capacity to inspire pupils to develop a greater talent than they thought they had.

"She savored and relished every precious moment of life. Her enthusiasm remained buoyant and youthful in spite of her years. She chose her own path in life and loved and valued life.

"She found God in nature and thrilled with all of the wonders of living life. A tiny wild flower, a freesia, highly scented, growing in her yard, was cherished by Leginska when she walked outdoors for a moment away from her piano.

"As she was sensitively aware of all living nature she respected those men and women who realized their potential in the arts and literature.

"She believed in life after death and wished to be reunited with loved ones long past gone.

"There will be music in heaven with her oncoming spirit.

"Life was action, and she would not want us to grieve for her, but to remember her through her great musical spirit and her musical achievements as an immortal, mortal woman."

---

* Unfortunately, all the efforts of the authors during the 1980s to locate Leginska's son Cedric, helped by several of her former students in Los Angeles and elsewhere working on our behalf, were unsuccessful. Several of Leginska's students believed he had been a dentist by profession but by the early 1980s when our work began no trace of him could be found in telephone directories, dental association lists of members, or by any other means. Mrs Margaret Stockbridge (née Liggins) has recently established during her researches into the Liggins family history that Cedric died on 7th September 1988 in Northern California, five days before his 80th birthday. His last residence had been at Shingletown, Shasta, California. This information is now available through the U.S. Social Security Death Index, via the Internet.

Certified copy of Ethel Leginska's death certificate. The fact that her date of birth and maiden surname are incorrect is not significant. It merely means that the informant (her attorney) did not know for certain. Her nationality as given (citizen of USA) is correct. Her social security number, correctly given, was acquired in 1952. Note that the cause of her death was shown as a) Cerebrovascular accident [stroke], b) Cerebral arteriosclerosis as a consequence of arteriosclerotic heart disease. The fact that she had undergone a mastectomy for cancer about ten years previously was also noted.

The seeming appropriateness of Leginska's fatal collapse occurring whilst she was seated at the piano was not lost on her former students. Beverly Carmen wrote: [4]

"It seems the Gods get us where we live . . . Beethoven's ears, Bach's eyes, Isadora's death-by-scarf (her trade mark). Leginska taught us to sit on the first part of the piano bench to get a more equal weight-distribution on all parts touching the floor, keys and bench. She herself sat on the very edge of the bench, and to get a really strong chord she would put her left leg so far back that the knee almost touched the floor. She was at the piano one night, and fell off the piano bench, lapsing into a coma. [*] It was no doubt from the edge she fell off. This position was one of her trade-marks, and it 'got her'. Ever since, I tell my students to sit on the first 1/3 to 1/2 of the bench."

Recently, it has been suggested that in the final period of her life Leginska might have been suffering from the early stages of Alzheimer's disease.[5] But there are several convincing pieces of evidence to suggest that Leginska did not have this illness:

a) Professor Marilyn Neeley, well-known concert pianist and former student of Leginska, assured the authors that Leginska "had gone on teaching, energetically, for some years after the operation [the mastectomy of 1960] and was teaching, full-time, when she died."[6]

b) Another concert pianist, Daniel Pollack, wrote to the authors:[7] "I visited her [Leginska] shortly before she died, about an article that I was writing on five great pianists (women) who were so influential – Leginska, Mme Lhevinne (my teacher at Juilliard),** Samaroff,[†] Vengerova,[††] and Kabos, [‡]." Professor Pollack confirmed in a telephone conversation with the co-author (Terry) on 5th June 2002 that when he met her on that occasion Leginska was perfectly lucid and entirely her normal self.

c) Anne Marie Biggs, who took the lead part in Leginska's opera *Joan of Arc* in the early summer of 1969 (a mere nine months before Leginska's death) worked closely with her during the preparations for the opera and found her delightful to work with. There was no suggestion in Miss Biggs's lengthy account [8] that Leginska was anything other than 100% alert mentally, though she was frail physically.

d) Christine Ammer, an authoritative American writer on music concludes, at the end of a three-page appraisal of Leginska's career: "A woman of considerable talent and energy, she remained active until she died, in 1970, at the age of eighty-three."[9]

---

* Bearing in mind Leginska's recent medical history, it is extremely probable that she did not fall spontaneously, but fell as the result of the stroke.
** Rosina Lhevinne (1880-1976), Russian-born pianist, was the wife of the famous Josef. She taught at the Juilliard School of Music and elsewhere for many years.
† Olga Samaroff, née Lucy Hickenlooper (1882-1948), was a famous Texan concert pianist until her career was cut short by an accident in 1925. Like Rosina Lhevinne she taught at the Juilliard School. She was married to the conductor Leopold Stokowski from 1911 to 1923.
†† Isabella Vengerova (1877-1956), born in Russia, had studied with Leschetizky and his former wife Annette Essipoff. She taught at the Curtis Institute in Philadelphia and in New York.
‡ Ilona Kabos (1893-1973) was a British pianist of Hungarian birth. She taught in London and at the Juilliard School in New York, and gave master classes in Europe and the USA. She married the Hungarian-born British pianist Louis Kentner in 1931; they were divorced in 1945.

e) Former Leginska student Beverly Carmen wrote, in response to a specific enquiry about the matter, that Leginska could not have been suffering from Alzheimer's disease because at the time of her death she was actively rehearsing for another production of one of her operas. Miss Carmen said she knows the pianists who worked with Leginska at the reheasals. [10]

Perhaps Leginska's behaviour, always rather impulsive and in the minds of some observers erratic, might have prompted misdiagnosis in the minds of unskilled observers. If a young or middle-aged person shows mildly eccentric traits it is often regarded as a feature of their personality, whereas if an old person shows the same tendencies people might think there must be something wrong with them due to their age. Leginska's personality had always been unusual – eccentric in the minds of some – and highly individual. And three cheers for that!

And so, in 1970, ended the life of this remarkable and talented woman at the age of 83 years and ten months. She had worked and taught virtually to the day of her final collapse and, as the manner of her demise indicates, had played her beloved piano right to the very end.

There remained the sad business of the disposal of her possessions. The authors understand from information received from a number of Leginska's former students in the Los Angeles area that Lucille Oliver, who had been Leginska's friend and companion since the early 1920s, was to have been her beneficiary, but Lucille died shortly before Leginska herself. According to Robert L. Watt, a French hornist with the Los Angeles Philharmonic Orchestra at the time, Leginska's musical possessions were then bequeathed to the Los Angeles Philharmonic Orchestra, an organisation with which she had never had a particularly close connection except to hire some of its members for the 'Leginska Little Symphony Orchestra' when she needed an orchestra for her students' recitals.[11] A private auction took place and many of Leginska's musical artefacts were purchased by members of the orchestra and other individuals.* Most of her private possessions were sold and her house was disposed of separately. (As noted earlier, the house and those surrounding it no longer exist.) Leginska's two bookcases full of operatic scores with the breathing marks used by singers in their opera performances marked, and her editions of piano music with the fingering used by other performers and teachers indicated on the pages, were all dispersed. A very sad state of affairs.

So nothing tangible remained at 254 South Hobart Boulevard to mark the final thirty years of the life of this dedicated musician.

---

* Mr Watt purchased Leginska's 'practice clavier' (a small upright piano-like instrument) and sent the authors a photograph of it.

Journey's End

How can we summarise the life of such a charismatic, magnetic, personality? It is not easy. When Leginska was born, Queen Victoria still had fifteen more years to reign, and horse transport was the order of the day everywhere, since the motor car had yet to be invented. Before she died, men had walked on the moon, The Beatles had come and all but gone, and daily life had changed almost beyond recognition. Between these two very different eras, she had packed nearly 80 years of outstanding musical activity, and had achieved many notable 'firsts', particularly with regard to the place of women in the world of music. Little Ethel Annie Liggins, the girl who skipped along the pavements of Hull's Pemberton Street, had crossed many bridges on her way to becoming Madame Leginska, the world-famous musician.

Now, more than thirty years after her death, we can stand back and look at her career objectively. As we have seen, she achieved distinction in four different realms of music: concert pianist, composer, conductor and teacher. As a pianist she was outstanding. She travelled the world and was acknowledged, between 1912 and the early 1930s, as one of the major figures on the concert platform. If she had done nothing else she should be remembered for that alone. Yet, in spite of her enormous success in that field and her huge popularity with the public, she never thoroughly enjoyed the life of a concert pianist. A total perfectionist, she could never bear to play a piece less well than she had played it on a previous occasion. This must have imposed a huge emotional burden on her and in this she was not alone. A brilliant pianist of the present day, Martha Argerich, once said, "I love playing the piano, but I hate being a pianist". Those words could have been uttered by Leginska herself. She loved playing the piano, right until her death, but she was never completely happy with the trappings of life as a concert pianist nor the stiff formality of concert performances. Nevertheless, she enjoyed remarkable success because of her outstanding talent and magnetic personality, always benefiting from a hugely loyal, dedicated band of adulatory followers – hardly surprising in view of her status, over a period of several years, as arguably the foremost female pianist of the day.

It is fortunate that Leginska made some recordings – a few on disc and rather more on piano roll – so that we have something tangible by which to remember her abilities as a pianist. Her Columbia discs, some of them recently re-issued on compact disc,[12] give a glimpse of her fine playing, uncluttered by foibles or affectations. Most of her recordings for the player piano, about 74 in number, may still be readily heard since many reproducing pianos in good working order are still in existence.

Leginska's days of glory recalled:
Publicity notices from 1918 (this page) and from the mid-1950s (opposite page)

Journey's End

Mme Ethel Leginska

Piano Virtuoso, Orchestra Conductor, Composer, Piano Pedagogue

Like nearly all of the great musicians, Leginska was a "Prodigy Child." Appearing as pianist at the age of six — a pupil of the master teacher, Leschetizky, at fourteen — she made her official debut as orchestral soloist when but sixteen years of age, under the baton of Sir Henry Wood in London. Following this auspicious commencement, she was engaged as soloist with practically all of the prominent orchestras in Europe and America. Besides this, Leginska has toured internationally as recitalist, attracting record-breaking audiences.

During this period, instead of resting in the summer time, she studied composition with Ernest Bloch and Symphonic as well as Operatic conducting with Professor Robert Heger (associate conductor of Bruno Walter) and Maestro Genaro Papi.

She became well known as a composer, her orchestral works having been performed by such prominent organizations as the Boston Symphony Orchestra, Boston, Pierre Monteux conducting; New York Symphony, New York, Albert Coates conducting; Berlin Philharmonic Orchestra, etc. Her Chamber Music works and Songs have been performed by such noted musicians as the London String Quartet, New York String Quartet, Madame Cahier, Greta Torpadie, and many other ensembles and artists.

Leginska was the first woman in musical history to be Guest Conductor of most of the world's greatest orchestras, and was the first of her sex to be engaged as grand opera conductor. London, Salzburg, New York, Boston and other cities heard her conduct such operas as "Madame Butterfly," "Tosca," "Rigoletto," "Carmen," "Louise," "Thais" and "Werther," to name but a few.

The Chicago Civic Opera Company engaged her to conduct her own one-hour opera, "Gale," with John Charles Thomas in the title role.

Leginska's second appearance as Guest Conductor of the Dallas Symphony Orchestra also made musical history; for she gave the first Texas performance of the Ninth Symphony of Beethoven with a chorus of 200, and an audience of 5500. She duplicated this event in Havana, Cuba, with the Philharmonic Orchestra.

A FEW PRESS OPINIONS OF LEGINSKA AS A PIANIST

"Ethel Leginska made upon me one of the strongest impressions I have been favored with for a long time. With the rarity of sparkling temperament, sensitiveness, spirited and elemental sense of rhythm, combined with the most beautiful singing touch and an enormous technique of floating grace and incomparable elasticity, which has pure, free, and unrestrained expression, the work of THIS THOROUGHBRED ARTIST IS IRRESISTIBLE.

A flood of encores was inevitable, after Leginska had reached her zenith and the public had sensed her power. Of them, an extraordinary achievement was the performance of the A minor and C minor Etudes of Chopin."—*Allgemeine Musikzeitung* (Berlin).

"She played Mozart's A Major Concerto with the utmost refinement and purity of style, and Liszt's Hungarian Fantasy with glowing temperament and triumphant technique, WITH A VIRTUOSITY WHICH FEW CAN EQUAL.—*Börsen Courier* (Berlin).

"She proved herself to be a Chopin and Liszt player OF THE FIRST RANK, and moved her hearers to tremendous enthusiasm through her brilliant virtuosity and the expressiveness of her temperamental playing . . ."—*Tageblatt* (Berlin).

". . . SHE IS A MASTER, THIS SPLENDID GENIUS. She played the Liszt Sonata, that mighty sea of tones, that unique piano symphony. Mind and heart, strength and fire, an absolutely demonical temperament and triumphant spirit, with immense pianistic skill. (I only have to recall the elementary strength of her octave technique, the lightness of the passage work.) All united to make this re-creation of the work a moving artistic experience of unforgettable value; Ethel Leginska, although you are English, you are always welcome in Munich; YOU ARE ONE OF THE GREATEST IN YOUR ART."—*Münchener Zeitung* (Munich).

"In her piano playing, SHE PRODUCES SOMETHING BIG; culture and colouring of touch and always eminent technique."—*München-Augsburger* (Munich).

". . . With technical mastery, perfection of touch and comprehension, she played the pianoforte Concerto in F minor of Bach and Weber's Concerto in C, conducting them from the piano with calmness and authority."—*Münchener Tageblatt* (Munich).

"She gives us real delight in the finely-chiseled perfection of her technique, in the beauty of her tone and the fascinating momentum of her rhythm. These were the qualities which came through so wonderfully in her playing of the Mozart Concerto — qualities which, added to a quite unusual colour-sense, REMINDED US CONTINUALLY OF RAOUL PUGNO."—*Daily Telegraph* (London).

"SHE PRODUCED SOME FAULTLESS PLAYING of Beethoven, Bach and Chopin. It penetrated their secrets and gave an intimate account of them. Her execution was fluent and her tone well graded and guarded. Leginska has the unusual power of uttering a forcible climax without becoming inarticulate." — *London Morning Post* (London).

". . . SHE IS A GREAT PIANIST and has much more in her than temperament and technique to match it. . . ."—*Evening Standard* (London).

"To be admired was her SUPERB TECHNIQUE and her TREMENDOUS MUSICAL QUALITIES."—*Echo de Paris* (Paris).

"Of the younger generation of pianists now before the public, LEGINSKA RANKS HIGHEST." — *New York Times* (New York City).

"Leginska is an artist of distinction, a player of exceptional merit, a woman with a perception of the spirit of the composers she interprets that sometimes is uncanny. She has a technical capacity that is unlimited."—*Tribune* (New York City).

"Leginska played like the MASTER SHE IS AND WON AN OVATION from a crowded audience."—*The Evening World* (New York City).

Few men have the power to move their audiences as she does. Yesterday SHE TOOK HER HEARERS BY STORM."—*New York Herald* (New York City).

Leginska Flames Through Chopin

"Technical and tonal splendor, poetic fire, romantic exaltation and stroke upon stroke of beauty or of power . . . AS FOR THE PLAUDITS, NONE SUCH HAVE BEEN HEARD EXCEPT WHEN PADEREWSKI PLAYED." — H. T. Parker, *Boston Transcript* (Boston).

Boston Enjoys Remarkable Work of Consummate Artist

"As a player of Chopin she stands close to de Pachmann. WE DOUBT IF HE COULD RIVAL HER IN THE PRELUDES."—Philip Hale, *Boston Herald* (Boston).

". . . the audience sat in one of those eloquent silences that attest alike the GREATNESS OF COMPOSER AND INTERPRETER." — *Sunday Globe* (Boston).

". . . Not for long in this city, it is safe to say, has Franck's music received a performance so ardent, or one more revealing of its pervading mood of exaltation."—*The Post* (Boston).

"Leginska is thrice gifted. She has mentality, temperament, superlative technical ability. HER PLAYING GLOWS WITH THE DIVINE FIRE THAT IS AKIN TO GENIUS." — *Herald-Examiner* (Chicago).

As a composer, Leginska achieved some success in her lifetime, but her work is rarely if ever performed in public now and one must await the judgment of posterity to discover whether any of it will be revived or will survive in the long term. Of the four facets of her career, her composition is probably the least important, though one feels she would not have shared that opinion herself.

During her lifetime Leginska was greatly respected by her musical contemporaries. In 1985 the Russian-born pianist Shura Cherkassky, who died in December 1995 aged 86, wrote to the authors: [13]

"Ethel Leginska was an exceptional personality, rather unusual, daring in her ways, but very convincing in what she wanted to project. Even though she was rather eccentric in her ways and manners, it somehow added to her interesting and fascinating personality. She was an excellent, thorough musician, and her intuition was remarkable. When I knew her during the second world war years, she was not then giving concerts professionally, but she was teaching, and she was very popular with her students. I regret that I never heard her play, except on some Duo-Art rolls."

The International Piano Archives at Maryland and the Hollywood Bowl Museum hold many letters sent to Leginska from well-known musicians.[14] The list of famous names of Leginska's correspondents includes the conductors Adrian Boult, Albert Coates, Walter Damrosch, Robert Heger and Landon Ronald. Leginska had worked with them and many others often over the years. Robert Heger, with whom Leginska had studied the art of conducting in the early 1920s, was still in touch with her in the 1960s. Well-known instrumentalists who wrote to Leginska include Harold Bauer, Fannie Bloomfield Zeisler, Frieda Hodapp, Josef Hofmann, James Kwast, (her teacher at Frankfurt), and Ernest Schelling (all outstanding pianists), Pablo Casals ('cello), and Boris Hambourg ('cello) with whom Leginska had shared the platform in chamber music in her younger days. All of their letters to Leginska were written in very cordial, friendly and some cases affectionate terms. Madelon Coates, wife of Albert, was clearly very fond of Ethel, starting her letters "Dearest baby" (!). Albert and Madelon were obviously very close friends of Leginska as well as musical collaborators.

These are just a few of the famous musicians known to have communicated with Leginska over the years. She was also on excellent terms with many of the notable pianists who were fellow-artists in the Duo-Art recording studios, sometimes appearing with them in joint concerts and recitals. Some of their names appear on page 147. Moreover, as indicated on page 242, Leginska's teaching studios were recommended and endorsed by a number of very eminent conductors and soloists.

In spite of Leginska's standing in the world of music over many years, in Britain she is nowadays hardly remembered. The authors have always found, when going into music shops to seek out sheet music or gramophone recordings, our enquiries draw a blank when Leginska's name is mentioned. "Ethel Leginska? No, I'm sorry, we've never heard of her". It is a well known saying that a prophet is not honoured in his or her own country and this certainly applies in Leginska's case. She was consistently ignored in the various editions of *Grove* until an offshoot, the *New Grove Dictionary of Women Composers* was published in 1994.[15] She then made a belated appearance in *Grove* itself in the new edition published in 2001 – 31 years after her death. In contrast, hundreds of lesser mortals, including many very obscure musicians, have appeared in successive editions of *Grove* over the years.

Moreover, as explained in the authors' preface (pages x to xi) the BBC declined our suggestion (made in a letter dated 16th May 1985) that the *Music Weekly* programme to be broadcast eleven months hence on 13th April 1986, Leginska's exact centenary, might devote a few minutes of its time to her life and career, including perhaps the playing of one of her records or piano rolls. Accompanying our letter was a copy of an article on Leginska that we had written, so no research on the BBC's part was required. However, the reply received six weeks later from the producer, supported by his co-producer, opined that "interesting though her career and achievements are, she is really too much of a marginal figure to be featured in *Music Weekly*".[16] Perhaps there might be some justification for Leginska having been forgotten in Britain since her work has not generally been widely known here (apart from her piano roll recordings) since the earlier part of the 20th century, unlike that of many British-born notables of the entertainment world who made their homes and careers in the USA. Names such as Charles Chaplin, Cary Grant, Bob Hope and Stan Laurel spring to mind, but they all benefited from the world-wide distribution of their films.

However, although Leginska lived nearly all of the last 57 years of her life in the USA, she has been remembered there little better than in Britain, though the recent re-issue of some her disc recordings of the 1920s on compact disc (see page 334) has helped a little in bringing her name once again before the musical public. Leginska has usually been included in the major American biographical dictionaries of musicians,[17] but she faded from the public eye when she became a full-time teacher in 1939 and by the date of her death she was almost unknown in the USA, except amongst her former students and older music-lovers who remembered her exploits as a pianist and conductor. Consequently she soon disappeared into historical semi-oblivion, though she is vividly recalled by those who knew her personally, especially her students, all of whom will remember her to their dying day. The authors are gratified that their own researches into Leginska's life beginning, so far as enquiries in the United States are concerned, in 1981, has acted as a catalyst for a revival of interest in this remarkable musician. Until then Leginska had remained in the background of people's minds and there were few plans to commemorate the centenary of her birth; indeed, until the authors put the record straight by quoting the birth certificate it was believed by many in the USA that she had been born in 1885 and hence her centenary would be in 1985.

Following a small re-awakening of interest, Leginska's centenary in 1986 was not allowed to pass un-noticed. In Britain it was marked by a meeting at the authors' home at which guests listened to Leginska's playing, through her Duo-Art piano rolls and a few of her 78rpm gramophone records (see opposite). In the USA, largely through the commendable efforts of Marguerite Heller and a small group of other former students of Leginska, a 'Leginska Centenniel Committee' was set up. Consequent on this, an exhibition in celebration of Leginska's life was held at the Hollywood Bowl Museum in 1986 and, as indicated in Chapters 16 and 17 of this book, a radio programme was broadcast in which a number of Leginska's former pupils paid tribute to her, recalling incidents that stood out in their memory.[18] There were also plans to institute a Leginska prize for young pianists, but as far as is known that has yet to come into being.

Never one to run with the herd, Leginska went her own way and did the things she believed in, irrespective of opposition and indifference. In doing so she enriched the world of music and was one of the most colourful, talented and compelling figures of her generation, possessing a magical charisma unique to herself. Her many notable achievements are a tribute to her personality and talent. In spite of all of this, she is now almost totally forgotten except to people owning player pianos who know her name through the rolls she made. It is hoped that this book will help to ensure that her achievements are at last recognised, thereby placing the name of this forgotten genius of music where it belongs, amongst the ranks of the great musicians of the past.

Journey's End

Celebratory Programme of Music – April 1986

Ethel Leginska's Duo-Art Piano Rolls:

The dates in the right-hand column (month/year) are the known dates of issue of the rolls. The indication ?11/14 indicates an educated guess by the Duo-Art roll historian Charles Davis Smith of Monrovia, California, USA as to the date of release of rolls known to have been issued before the publication of the first 'Catalogue of Duo-Art Piano Music' which appeared in January 1915. All the rolls so marked are in that catalogue. Leginska was one of 32 pianists whose photograph appeared in the catalogue.

6999	Weber	*Oberon* Overture	5/26
5585	Mendelssohn	Songs Without Words, No. 30, Op.62, No. 6 (*Spring Song*)	?11/14
6743	Beethoven	Minuet, No. 2 in G	4/24
5644	Chopin	Ballade (1st) in G minor, Op. 23	5/15
5587	Rubinstein	Valse Caprice in E flat	?11/14
5586	Schumann	*Träumerei*, from *Kinderszenen*, Op. 15, No. 7	?11/14
6217	Rameau	Gavotte and Variations (tr. Leschetizky)	12/19
6539	Leschetizky	*The Two Larks* (Impromptu), Op. 2, No. 1	6/22
6707	Chopin	Valse in E minor (Posthumous)	1/24
7137	Mendelssohn	Songs Without Words, No. 44, Op. 102, No. 2 and No. 10, Op. 30, No. 4	7/27
6957	Beethoven	Eight Variations on the theme *Tändeln und Scherzen*	1/26
6731	Liadov	*The Music Box* (*Une Tabatière à Musique*), Op. 32	3/24

Interval – Tea

6549	Rimsky-Korsakov	*Hymn to the Sun* from *The Golden Cockerel*	9/22
6388	Leschetizky	Arabesque en Forme d'Étude, Op. 45, No. 1	2/21
5584	Schubert	Marche Militaire, Op. 51, No. 1 (arr. Tausig)	?11/14
6159	Moszkowski	Valse in A flat, Op. 34, No. 1	6/19
6592	Strauss	Concert Arabesques on Motives from the Waltz *By the Beautiful Blue Danube* (tr. Schulz-Evler)	1/23
7396	Liszt	Hungarian Rhapsody, No. 8 in F sharp minor (Capriccio)	5/30
6822	Leginska	*Cradle Song* *	12/24

* The roll of Leginska's own composition *Cradle Song* was played as a tape recording, courtesy of Mr G. C. Stonehill, as the authors do not have the roll. Marguerite Broadbent also played it 'by hand' from the sheet music.

The programme of piano rolls was followed by the playing of some of Leginska's Columbia recordings of Schubert's Impromptus and Moments Musicaux (78rpm discs), all recorded and issued in 1928.

Programme of music played in the company of a group of friends at a special meeting of The North West Player Piano Association at the authors' home on Saturday, 12th April 1986, to celebrate Leginska's centenary the following day. The rolls were played on a Steinway Duo-Art player piano.

Ethel Leginska

(b. Ethel Liggins, Hull, England, Apr. 13, 1886; d. Los Angeles, Feb. 26, 1970)

On August 4, 1925, Ethel Leginska became the first woman conductor at the Hollywood Bowl, where she received nine curtain calls from a large, enthusiastic audience. Bruno David Ussher, reviewing the concert in the Los Angeles *Express*, noted that Leginska "has a decided contribution to make to an art in which a blending of tradition and individuality is priceless . . . " What made the evening even more notable was that the concert also featured Leginska as both piano soloist and conductor. Critic Patterson Greene wrote "her pianism merits unqualified praise" and Ussher felt that her composition *Six Nursery Rhymes* was "poetic, virile, sensitive and imaginative".

Leginska began her career as a pianist. She studied at the Frankfurt Conservatory and then subsequently with the great Theodor Leschetizky in Vienna. Her regular tours throughout Europe brought her great acclaim as a virtuosa and eventually brought her to America, where she first appeared in 1913. Leginska began to study conducting in 1920 and, three years later, was invited to conduct the Munich Symphony.

Encouraged by the enthusiastic response of the German audiences and musicians, she increasingly pursued a conducting career, making her first appearances on the podium in America in 1924. After appearing at the Hollywood Bowl, she formed her own orchestra, the Boston Philharmonic, and then became the conductor of the newly-formed Women's Symphony Orchestra of Chicago. In 1932 she conducted at Carnegie Hall. During the 1930s, she was often engaged as an opera conductor and she made guest appearances with many of the world's leading orchestras, among them the New York Philharmonic, the Berlin Philharmonic, the London Symphony and the Paris Conservatory Orchestra.

Leginska began composing in 1918 and, in 1920, won a prize in the Berkshire [USA] Chamber Music Festival Competition for her *Four Poems for String Quartet after Tagore*. Other works from the 1920s included *From a Life* (1922, for chamber ensemble), *Two Short Pieces* for orchestra (1924, performed by Pierre Monteux and the Boston Symphony) and *Quatre Sujets Barbares* (1924), an orchestral suite inspired by the paintings of Gauguin. Leginska's opera *Gale* was performed by the Chicago Civic Opera in 1935 with John Charles Thomas heading the cast. She wrote two other operas – *The Rose and the Ring* and *Joan of Arc* – both of which were performed in Los Angeles late in the composer's life.

In 1938, Leginska settled permanently in Los Angeles where she concentrated on teaching. She was an influential figure for many talented young musicians, always stressing that technique was only the means to an expressive end. Among the many pianists she trained were Lucille Oliver, Ralph Pierce, Jon Robertson, Marilyn Neeley and Daniel Pollack.

Ethel Leginska was a gifted musician, acclaimed in the multiple facets of her long career – virtuosa, composer, conductor and pedagogue. Her achievements were all the more remarkable because her career came at a time when few women were accepted as equal professionals in the world of music. In 1986, the centennial of her birth, we celebrate Ethel Leginska not only for her many accomplishments but also for her pioneering efforts on behalf of women in musical life.

A page from the Hollywood Bowl Museum's booklet 'Sound Waves' published at the time of Leginska's centenary in 1986. The booklet features many of the notable musicians who had appeared at the Bowl over the years. On the facing (left-hand) page was Alex Heller's photograph of Leginska, which is shown on page 251 of this book. The page has been re-typed to convert it from 'landscape' to 'portrait' format.

Journey's End

75 years of music-making: A few milestones in Ethel Leginska's career

Age 8: "On Wednesday the numerous pupils of Mrs Russell Starr (Miss Martin) and Mr Lancelot gave a concert. A very small performer was Miss Ethel Liggins, only eight years of age, but considerably to the front in ability, who played Hummel's Rondo in B flat, for which she received an encore." *Hull News, 23rd June 1894.*

Age 10: "The ten-year-old Miss Ethel Liggins's pianoforte recital contained a very ambitious programme. The child, a very serious-looking pretty little thing, plays indeed, for her age, with great musical understanding and technic." *Musical Courier, 25th June 1896.*

Age 20: "Miss Ethel Leginska increased the number of her admirers by her vivacious and clever pianoforte playing at her orchestral concert, conducted by Henry J. Wood at Queen's Hall on June 14. She is to be commended for having revived Henselt's Concerto in G minor; in this and in Rubinstein's Concerto in D minor the young artist played with great brilliance and intelligence." *Musical Times, 1st July 1906.*

Age 26 (New York debut): "Young English pianist plays with brilliancy and poetic feeling: She soon showed herself to be an artist of unusual gifts and attainments. Her artistic sympathies are eager, her playing is impetuous and hot-blooded, full of high lights and deep shadows, and yet not lacking in artistic tenderness." *New York Times, 21st January 1913.*

Age 35: "She is a composer of excellent technique and ideas. 'Three Poems' for string quartet contained passages that were extremely beautiful and others that were strikingly effective from other points of view." *Evening Standard (London), 16th June 1921.*

Age 38: "History, musically speaking, was made at the Symphony Hall last night when Ethel Leginska led the orchestra through its 21st and final concert of the season. It was a triumph both for the band itself and its doughty guest conductor." *Boston Post, 6th April 1925.*

Age 40: "Yesterday she won her first great triumph. She and the Boston Philharmonic Orchestra gave 5000 people a brilliant and enjoyable concert." *Boston Globe, 25th October 1926* (reporting the inaugural concert of Leginska's new Boston Phil. Orchestra).

Age 43: "Once more yesterday, Ethel Leginska and her [Boston Women's Symphony] orchestra played before Jordan Hall sold-out. A large company did at all events hear an excellent programme admirably performed, and derived therefrom it was plain to see, rare pleasure." *Boston Herald. 14th October 1929.*

Age 49: "The world premiere of Leginska's 'Gale' was the high point of a crowded Saturday at the Civic Opera House. For the first time in history a woman composer of opera appeared in a major house to conduct her own work." *Chicago Sunday Tribune, 24th November 1935.*

Age 74: "Leginska program well received: Ethel Leginska, one of the world's distinguished musicians, last night presented a program of her own compositions. Acting as both accompanist and conductor, she selected music from her long list of creative works." *Los Angeles Herald and Express, 13th May 1960.*

Age 83: "Her [Leginska's] 'Joan of Arc' received a world premiere by the Los Angeles Lyric Opera last night." *Los Angeles Times, 12th May 1969.*

References: Chapter 19

1. Information on the circumstances of Leginska's death was sent by former Leginska student Beverly Carmen in a letter dated 30th November 1984.
2. Certified copy of Leginska's death certificate, dated 4th March 1970, purchased in 1985 from the County Registrar-Recorder, Los Angeles County, 5th October 1984 (certificate shown on page 300).
3. Information about Leginska's funeral was sent to the authors in the mid 1980s by Beverly Carmen, Marguerite Heller, and other former students.
4. As reference 1.
5. Marina A. Ledin, the writer of the sleeve notes of the Ivory Classics compact disc, *Ethel Leginska: The Complete Columbia Masters, 1926 -1928* (CD 64405-72002) asserts: "Her last years were difficult, as those closest to her have claimed, some have even gone so far as to suggest she may have been an undiagnosed Alzheimer's sufferer."
6. Letter from Marilyn Neeley to the authors dated 13th December 1982, in which she answered various questions we had asked.
7. Letter from Daniel Pollack to the authors, dated 27th June 1984.
8. Letter to the authors from Anne Marie Biggs, dated 16th April 1985.
9. Christine Ammer: *Unsung: A History of Women in American Music.* Greenwood Press, Westport, Connecticut, pages 109-111. The reference to Leginska remaining "active until she died" comes at the end of the passage.
10. Letter from Beverly Carmen dated 15th December 2001.
11. Letter from Robert L. Watt dated 3rd February 1984.
12. Ivory Classics CD referred to in reference 5. Pavilion Records compact disc: *Pupils of Leschetizky* (Opal 9839) includes two of Leginska's disc recordings.
13. Letter sent by Shura Cherkassky from the White House, London. 15th September 1985.
14. Copies of various letters were kindly supplied by IPAM's Curator, Donald Manildi and the Hollywood Bowl Museum's Curator Dr Carol Merrill-Mirsky.
15. *The New Grove Dictionary of Women Composers*, Ed. Julie Anne Sadie and Rhian Samuel. Macmillan, London, 1994.
16. Letter from Andrew Lyle, producer of the BBC's *Music Weekly*, dated 26th June 1985.
17. For example, *Baker's Biographical Dictionary of Musicians*, various editions, and earlier editions when it was known as *The International Cyclopedia of Music and Musicians*; *Notable American Women: The Modern Period*, Harvard University Press, Cambridge, Mass, 1980; *International Cyclopedia of Women Composers*, Ed. Aaron I. Cohen, R.R. Bowker Co., New York, 1981; *The Piano in Concert*, compiled and annotated by George Kehler (in 2 volumes), Scarecrow Press Inc., Metuchen, New Jersey, 1982.
18. Radio programme *Tribute to Ethel Leginska*; part of the 'Music of the Americas' series, broadcast by KPFK, Los Angeles, on Sunday, 6th April 1986.

Bibliography

The books and periodicals in the first two lists below all contain references to Leginska, albeit in many cases very brief (a few lines only). Several of them contain inaccuracies, often concerning such basic facts as Leginska's date of birth, dates of important landmarks in her career such as her studies in Frankfurt and London Promenade Concert debut, her marriage and divorce, etc. However, they are listed nevertheless in view of the sparsity of published material on Leginska prior to this biography .

Dictionaries and encyclopaedias of music:

Listed in reverse chronological order

1. *The New Grove Dictionary of Music and Musicians*, edited by Stanley Sadie and John Tyrrell, 2nd edn., Macmillan, London, January 2001.
2. *The New Grove Dictionary of Women Composers*, edited by Julie Sadie and Rhian Samuel. Macmillan, London, 1994.
3. *A Biographical Dictionary of Composers and Musicians* (*The Concise Baker's*), edited by Nicolas Slonimsky. Simon Schuster, London, 1988. Also *Baker's Biographical Dictionary of Musicians*, 7th edn. (a more comprehensive version of the concise version quoted above), Oxford, 1984. Also various earlier editions of the book when it was known as *The International Cyclopedia of Music and Musicians* and published by J.M.Dent & Sons Ltd. Edited in earlier editions by Oscar Thompson and in later editions by Nicolas Slonimsky.
4. *Musik Lexicon*, edited by Williblad Garlitt. H. Riemann; B. Schott's Sohne, Mainz, 1972-75.
5. *Index to Biographies of Contemporary Composers* by S. Bull. Scarecrow Press, Metuchen, New Jersey, 1974.
6. *Biographical Dictionary of American Music* by C.E. Claghem. Parker, New York, 1973.
7. *Musik von A-Z vom Gregorianischen Choral zu Jazz und Beat* by A. Goodman. Sudwest Verlag, Munich, 1971.
8. *Dictionary of American Women Composers with Selected Music for Senior and Junior Clubs*. National Federation of Music Clubs, Chicago, 1970.
9. *Encyclopedia of Concert Music* by David Ewen. Peter Owen Ltd., London, 1961.
10. *Muzicka Encikopedija*. Izdanje Naklade, edited by J. Andreis. Leksikografskog Zovoda Fnrk., Zagreb, 1958.
11. *Lexikon der Neuen Musik* by F.K. Prieberg. Alber, Munich, 1958.
12. *Music Lovers' Encyclopaedia*, compiled by Robert Hughes, revised and edited by Deems Taylor and Russell Kerr. Macdonald, London, 1955.
13. *Encyclopaedia van Muziek*. El Seviev, Amsterdam, 1951-57.

14. *The New Encyclopaedia of Music and Musicians*, edited by Waldo Selden Pratt. Macmillan, New York, 1943.
15. *The Macmillan Encyclopaedia of Music and Musicians*, compiled by A.E. Weir. Macmillan, London, 1938.
16. *A Dictionary of Modern Music and Musicians*, edited by A. Eaglefield-Hull. J.M. Dent & Sons Ltd., London, 1924.
17. *Black's Dictionary of Music and Musicians*, compiled by L.J. de Becker. A. & C. Black Ltd., London, 1924.

Other biographical dictionaries (not all specific to music), various music books, articles, etc. with references to Leginska:

1. *Women in Music: An Anthology of Source Readings*, edited by Carol Neuls-Bates. Harper & Row, New York, 1982.
2. *Unsung: A History of Women in American Music* by Christine Ammer. Greenwood Press, Westport, C.T. 1980.
3. *Notable American Women: The Modern Period.* Harvard University Press, Cambridge, Mass. and London, 1980.
4. *Women in American Music: A Bibliography of Music and Literature* by Adrienne Block and Carol Neuls-Bates. Greenwood Press, Westport, C.T., 1979.
5. *Famous Pianists and their Technique* by R.C. Gerig. David & Charles, Newton Abbot and London, 1976.
6. *Contemporary American Composers*, compiled by Ruth E. Anderson. G.K. Hall, Boston, Mass., 1976.
7. *20th-Century Opera in England and the USA* by C. Northouse. Hall, Boston, Mass., 1976.
8. *Consider These Creators* by M.S. Green. *American Music Teacher*, July/August 1974.
9. *Women in Music* by D. Hennersee. Scarecrow Press, Metuchen, 1974.
10. *The Distaff'd Composers* by D. Burns. Music Journal, March 1974.
11. *Who's Who of American Women*, 3rd edition. Marquis Who's Who, Inc., Chicago, 1964.
12. *Etude* Historical Musical Portrait Series. *Etude*, January 1932 to October 1940.
13. *American Women in Creative Music* by E.N.C. Barnes. Music Education Publishers, Washington, D.C., 1936.
14. *Woman's Work in Music* by A. Elson and E. Truette. Page, Boston, Mass, 1931.
15. *Noted Names in Music* by W.J. Baltzell. (Selected composers to 1927). O. Ditson, Boston, Mass., 1927.

Bibliography

Ethel Leginska's disc recordings – documentation:

See Pathé record catalogues, early 1920s and Columbia record catalogues, late 1920s and early 1930s.

Leginska's gramophone recordings are listed in Appendix 5(a), page 330.

Piano rolls recorded by Ethel Leginska – documentation:

Duo-Art: *Duo-Art Piano Music: A Catalogue of Reproducing Piano Rolls.* The Aeolian Company, New York, 1927, with a supplement published in 1932. *Catalogue of Duo-Art Piano Rolls* by Charles Davis Smith. The Player Shop, Monrovia, California, 1987.

Ampico: *A Catalogue of Music for the Ampico.* The Ampico Corporation, New York, 1925.
The Complete Catalogue of Ampico Reproducing Rolls by Elaine Obenchain. Wm. H. Edgerton, New York, 1977.

Artrio: *Catalogue of Rolls for the Artrio-Angelus Reproducing Piano.* Wilcox & White Company, Meriden, Connecticut, 1922.

Also, *The Classical Reproducing Piano Roll: A Catalogue Index* by Larry Sitsky (in two volumes). Greenwood Press, Westport, Connecticut and London, 1990. This covers all makes of rolls made for the 'reproducing piano'.

Leginska's piano roll recordings are listed in Appendix 5(b), page 332.

During their researches the authors have had access to hundreds of press cuttings and other documents relating to Ethel Leginska. Specific references to books, articles, newspaper reports and reviews and other sources are given at the end of each chapter.

Appendix 1(a): The Liggins family tree

This is a more detailed version, with more names, than the one shown on page 7.

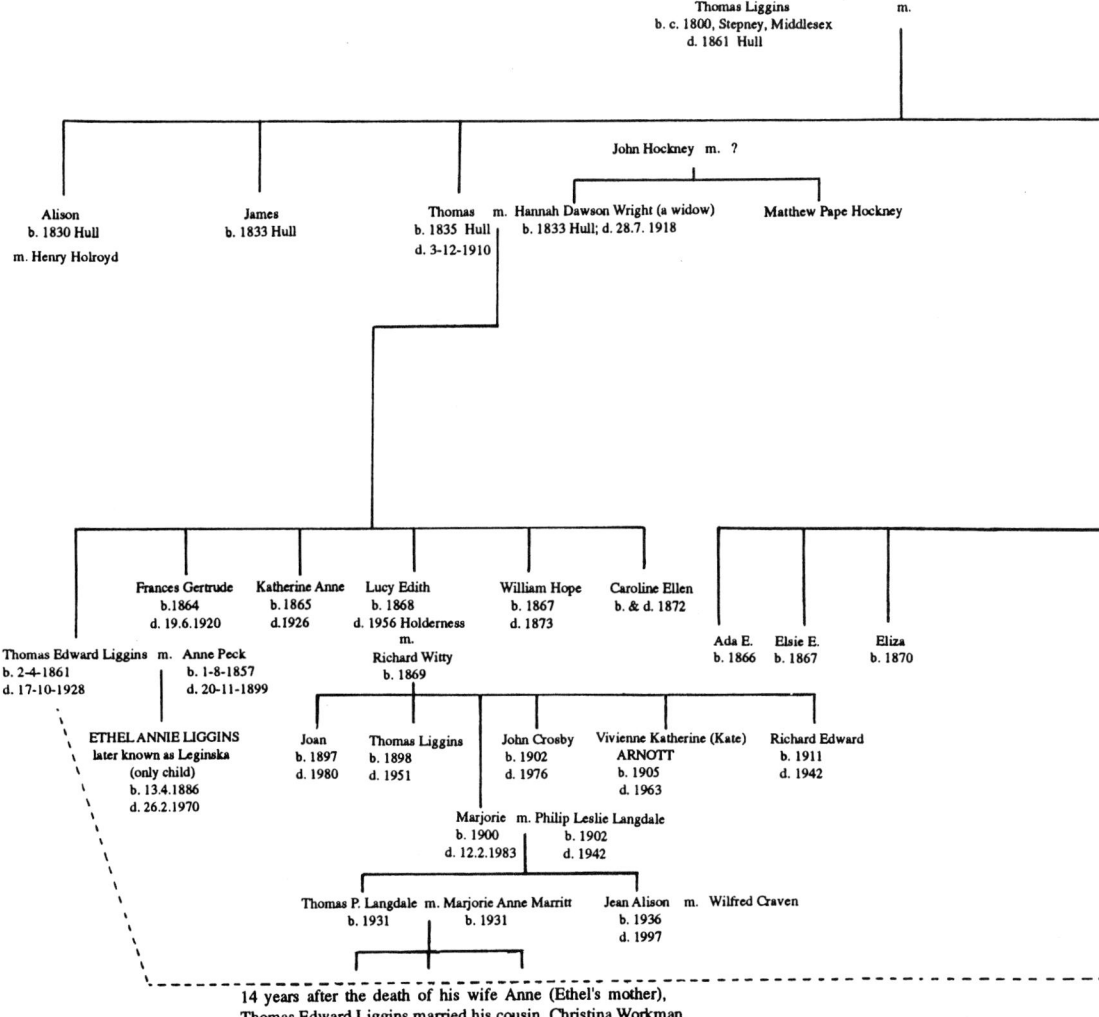

Where dates are given in full the English system is used; day-month-year.

Appendix 1(a): The Liggins Family Tree

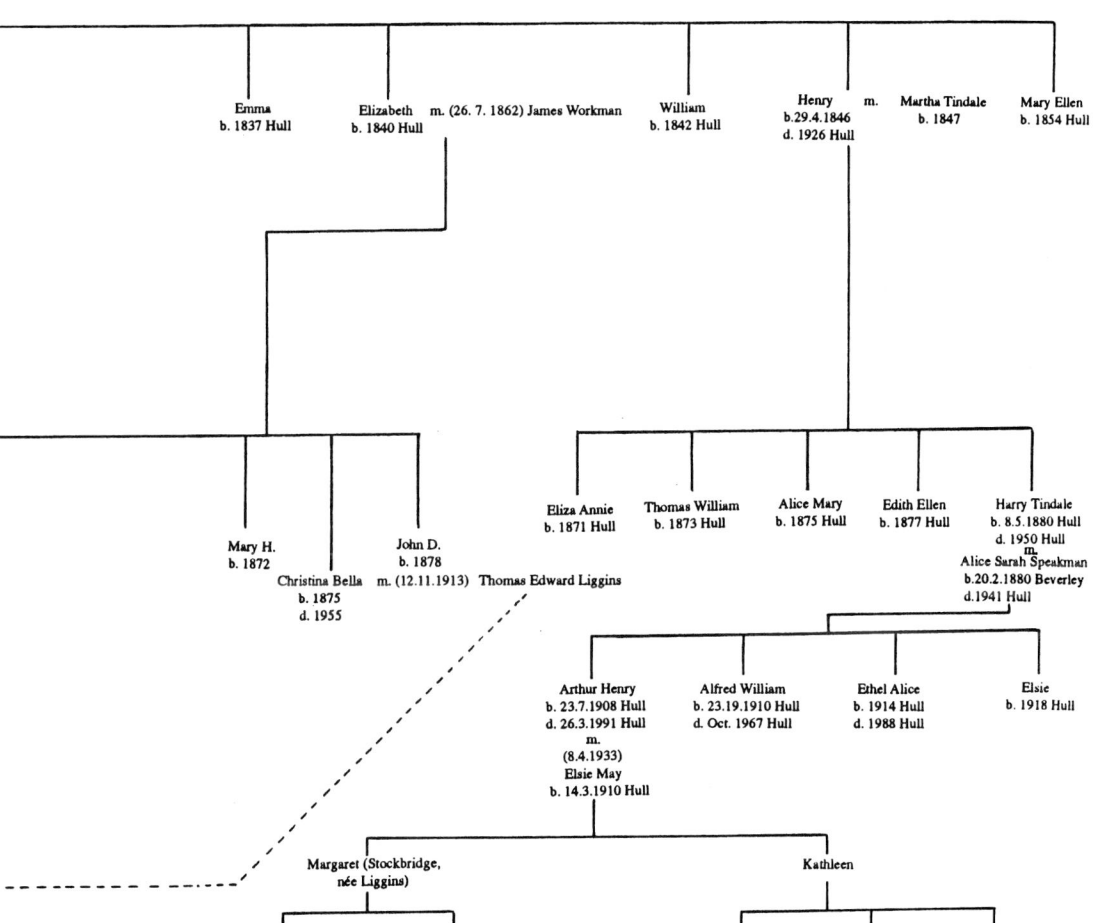

The authors are indebted to Mr Tom Langdale of Beverley and Mrs Margaret Stockbridge of South Cave, near Hull, both distantly related to Ethel Leginska and who appear on this family tree, for carrying out the family research that enabled the tree to be established.

Appendix 1(b): The Liggins paternal forbears

The names Liggins and Hockney (the Hockneys were related to the Liggins family by marriage - see family tree - as well as being business partners) appear in several town and business directories of the late 19th and early 20th centuries. Relevant extracts giving names, addresses, occupations, etc. are listed below, along with the date of the directory entry.

Relationship to Ethel Liggins (Leginska)	Name	Date	Address and occupation
Great grandfather	Thomas Liggins	1818/1829	Gunmaker, small gun office, Tower of London, aged 22. (Believed to be E.L.'s great grandfather but not absolutely certain)
Great grandfather	Thomas Liggins	1831	Master armourer
Great grandfather	Thomas Liggins,	1851	Armourer, garrison
Great grandfather	Thomas Liggins	1858	Master armourer, Garrison Light Office, Custom House, Whitefriargate, London
	John Hockney	1858	Joiner and builder, Witham (a district of Hull) (possibly father of Matthew)
Grandfather	Thomas Liggins	1863	Son of Thomas. Firm of Hockney & Liggins mentioned
	Matthew Hockney	1863	Hockney & Liggins, joiners, builders, undertakers, Gt. Union Street Steam and Saw Mills, Witham
		1874/75	Hockney & Liggins, contractors, 13, Great Union Street
		1882	Hockney & Liggins, builders, contractors, saw mills and house and ship joiners, 1, Great Union Street and Witham
Grandfather	Thomas Liggins	1882 & 1885	Builder. Residence 10, East Parade, Holderness Road
	Matthew Pape Hockney	1882 & 1885	Residence 7, Somerstown, Holderness Road
Father	Thomas Liggins	1897	Surveyor. Residence 22, Pemberton Street
Grandfather	Thomas Liggins	1897 & 1903	Residence 408, Holderness Road
		1889 & 1901	Hockney & Liggins, builders, saw mills, contractors and house and ship joiners. Great Union Street and Witham.
Father	Thomas Edward Liggins	1900	Residence 22, Pemberton Street
Father	Thomas Edward Liggins	1908 & 1913	Architect and Surveyor, 43, George Street
Grandfather	Thomas Liggins	1904	Residence 403, Holderness Road. Hockney & Liggins.
Grandfather	Thomas Liggins	1905 & 1906	Residence Wilton House, Wilton Terrace, Hornsea (presumably retired)
Father	Thomas Edward Liggins	1909	Hockney & Liggins, builder and contractors (Thomas Liggins (E.L.'s grandfather) not listed)

This family research was carried out by Mrs Margaret Stockbridge (née Liggins, see family tree on the previous two pages) to whom the authors are indebted for the information.

Appendix 1(c): Dates of Birth and Death of the members of Ethel Leginska's family

Grandparents:

Thomas Liggins	b. 1835	d. 3rd December 1910 (at Skirlaugh)	Age: c. 75
Hannah Liggins	b. 1833	d. 28th July 1918	Age: c. 85
George Peck	b. c. 1821	d. 4th December 1894 (Hedon)	Age: 73
Maria Peck	b. c. 1819	d. 20th July 1911 (Hedon)	Age: 92

Parents:

Thomas E. Liggins	b. 2nd April 1861 d. 17th Oct 1928 (Bridlington)	Age: 67
Ann(i)e Liggins	b. 1st August 1857 d. 20th Nov 1899 (Hull, Sutton)	Age: 42

Stepmother:

Christina Bella Liggins (née Workman)
  b. 1875   d. 16th March 1955 (Bridlington)   Age: 79

Deaths in chronological order, and the stage that Ethel had then reached in her career:

	Age	Ethel's age at the time
4th December 1894: George Peck (maternal grandfather)	73	8

Ethel had already played at a public recital in Hull.

20th November 1899: Anne Peck (mother)	42	13

Ethel had given important public recitals at the Assembly Rooms in Jarratt Street, Hull and at the Queen's Hall in London, and was now a notable pupil at the Hochschule in Frankfurt.

3rd December 1910: Thomas Liggins (paternal grandfather) c. 75		24
and		
20th July 1911: Maria Peck (maternal grandmother)	92	25

By the time these two grandparents died Ethel had become a well-known, established concert pianist throughout Britain and the continent.

28th July 1918: Hannah Liggins (paternal grandmother)	c. 85	32

Ethel had, by July 1918, achieved huge success in the USA, she had already played six times at Carnegie Hall, and had been dubbed "The Paderewski of Women Pianists".

17th October 1928: Thomas E. Liggins (father)	67	42

Ethel's great success as a top-class pianist had continued over a period of more than twenty years and she had now branched out into conducting, having established her own orchestra.

16th March 1955: Christina Liggins (stepmother)	79	68

Ethel had given up her performing career sixteen years previously and since 1939 had been a successful teacher in Los Angeles. Christina's lifetime thus encompassed most of Ethel's musical career.

Appendix 2: Leginska the pianist

2 (a) A selection of typical recital programmes

Leginska believed in offering substantial recital programmes, thus giving her audiences their money's worth, as the following examples show.

Frankfurt, 17th January 1911

Schubert	Sonata in E flat, Op. 122
Glazunov	Sonata No. 1, Op. 74
Ravel	Jeux d'Eau
Whithorne	A Night Thought (Whithorne was Leginska's husband at the time)
Leschetizky	Étude Héroique
Fauré	Nocturne in E flat minor
Liszt	'Mazeppa' Étude

Aeolian Hall, New York, 20th January 1913 (Leginska's debut recital in the United States, see review on page 78).

Beethoven	Rondo à Capriccio in G, Op. 129 ('Rage over a Lost Penny')
Beethoven	Andante Favori in F, Op. 170
Brahms	Variations on a Theme of Paganini, Op. 35
Brahms	Sonata No. 3 in F minor, Op. 5
Chopin	A group of pieces (unspecified)
Liszt	'Mazeppa' Étude

Aeolian Hall, New York, 11th December 1913

Bach	Prelude and Fugue in E
Scarlatti	Capriccio in E
Mozart	Adagio from Sonata in F
Beethoven	Sonata in C, Op. 53 ('Waldstein')
Weber	Rondo in C ('Perpetual Motion')
Schubert	Moment Musical, Op. 94, No. 6
Mendelssohn	Scherzo (Capriccio) in E minor, Op. 16, No. 2
Chopin	Prelude in D flat, No. 15 ('Raindrop')
Schumann	Toccata in C
Brahms	Intermezzo in E flat, Op. 117, No. 1
Paganini-Liszt	La Campanella
Reger (Max)	Humoresque in D, Op. 20
MacDowell	'With Sweet Lavender', from 'New England Idyls', Op. 62
Ravel	Jeux d'Eaux
Scott (Cyril)	Water Wagtail, Op. 71, No. 3
Debussy	Toccata, from 'Pour le Piano'

Carnegie Hall, 19th March 1915

Scarlatti, D	Katzenfuge (Cat's Fugue)
Scarlatti, D	Sonata in E minor
Daquin	Le Coucou
Borodin	In a Convent
Rameau, J	Pièces de Clavecin en Concerts
Rameau, J	Nouvelles Suites de Pièces de Clavecin: Gavotte avec 6 variations
Schumann	Piano Sonata No. 2 in G minor, Op. 22
MacDowell	Piano Sonata No. 4 in E, Op. 59 ('Keltic')

contd...

Appendix 2: Leginska the Pianist: Typical Concert Programmes

Rubinstein	Étude in E flat major
Liszt	Hungarian Rhapsody No 8 in F sharp minor, R. 106
Leschetizky	Les Deux Alouettes (The Two Larks)
Schulz-Evler	Arabesques on themes by Johann Strauss II ('The Beautiful Blue Danube' Waltz)

Carnegie Hall, 31st March 1916

Bach-Busoni	Organ Toccata and Fugue in D minor, BWV 913
Bach	Two Inventions, in F (BWV 779) and in B flat (BWV 785)
Beethoven	Sonata in A, Op. 2, No. 2
Chopin	Scherzo in B minor, Op. 20
Chopin	Ten Preludes from Op. 28 (No. 3 in G major; No. 2 in A minor; No. 8 in F sharp minor; No. 7 in A major; No. 14 in E flat minor; No. 11 in B major; No. 16 in B flat minor; No. 22 in G minor; No. 23 in F major; No. 24 in D minor.)
Leschetizky	Étude Héroique, Op. 48
Liszt	Legend (St Francis Walking on the Waves)
Paganini-Liszt	La Campanella

Carnegie Hall, 2nd November 1916 (a recital described by the critics as "severely classical")

Bach	Concerto in the Italian Style, BWV 971
Brahms	16 Valses, Op. 39, arranged for solo pianoforte
Beethoven	Ecossaise in E flat major, WoO 86
Beethoven	Piano Sonata No. 8 in C minor, Op. 13 ('Pathétique')
Brahms	Variations on a theme by Paganini, in A minor, Op. 35

Carnegie Hall, 1st December 1916 (One of Leginska's famous 'all-Chopin' recitals)

Chopin	Ballade in G minor, Op. 23
Chopin	Bolero in C major, Op. 19
Chopin	18 Preludes from Op. 28 (No. 1 in C major; No. 2 in A minor; No. 3 in G major; No. 4 in E minor; No. 6 in B minor; No. 7 in A major; No. 8 in F sharp minor; No. 9 in E major; No. 11 in B major; No. 13 in F sharp major; No. 14 in E flat minor; No. 15 in D flat major; No. 16 in B flat minor; No. 17 in E flat major; No. 21 in B flat major; No. 22 in G minor; No. 23 in F major; No. 24 in D minor.)
Chopin	Sonata in B flat minor, Op. 35
Chopin	Four Études; Op. 10 (No. 12 in C minor; No. 7 in C major) and Op. 25 (No. 11 in A minor; No. 12 in C minor).

Columbia University, 2nd February 1917

Rameau	Gavotte and Variations
Daquin	Le Coucou
Beethoven	Two German Dances
Beethoven	Rondo à Capriccio, Op. 129 ('Rage over a Lost Penny')
Chopin	Nocturne in C minor, Op. 48
Chopin	Scherzo in B minor, Op. 20
MacDowell	Sonata Keltic, Op. 59
Leschetizky	Étude Héroique
Liszt	Legend (St. Francis Walking on the Waves)
Paganini-Liszt	La Campanella
Liszt	Hungarian Rhapsody No. 8

Carnegie Hall, 16th March 1917 (Benefit: People's Symphony Concerts)

Scarlatti-Tausig	Pastorale
Daquin	Le Coucou
Borodin	Au Couvent
Beethoven	Dances
Beethoven	Rondo à Capriccio in G major ('Rage over a Lost Penny')
Rameau	Le Rappel des Oiseaux (Call of the Birds)
Rameau	Gavotte and Variations
Chopin	Nocturne in C minor, Op. 48, No. 1; Scherzo in B minor, Op. 20
Schumann	Sonata in G minor, Op. 22
MacDowell	Sonata Keltic
Rubinstein	Sonata for Left Hand
Liszt	Hungarian Rhapsody No. 8
Leschetizky	Les Deux Alouettes (The Two Skylarks)
Schulz-Evler	Arabesques on the Blue Danube Waltz

Carnegie Hall, 11th March 1918 (Benefit: Y.W.C.A. New York Hostess House)

Paradies	Sonata No. 10 in D minor
Scarlatti	Pastorale and Capriccio
Liszt	Piano Sonata in B minor, R. 21
Godowsky	Angelus (premiere)
Balakirev	Islamey (Oriental Fantasy)
Chopin	Polonaise in A major, Op. 40, No. 1
Chopin	Berceuse in D flat major, Op. 57
Liszt	Transcendental Étude no. 4, R. 2B ('Mazeppa')

Two days later Leginska played the same programme, with the addition of Sonata No. 10 in D by Paradies, at Jordan Hall, Boston, Mass.

Carnegie Hall, 16th April 1918 (Benefit: Humanitarian Cult)

Schumann	Piano Sonata No 2 in G minor, Op. 22
Chopin	Etudes: A minor, Op. 25, (Whether No. 6 or No. 11 not specified); C minor, Op. 10, No. 12; E major, Op. 10, No. 3.
Verdi	'Rigoletto' Paraphrase, R. 267

These items were interspersed with speeches on 'The Liberty Loan' and 'The Simple Life – Its Relation to the War'.

Carnegie Hall, 20th February 1923

Beethoven	Six variations in F major on the theme 'Tändeln und Scherzen' by Franz Süssmayr *
Bach	Prelude in C major
Chopin	Nocturne in B major, Op. 62, No. 1
Chopin	Scherzo in B minor, Op. 20
Leginska	Dance of the Little Clown (New York premiere); Cradle Song; Scherzo after 'O Mad Superbly Drunk'; At Night (An Etching) (New York Premiere)
Ravel	Valses Nobles et Sentimentales
Berners	A Little Funeral March for a Rich Aunt (New York premiere)
Goossens	The Hurdy-Gurdy Man (New York premiere); Three Nature Poems, Op. 25, 'Bacchanal'
Liszt	St. Francis Walking on the Water; La Campanella

*Sometimes spelt Süssmayer

Appendix 2: Leginska the Pianist: Typical Concert Programmes

Carnegie Hall, 7th November 1923

Beethoven	Piano Sonata No. 12 in A flat major, Op. 26
Beethoven	Rondo à Capriccio in G major, Op. 129 ('Rage over a Lost Penny')
Leginska	Gargoyles of Notre Dame; Dance of a Puppet (New York premiere)
Liszt	Ballade No. 2 for Piano in B minor, R. 16
Chopin	Waltz in E minor, Op. Posth.; Prelude in A flat major, Op. 28, No. 17; Étude in A minor, Op. 25; Étude in E major, Op. 10, No. 3; Ballade in G minor, Op. 23; Polonaise in A major, Op. 40, No. 1.
Schulz-Evler	Arabesques on the Blue Danube Waltz

Appendix 2 (b)
Leginska's appearances as a soloist in concerts at Carnegie Hall

Since Leginska's nine appearances as a solo recitalist at Carnegie Hall have all been quoted above, it seems logical to also list her six appearances there as soloist in concerts. In the following list, the musical item in which Leginska was the soloist is indicated by an asterisk (*). Leginska was also the conductor of the orchestra, as well as the soloist, in the last two of these concerts (9th January 1925 and 12th March 1932).

6th February 1915: Young People's Concert – Symphony Society of New York
Conductor, Walter Damrosch

Schumann	Symphony No. 3 in E flat major, Op. 97 ('Rhenish')
Rubinstein	* Piano Concerto No. 4 in D minor, Op. 70
Dvorak	Nocturne for Strings in B major, Op. 40
Grieg	Peer Gynt, Op. 23, No. 2 (Solvejg's Cradle Song)

24th October 1915: People's Symphony Concert
Conductor, Franz X. Arens

Beethoven	'Egmont' Overture, Op. 84
Bach	Orchestral Suite No. 3 in D major, BWV 1068, Air (on the G string)
Liszt	* Fantasia on Hungarian Folksongs, R. 458
Tchaikovsky	Symphony No. 5 in E minor, Op. 64

24th February 1917: Young People's Concert – Symphony Society of New York
Conductor, Walter Damrosch

Beethoven	Overture 'Fidelio'; Overture 'Leonore'
Stanford	Symphony No. 3 in F minor, Op. 28 ('Irish')
Rubinstein	* Piano Concerto No. 4 in D minor, Op. 70
Wagner	'Die Meistersinger': Preislied; Prelude

22nd December 1918: Philharmonic Society of New York
Conductor, Joseph Stransky

Smith	The Star Spangled Banner
Kalinnikov	Symphony No. 1 in G minor
Rubinstein	* Piano Concerto No. 4 in D minor, Op. 70
Rimsky-Korsakov	Capriccio Espagñol, Op. 34

9th January 1925: Symphony Society of New York
Conductor and soloist, Ethel Leginska (See page 161 for more details)

Weber	Oberon Overture
Beethoven	Symphony No. 7 in A major, Op. 92
Bach	* Concerto for harpsichord in F minor, BWV 1056
Leginska	Two Short Poems after Tagore (New York premiere)
Wagner	Die Meistersinger von Nürnberg – Prelude

12th March 1932: National Women's Symphony Orchestra
Conductor and soloist, Ethel Leginska (See page 213 for more details)

Glinka	Overture, Russlan and Ludmilla
Schumann	'Spring' Symphony in B flat major
Mozart	* Piano Concerto in A major, K. 488
Rimsky-Korsakov	Russian Easter
Debussy	Cortège et Air de Danse (from Cantata "L'Enfant Prodigue")
Wagner	Overture, 'Rienzi'

Leginska's interpretation of Rubinstein's Piano Concerto No. 4 must have been very well received because she played it at no less than three of the six concerts in which she was piano soloist at Carnegie Hall, presumably at the request of the management.

Programmes of the first season of concerts of the Boston Philharmonic Orchestra, founded, managed and conducted by Ethel Leginska, are listed in Appendix 3 (page 326).

———————— * * * ———————— * * * ————————

The programme of the recital which Leginska was scheduled to give at Carnegie Hall on 26th January 1925, but did not give (see Chapter 12) was as follows:

Chopin	Prelude in F sharp major, Op. 28, No. 13
Liszt	Piano Sonata in B minor, R 21
Chopin	Preludes, Op. 28: No. 8 in F sharp minor; No. 2 in A minor; No. 23 in F major; No. 21 in B flat major; No. 22 in G minor.
Chopin	Études, Op. 25: No. 9 in G flat major; No. 12 in C minor.
Chopin	Scherzo in B minor, Op. 20
Chopin	Prelude in D flat major, Op. 28, No. 15
Chopin	Polonaise (unspecified)
Liszt	Hungarian Rhapsody No. 8 in F sharp minor, R. 106

Appendix 2: Leginska the Pianist: Typical Concert Programmes

Biographical notes on the three conductors with whom Leginska worked in the Carnegie Hall concerts of 6th February 1915, 24th October 1915, 24th February 1917 and 22nd December 1918:

Walter Johannes Damrosch was born in Breslau on 30th January 1862 and was brought to the USA along with his brother Frank by their musician father Leopold in 1871, both boys later becoming American citizens by naturalisation. In 1894 he created the Damrosch Opera Company which toured the USA for five seasons and in 1903 he organised the Symphony Society of New York into a permanent orchestra (The New York Symphony Orchestra) and remained its conductor until his retirement in 1927. In 1925 he became a pioneer of radio by conducting the first symphonic concert to be relayed across the whole of the USA. He died in New York on 22nd December 1950 aged 88. (He conducted Leginska's Carnegie Hall concerts of 6th February 1915 and 24th February 1917. He also conducted many other concerts of the New York Symphony Orchestra at other venues in which Leginska was piano soloist.)

Franz Xavier Arens was born in Neef (Rhenish Prussia) on 28th October 1856 but was brought to Milwaukee, USA by his family when he was very young. He studied in the USA and returned to Germany for further study with Rheinberger. On his return to the USA he was active in many musical enterprises and in 1900 he established a series of People's Symphony Concerts, a feature of which was low admission prices. Leginska's Carnegie Hall concert of 24th October 1915 was part of this series. He died in Los Angeles on 28th January 1932 aged 75.

Josef Stransky was born in Humpoletz, Bohemia, on 9th September 1872. He studied medicine, qualifying as a Doctor of Medicine at the University of Prague in 1896, and also studied music with Bruckner and Dvorak. After a number of musical appointments in Europe, he was appointed in 1911 as Mahler's successor as conductor of the New York Philharmonic Orchestra, a post he held until 1923. He died in New York on 6th March 1936 aged 63. (See Leginska's Carnegie Hall concert of 22nd December 1918.)

Sources of the information in this appendix:

Much of the information in this appendix is contained in the authors' file of press cuttings which include many press reviews, extracts of some of which are quoted in the text of the various chapters. The programmes of the concerts or recitals of 17th January 1911, 11th December 1913, 31st March 1916, 2nd November 1916, 1st December 1916, 2nd February 1917, 16th March 1917 and 11th March 1918 are quoted in *The Piano in Concert* (a book in two volumes consisting entirely of concert programmes) compiled and annotated by George Kehler, published by Scarecrow Press inc., Metuchen, New Jersey, 1982.

A printout of all of Leginska's Carnegie Hall concert programmes except the last (on 12th March 1932) was kindly supplied to the authors by Mr Gino Francesconi, the present Archivist of Carnegie Hall. The list includes the programme of the recital of 26th February 1925 which Leginska was scheduled to give but for which she failed to appear.

Appendix 3: Programmes of the first season of concerts in Boston of the Boston Philharmonic Orchestra, founded and conducted by Ethel Leginska, 1926-1927

All held on Sunday afternoons at 3.15pm.

Initial concert: 24th October 1926. Mechanics Hall

Weber	Overture 'Oberon'
Beethoven	Symphony No. 5 in C minor, Op. 67
Peterka	Prelude, Op. 8, 'Triumph of Life' (First performance in the USA)
Liszt	Hungarian Fantasie for piano and orchestra (Leginska played as well as conducted)
Wagner	Overture 'Tannhäuser'

Second concert: 31st October 1926. Mechanics Hall

Wagner	Prelude 'Die Meistersinger von Nuremberg'
Mahler	Das Lieder eines Fahrenden Gesellen (Songs of a travelling journeyman) for voice and orchestra

Leginska	Three Nursery Songs
	    Sleep, Baby, Sleep
	    Three Mice went into a Hole to Spin
	    Old King Cole
	(Madame Charles Cahier, contralto)

Dvořák	Symphony No. 5 in E minor, Op. 95 (from the New World)

Third concert: 21st November 1926. Mechanics Hall

Brahms	Academic Festival Overture
Mendelssohn	Capriccio Brillante in B minor, Op. 22 for piano and orchestra Piano part played by Justin Sandridge
Korngold	Suite for Orchestra (Incidental Music to 'Much Ado about Nothing') (First performance in orchestral form)
Rimsky-Korsakov	Suite, 'Scheherazade', Op. 35

Fourth concert: 28th November 1926. Mechanics Hall

Weber	Overture 'Der Freischütz'
Mozart	Concerto in A major for piano and orchestra, K. 488 (Leginska played the piano part as well as conducted)
Liszt	Symphonic poem, 'Les Preludes'
Leginska	Marche Funebre from 'Quatre Sujets Barbares'
Tchaikovsky	Slavic March

Appendix 3: Programmes of Leginska's Boston Concerts, 1926-1927

Fifth concert: 23rd January 1927. Boston Opera House

Schubert	Symphony No. 8 in B minor (Unfinished)
Salzedo	Symphonic Poem, 'The Enchanted Isle' for harp and orchestra. Solo part played by the composer, Carlos Salzedo
Wolf-Ferrari	Overture 'Susanna's Secret'
Coleridge-Taylor	'Onaway! Awake, Beloved'. Air from 'The Wedding Feast of Hiawatha', Op. 31, No. 1

Strauss (Richard)	Two songs:
	     To You
	     Cacilie
	     Soloist Rafael Diaz (tenor) of the Metropolitan Opera Company, New York

Wagner	Overture 'Rienzi'

Sixth and final concert of the season. 10th April 1927, Boston Opera House

Weber	Overture 'Euryanthe'
Beethoven	Concerto in C minor, Op. 7 for piano and orchestra First movement, Allegro con brio. (Piano part played by a Duo-Art reproducing piano from a Duo-Art roll previously recorded by Leginska. *) Beethoven's cadenzas used. Second Movement: Largo } These two movements played by Third movement: Rondo } Ethel Leginska in person (not a piano roll) She also conducted the orchestra in the whole concerto.

Malipiero	'The Princess Ulahlia' (for two soloists, chorus of mixed voices and orchestra)
	     Soloists: Dorothy Peterson Raynor (soprano)
	             Joseph Lautner (tenor)

Berlioz	'Rakoczy' from 'Damnation of Faust'

    It will be noticed that each concert included a composition that was new in 1926-27, Leginska herself being the composer of the modern work played in the second and fourth concerts (pieces composed c. 1923 in each case). In the other concerts the new works were composed by:

First concert: Rudolf Peterka (1894-1933), German composer. 'Triumph of Life' was written in 1924.

Third concert: Erich Korngold (1897-1957) German composer who settled in the USA and later became famous for his film music. His music for 'Much Ado about Nothing' was written in 1919.

Fifth concert: Carlos Salzedo (1885-1961), French-American composer and harpist. 'The Enchanted Isle' was written in 1917.

Sixth concert: G. Francesco Malipiero (1882-1973), Italian composer. 'The Princess Ulahlia' was written in 1925.

* The Duo-Art rolls used on occasions such as this were ones specially recorded for concert performances, not the ordinary rolls available for purchase by the public as listed in Appendix 5(b).

Appendix 4: Musical compositions by Ethel Leginska

Four Songs:
1. *Bird Voices of Spring* (or *Spring Song*) (words by C.S. Whittern).
2. *The Gallows Tree*.
3. *The Frozen Heart* (or *Winter*) (words by Otto Julius Bierbaum, English version by F.H. Martens).
4. *At Dawn* (words by A. Symons).
   All four published by G. Schirmer, 1919.

Other songs (from Leginska's early years as a composer):
Forgotten; An Island River; Sorrow;
I have a Rendevous with Death (words by Alan Seeger who died fighting in France in World War I);
Kälte (words by Otto Julius Bierbaum);
Love Song, A Song of Knowledge, Oh Lovely Moon, Set His Heart (all with words by C.A. Dawson-Scott);
Ode to the West Wind (words by P.B. Shelley);
Invocation; Light; Meadow Grass;
Desire (words by Philip Lindsey)
Four songs with words by Arthur Guiterman: *Mumps, A Tract for Autos, The Ambitious Dog, A Fable with a Moral*.

Gargoyles of Notre Dame (for piano), written 1918.
Published by G. Schirmer, New York, Boston, 1919. An interesting example of Leginska's work. Each hand is written in a different key.

Oh! Mad, Superbly Drunk (a scherzo for piano, after Tagore), c. 1920. Dedicated to Rudolph Ganz and published by G. Schirmer.

String Quartet. After four poems of Tagore. Composed c. 1920-21.
Performed at Boston, Mass, 25th April 1921.
Performed at Aeolian Hall, London, 14th June 1921.

From a Life (for 13 instruments).
Performed New York, 9th January 1922.

Beyond the Fields We Know (symphonic poem), written c. 1919.
Performed New York, 12th February 1922.

Cradle Song (for solo piano). J. Church Co., Cincinnati, 1922. Written for
Tamara Coates (daughter of the conductor Albert Coates).

Two Short Pieces for Orchestra, 1922. First performed by the Boston Symphony
Orchestra, 29th February 1924, Pierre Monteux conducting.

Dance of a Puppet (for solo pianoforte)
J. Church Co., Cincinnati, 1924.
Dedicated to Ethel's pupil, Evelione Taglione.

Quatre Sujets Barbares. A four-movement suite for orchestra, inspired by Gauguin, 1923.
Performed Munich, 13th December 1924, Leginska conducting.

Appendix 4: Leginska's Musical Compositions

        Six Nursery Rhymes (songs for soprano and small orchestra),1923. Published by J. Church Co., Cincinnati, 1925 and performed by the Boston Philharmonic Orchestra, 1926. They comprise:
Gorgy-Porgy (dedicated to "Kewpie"); *Sleep, Baby, Sleep* (to "Baby"); *Little Boy Blue* (to "She-She"); *Three Mice Went Into a Hole* (to "Pussy"); *Jack and Jill* (to "Toie"); *Old King Cole* (to "Shorty").
        All available separately.

Fantasy (for Orchestra and Piano)
        Written c. 1922. Performed New York, 3rd January 1926.

Triptych (for 11 instruments).
        Performed Chicago, 29th April 1928.

In a Garden (song), 1928. Words by David Morton.

Americans are Always Marching On. (Setting of a poem by Stephen Vincent Benét.
        For mixed chorus, solo voices and piano. Won the Mu Phi Epsilon award for chamber music works, 1959.

Other music for piano:
Three Victorian Portraits. Published by Composer's Press, 1959.
        Performed by Joanna Hodges at the New York Town Hall, 10th November 1959.
        Comprises:
             Nostalgic Waltz; Dirge; Heroic Impromptu; At Night; Dance of the Little Clown; Impromptu; Scherzo.

Moments Musicaux, Op. 5. Date unknown.

Operas:
        The Rose and the Ring (based on a satire by W.M. Thackeray). Composed 1931-32.
Libretto adapted by Edith E. Ohlson. Miss Ohlson, who was born in London in 1865, was a friend of Leginska. At the time *The Rose and the Ring* was being written and composed, she lived at 'Loretto', 36, Sanyhils Avenue, Patcham, Brighton, and she and Leginska (who was living in England at that time) used to meet in London periodically to discuss matters. *The Rose and the Ring* lay unperformed for 25 years until Leginska conducted the premiere in Los Angeles on 23rd February 1957. In 1936 Leginska and Edith Ohlson also discussed the possibilities of *Joan of Arc*, using Mark Twain's book as a basis for the libretto.

        Gale (The Haunting).
Presented at the Chicago Opera House by the Chicago Civic Opera Company on 23rd November 1935, Leginska conducting.

        Joan of Arc (Libretto by Mark Twain).
Presented at the Wilshire Ebell Theatre, Los Angeles, on 10th May 1969.

Appendix 5 (a): Leginska's gramophone recordings

Recordings made for British Pathé, c. 1920: 12" acoustic recordings

Record No.	Matrix	Composition
5634	67524	Liszt: Hungarian Rhapsody, No. 13
	67525	Moszkowski: Waltz in E major
5390	67523	Leschetizky: Gavotte
	67528	Chopin: Étude, Op. 25, No. 11 (*Winter Wind*)
5583	*	MacDowell: *Hexentanz* (*Witches' Dance*)
	*	Arensky: Study in F sharp
		MacDowell: *Shadow Dance*

     *   Matrix Nos. unknown but presumed to be 67526 and 67527.

  These Pathé records would have been of the 'centre start' type (see pages 136-137). No copies have been found by the authors, and the appropriate section of the British Library (formerly known as The British Institute of Recorded Sound) does not have copies either. However, the British Library is confident that the records were definitely made and released.

Recordings made for Columbia (USA), 1926-27. 12" electric recordings

7176M/5068M	{Rachmaninov: Prelude in C sharp minor, Op. 3, No. 2
	{Rachmaninov: Prelude in G minor, Op. 23, No. 5
7177M/5074M	{Chopin: Polonaise, Op. 40, No. 1 in A (*Military*)
	{Chopin: Prelude, Op. 28, No. 5 in D
7178M/5072M	Liszt: Hungarian Rhapsody, No. 8 (Parts 1 and 2)
7179M/5086M	Schubert: Marche Militaire, Op. 51, No. 1 (2 parts)

  These Columbia discs of 1926-27 were not issued in Britain

  See page 334 for the exact dates when the above Columbia discs were recorded.

Appendix 5(a): Leginska's Gramophone Recordings

Recordings made for Columbia (USA), c. 1928. 10" electric recordings

Schubert: Moments Musicaux, Op. 94, as follows:

17013D	No. 1, Part 1
	No. 2, Part 1
17014D	No. 2, Part 2
	No. 4, Part 1
17015D	(a) No. 4, Part 2
	(b) No. 3 and No. 5
16016D	No. 6, Part 1
	No. 6, Part 2

The above four records were issued in Britain as 4887 - 88 - 89 - 90. They were deleted from Columbia's British catalogues after 1934.

Records made for Columbia (USA), c. 1928. 12" electric recordings

Schubert, Impromptus, Op. 142, as follows:

Record No.	Matrix	
67445D	W98483	No. 1, Part 1
	W98484	No. 1, Part 2
67446D	W98486	No. 2
	W98469	No. 3, Part 1 (*Rosamunde*)
67447D	W98470	No. 3, Part 2 (*Rosamunde*)
	W98514	No. 4

The above three records were issued in Britain as 9476 - 77 - 78. They were in Columbia's British catalogues until 1938 - 39.

The 1928 Schubert recordings were issued as part of a centenary tribute to Schubert, who died in 1828. See page 334 for the exact dates when the above Columbia discs were recorded.

Appendix 5 (b): Leginska's piano roll recordings

Roll No.	Composer	Title	Date of issue
Duo-Art:			
6885	Bach	Prelude and Fugue from *The Well-Tempered Clavier*, No. 3 in C	6/25
6743	Beethoven	Minuet, No. 2 in G	4/24
		[Also issued as A-7 and D-651, each annotated by Conrad; as D-55 (annotated by Lowe), and as D-1017 ('Playtime' series for children, with words, music and pictures).]	
6957	Beethoven	Eight Variations on the theme *Tändeln und Scherzen* arranged by Franz Süssmayr	1/26
5644	Chopin	Ballade (1st) in G minor, Op. 23	5/15
7075	Chopin	Nocturne in E flat, Op. 9, No. 2	11/26
6707	Chopin	Valse in E minor (Posthumous)	1/24
6822	Leginska	*Cradle Song*	12/24
6388	Leschetizky	Arabesque en Forme d'Étude, Op. 45, No. 1	2/21
6539	Leschetizky	*The Two Larks* (Impromptu), Op. 2, No. 1	6/22
		[Also issued as D-207, annotated by Forsyth.]	
6731	Liadov	*The Music Box* (*Une Tabatière à Musique*), Op. 32	3/24
		[Also issued as A-26 (children's roll annotated by Woods); as D-641 (annotated by Woods or McNaught (the Aeolian Company's monthly bulletin says Woods but their catalogue says McNaught)), and as D-9 (children's roll with introduction by Reed).]	
7396	Liszt	Hungarian Rhapsody, No. 8 in F sharp minor (Capriccio)	5/30
5585	Mendelssohn	Songs Without Words, No. 30, Op. 62, No. 6 (*Spring Song*)	?11/14
7137	Mendelssohn	Songs Without Words, No. 44, Op. 102, No. 2 and No. 10, Op. 30, No. 4	7/27
6159	Moszkowski	Valse in A flat, Op. 34, No. 1	6/19
		[Also issued as A-122 and as D-837, (each annotated by Jacquet)]	
1106	Mozart	Sonata for two pianos, K.448, 1st movement	4/23
1107	Mozart	Sonata for two pianos, K.448, 2nd movement	4/23
1108	Mozart	Sonata for two pianos, K.448, 3rd movement	4/23
		[In the above three Mozart rolls Leginska plays the <u>second piano part only</u>. These are instructional rolls intended to assist pianists who are learning to play the piece.]	
6217	Rameau	Gavotte and Variations (tr. Leschetizky)	12/19
6549	Rimsky-Korsakov	*Hymn to the Sun* from *The Golden Cockerel* (*Le Coq d'Or*)	9/22
5587	Rubinstein	Valse Caprice in E flat	?11/14
5583	Rubinstein	Melody in F, Op. 3, No. 1	?11/14
5584	Schubert	Marche Militaire, Op. 51, No. 1 (arr. Tausig)	?11/14
5582	Schubert/Liszt	*Hark! Hark! The Lark!* (transcription by Liszt)	?11/14
5586	Schumann	*Träumerei*, from *Kinderszenen*, Op. 15, No. 7	?11/14
6592	Strauss	Concert Arabesques on Motives from the Waltz *By the Beautiful Blue Danube* (tr. Schulz-Evler)	1/23
7352	Tchaikovsky	*Autumn Song*, Op. 37A, from *The Seasons* (No. 10 - October)	10/29
7359	Tchaikovsky	*Festival Overture "1812"*, Op. 49	11/29
6999	Weber	*Oberon* Overture	5/26
		[Also issued as A-68 and D-739, each annotated by Percy A. Scholes.]	

Appendix 5(b): Leginska's Piano Roll Recordings

Leginska also contributed, with Harold Bauer, Josef Hofmann and Albert Stoessel, to two Biographical Rolls of Beethoven, with commentary by Mackenzie: A-51A and D-333 (Part 1) and A-51B and D-335 (Part II) – 10/26. She also contributed to *Chopsticks* in 1925 (see p. 145).

Ampico:
52553	Daquin	*Le Coucou*	by 7/20
55396	Liszt	Hungarian Rhapsody, No. 8 in F sharp minor (Capriccio)	by 7/20
53927	Strauss	*Blue Danube* - Concert Arabesque (tr. Schulz-Evler; arr. Leginska)	by 7/20

Artrio: Dates of issue of these Artrio rolls is unknown but they were all in the 1922 catalogue.
7600	Beethoven	Rondo à Capriccio, Op. 129 (*Rage over a Lost Penny*)
7568	Chaminade	Air de Ballet, Op. 41 (*Pierrette*)
7576	Chaminade	*Automne*, Op. 35, No. 2
7593	Chaminade	*Elevation*, from *Romances Sans Paroles*, Op. 76, No. 2
7827	Chopin	Nocturne, Op. 48, No. 1
7518	Chopin	Prelude, Op. 28, No. 24 in D minor
7564	Donizetti	*Lucia di Lammermoor*. Sextette
7615	Godard	Second Mazurka, No. 2, Op. 54
7616	Granados	Danzas Españolas, No. 4. *Villanesca*
7513	Leginska	Moment Musical, Op. 5, No. 1 (*Love*)
7510	Leschetizky	*The Two Larks* (Impromptu), Op. 2, No. 1
7640	Leschetizky	*Souvenirs d'Italie*, Op. 39, No. 1, Ballade Venetienne
7641	Leschetizky	*Souvenirs d'Italie*, Op. 39, No. 2, Scherzo (Como)
7642	Leschetizky	*Souvenirs d'Italie*, Op. 39, No. 3, Canzonetta all' Antica (Firenze)
7643	Leschetizky	*Souvenirs d'Italie*, Op. 39, No. 4, Mandolinata (Roma)
7644	Leschetizky	*Souvenirs d'Italie*, Op. 39, No. 5, Tarantella (Napoli)
7645	Leschetizky	*Souvenirs d'Italie*, Op. 39, No. 6, Siciliana all' Antico (Cantanio)
7557	Liszt	Hungarian Rhapsody, No. 2
7542	Liszt	Hungarian Rhapsody, No. 8 in F sharp minor (Capriccio)
7511	MacDowell	*Sea Pieces*, Op. 55, No. 5
7545	MacDowell	*Witches' Dance (Hexentanz)*, fr. *Two Fantastic Pieces*, Op. 17, No. 2
7569	MacDowell	Shadow Dance
7629	Moszkowski	*Guitarre*, Op. 45, No. 2
7537	Moszkowski	*La Jongleuse (The Juggleress)*, Op. 52, No. 4
7519	Moszkowski	Waltz, Op. 34, No. 1
7590	Nevin	*Water Scenes*, Op. 13, No. 4 (*Narcissus*)
7514	Paderewski	Nocturne, Op. 16, No. 4
7649	Rubinstein	Barcarolle, No. 1; Op. 30 in F minor.
7598	Rubinstein	*Kamennoi-Ostrow*, Op. 10, No. 22
7574	Seeling	*The Lorelei*, Op. 2
7533	Sieveking	Valse Lente, Op. 10
7553	Tchaikovsky	*The Seasons*, Op. 37a, No. 6 (*June*)
7512	Verdi	*Rigoletto* (Paraphrase; transcription by Liszt)
7562	Wagner	*Tristan und Isolde. Isolde's Love Death* (transcription by Liszt)

Recordo: Dates of issue unknown.
613550	Chaminade	*Elevation*, Op. 76, No. 2
613530	Chopin	Nocturne, Op. 48, No. 1
612900	Leschetizky	*The Two Larks* (Impromptu), Op. 2, No. 1
613750	MacDowell	*Sea Pieces*, Op. 55, No. 5
613890	Moszkowski	Waltz, Op. 34, No. 1
613540	Nevin	Three Characteristic Dances, Op. 6, No. 2
614140	Sieveking	Valse Lente, Op. 10

Appendix 5(c)
Currently-available compact disc re-issues of Leginska's gramophone recordings

At the time of writing only two compact discs of Leginska's recordings are available. The details are:

Ivory Classics. Ethel Leginska: The Complete Columbia Masters, 1926-1928. Disc Number 64405-72002. Issued 2001.

The recordings on this disc are:

Schubert: Four Impromptus, Op. 142 (D. 935)
    No. 1 in F minor   (Recorded 9 March 1928)
    No. 2 in A flat major   (Rec. 20 February 1928)
    No. 3 in B flat major   (Rec. 20 February 1928)
    No. 4 in F minor   (Rec. 5 April 1928)
Schubert: Six Moments Musicaux, Op. 94 (D. 780)
    No. 1 in C major
    No. 2 in A flat major
    No. 3 in F minor   All the Moments Musicaux
    No. 4 in C sharp minor   were recorded on 8 March 1928
    No. 5 in F minor
    No. 6 in A flat major
Schubert, arranged Carl Tausig:
    Marche Militaire in D major, Op. 51, No. 1 (D. 773) (Rec. 5 April 1928)
Chopin:
    Polonaise in A major, Op. 40, No. 1 ('Military')   (Rec. 3 June 1927)
    Prelude in D flat major, Op. 28, No. 15 ('Raindrop')   (Rec. 3 June 1927)
Rachmaninov:
    Prelude in G minor, Op. 23, No. 5   (Rec. 21 December 1926)
    Prelude in C sharp minor, Op. 3, No. 2   (Rec. 21 December 1926)
Liszt:
    Hungarian Rhapsody no. 8 in F sharp minor (abridged)   (Rec. 19 June 1926)
    Total Playing time: 72 min. 44 sec.

Opal (Pavilion Records Ltd): Pupils of Leschetizky.
Disc Number: Opal CD 9839. Issued 1988.

This disc consists of contributions by (in order) Ethel Leginska, Benno Moiseiwitsch, Mark Hambourg, Ossip Gabrilowitsch, Ignace Paderewski, Ignaz Friedman, Frank La Forge, Marie Novello, with an additional recording (from a piano roll) of Theodor Leschetizky himself.

The two recordings of Ethel Leginska included on this disc are:

    Schubert: Impromptu in A flat, Op. 142, No 2
    Liszt: Hungarian Rhapsody No. 8 in F sharp minor (abridged)

These two recordings have the same matrix numbers as the corresponding ones on the Ivory Classics disc and are therefore evidently the same 'takes'.

The total playing time of these two pieces is 9 min. 37sec.

Appendix 6: Musical compositions by Emerson Whithorne
(Ethel Leginska's husband from 1907 to 1918)

The date of composition is followed by the place of first performance, where known.

For orchestra
The Rain (for orchestra, 1912). (Detroit, February 1913).
New York Days and Nights, Op. 40 (representing the USA, very successfully, at the Salzburg Festival, 1923. New York Premiere in 1927). Often played by jazz bands as well as symphony orchestras.
The Aeroplane (Birmingham, UK, 1926). This was an orchestral version of a piano piece written in 1920, one of the earliest examples of 'machine music'.
Several works based on Japanese and Chinese themes, e.g. *Adventures of a Samurai*, *The Yellow Jacket*, *The Typhoon*.
In the Court of the Pomegranites (Colonne concerts, Paris, 1925).
Saturday's Child (for mezzo soprano, tenor and small orchestra). New York, 1926. Set to the poems of the Negro poet Countee Cullen; commissioned by the League of Composers.
Poem (for piano and orchestra), Op. 43. Chicago, 1927 with Walter Gieseking as soloist.
Fata Morganna (symphonic poem), Op. 44. New York, 1928.
Marco Millions (1928).
Symphony No. 1 (1929; Cincinnati, 1934).
The Dream Pedlar (symphonic poem), Op. 50, 1930. Los Angeles, 1931.
Violin Concerto (Chicago, 1931).
Fandango (for orchestra). New York, 1932, conducted by Sir Thomas Beecham.
Moon Trail (symphonic poem). (Boston, 1933).
Symphony No. 2, Op. 56 (Cincinnati, 1937).
Sierra Morena (New York, 1938).

Chamber music
Greek Impressions (string quartet) 1917.
Piano Quintet, Op. 48 (1928).
String Quartet, Op. 51 (1930).
Violin Sonata.
The Grim Troubador is another setting of a Cullen poem and was an attempt to express the rhythmic feeling of Negro music. Set for string quartet and baritone (1937).

For piano
El Camino Real (piano suite) 1937.

For violin
Violin Sonata, 1932.

For the theatre
Sooner and Later, ballet for chamber orchestra and chorus (1925).
Incidental music to the New York Theatre Guild production of *Marco Millions*.

Vocal
Two Chinese Poems, Op. 18 and two Chinese Nocturnes, Op. 34.

Whithorne also composed three tone poems and many other pieces including other chamber music, piano pieces and songs. Whithorne's compositions were often performed during his lifetime but have rarely been played since his death.

Appendix 7: Article by Bruno David Ussher, 1925.
A contemporary account of Leginska as conductor/composer/pianist

Music
By Bruno David Ussher

Lo! a little woman shall lead them. There were, doubtless, 30,000 people at the Hollywood Bowl when Ethel Leginska appeared as conductor, pianiste and composer, with the symphony. One need not be a feminist to delight in this remarkable achievement of the lion-maned, quick moving bit of a girl who in black coat and skirt flamed music gently, broadly, dramatically, in short, convincingly. It may be said that Leginska truly triumphed, not merely by attracting the largest concert audience at the Hollywood Bowl, being recalled nine times, but her greatest attainments were notable performances of great classic works with an orchestra to a large extent in quizzical, if not worse, mood.

While the Philharmonic Orchestra played well and often with surpassing beauty of tone, one sensed easily the contest of a decidedly masculine inclined group of performers, who eyed the woman conductor with none too ready acceptance. In fact, there were players whose unfriendly or openly derisive attitude towards Leginska proved decidedly annoying to an audience which had faith – and justly so – in her artistry. To anticipate, Leginska's technic of the stick may not always have equal power of holding and compelling an ensemble used to a baton of rather unbending insistence. There were effects which might have gained with greater forcefulness. Both will come with a few years of opportunity and ample rehearsals.

Leginska, to succeed in a program of demanding classics, difficult, because so transparent and well known, customary to the orchestra to the degree of convention, proved her specific qualities as a leader in producing readings notable for their purity of style, plasticity, and poetic elegance of phrasing. Her detail of tempo conceptions, such as in the works mentioned, is but one instance of her knowledge of score, her interpretive forethought and executive consistency. Leginska, after years of pianistic success, following an amazingly short period of baton experience, comes to us with readings which to a large extent actually and potentially reveal her as the possessor of conductorial qualities not a few more routined directors have lost in the years of gaining control.

Leginska "individualizes" her music. Her Beethoven symphony, and it was "unbuttoned", joyously abandoned Beethoven in the quick movement, delicate, mysterious in the slow movement. Weber's "Oberon" was truly Weber with that touch of Shakespearean Midsummer Night's Dream which makes this distinctively "Oberon" music. Rarely has Wagner's "Meistersinger" prelude glowed more splendidly. The festive pompousness of those "Meistersingers" had grown threadbare in the hands of many conductors. The genuine pride of those burgher-singer-poetasters, the precious sweetness of those love themes, the quaintly gothic angularity, the happy, festive whirl of medieval Nuremberg, came to life in a manner that was as atmospheric as one hears it but seldom in a concert, as it wells up so indefinably only in a darkened opera house, as this great overture is intoned from the pit.

If Leginska can feel the soul of "Meistersingers" as she did last Tuesday, make live again the almost naive happiness of Beethoven, exult with him in the last movement as she did, then one anticipates keenly the Leginska who will, in a few years of routine, have added that authoritiveness of feeling and expression, which is already in her, but which, sensitive as she is, is yet retarded psychologically. It is not how Leginska conducts. It matters little that often she does not use the baton arm at all. It is significant only inasmuch as it bespeaks her economy of means, her interpretive self-control.

Once the concert was well under way, there seemed to exist closer contact between maestra and players. Orchestral playing had fine precision and for the most part good balance. The latter was due, not a little, to Miss Leginska grouping the instrumental sections according to old-fashioned customs, violin to the left and right, cellos and violas in front, double basses to the left, woodwind in the center, the darker-toned

Appendix 7: Article by Bruno David Ussher, 1925

instruments linking up with the heavy brass. Not for a long time has one heard so much soaring tone as in this arrangement, individual string tone from the different groups, yet blended in ensemble. Leginska's rhythms are as supple as they can be incisive and broadly vigorous. She directed and phrased as she would sing, with a natural urge and beauty of flow and thematic blend.

To all extents she directs with much gusto. She enjoys it. Where she inspires confidence is in moments of musical suspense or rich sonority, when she does not overexert herself. She darts her accents, but again she produces a legato and continuity of thematic progress which is captivating. Leginska mainly conducts with hand and full arm, but now and again her body stiffens, or relaxes, bends forward, or a motion toward the players, a turn to the strings. She listens well for tone quality and her left hand was busy shading. Just as in her compositions she has a keen sense for instrumental color and rhythm and that also marks her readings. Those transition and development periods in the Beethoven symphony never lacked interest, yet they remained unadulterated Beethoven. One enjoyed her feeling for sentiment, never dragged down into sentimentality.

Leginska knows what she wants and with fuller rehearsal time would have gained it more completely. She has been called sensational. Yes, she is, genuinely so, by her sincerity and lack of musical affectation. Although she has most evidently the complete exposition of a work in mind, driving at once for detail and bigness, she avoids two conductorial sins. She does not toy with tonal effects, or rhythmic or tempo exaggerations, tempting as they may be. Her faithfulness to style distinctly impresses her public. So much for Leginska the conductor. To add only a single side-thought, opportunely expressed in Mrs Carter's announcement from the stage, that Leginska, while honestly coveting baton success, cherishes more yet her opportunity of pioneering for woman musicians, both to occupy the rostrum and the players' seats.

Leginska the pianist needs little comment, as she has long been recognized. To see and hear her revive the old custom of directing from the piano bench made the Weber concerto No. 1 opus 11 in C-major an all the more delightful experience. Not often has piano tone sounded so well in the Bowl. Her solo work at the keyboard, interrelated with occasional directions, made the performance historically true chamber music on a larger basis. Here the orchestra lent itself more affably to artistic inter-relation, and especial credit must go to Ilya Bronson whose cello in the all-too-lovely, because so short, middle movement, found him playing with telling devotion and beautiful tone. It is a peculiarly Mozartian work, arresting in its lyric playfulness. Incidentally, this Weber concerto is practically unknown and was played from manuscript. Not a virtuoso work of the flashy type, the sincerity of its simplicity, inherent to the work as true of rendition, won Leginska some of the greatest ovations in an evening of triumph.

Last but not least, Leginska the composer. These "Six Nursery Songs for Chamber Orchestra and Soprano" are highly original, whimsical, dreamy, wistful, mockingly sad and grotesque. There is "Gorgy-Porgy", only nine bars long, but even then Leginska (musical tom-boy that she is) insinuates cleverly how running away does not help pie-eating, girl-kissing Gorgy, that fat little coward, who is thrashed in the end. "Sleep, Baby, Sleep" is more seriously artistic and uncommonly ingenious, based only on triads without intermodulatory chords of other intervallic nature. It is a crooning song which has much of the folk-like.

Altogether these are songs of characteristic English humor. "Little Boy Blue" is a shimmering dream picture into which the muted bleating of the sheep carries a clever touch of realism. "Three Mice went into a Hole", indeed! But one fairly sees meowing pussy crouch and slide and finally land her prey after the instruments nimbly have done their spinning. There is a pseudo-sadness, a crocodile's tear, in the closing harmonies when pussy lays out her victims. "Jack and Jill" is a little holter-polter epic, naive and drastic. Finally, robust, swashbuckling "Old King Cole".

Leginska has given us here miniatures of exceeding artistry and poetic subtleness. It bespeaks her fine touch when she gives the role of honor in the poem to the flute, thus making the suggestion more dream-like. Mrs Carter is to be congratulated upon bringing Ethel Leginska, and finding for her the opportunity to reveal her lovable triple-personality. She is a genius who gives herself so wholly that one prays to her guardian angel to take especial care of this generous little body with so big and vivid a heart.

* * * * *

This is a newspaper cutting in the authors' possession, re-typed to fit two pages. The newspaper from which it came is unknown because the cutting was unattributed. However, Bruno David Ussher wrote for The Evening Express *(Los Angeles) and the* California Graphic *so it may have come from one of those. Mr Ussher also wrote programme notes for the Hollywood Bowl's symphony concerts. The concert referred to was held on 4th August 1925. Whatever the source, Mr Ussher's review is duly acknowledged.*

The page opposite shows the artistic front cover of the various pieces comprising Leginska's 'Six Nursery Rhymes', a good description of which is given in the final column of Bruno David Ussher's article on page 337.

The six nursery rhymes were all available separately, each one having the same cover, as shown. In accordance with the usual custom in such cases, the title of the particular one being sold was underlined on the front cover. The words of all the nursery rhymes are quoted on pages 342 and 343.

Front Cover of Leginska's 'Six Nursery Rhymes'

Appendix 8: Programme of a concert given on 12th May 1960: Leginska conducting her own compositions

HUTTENBACK ARTIST BUREAU

Presents

LEGINSKA

CONDUCTING A PROGRAM OF

HER COMPOSITIONS

Assisted by

THE ARIOSO STRING QUARTET

CHAMBER MUSIC ORCHESTRA

AND SOLOISTS

WILSHIRE EBELL THEATRE

THURSDAY, MAY 12th 8:30 P.M.

This page and pages 341, 342 and 343: This is the concert described at the beginning of Chapter 18. Its importance lies in the fact that it seems to have been the last time that Leginska appeared on stage as a performing artist (she accompanied the various songs at the piano). The programme is reproduced here because the words of several of Leginska's songs are quoted – information which is not easy to access unless the sheet music is available.

(Copy of the programme kindly supplied by Marguerite Heller)

Appendix 8: Concert Programme, 1960

PROGRAM

"From a Life" Chamber Music Work for Eleven Instruments
(first Los Angeles performance)

    a) Lento — Allegro energico — Andante
    b) Grandioso — Lento dolentissimo
    c) Vivace

To be played without intermission
Composer Conducting

1st Flute — Arthur Gleghorn	1st Violin — Ralph Schaeffer
2nd Flute — Louise DiTullio	2nd Violin — Joseph Livoti
Oboe — Bert Gassman	Viola — Abraham Weiss
1st Clarinet — Kalman Bloch	Cello — Nino Rosso
2nd Clarinet — Merritt Buxbaum	Piano — Natalie Limonick
Bassoon — Norman Herzberg	

Songs
    a) "Kaelte"
    b) "Ode to the West Wind"   *First Los Angeles Performance*

    c) "Set His Heart"
    d) "Love Song"   *World Premiere*
    e) "A Song of Knowledge"

Soloist: KATHERINE HILGENBERG
Composer at the Piano

KÄLTE
Meine armen Veilchen sind erfroren,
Liegen nun im Schnee vorm Fenster draussen
Nass und duftlos.
Meine holde Hoffnung ist gestorben.
Einsam weiter durch das leere Leben
Mit erfrornen Herzen einsam weiter
Irgend wo in einem tiefen Walde
Sink ich nieder.
                Otto Julius Bierbaum

ODE TO THE WEST WIND
Oh, wild West Wind, thou breath of Autumn's being,
Make me thy lyre.
What if my leaves are falling like its own!
The tumult of thy mighty harmonies
Will take from both a deep, autumnal tone,
Sweet tho' in sadness. Be thou, Spirit fierce, My Spirit!
Be thou me, impetuous one!
Drive my dead thoughts over the universe
Like withered leaves to quicken a new birth!
Scatter my words among mankind!
Be, through my lips to unawakened earth,
The trumpet of a prophecy! Oh Wind,
If Winter comes, can Spring be far behind?
                Percy B. Shelley

SET HIS HEART
Set his heart 'tween the sunset and my thought,
Lest, under the white moon I see it ivory and dead.
Let his silence stand 'twixt tree and waterfall,
That I may hear murmur of life.
Warm the dark earth with sun ere you scatter it o'er my sleeping
That I may dream 'tis his hand on mine.
                C. A. Dawson Scott

LOVE SONG
A low fire burns,
Dreaming upon the hearth
While the stars swing across the sky.
Your flaming thought
Leaps through the dark and the stars set.
But for the comfort of my human fears,
Your low fire burns.
                C. A. Dawson Scott

SONG OF KNOWLEDGE
The Spring has hung a veil of green,
My eyes and the dark wood between,
The leaves have cloaked the poplar tall —
Dear leaves, I shall not see them fall.
When rough November's breath has set the gallop of their death,
Did all the winds of Autumn blow about my bed, I should not know.
The thick rank grass will wave around my dreaming earth,
And if your love, pass with my passing, be it so,
Faithful or false, I shall not know!
If love, should call to love? Dear heart,
We shall not be so far apart,
But that your welcome cry, would grow out of the hush,
And I should know, should know.
                C. A. Dawson Scott

Four Poems for String Quartet *(after Tagore)* (First Los Angeles performance)

ARIOSO STRING QUARTET

Ralph Schaeffer, *Violin*   Abraham Weiss, *Viola*
Joseph Livoti, *Violin*   Nino Rosso, *Cello*

(a)
"You left me and went on your way;
I thought I should mourn for you, and set your solitary image in my heart, wrought in a golden song.
But ah, my evil fortune, time is short."

"Then come, my rainy night, with pattering feet;
Smile, my golden Autumn; come, careless April; scattering your kisses abroad.
You come, and you, and you also!" etc.

(b)
"You are the evening cloud floating in the sky of my dreams.
I paint you, and fashion you, ever with my love longings.
You are my own, my own, Dweller in my endless dreams!" etc.

(c)
"I run as a musk-deer runs in the shadow of the forest, mad with his own perfume.
The night is the night of Mid-May, the breeze is the breeze of the south.
I lost my way and I wander, I seek what I cannot get, I get what I do not seek." etc.

(d)
"We are to play the game of death to-night, my bride and I.
The night is black, the clouds in the sky are capricious, and the waves are raving at sea." etc.
                Rabindranath Tagore

Songs: "O Lovely Moon" }
       "Desire"   }   *World Premiere*
       "In a Garden"
       "I have a Rendezvous with Death"   *World Premiere*

SOLOIST: STEVE STAGNER
Composer at the Piano

O, LOVELY MOON

O, Lovely Moon,
Sailing serene above the Ocean's fret,
Hear the sad crying of the curlews and a lonelier cry,
We, stumbling 'neath a burthen in the dark,
Look up to pray
The benison of thy peace.
O, Lovely Moon.
C. A. Dawson Scott

DESIRE

Better to hold you in hell's flame,
   our bodies flame, why should we care?
Than to suffer empty pain of heav'n
   without you there.

Better to freeze in hell's deep ice,
   ah, ice could never cool our lips,
Touch of your fingers would suffice
   for all the devil's angry whips.

Heav'n is hell with you away,
   hell turns heav'n when you're by.
I don't care what the prophets say,
I shall desire you when I die.
Philip Lindsay

IN A GARDEN

Who knows, who knows,
But in this perfect place of peace, of parting's pain,
Where I have touched your lips, your face.
Who knows, who knows,
But we shall come again,
You as the thirsting Rose and I the Rain.
David Morton

I HAVE A RENDEZVOUS WITH DEATH

I have a rendezvous with Death
At some disputed barricade,
When Spring comes back with rustling shade
And apple blossoms fill the air —
I have a rendezvous with Death
When Spring brings back blue days and fair.

It may be he shall take my hand
And lead me into his dark land
And close my eyes and quench my breath —
It may be I shall pass him still.
I have a rendezvous with Death
On some scarred slope of battered hill,
When Spring comes round again this year
And the first meadow flowers appear.

God knows, 'twere better to be deep
Pillowed in silk and scented down,
Where Love throbs out in blissful sleep,
Pulse nigh to pulse, and breath to breath,
Where hushed awakenings are dear . . .
But I've a rendezvous with Death
At midnight in some flaming town,
When Spring trips north again this year,
And I to my pledged word am true,
I shall not fail that rendezvous.
Alan Seeger
(Young American poet, member of the Foreign Legion, died fighting in France, World War 1)

INTERMISSION

"Triptich" *Chamber Music Work for Eleven Instruments*

   Lento — Allegro
      Lento dolentissimo
         Allegretto (molto ritmico e con umore)

Composer Conducting

Arthur Gleghorn — Flute	Ralph Schaeffer — 1st Violin
Bert Gassman — Oboe	Joseph Livoti — 2nd Violin
Kalman Bloch — Clarinet	Abraham Weiss — Viola
Norman Herzberg — Bassoon	Nino Rosso — Cello
Sinclair Lott — French Horn	Richard F. Kelley — Bass
	Natalie Limonick — Piano

Cycle of Six Nursery Rhymes, *for Soprano and Chamber Music Orchestra*

        (a) "Jack and Jill"   (d) "Gorgy-Porgy"
        (b) "Three Mice went into a Hole to spin"   (e) "Little Boy Blue"
        (c) "Sleep, Baby, Sleep"   (f) "Old King Cole"

SOLOIST: KRISTINA KOHLER
Composer conducting

(a)
Jack and Jill went up the hill to fetch a pail of water;
Jack fell down and broke his crown;
And Jill came tumbling after.

(b)
Three mice went into a hole to spin;
Puss passed by, and Puss looked in.
"What are you doing my little men?"
"Weaving coats for gentlemen."

"Please let me help you to wind off your threads."
"Ah, no, Mistress Pussy, you'd bite off our heads,

SAYS PUSS:
"You look so wondrous wise, I like your whiskers and bright eyes;
Your house is the nicest house I see,
I think there is room for you and me."
The mice were so pleased that they opened the door;
And pussy soon laid them all dead on the floor.
And pussy soon laid them all dead on the floor.

Appendix 8: Concert Programme, 1960

(c)
Sleep, baby, sleep.
Our cottage vale is deep;
The little lamb is on the green, with snowy fleece so soft and clean;
Sleep, baby, sleep.
Sleep, baby, sleep,
I would not, would not weep.
The little lamb, he never cries; for bright and happy are his eyes.
Sleep, baby, sleep.
Sleep, baby, sleep,
Near where the woodbines creep.
Be always like the lamb so mild, a sweet and kind and gentle child.
Sleep, baby, sleep.

(d)
Gorgy-Porgy, puddingy pie,
Kissed the girls and made them cry.
When the boys came out to play,
Gorgy-Porgy ran away.

(e)
Little Boy Blue, come blow your horn;
The sheep's in the meadow, the cow's in the corn.
Where's the boy who looks after the sheep?
He's under the haycock fast asleep.
Will you wake him? No, not I,
For if I do, he'll be sure to cry.

(f)
Old King Cole was a merry old soul,
And a merry old soul was he;
And he called for his pipe,
And he called for his bowl,
And he called for his fiddlers three.

Every fiddler had a fiddle fine,
A very fine fiddle had he;
Then tweedle-dee went the fiddlers three,
And so merry we will be.

Two Short Duets from the Opera Buffa "The Rose and the Ring"
 for Soprano, Tenor and Chamber Music Orchestra
Soloists: KRISTINA KOHLER and STEVE STAGNER
Composer conducting

Duet I
We must not part, as others do,
With sighs and tears, as we were two.
We keep each other in our heart.
True love hath wings, and can as soon survey the world
As sun or moon.
We keep each other in our heart.

Words Anonymous (written before 1650)

Duet II
Were I as base as is the lowly plain,
And you, my Love, as high as heav'n above,
Yet should the thoughts of me, your humble swain,
 Ascend to heav'n in honour of my love.
Were you, dear Love, the earth and I the skies,
My love should shine on you like to the sun,
And look upon you with ten thousand eyes,
'Till heav'n waxed blind, and 'till the world were done.
Where e'er I am my heart shall truly love but you.

J. Sylvester, (about 1730)

CHAMBER MUSIC ORCHESTRA

VIOLIN
Ralph Schaeffer, *Concertmaster*
*Harold Dicterow
Joseph Livoti
Nathan Ross

VIOLA
Abraham Weiss
Albert Falkove

CELLO
*Nino Rosso
David Filerman

BASS
*Richard F. Kelley

FLUTE
Arthur Gleghorn
Louise DiTullio

OBOE
*Bert Gassman
*Joseph Fishman

CLARINET
*Kalman Bloch
*Merritt Buxbaum

BASSOON
Norman Herzberg
Robert Swanson

HORN
*Sinclair Lott
*Ralph Pyle

TRUMPET
Vladimir Drucker
*Norman Williams

PIANO
Natalie Limonick
Jon Robertson

HARP
Dorothy Remsen

PERCUSSION
*William Kraft
*Walter Goodwin

* Member of Los Angeles Philharmonic Orchestra

Philip Kahgan, *Orchestra Manager*

STEINWAY PIANO — COURTESY OF PENNY-OWSLEY MUSIC CO.

Index

This index includes the names of people mentioned in the Authors' Preface and in the text of the 19 chapters. Mentions occurring in the Acknowledgments, List of Illustrations, Picture Credits, Bibliography, Appendices and the lists of references at the ends of chapters are excluded from the index, in accordance with standard practice.

Composers' names are included in the index where the reference in the text is an important part of the story, but not when it is only to one of their compositions, unless it is considered to be particularly significant. Leginska's three operas are quoted in the index but not her other compositions since they are so numerous.

Page numbers in italics refer to photographs or illustrations.

Aeolian Company, New York & London, (Duo-Art piano rolls), 92, 93, 94-95, 140-148, 151, 160, 188, 189, 306, 308, 309
d'Albert, Eugen, 33
Alda, Frances, 105
Aldrich, Richard, 78
Alexandra, H.M. The Queen, 64
Allan, Maud; see Maud Allan Dance Company
Allen, Maud Perceval, 54, 55
Allert, Adrienne, 252
American Piano Company, New York, (Ampico piano rolls), 94, 148, 169, 183
Ammer, Christine, 301
André, Madame von, 21
Apollo Piano Company, De Kalb, Illinois, (Artecho piano rolls), 94
Argerich, Martha, 303
Armand, I.O., see Knorr, Iwan
Arrau, Claudio, 152
Artecho piano rolls; see Apollo Piano Co.
Artrio piano rolls; see Wilcox & White Co.
Ashley-Cooper, Maud; see Warrender, Lady Maud
Associated Humber Lines (shipping company), 13
Avramov, Bogidar, 288
Ayers, Captain John, 174

Bach, J.S., 81, 97, 98, 140, 161, 176, 231, 236, 256, 301
Backhaus, Wilhelm, 106
Barry, Edward, 219
Bauer, Harold, 55, 145, 146, 237, 306
Baum, Marguerite; see Heller, Marguerite
Bauszern, W.E., 28
Baylis, Lilian, 224
Beatles, The, 287, 303
Bechstein, Carl; piano manufacturing company, 94
Beethoven, Ludvig van, 41, 53, 97, 98, 132, 133, 140, 148, 161, 169, 181, 188, 216, 217, 234, 263, 268, 301
Benét, Stephen V., 260
Bennett, William Sterndale, 16
Bergh, Haakon, 254
Berlin, Irving, 151
Berlioz, Hector, 194
Bernhardt, Henry, 55
Bey, Viana, *245*, *246*
Biggs, Anne Marie, 288-296, *289*, 301
Biggs, Anne Marie's son John, 292
Biggs, Dr Richard Keys, 288, 290, 292, 296
Bishop & Starr, organ builders, 17
Bizet, Georges, 195
Bliss, Cornelius, 146
Bloch, Ernest, 118, 119, 120, 122, 125, 129, 156

344

Index

Bloch, Ivan, 118
Bloch, Lucienne, (Bloch Dimitroff after her marriage), 118, 120
Bloch, Suzanne, 118
Bloomfield Zeisler, Fannie; see Zeisler, Fannie Bloomfield
Boardman, Reginald, 191
Böhme, Ferdinand, 29
Bolognini, Ennio, 254
Borodin, Alexander, 145, 146
Boult, Adrian (Sir Adrian from 1937), 224, 306
Brahms, Johannes, 29, 97, 98, 132
Brée, Malwine, 268
Breitkopf & Härtel, music publishers, 71
Brendel, Alfred, 152
Brenner, Morris, 254
Brica, Antonia, 158, 203
Britain, Radie, 166, 176, 194-195, 268, 280, 281
Broadbent, Marguerite, vi, 309
Brogden, Gwendoline (or Gwendolen; spellings vary), 13, 49
Brontë sisters, 13
Brooke, Lady Daisy, 14
Brougham, Lord and Lady, 21
Brower, Harriette, 87, 88, 92
Bruch, Max, 194
Burton, Lord and Lady, 21
Busoni, Ferruccio, 42, 106, 139, 140, 169, 270

Cahier, Charles, 186
Cahier, Mme Charles, 186
Cahn, Dr Peter, 35
Carl Rosa Opera Company, 10, 210
Carmen, Beverly, 176, *235*, 236-238, 239-240, 262, 263, 265-267, *267*, 280, 298, 301, 302
Carreño, Teresa, 42, 55, 71, 75, 114, 158
Caruso, Enrico, 39, 119
Casals, Pablo, 306
Chaplin, Charles, 266, 307
Cherkassky, Shura, vi, 306
Chopin, Frederic, 41, 53, 83, 85, 98, 103, 104, 133, 137, 140, 148, 168, 169, 264, 270

Christie, Agatha, 178
Clarke, Sir Edward, 14
Cleghorn, Arthur, 283
Clemens, Clara, 40
Clemens, Samuel, see 'Mark Twain'
Coates, Albert, 132, 242, 296, 306
Coates, Madelon (wife of Albert), 132, 306
Coates, Tamara (their daughter), 132
Colonne, Édouard J., 74
Columbia Phonograph Co. Inc., (the American branch of Columbia), 137-139, 152-153, 203, 204, 207, 303, 309
Contos, Catherine, 158, 203
Cooper, James Fenimore Jr., 99
Copland, Aaron, 125, 256
Cortot, Alfred, 151
Corzo, Ysidoro, 106
Cramer, Stuart, 61
Crofts, William H., 5
Cui, César A., 145, 146
Culver, Barbara Dell, 252
Curtis, Thomas, 275, 278
Curzon, Clifford, 152
Czerny, Carl, 36, 39, 41, 268

Dagg, Lynnore, 263
Damrosch, Walter, 85, 102, 117, 188, 242, 306
Dare, Zena, 55
Davies, Rev J. Vivian, 204
Dawimirska, Mrs, née Donimirska Benislavska (Mrs Theodor Leschetizky III), 41
Dawson, Charles, 204
Dawson, Peter, 55
Dawson-Scott, Mrs C.A., 219
Debussy, Claude, 81
Devries, Herman, 220
Devries, Rene, 191, 222
Diaz, Rafael, 119
Dolores, Antonia, 53
Donaldson, Herbert, 222, 254
Dresser, Marcia van, 119
Drucker, Vladimir, 283
'Duca' and 'Ducartist' piano rolls; see J.D. Philipps & Söhne

345

Duncan, Isadora, 301
Dunsany, Lord, 123
Duo-Art piano rolls; see Aeolian Company
Dupré, Marcel, 194
Dvorák, Antonin, 125
Dylan, Bob (Robert Allen Zimmerman), 287

Edward VII, H.M. The King, 65
Edwards, Arthur F., 292
Elgar, Lady Alice, 48
Elgar, Sir Edward, 140
Elizabeth II, H.M. The Queen, 224
Ellerman, Sir John, 13
Ellerman's Wilson Line Ltd., (shipping company), 13
Ellis, Richard, 252
Emerson, Ralph Waldo, 299
Enos, Joseph, 132, 176, 180, 230, 231-232, 234, 239, 263, 280
Erpelding, John W., 298
Essipoff, Annette; (Mrs Theodor Leschetizky II), 41, 158

Fera, Dominick, 254
Fisher, Elliott, 254
Franck, César, 274
Franz Ferdinand, Archduke of Austria, 47
"Frau Musica", 21
Friedberg, Carl, 28
de Friedebourg, Anna (Mrs Theodor Leschetizky I), 41
Friedheim, Arthur, 141
Friedman, Ignaz, 36, 106, 152
Fuchs, Robert, 62
Furtwängler, Wilhelm, 156

Gabrilowitsch, Ossip, 33, 36, 40
Gagen, Ray, 292
Gale (opera), 219-222, 224, 310, 311
Ganz, Rudolph, 106, 123, 146, 188
Gardiner, Henry Balfour, 32
Gaskell, Elizabeth, 13
Gauguin, Eugène, 132, 310
Gault, Arthur, 254
Gayner, Suzanne, *245, 246*

Germain, Karl (real name Charles Mattmueller), 61, 62, *62*, 63
Gershwin, George, 151
Gibson, Dr John Hare, 17
Gluck, Marcel, 69
Godowsky, Leopold, x, 77, 106, 117, 151, 194
Goldmark, Rubin, 125
Goldschmidt, Paul, 117
Goodson, Katharine, 36
Goossens, Eugene, 128, 129, 133, 156
Gordon, John, 170
Gordon-Cumming, Lt. Colonel Sir William, 14
Gough, James, 16
Gough & Davy Music Co., 16
Gowdy, Alma, 255, 283
Grainger, Percy, 32, 33, 34, 64, 141, 143
Grainger, Rose, 34
Gramophone and player piano compared, 138-140
Granados, Eduardo, 148
Grant, Cary (Archibald Leach), 307
Gray, Lydia M., 190
Green, Sophie D., 3
Greene, Gloria, *235, 259*
Greene, Patterson, 285, 310
Grey, Earl de (Marquess of Ripon), 42, 64
Grey, Lady de (Constance Gladys), 42, 64
Grieg, Edvard, 32, 124, 143
Gruber, Owen, 255
Gruenberg, Louis, 222
Guys, Mrs, 266

Hackett, Charles (singer and music critic), 209
Haensel, Fitzhugh William, 168
Haensel & Jones, concert agents, 105, 168
Hale, Philip, 96, 109
Hambourg, Boris, 53, 80, 306
Hambourg, Jan, 80
Hambourg, Mark, 36, 40, 53, 55
Hambourg, Michael (father of Boris, Jan and Mark), 53

Index

Hamilton, Roberta, 274
Hanon, Charles L., 268
Harrison, Percy, 50
Harty, (Herbert) Hamilton (Sir Hamilton Harty from 1925), 69
Haydn, Josef, 140
Hedman, Martha, 109
Heger, Robert, 156, 157, 271, 306
Heller, Alex, 250, 251
Heller, Marguerite (née Baum), 240, 247, *247*, 248-249, *250*, 269, 278, 280, 299, 308
Henderson, W.J., 109, 213, 215
Henselt, Adolf von, 42, 53, 54-55, 311
Hepburn, Katharine, 226
Hess, Lydia, 221
Hess, Myra (Dame Myra from 1941), 146
Hilgenberg, Katherine, 282, 283, 285, 286
Hiller, Ferdinand, 29
Hindemith, Paul, 28
His Master's Voice (HMV), record company, 139
Hitler, Adolf, 225
Hoch, Joseph P., 28
Hockney, John (Ethel's great-grandfather), 1
Hockney, Matthew Pape, 1, 3
Hockney & Liggins, builders, 1
Hodapp, Frieda; see Kwast, Mrs James II
Hodges, Joanna, 256
Hoffman, Eugene, 252
Hofmann, Josef, x, 77, 106, 141, 145, 146, 151, 169, 186, 306
Holloway, Mary-V., 242, *250*, 252
Hope, Bob (Leslie Townes Hope), 307
Horowitz, Vladimir, 178, 237
Hoss, Wendel, 254
Hugo, Victor, 121
Hummel, Ferdinand, 18, 311
Humperdinck, Engelbert, 28
Humphrey, Laning, 208-209
Huneker, James, 122
Hupfeld Co., Leipzig, (player piano actions and rolls), 94, 148
Hutcheson, Ernest, 146

Imperial Company; see Recordo piano rolls
Ireland, John, 129
Ivory Classics Record Company, 138, 152

Jackson, Mrs Irene, 287
James, Mr and Mrs W., 21
Joan of Arc, 114
Joan of Arc (Opera), 274, 288-296, 298, 310, 311
Johnson, Amy, 210
Johnson, James P., 117
Johnson, Samuel, 158
Jonás, Alberto, 106, 117
Jones, Allan, 212
Jones, Mary, 3
Jones, Rev W.H., 3
Joseffy, Rafael, 125
Joy, Charmian, 252

Kabos, Ilona, 301
Kaplan, Esther Lee, 238, *238*, 254, 264, *276*
Kempter, Lothar, 156
Kentner, Louis, 301
Kerr, Muriel, 231
Kindler, Hans, 128
Klemperer, Otto, 28, 242
Knorr, Iwan, 28, 29, 30, *31*, 34, 118
Knowles, Charles, 54
Kohler, Kristina, 255, 283, 285, 286
Koussevitzky, Serge, 242
KPFK (Los Angeles) radio station and programme, 262, 268-271, 274-275
Krehbiel, H.E., 109
Kreisler, Fritz, 96
Krimer, U.L., 63
Kwast, Antonia (Mrs James Kwast I), 29
Kwast, Frieda, (née Hodapp) (Mrs James Kwast II), 306
Kwast, James, 29, 30, *31*, 33, 34, 75, 306
Kwast, Mimi, 34

Lamond, Frederic, 33
Lancelot, Mr, 18, 311
Langdale, Marjorie, 83

Langdale, Thomas P., 49, 52, 218
Langtry, Lily, 55
Laurel, Stan (Arthur Stanley Jefferson), 307
Ledin, Marina A., 152
Leginska, Ethel; née Liggins, Ethel Annie (entries in roughly chronological order), photographs of, *17, 25, 62, 65, 66, 67, 82, 85, 88, 90, 93, 99, 100* (X-ray of hand), *105, 115, 118, 120, 126, 128, 142, 144, 147, 150, 160, 163, 183, 197, 200, 202, 211, 214, 218, 221, 233, 250, 251, 290, 291*; silhouettes or drawings of, *front and back covers, 184, 185, 196, 221*; ancestry and family background, 1-5; birth of, 5, 8; baptism, 5; early fascination with music, 10; starts to play the piano at age two, 10; taught at home by mother, 12; begins to teach at age six, 12; 'taken up' by Mary Wilson, 13; her early piano recitals at Tranby Croft, 14; enrolled as a pupil of Mrs Russell Starr at six, 16-18; early public appearances as pianist in Hull, 18; London debut aged 10, 19-21; similar recital in Hull, 21-22, 24-25; friend's assessment of Ethel as a child pianist, 23; personal appeal and magnetism of, x, 23, 80, 87, 104, 162, 207, 208, 236, 278, 282, 303; enrols at Hoch Conservatory in Frankfurt, 28; her fellow-students at Frankfurt, 32; Ethel's concerts and recitals at Frankfurt, 30, 34, 35; dissatisfaction with the Frankfurt Conservatory, 34; flees Frankfurt for Vienna, 36; audition with Leschetizky, 37-38; enrolled as a student by Leschetizky, 38; period of study with Leschetizky, 39-43; gift from Leschetizky, 42; petite physique of throughout life, x, 46, 80, 81, 85, 95, 98, 105, 109, 110, 125, 164, 195, 207, 210, 213, 225, 262; death of mother from smallpox, 46; adopts the name 'Leginska', 47; influence of Lady Maud Warrender on career, 47-48; Liggins family purchases a house in Hornsea, 49; visits to Tranby Croft, 49; based in London from 1904 to 1912, 50 *et seq*.; engaged for London recitals and provincial UK tour in 1904-1905, 50; recitals at Bechstein Hall, London, 53; recital in Hull, 53; appears in a Henry Wood concert at Queen's Hall, 53, and in a Henry Wood 'Prom', 54-55, 56-58; recitals at seaside holiday resorts, 55; forceful personality of, 61; romantic attachments to Karl Germain, 61-62 and Emerson Whittern, 62-63; marriage to Emerson Whittern, 63; was citizen of the United States from 1907, 63, 111, 225, 260, 286; recitals at Aeolian Hall and elsewhere, 63, 65; first visit to USA at age of 21, 65; plays in Cleveland, Ohio, 65; a son (Cedric Villiers) born in London, 65; series of recitals of music of different eras, 69; disappears and is lost for four and a half days, 69-70; highly-strung nature of, 69, 170, 173, 175; continuation of recitals, 70; prepared her programmes in Yorkshire, 70; recital/concert tours of Britain, Germany, France and Austria, 70-71, 74; views on piano technique, 75; goes to USA, 75; official New York debut, 78-79; quickly becomes a favourite performer in USA and Canada, playing many concerts and recitals, 80-85; father re-marries, to a cousin, 83; all-Chopin recital in New York, 83; adulatory poem in her honour, 84; regarded by many as foremost woman pianist of the day, 87; views on concert attire, 87-89; views on women's place in music, 89, 92; records her first Duo-Art rolls for the Aeolian Co., 92-95; able to guarantee a 'full house' at Carnegie Hall, 95 *et seq*.; contemporary analysis of her 'remarkable qualities', 95; reviews of concerts and recitals,

Index

96-98, and sobriquet "The Paderewski of Women Pianists", 98; another adulatory poem, 99; always in public eye, 100; damages finger in train door, 100; injured in train crash, 102; more reviews, 102 *et seq*.; movie film of Leginska, 105; interest in composition, some of her early compositions (1914, when aged 27) and description of them, 105; love of teaching, 106; performs in Cuba, 106-107; studies with Alberto Jonás, 106; wartime charity concerts, 107; divorce proceedings, 107 *et seq*.; actress Martha Hedman named in divorce case, 109; loses custody of Cedric, 110; Cedric's letters to his mother, 112-113; career unaffected by divorce, 113-114; her generous gifts to relatives in Hull, 115; widening interests, 117 *et seq*.; studies with Ernest Bloch, 118; performances of own compositions, 119 *et seq*.; takes up golf, 121; teaches in New York, 122; role model for young women and temporary withdrawal from concert platform, 122; public performances by her students, 123; moves from New York to Boston, 124; sought 'larger service to music', 124, 125, 127; studies with Rubin Goldmark, 125; views on admission prices to concerts, 127; desire to further widen career, 127; appearances in Great Britain in 1920s, 128-129; friendship with conductor Albert Coates and his wife Madelon, 132; her composition *Cradle Song* and its analysis, 130-132; description of *Six Nursery Rhymes*, 133; own compositions usually included in recitals, 133; records discs for Pathé, 136-137; records discs for Columbia, 137-138; *The Musical Times'* review of her Schubert recordings, 138; her Duo-Art piano-roll recordings, 92-95, 140-147, 151; records piano rolls for Ampico, 148; records piano rolls for Artrio, 148-149; records piano rolls for the Recordo Company, 149-150; summary and review of her recorded work on piano roll and disc, 151-153, 207; multiple role as pianist, composer, conductor and teacher, 156 *et seq*., 207; studies conducting with Robert Heger, 156-157 and Gennaro Papi, 157; conducts several major European orchestras, 157; prejudice against women conductors, 158-159, 180, 201, 203, 208; conducts in Great Britain and in Berlin, 159; reviews of Leginska as conductor, 159, 161, 162; conducts at Carnegie Hall, 161; conducts at Hollywood Bowl, 162; fails to appear for a piano recital at Carnegie Hall and is missing for six days, 168-175; two uncles (her mother's brothers) were living in New York, 173-174; probable reasons for Leginska's disappearance, 175-176; comparison of her disappearance with that of Agatha Christie, 178; sets up own orchestras, 180 *et seq*.; founds Boston Philharmonic Orchestra, 180; conducts and plays piano in concerts of Boston Philharmonic Orchestra, 181-190; description of programmes, and critics' reviews, 181-190; shares solo role in a concert with Duo-Art piano, 188-189; Boston Philharmonic Orchestra disbanded, 190; founds and conducts Boston Women's Symphony Orchestra, 190; conducts Women's Symphony Orchestra of Chicago, 191; conducts and plays piano in performances of Boston Women's Symphony Orchestra, 191-201; death and funeral of father, 203-205; an all-round musician, 207-209; anecdotes concerning Leginska as conductor, 208; tour of United Kingdom in 1930 in which she conducts operas, 209-210; praise from aviation pioneer Amy Johnson, 210; Leginska's skill as a conductor of operas, 195, 198, 210-213; founds and conducts National Women's Symphony Orchestra, 213-216; rents cottage in Suffolk in order to work in quiet surroundings, 217; writes opera, *The Rose and the Ring*, 217; conducts in Cuba, 217; writes her second opera, *Gale*, which is staged in Chicago, Leginska conducting, x, 217, 219-222; guest conductor of many opera companies, 223; resident in London in years 1936-39, 223-226; reluctance of concert managements to present *Gale* in the UK, 224-225; decision of future needed with war imminent, 225-226; decides to give up performing career in favour of full-time teaching, 225; proposed film about Clara Schumann starring Leginska, 226; leaves Britain for good and sets up teaching studio in Los Angeles, 228; students' accounts of Leginska's teaching, 228-240, 262-278; professional orchestral players hired for students' performances to form 'Leginska Little Symphony', 231, 242, 266, 278, 302; followed Leschetizky's teaching methods, 234, 236, 238, 239, 268; 'pep talks' to prepare students before their recitals, 237-238, 274; founds and runs 'New Venture in Music', 242 *et seq.*; her studios endorsed by many famous musicians, 242; vacations at Laguna Beach, 252; death of stepmother, 253; activities still reported in Hull in late 1950s, 253; production of opera *The Rose and the Ring*, 254-256; recalls early years in Yorkshire in her compositions, 256; role in Los Angeles 'Musicale' series, 256, 259; wins Mu Phi Epsilon award, 260; was lifelong heavy smoker, 262; her lessons expensive, 265; retained English accent, 266; KPFK radio programme featuring her students' recollections, 268 *et seq.*; 'An Evening with Leginska' concert of May 1960, 282-286, 287; this concert reported in Hull, 286-287; mastectomy for breast cancer, 287; production of *Joan of Arc*, 288-296; death, 298; death certificate, 300; funeral, 298-299; rejection of view that Leginska might have had Alzheimer's disease, 301-302; sale of personal effects, 302; review of life and career, 303-308; is currently largely forgotten in spite of her huge achievements, 306-307; some recent revival of interest in her, 307-308; piano recital marking centenary of death, 309; Hollywood Bowl Tribute, 310; some career landmarks, 311

Leschetizky, Anna (Mrs Theodor Leschetizky I, née de Friedebourg), 41

Leschetizky, Annette (Mrs Theodor Leschetizky II, née Essipoff or Essipova), 41, 158

Leschetizky, Donimirska (Mrs Theodor Leschetizky III, formerly Dawimirska, née Benislavska), 41

Leschetizky, Marie Gabriela (Mrs Theodor Leschetizky IV, née Rozborska), 41

Leschetizky, Theodor, 34, 36, 37, 38, *38*, 39, 40, 41, 42, 43, 46, 47, 50, 53, 61, 62, 63, 70, 75, 79, 89, 111, 117, 149, 234, 236, 238, 239, 252, 268, 271, 296, 301, 310

Lhevinne, Josef, 106, 151, 265, 270, 301

Lhevinne, Rosina, 265, 270, 301

Liadov, Anatol, 145, 146

Liapounov, Serge, 102, 103, 104, 199, 209, 264

Liggins, Anne (née Peck) (Ethel Leginska's mother), 2, 3, 4, 5, 10, 11, 12-13, 46, 47, 83, 203, 253

Liggins, Caroline Ellen, 2

Liggins, Christina Bella, (née Workman) (Ethel Leginska's stepmother), 83, 203, 204, 205, 253, 286, 287

Liggins, Ethel Annie; see Leginska,

Index

Ethel
Liggins, Frances Gertrude (Ethel Leginska's aunt), 2, 49, *52*
Liggins, Hannah Dawson (formerly Wright) (Ethel Leginska's paternal grandmother), 1, 2, 23, 49, 253
Liggins, Katherine Anne (Ethel Leginska's aunt), 2, 49
Liggins, Lucy Edith (Ethel's aunt; name 'Witty' after marriage), 2, 114-115, 218
Liggins, Thomas (Ethel Leginska's grandfather), 1, 2, *23*, 49
Liggins, Thomas Edward (Ethel Leginska's father), 2, 3, 4, 5, 10, 11, 12, 49, 63, 70, 83, 111, 153, 203-204, 205, 253, 286, 287
Liggins, William, 2
Limonick, Natalie, 283, 285
Liszt, Franz, 33, 50, 64, 75, 89, 95, 104, 114, 133, 137, 140, 145, 146, 151, 168, 169, 181, 182, 184, 252, 270
Livoti, Joseph, 283
Loeb, Magda, 264
Logan, Marie, 264
Logan, Robert, 240, 264, 280
Lonsdale, 4th Earl of, 42
Loredo, Armando, *235*, 264, 265
Lupu, Radu, 152

McCormack, John (initially known as J.F. McCormack), 55, 96
MacDonald, Jeanette, 212
McFarland, Ronald, 78, 226, 271, 274, *277*, 280, 281
Macfarren, Walter, 16
Mahler, Gustav, 186
Mar and Kellie, Lord and Lady, 21
Marsh, Jack, 254
Martin, Annie Jane; see Starr, Mrs Russell
Maskelyne and Devant Show, 51
Mattmueller, Charles; see Germain, Karl
Maud Allan Dance Company, 118
Mayer, Daniel, 19
Meggett, Joan M., 263
Mendelssohn, Felix, 132, 193, 270
Menuhin, Yehudi, 75

Mérö, Yolanda, 146
Metro-Goldwyn-Mayer (MGM) film company, 226
Middleton, Arthur, 119
Milhaud, Darius, 242
Millar, Gertie, 55
Mlynarska, Aniela, 169
Moiseiwitsch, Benno, 36, 37-38, 40, 239
Monteux, Pierre, 132, 242, 296, 310
Morgana, Nina, 119, 120
Morris, Paul, 98
Morton, Rachel, 282
Moschelles, Ignaz, 29
Moszkowski, Moritz, 148
Mozart, Wolfgang Amadeus, 32, 129, 132, 191, 215, 231, 244, 263
Mu Phi Epsilon Award, 260
Muck, Carl (or Karl), 104, 199
Munz, Mieczyslaw, 168-169, 173

Naish, Ted, 266
Neeley, Marilyn, 228, 230-231, 263, 268, *276*, 280, 281, 301, 310
Nevin, Ethelbert, 148
'New Venture in Music', 242-244, 252
Newcomb, Ethel, 39
Newman, Robert, 54
Ney, Elly, 36
Niemann, Walter, 74
Novaës, Guimar, 146

Ohlson, Edith E., 255, 274
Oliver, Lucille, 123, 166, 168, 170, 171, 172, 174, 175, 176, 190, 252, 263, 266, 302, 310
O'Neill, Marion, 63
O'Neill, Norman, 32
Ornstein, Leo, 124

Pabst, Arthur, 254
Pachmann, Vladimir de, 78, 151, 270
Paderewski, Ignace, x, 36, 48, 53, 77, 89, 96, 98, 100, 102, 106, 109, 207, 210, 234
Papi, Gennaro, 157
Pardee, Paula, 120

Parish, J.R., 212
Parker, H.T., 109
Pathé Frères Record Company, 136-137, 204, 207
Pavlova, Anna, 296
Pearson, Judge, 110
Peck, Anne; see Liggins, Anne (Ethel Leginska's mother)
Peck, Emma (Ethel's aunt), 2
Peck, Frederick W., (Ethel's uncle), 2, 173, 174
Peck, George (Ethel's maternal grandfather), 2, 3
Peck, George W. (Ethel's uncle), 174
Peck, Maria, late Orton, formerly Spink (Ethel's maternal grandmother), 2
Peck, Maria (Ethel's aunt), 2
Peeler, Clare, 121, 122
Pembroke, 13th and 14th Earls of, 42
Pepys, Samuel, 158
Peterka, Rudolph, 181, 182
Pfitzer, Hans, 28
Philipp, Isidor, 268
Philipps, J.D. & Söhne, Frankfurt-am-Main, (Duca and Ducartist piano rolls), 29, 94, 117
Pierce, Ralph, *235*, *259*, 310
Pitts, M.R., 212
Player piano and gramophone compared, 138-140
Pleyel Piano Co., Paris, (Pleyela piano rolls), 94
Pollack, Daniel, 244, *245*, *246*, 254, 268, 270-271, *276*, 278, 280, 281, 301, 310
Pollak, Robert, 220
Porter, Cole, 151
Presley, Elvis, 296
Prokofiev, Serge, 141, 264
Pym, Captain A.R., 48

QRS piano roll company; see Recordo piano rolls
Quilter, Roger, 32

Rachmaninov, Serge, 137
Raff, J.J., 28
Ravel, Maurice, 81

Recordo piano rolls, 149-150
Reese, Henry, 254, 288
Reger, Max, 81
Reinecke, Carl, 29
Reiner, Fritz, 242
Remsen, Dorothy, 254
Remsen, Lester, 254
Reszke, Jan de, 186
Reynolds, Jane (Emerson Whithorne's second wife), 111
Richardson, Rev John H., 3
Richter, Hans, 29
Rimsky-Korsakov, Nicolas Andrei, 145, 146
Robertson, Jon, 274-275, *276*, 278, 280, 281, 310
Robinson, Frederick Arthur; see de Grey, Earl
Rogers, J.H., 62
Ronald, Landon (Landon Ronald Russell; Sir Landon Ronald from 1922), 224, 306
Ronalds, Mrs and the Brazilian Minister, 21
Roosevelt, Franklin D., 216
Rosa, Carl; see Carl Rosa Opera Company
Roschore, Mrs Charles, 172
Rose and the Ring, The (opera), 217, 254, 256, 274, 283, 285, 310
Rosenthal, Moriz, 95, 106, 270
Rosso, Nino, 283
Rozborska, Marie Gabriela (Mrs Theodor Leschetizky IV), 41
Rubinstein, Anton, 36, 50, 53, 54, 104, 110, 117, 236, 311
Rubinstein, Artur, 169, 237, 226, 242

Samaroff, Olga, 301
Sandridge, Justin, 187
Sauer, Emil, 55, 106
Saunders, Richard D., 285
Scarlatti, Dominico, 81
Schaeffer, Ralph, 283
Scharrer, Irene, 55
Schelling, Ernest, 146, 306
Schiff, Andras, 152

Index

Schillinger, Julius, 156
Schirmer, G. Inc, New York, music publisher, 120, 121, 268
Schmidt, Leopold, 74
Schnabel, Artur, 36, 62, 106, 117, 132
Schoenberg, Arnold, 271
Scholz, Bernhard, 28, 29, 30
Schubert, Franz, 95, 132, 137, 138, 152, 199, 203, 252
Schulz-Evler, Andrei, 95, 133
Schumann, Clara (née Wieck), 28-29, 158, 226
Schumann, Robert, 28, 75, 140, 194, 226
Scott, Cyril, 32, 81
Sechter, Simon, 36
Seifert, Evelyn, 285, 286
Sekles, Bernhard, 28, 30
Seydel, Irma, 194
Shaftesbury, 8th Earl of, 47
Sharrar, Alice, 13
Shaw, G.B., 274
Shubow, Ruth, 192
Siloti, Alexander, 146
Smith, Charles Davis, 309
Smith, Mr and Mrs Frank, 171
Smolian, Arthur, 74
Spink, George, 3
Stagner, Steve, 255, 256, 282, 285, 286
Starr, Russell, 16
Starr, Mrs Russell (née Martin, Annie Jane), 16, 17, *17*, 18, 19, 20, 21, 22, 28, 75, 175, 311
Steinberg, Sybil, *245, 246*
Steinway & Sons, piano manufacturers, 94, 151, 213, 214, 216, 309
Stockbridge, Margaret, 83, 205
Stockhausen, Julius, 28
Stoessel, Albert, 145
Stokowski, Leopold, 188
Stonehill, Gerald C., 309
Strauss, Johann (the younger), 143
Strauss, Richard, 156
Stravinsky, Igor, 203
Suppé, Franz von, 211
Szigeti, Joska, 55

Taglione, Evelione, 123, 171

Tagore, Rabindranath, 123, 282, 283, 285, 286
Tausig, Carl, 95
Taylor, Deems, 203
Tchaikovsky, Peter Ilyich, 222, 231
Tempest, Marie, 55
Tetrazzini, Luisa, 119
Thackeray, William Makepeace, 217, 254, 255, 256, 285
Thomas, John Charles, 219-220, 222, 292, 310
Toscanini, Artur, 157, 195
Trebelli, Zelia, 53
Triphonola piano rolls; see Hupfeld Co., Leipzig
Twain, Mark (Samuel Langhorne Clemens), 40, 274, 288, 290, 292
Tweedmouth, Lord and Lady, 21

'Uncle Ted'; see Naish, Ted
Ussher, Bruno David, 133, 162, 255, 310

Vengerova, Isabella, 301
Victor Talking Machine Co., 290
Victoria, H.M. The Queen, 255, 287, 303
Vidor, King, 296
Virtuola Co., Holland or Germany, (manufacturers of piano rolls), 94

Wagner, Charles L., 211, 212, 213
Wagner, Richard, 181, 222, 256
Wagner, Roger (Roger Wagner Master Chorale), 288, 296
Wales, Prince of (later King Edward VII), 14, 15, 64, 244
Walker & Spink, solicitors, 3
Waller, Thomas 'Fats', 117
Walter, Bruno, 156, 242, 271
Warrender, Sir George (6th Baronet), 47
Warrender, Sir George (7th Baronet), 47, 48
Warrender, Harold, 48
Warrender, Lady Maud (née Ashley-Cooper), 47, 48, 49
Warrender, Sir Victor (Lord Bruntisfield), 48
Watt, Robert L., 265, 302

Weaver, Powell, 194
Weber, Carl Maria (Friedrich Ernst) von, 181
Weber Piano Company, 146
Weinlich, Josephine, 158
Weiss, Abraham, 283
Welte, M. & Söhne, Freiburg (piano rolls), 29, 94, 148
Whithorne, Cedric Villiers (Ethel Leginska's son), (his name was registered as Whithorne, not Whittern, on his birth certificate), 64, 66, 69, 73, 77, 108, *108*, 110, 111, *112*, *113*, 174, 263, 266, 278, 298-299
Whithorne, Roy Emerson; see Whittern, Roy Emerson
Whittern, Charles Stroud, 62, 63
Whittern, Roy Emerson; surname changed later to Whithorne (Ethel Leginska's husband; name given as 'Whittern' on his marriage certificate, in 1907, but as Whithorne on his son Cedric's birth certificate the following year), 62, 63, 64, *66*, 68, 69, 70, 71, *72*, 74, 77, 107, 108, 109, 110, 111, 266
Wieck, Clara; see Schumann, Clara
Wightman, Elaine, *235*, 244
Wilcox & White Co., Meriden, Connecticut, (Artrio piano rolls), 94, 148-50
Wilkie, Earl, 292

Wilshire, Henry G., 282
Wilson, Arthur, 13
Wilson, Arthur Stanley (son of the above; always known within the family as 'Jack'), 14, 15, 256
Wilson, Charles Henry, 13
Wilson, Jack; see Wilson, Arthur Stanley
Wilson, Mary Emma (Mrs Arthur Wilson), 13, 15, 21, 42-43, 49
Wilson, Thomas, 13
Wilson, Thomas, Sons & Co., ship owners, 13
Witty, Lucy; see Liggins, Lucy E.
Witty, Thomas, 115
Witty, Vivienne Katherine, *52*
Wolfenstein, Isabel, 84
Wolseley, Lord and Lady, 21
Wood, Henry (Sir Henry from 1911), 47, 50, 53, 54, 55, 56, 63, 136, 252, 296, 311
Wood, Mabel Hill, 194
Workman, Christina Bella (Ethel Leginska's stepmother); see Liggins, Mrs C.B.
Wright, Hannah Dawson; see Liggins, Hannah

Yon, Pietro, 194

Zeisler, Fannie Bloomfield, 306